D0214947

THE WAR FOR THE PUBLIC MIND

Political Censorship in Nineteenth-Century Europe

Edited by
Robert Justin Goldstein

PRAEGER

Westport, Connecticut
London

Library of Congress Cataloging-in-Publication Data

The war for the public mind : political censorship in nineteenth-century Europe / edited by Robert Justin Goldstein.

p. cm.

Includes bibliographical references and index.

ISBN 0-275-96461-2 (alk. paper)

1. Censorship—Europe—History—19th century. 2. Europe—Politics and government—1789-1900. 3. Communication in politics—Europe—History—19th century.

I. Goldstein, Robert Justin.

Z658.E85W37 2000

363.3'1—dc21 99-046307

British Library Cataloguing in Publication Data is available.

Library of Congress Catalog Card Number: 99-046307
ISBN: 0-275-96461-2

First published in 2000

Praeger Publishers, 88 Post Road West, Westport, CT 06881
An imprint of Greenwood Publishing Group, Inc.
www.praeger.com

Printed in the United States of America

The paper used in this book complies with the Permanent Paper Standard issued by the National Information Standards Organization (Z39.48-1984).

10 9 8 7 6 5 4 3 2 1

This book is dedicated
to all those who have taken up the pen
in hopes of avoiding the sword.

Contents

Preface

In one sense, this book has been gestating for almost 200 years, since it deals with developments in Europe during the nineteenth century (defined here, as historians tend to, as covering the period from the end of the Napoleonic Wars in 1815 until the outbreak of World War I in 1914). Even its more recent origins date back well over ten years to the reseach that went into my 1989 book *Political Censorship of the Arts and the Press in Nineteenth-Century Europe*. That book's purpose was to collect in one place information about political censorship of a wide variety of media—press, theater, caricature, and cinema—in nineteenth-century Europe.

Having studied the subject for a lengthy period, it was obvious to me that, given the amount of energy expended by nineteenth-century European authorities in their vigorous censorship activities, this was an important and relatively neglected subject, at least partly because information related to it was scattered in literally thousands of books and articles and never before integrated in one volume. But I was acutely aware at the time that I was limited in my ability to compile a book on this intriguing subject since I read only English and French and my archival work was limited to France. As I pointed out in the preface to that earlier book, had I "mastered all 25 or so European languages" and "burrowed through the archives of all of the European countries" before writing it, the volume "would have been a better book, but it also would never have been written" as such a task would consume "several lifetimes, no doubt explaining why historians perhaps better qualified to perform it than I have failed to do so."

All of this is a lengthy way of saying that, although I like that earlier book and think it made a real contribution to scholarship, I never strayed from the view that the subject demanded additional treatment, such as a collection of articles written by specialists on each of the major European countries designed to provide for English-language readers a comprehensive account based on the latest scholarly materials. This book reflects that hope: it is co-authored by six professors living in four countries in Europe and North America who have each specialized in one of the major countries of Europe, know the national language, and have done the appropriate archival work. Unlike my earlier book, in which each chapter focused on a particular type of censored media, this volume covers multiple media within chapters that are organized around censorship within a particular country.

In sending out the call for contributors to this volume more than five years ago, I asked the authors to be certain to include in their chapter some background information about their country (to help those whose primary interest is in censorship rather than in particular nations). Since the intended audience for this volume includes both scholars and interested laypersons, in order to avoid flooding the book with thousands of footnotes I suggested that notes be limited primarily to the sources of direct quotations and obscure statistical material and generally grouped together at the end of each paragraph. To provide further guidance to readers, each author has included at the end of his chapter a short bibliographical essay, emphasizing, where possible, material in English, but also including the most important foreign language sources.

Finally, I have written an introductory chapter that is designed to provide some general background context and highlight common developments across countries for readers who are interested in comparative aspects of nineteenth-century European political censorship. It includes information about European countries that are not covered in subsequent chapters (usually to emphasize similar developments across countries). Although it has been massively informed by the chapters in this book, it is also heavily based on my own research; I have deliberately tried to avoid excessive citing of specific information, examples, and quotations that readers will be able to find elsewhere in this volume.

I am deeply indebted to the contributors, without whom, to put it mildly, this volume would not have been possible. I also want to thank Greenwood Publishing Group, especially my editors, Heather Staines and Peter Kracht, for their staunch and continuing support of scholarly research in the United States and their resistance to the continuing censorship pressures that the marketplace can impose with even greater ruthlessness than the authorities.

1

Introduction

Robert Justin Goldstein

THE TRANSFORMATION OF LIFE IN NINETEENTH-CENTURY EUROPE

"In waging our war, we do not throw bombs," declared the socialist *Hamburger Echo* of September 27, 1910. "Instead, we throw our newspapers amongst the masses of the working people. Printing ink is our explosive." As if in direct response, the Russian Bolshevik leader Vladimir Lenin, who in opposition had frequently thrown ink "bombs," rhetorically asked once in power, "Why should freedom of speech and freedom of the press be allowed? . . . [A government] would not allow opposition by lethal weapons. Ideas are much more fatal things than guns."[1]

These two quotations capture well the widespread feeling in nineteenth-century Europe that governments and oppositions were engaged in a "war," which, although occasionally taking the form of physical combat, more frequently was fought as a nonviolent but just as serious battle of ideas for the minds of the population. Primarily due to the whole cluster of developments summarized by the concept of "modernization"—namely, essentially simultaneous, rapid, and massive advances in literacy, urbanization, industrialization, transportation, and communication—as the nineteenth century progressed the common man increasingly became a significant figure on the political stage. Politics was still dominated by elites, but while before the nineteenth century ordinary citizens were politically largely invisible and powerless, by 1914 this was no longer so anywhere in Europe. In a statement that has become famous to modern historians because it so aptly captures both the political emergence of ordinary citizens and the horror that that evoked among ruling elites, French legislative deputy Saint-Marc Girardin warned his colleagues in the early 1830s that "the barbarians which threaten society are [the working classes] in the faubourgs [outlying districts] of our manufacturing towns, not in the Tartary of Russia [a reference suggestive of Mongol hordes]." And even in Russia, where, by all measures of modernization and the political mobilization of ordinary citizens that everywhere accompanied it, conditions remained extremely backward, rapid change was thrusting the common man forward by the end of the century. On the eve of the 1905 revolution there, the jurist A. F. Koni wrote to a friend:

> The current situation in Russia is strange and, I have to say, frightening. Society is bursting out of its swaddling clothes, in which it was forcibly kept [by backwardness and repression] and which dulled the mind and atrophied any feelings of self-dignity. But it already wants to run, although it doesn't yet know how to walk, and indeed to stand on its own feet.[2]

Society began to burst "out of its swaddling clothes" with great rapidity during the nineteenth century because both the ideological and material surroundings of everyday life were undergoing the greatest and fastest transformation in human history. Ideologically, the French revolutionary slogans of "liberty, equality, and fraternity" posed a fundamental challenge to a European order that had been based for over a millennium on profound political, social, cultural, and economic distinctions and inequalities between classes that made "equality" and "fraternity" inconceivable concepts and reserved any significant kind of "liberty" or power almost exclusively for royalty and aristocrats. Materially, although reliable statistics for even the most basic indicators of everyday life (such as life expectancy) become available for many European countries only around 1850 or later (itself a reflection of the rapid and profound changes that were occurring), we can quickly glimpse this transformation through rough approximations such as the following for the entire continent for the 1815–1914 period: adult literacy grew from less than 30 percent to more than 70 percent; life expectancy leapt from well under forty years to almost fifty; the infant mortality rate (the number of children born alive who died before age one per 1,000 births) dropped from about 200 to about 150; the population living in towns of 20,000 or more jumped from about 5 percent to about 20 percent; and the labor force engaged in industry of any kind increased from about 15 percent to about 30 percent. (Because modernization began earlier and advanced most speedily in northwestern Europe, while lagging elsewhere, such figures can be very misleading for individual states: in 1870, for example, Swedes had a life expectancy of about forty-five years and 95 percent of adults were literate, while Russians lived on average only twenty-five years and 85 percent of adults could not read.)[3]

Coupled with revolutionary advances in transportation and communication, especially the post-1840 rapid spread of railroads and the telegraph, and the simultaneous emergence of the first truly mass press, these ideological and material developments opened up new mental and physical horizons for the European masses, who had previously typically lived out their lives encased in narrow geographical, vocational, and ideological "swaddling clothes" that had made it almost impossible for them to envision, much less demand, different and better lives from their rulers. John Stuart Mill observed in England in 1848 that the working classes would no longer accept a "patriarchal or paternal system of government" and had irrevocably "taken their interests into their own hands" once "they were taught to read, and allowed access to newspapers," brought "together in numbers to work socially under the same roof," and enabled by railways to "shift from place to place." Or in the astonishingly eloquent words of the peasant Albert Szilagi, testifying before a government commission investigating sudden outbursts of peasant unrest in Hungary in the 1890s, "The rightful demands of the laborers increased because the people of the land study more, know more, see more. How can you blame us? We have learnt how to read and write. We would now like to wear better clothes, eat like human beings and send our children to schools."[4]

CENSORSHIP MEDIA AND MOTIVATIONS: FEARS OF THE "DARK MASSES"

The eruption of the masses onto the public stage in the wake of the French Revolution was a development deeply feared by the relatively small and largely hierarchical and closed elite that dominated European society, politics, and culture in 1800. Thus, Napoleon's secret police chief Joseph Fouché expressed concern about "the previously unknown pressure of public opinion," while Friedrich Gentz, secretary to Austrian Foreign Minister Klemens von Metternich (1809–48), who masterminded the reactionary politics of the pre-1848 era, declared, "We do not by any means desire the great masses to become wealthy and independent, for how could we [then] govern them?" Danish King Frederick VI declared in 1833, "The peasant should learn reading and writing and arithmetic; he should learn his duty toward God, himself and others, and no more. Otherwise he gets notions into his head." When the reactionary Spanish Prime Minister Juan Bravo Murillo (1851–52) was asked to provide schools for the poor, he responded, "You want me to authorize a school at which 600 working men are to attend? Not in my time. Here we don't want men who think, but oxen who work."[5]

The fears of the ruling classes were especially centered on the impact of new ideas on the lower classes. Compulsory free elementary school education was not introduced in much of central and western Europe (and there only) until after about 1850, and was entirely lacking above that level throughout the era before World War I (in 1914 less than 3 percent of children aged fourteen to eighteen were enrolled in school in even the most advanced countries). Therefore, elite concerns centered less on controlling what little popular education existed than on restraining the press and other forms of communication, especially media such as caricature, theater, and (after 1900) cinema, which could reach a broad, even illiterate, lower-class audience. The purpose of education was generally perceived as teaching rudimentary skills necessary for the masses to contribute to the strength of the country and, especially, developing patriotism and refuting subversive ideas that might be percolating among the lower classes. Thus, French politician Adolph Thiers, who served King Louis-Philippe (1830–48) and later became president (1871–73), defined the purpose of education as teaching that "suffering is necessary in all estates" and that "when the poor have a fever, it is not the rich who have sent it to them." The great dilemma for the ruling classes was that it became increasingly obvious as the century progressed that their countries would fall behind others without broad popular education, yet the latter inevitably seemed to provoke demands for fundamental change. As Russian Finance Minister Sergei Witte (1892–1903) lamented, "Education foments social revolution, but popular education loses wars."[6]

Despite such dilemmas, education at least was overwhelmingly state-controlled (and where not was generally administered by the Catholic church, which in matters of politics could generally be counted on to be "more patriotic than the king"). What could not be controlled nearly so easily, and therefore became the subject of rising alarm and constant attempts to constrain, was the rising desire and ability of the masses to read, the emergence of newspapers that sought a popular audience, and the simultaneous growth of other media such as theater and caricature that could be comprehended even by the illiterate, who typically constituted a large, impoverished, alienated, and therefore potentially deeply subversive element. The alarm of the ruling elements at the rising tide of literacy, reading, and demands for knowledge among the lower classes is a marked theme of 1815 to 1914 throughout Europe, as fears of lower-class uprisings (such as another French Revolution or outbreaks like those across Europe in 1848 or in Paris during the 1871 Commune) were pervasive and reflected in numerous aspects of censorship policy. Thus, Russian Minister of Education S. S. Uvarov warned during the 1830s that "the taste for reading and literary activity, which earlier was confined to the upper middle classes is now spreading *even* further." A conservative French newspaper writer complained in 1829 that "the rage to read has invaded everywhere. . . . Reading has now reached the blacksmith's shop, the quarries, the sheds of wood-joiners' apprentices, and the stonemason's closet under the stairs [of the wealthy who lodged servants]." In Germany, conservatives complained about "excessive reading" (*Zuviel-Lesen, Zeitungslerei, Lesesucht*) and blamed this for social unrest, moral decline, and (according to historian James Sheehan) "physiological, psychological and social disabilities, to which disrespectful servants, overtrained teachers, nervous youths, and loose women were especially susceptible."[7]

The press was repeatedly described by the ruling elements as a disease or a mental poison that threatened society and therefore required strict controls. Metternich termed the press a "scourge," which was the "greatest and consequently the most urgent evil" of his time, while Austrian Police President Count Joseph Sedlnitzky warned in the 1840s that a loosening of controls over the press threatened that "people will read themselves into criminals." Metternich's assistant Gentz proposed in 1819 that "as a preventative measure against the abuses of the press, absolutely nothing should be printed for years. . . . With this maxim as a rule, we should in a short time get back to God and the truth." The Spanish general Ramon Narváez, who dominated his country's politics at mid-century, had an even more drastic remedy, declaring, "It is not enough to confiscate papers; to finish with bad newspapers you must kill all the journalists." The reactionary French legislative deputy Vicomte de Bonald told his colleagues in 1827 that censorship was a "sanitary measure to protect society from the contagion of false doctrines, just like measures to prevent the spread of the plague"; three years later a ministerial report to French King Charles X declared that the "agitations" and "dangerous and subversive doctrines" that were beginning to "penetrate the foundations and stir the popular masses" were "almost exclusively produced and excited by the liberty of the press," which served, by "nature," as "only an instrument of disorder and sedition." In his 1832 encyclical *Mirari Vos*, Pope Gregory XVI (1831–46) termed liberty of the press "a detestable and execrable moral scourge," while a university professor arrested in the Kingdom of the Two Sicilies (Naples and Sicily) after the failed 1848 revolution was told by his persecutors that the "three worst enemies of man are pen, ink and paper."[8]

Although the fears and hatred directed toward the press were substantial and intense, the authorities were even more alarmed by media such as caricature, theater, and cinema that communicated with an audience broader and poorer than that reached by the press, even encompassing the dreaded, often illiterate "dark masses" who could not read but were not blind or deaf. Moreover, even the literate poor could afford less expensive theaters far more easily than newspapers (especially before 1850, when the latter rarely reached circulations exceeding several thousand, largely due to the general practice of selling newspapers only via long-term and expensive subscriptions). Drawings, plays, and films were perceived as more powerful and threatening than the written press not only because of their broader reach, but also because it was generally agreed that they had greater impact; moreover, in the case of theater and cinema, their audience was a collective one that might be stirred to immediate mob action.

That these visual media were perceived as greater threats than the printed word is clear because prior censorship of caricature, theater, and cinema often continued long after the press was freed from prior restraints (although not necessarily from possible post-publication prosecution). Thus, a number of countries (including France, Portugal, and Russia) continued caricature censorship long after ending prior press censorship; every major country continued prior theater censorship after press censorship was abolished; and even countries that abolished caricature and theater censorship before World War I nonetheless subsequently introduced movie censorship. France is a particularly clear example: prior press censorship was never enforced after 1822, yet caricature censorship was abolished only in 1881, theater censorship continued until 1906, and film censorship was *introduced* in 1916. Similarly, in Russia the press was finally completely freed from prior censorship only in 1905, yet theater and caricature censorship continued until the overthrow of the tsars and film censorship was introduced early in the twentieth century.

Nineteenth-century European authorities were not shy about explaining why they feared visual media more than the printed word. When France's Minister of Justice Jean-Charles Persil successfully urged legislators to impose prior censorship for theater and drawings but not for the written word in 1835, he characterized the former media as posing a special danger because instead of addressing the "mind," they spoke to the "eyes" and thus amounted to "opinions converted into actions," and "a *deed, an action, a behavior*," rather than "the expression of an opinion." Moreover, print was perceived to be primarily consumed by relatively educated people who would not be immediately affected even by subversive matter, and therefore, if a publication proved dangerous, there would be time to confiscate unsold copies before its effects were evident, while drawings and theatrical presentations were considered immediate and irremediable in their impact. Thus, in 1822 French legislator Claude-Joseph Jacquinot-Pampelune defended abolishing press censorship but continuing caricature censorship by telling his colleagues that while printed matter "requires a considerable time for that writing to produce its effect" and the "vigilance of the magistrates can prevent the continuation of a scandal by seizing it . . . it isn't the same with engravings and illustrations" since "as soon as they are exhibited in public, they are instantly viewed by thousands of spectators and the scandal has taken place before the magistrate has had time to repress it." Throughout the nineteenth century, advocates of stage censorship cited the widespread belief that presentation of the opera *La Muette de Portici* triggered the successful 1830 revolution in Belgium against Dutch rule. The effect of subversive theater could apparently be quite instantaneous: according to a French prison director, "When they put on a bad drama, a number of young new criminals soon arrive at my prison."[9]

For caricatures and drawings, their power and speed of impact, especially on an illiterate or poorly educated lower-class audience, were clearly special foci of concern. For example, in 1843 the Prussian Minister of the Interior, Count von Arnim-Boitzenburg, successfully urged King Frederick William IV to reimpose the recently abolished censorship of drawings by arguing that caricatures "prepare for the destructive influence of negative philosophies and democratic spokesmen and authors," especially since the "uneducated class do not pay much attention to the printed words" but they do "pay attention to caricatures and understand them" and to "refute [a caricature] is impossible, its impression is lasting and sometimes ineradicable." In France, in 1829 the interior minister warned his subordinates that drawings were especially dangerous because they "act immediately upon the imagination of the people, like a book which is read with the speed of light." In 1852 the French police minister told his subordinates that drawings were "one of the most dangerous" means employed "to shake and destroy the sentiments of reserve and morality so essential to conserve in the bosom of a well-ordered society . . . because the worst page of a bad book requires time to read and a certain degree of intelligence to understand, while a drawing offers a sort of personification of thought, it puts it in relief, it communicates it with movement and life, in a translation which everyone can understand." In 1880, one year before French caricature censorship was finally abolished, French legislator Emile Villiers told his colleagues that while an unregulated print press posed "problems and dangers, the unlimited freedom of drawings presents many more still," as the latter startled "not only the mind but eyes" and were a "means of speaking even to the illiterate, of stirring up passions, without reasoning, without discourse."[10]

Theater, opera, film, and other forms of oral-visual presentations such as popular songs were also viewed as more threatening than print, not only because they were perceived as exceptionally powerful media accessible to an illiterate lower-class audience, but also because they were presented to a *collective* audience, and thus far more likely to provoke *immediate* action than printed matter typically read in the privacy of (often middle-class) homes. Such reasoning was explained by a high-ranking Austrian censorship official in an 1795 memorandum:

> Censorship of the theater must be much stricter than the normal censorship of printed reading matter, even if the latter may consist of dramatic works. This is a consequence of the different impression which can be made on the minds and emotions of the audience by a work enacted with the illusion of real life, by comparison with that which can be made by a play that is merely read at a desk. The impression

made by the former is infinitely more powerful . . . [because it] engages the eyes and ears and is intended even to penetrate the will of the spectator in order to attain the emotional effects intended; this is something that reading alone does not achieve. Censorship of books can restrict their circulation and made them accessible only to a certain kind of reader whereas the playhouse by contrast is open to the entire public, which consists of people of every class, every walk of life, and every age.[11]

In 1820 the Viennese actor Friedrich Ziegler similarly argued that drama that attacked "religion, law, and monarchy" had done more damage than "all the political pamphlets" together, as the "inspiration of the spoken word, heard by many thousands, strikes more deeply than any cold political writings read only by a few." The president of the French Society of Dramatic Authors, Baron Isidore Taylor, succinctly summarized such arguments when he defended theater censorship before an 1849 state inquiry on that subject: he declared that the stage "produces, among all those watching, a sort of electric communication, even more seductive for the masses than a speech, and one thousand times more dangerous than the most vehement article in the daily press." The impact of such arguments was explicitly reflected in an 1822 decree issued in Tuscany, which ordered that restrictions that applied to printed matter that disseminated "subversive" ideas that threatened to "weaken or destroy veneration for Religion or for the Throne" should be "applied more strictly to theatrical performances."[12]

Fear of the theater's potential subversive power was especially marked before the advent of compulsory primary education because the stage was then widely considered the most important form of mass education for the lower classes. During the reign of French King Louis-Philippe (1830–48), theater inspectors were directed to report to their superiors in great detail about what they observed in theaters "in which the coarsest classes of people gather" since such venues had "become the only school in which the lower class of society goes to learn its lessons." Similarly, an 1819 decree in Wallachia, the Turkish-controlled province that later formed part of Rumania, declared that theater censorship was required because while the stage could be a school for "good morals, commensurate in its zeal and power with its endeavor to combat wickedness and make virtue triumph," when "the selection of plays is poorly made, they abuse the law, become a school for laxity and bad habits and defile civic custom."[13]

Most nineteenth-century European regimes carefully censored and regulated the performance of songs in cafés, cabarets, and other gathering spots for the same reasons that caused them such alarm about the theater. For example, when the great popular French poet and song writer Pierre Béranger was convicted and jailed in 1821 (as would occur again in 1828) for sedition (thereby making him a popular martyr whose songs were memorized and declaimed throughout the country), the prosecutor declared that songs were "1,000 times more contagious" than pamphlets and could "even infect even the air one breathes," especially as the "most guilty pamphlet only influences a narrow circle with its bad influence," while songs "circulate with rapidity, penetrate the villages and the hamlets, and equally encompass all classes."[14]

Although France abolished stage censorship in 1906, and several other European countries, including Sweden and Denmark, did likewise before World War I, none of these regimes perceived any contradiction in introducing film censorship *after* they had freed the theater, because cinema was seen as more powerful yet than the stage, was far less expensive, and attracted a more popular audience. Thus, in 1913 a French court rejected a challenge to the legality of film censorship, declaring that movies were "not just the image or photograph of the dramatic work [on which they might be based]; they are not made for the same audience; infinitely more varied, proceeding by means different from those used by dramatic authors, films attempt to excite and sometimes to astonish public curiosity, rather than to awaken and develop the aesthetic feeling of the spectators." In 1931 French writer Georges Altman made the same point, maintaining that even when a movie "copies the drama, it isn't ordinary theater," but rather a "more powerful theater, an enraged theater, a theater squared," that depicts life "enhanced to the Nth degree, life through a magnifying glass, life enlarged 100 times, nearly a thousand times larger and stronger than life as lived."[15]

Not only were communications media perceived as especially accessible to lower-class audiences particularly strictly surveilled, but even *within* each media category material that the authorities viewed as particularly targeted at the "dark masses" was often more strictly controlled than that aimed at a more elite, educated, and upper-class audience. Thus, as John House notes in a recent study of the censorship of images in France in the 1860s, while the authorities were in general "particularly wary of the potency of visual experience, in the form of a print or a stage representation or a performance of a popular café-concert songs," the "question of class—of determining what types of material should be permitted for which social groups—seems to have been the most fundamental concern."[16]

For example, newspapers and short, cheap pamphlets that were especially affordable and accessible to literate lower-class elements (as opposed to longer, more expensive books targeted at the more educated and wealthy) were the primary targets of conservatives who fulminated against the newly emerging disease of "excessive reading." Thus, the French press law of 1814, the notorious Carlsbad Decrees of 1819, which applied to the German Confederation (including large segments of the Austrian Empire), and the Russian press decree of 1865 all excluded from prior censorship lengthy books, but required prior approval of newspapers and short books and pamphlets. Prussian King Frederick William IV's close advisor Joseph von Radowitz advised him during the 1840s that books were "never really dangerous" and required no prior censorship but newspapers and pamphlets were "one of the so-called dangerous trades, which, like the making of gunpowder and the mixing of drugs, we do not allow to be practiced without constant police supervision," including the assurance that only "truly respectable men" were allowed to own newspapers. In 1834, when Russian censorship officials recommended that Tsar Nicholas I forbid all cheap secular magazines comparable to the British "penny press" aimed at a "lower-class reading public," as the entire concept of exposing ordinary people to such material was incompatible with "our existing order," Nicholas concurred, proclaiming, "Completely true. By no means allow."

After 1865, as the public demand for reading material gradually increased and press controls were moderately eased, the Russian interior ministry regularly sent out directives urging the "strictest attention to censoring the publications destined for the general public." Due to such class-differentiated censorship, while 2 percent of all books intended for publication were forbidden in Russia in the late nineteenth century, 25 percent of those specifically intended for the lower classes were banned. Because of such class distinctions, Karl Marx's *Das Kapital* was given censorship approval in Russia in both the original German and in translation during the 1870s because, the censors concluded, it was a "difficult, inaccessible, strictly scientific work" and few would "read it and even fewer will understand it" as its socialist message was imbedded in a "colossal mass of abstruse, somewhat obscure politico-economic argumentation." Although prior censorship of all print media was finally terminated in Russia in 1905, a recent study concludes (and Professor Ruud documents in this volume) that while thereafter "moderate liberal, conservative, and reactionary" newspapers were able to publish quite freely, the tsarist authorities conducted a crushing campaign of post-publication harassment against the "extreme left" and "workers" press that represented the "urban lower classes and their political organizations."[17]

In pre-1850 Austria, books might be approved for all audiences ("Admittur") or banned for all ("Damnatur"), but could also be placed in several intermediate categories that effectively limited access to only an educated audience; although restrictions on the granting of licenses to booksellers were generally eased in Austria after 1860 (resulting in a tripling of such outlets between 1860 and 1875), requests for such licenses in working-class districts of Vienna were routinely denied until about 1900 on the grounds that there was no "local demand" for such outlets. In 1829 the French interior minister instructed his subordinates with regard to the proposed circulation of Napoleonic imagery that "in general, that which can be permitted without difficulty when it is a question of expensive engravings, or lithographs intended only to illustrate an important [i.e., expensive] work, would be dangerous and must be forbidden when these same subjects are reproduced in engravings and lithographs at a cheap price." Similarly, in 1843 Prussian King Frederick William IV directed his officials to treat erudite books leniently, but not to allow the spread of "seductive errors and corrupt theories" via "newspaper scribbling" that would be accessible to a "class of the population" to whom such popular writing "is more appealing" than the "products of serious examination and thorough scholarship."[18]

In Russia, beginning in 1888 inexpensive popular theaters were subjected to a harsher, separate censorship than that applying to a more educated drama audience; hundreds of plays approved for the latter were banned from the former (or, if it was a matter of particular words, the censors lined out with red ink material forbidden from all theaters and with blue ink excisions only applying to the popular stage). For example, the 1891 play *A Happy Day*, co-authored by the prominent dramatist Alexander Ostrovsky, which dealt with a scheming corrupt provincial official who was plotting to marry off his daughters, was cleared as a "harmless farce" for the regular stage, but, according to the censors, could not be tolerated in the popular theaters since "to depict before the ignorant crowd the lowest-ranking representatives of the government in a ridiculous light, to have them commit crimes with impunity—this is extremely inappropriate."[19]

In France, similarly, plays that might be approved for "legitimate" state-subsidized theaters were often barred from the popular stage: the censors' reports repeatedly contain phrases such as "this appears to us to contain passages which could be troublesome given the [working-class] theater for which this work is destined" and "there is reason to fear that, in [a theater] currently frequented by the working class, such a spectacle would only arouse [class] animosities." For example, an 1837 play about the death penalty, *La Mort en loterie*, intended for the popular Gaîté, was banned because, according to the censors, "if reform ideas which attack one of our penal institutions are admissible in the sphere of politics and philosophy, they are out of place in a vaudeville intended for a Boulevard [i.e., popular] theater." The great German director Max Reinhardt played on such official orientations in appealing in 1906 for censorship approval of Frank Wedekind's controversial drama, *Spring Awakening*, which touched on sexual themes. Reinhardt assured the censors that the play would not be performed "for the general public" but "in the Kammerspiele, a theater which seats only some 300 and which, owing to the high prices, will draw its public from the most exclusive social circles."[20]

Additional concern for perceived highly susceptible lower-classes sensibilities was reflected in special restrictions in many nineteenth-century European countries on materials sold by itinerant peddlers (known as *colporteurs* in France) and hawked at railway stations, street kiosks, and available in libraries, since the lower classes were seen as their primary consumers. For example, for decades after 1850 French and Austrian peddlers were restricted to selling only specifically approved publications. In France, according to an 1869 article in the newspaper *Siècle*, this ban effectively deprived rural France of access to "books, the food of thought." In Austria, according to an 1891 publication by socialist leader Viktor Adler (who was jailed himself several times for press offenses), due to these restrictions:

> It is no exaggeration to say that for a very large part of our nation Gutenberg's invention simply does not exist. Our country dwellers forget how to read as they have no opportunity to practice reading. . . . one does not want [opposition] writings to circulate among the people, even though the keenest public prosecutor can find nothing dangerous in them. What is meant to reign is the "intelligence" of the few, not the "brutal instincts" of the masses.[21]

In Germany and France, for decades after the ending of prior press censorship, the authorities regularly claimed the right to ban otherwise legally published material from sale at street kiosks and railway stations; thus, Prussian authorities banned the leading caricature journal *Simplicissimus* from railway sales after 1898, and French authorities periodically refused to allow street sales of their nation's equivalent, *L'Assiette au Beurre*. In Russia, only specifically approved books could be read to public audiences or admitted to public libraries; these restrictions were so severely applied that only 3 percent of all legally produced materials could be found in the nation's public libraries. Much of the banned material was rejected due to the perception that it might stimulate mass unrest. Thus, an 1899 short story, "Feodosevna," about a poor old women who freezes to death on the road, was banned by a censor with the comment, "An appalling plot for a short story meant to be read by children and the masses!"[22]

CENSORSHIP LAWS AND MECHANICS

Until the concept of continuing, organized opposition political groupings was accepted as legitimate—a development that came only after 1850 in most European countries—the press was by far the most important source of potential or actual persistent critical commentary about the ruling elements, and therefore it everywhere became the focus of virtually never-ending debate as to how to best regulate it. As historians Daniel Rader and Maryse Maget-Dodominici note with regard to Restoration (1815–30) France, because the press "represented the sole means by which adversaries of the regime could express their views" and was thus "frequently more important than the legislative chambers as the nation's forum of opinion," the subject of press regulation "monopolized the attention of the French," "never ceased being the object of successive legislation," and represented "one of the most important stakes in the political struggle." The mid-century liberal German parliamentarian Georg von Bunsen declared:

> The freedom of the press is to the nineteenth century what spiritual freedom was to the Christian of the first century and religious freedom to the sixteenth and seventeenth centuries. It is the political question of life and death in our time, the question that wrecks governments and reduces kingdoms to death, or gives them the strength to rise. The fight for the freedom of the press is a holy war, the holy war of the nineteenth century.

When censorship temporarily collapsed amidst the 1848 German revolutions, the *Vossische Zeitung* published an extra edition with the headline, "THE PRESS IS FREE!"[23]

European authorities devoted immense amounts of time, energy, and personnel to attempting to control the press and other forms of communication. In Spain, at least fifteen major press laws were enacted between 1810 and 1853. A prominent late nineteenth-century Russian journalist complained that his newspaper had to hire a specialist to keep up with the over 13,000 bureaucratic circulars that the authorities promulgated to provide the press with "guidance." The landmark 1881 liberal French press law replaced forty-two laws containing 325 separate clauses that had been passed during the previous seventy-five years by ten different regimes; French censorship regulations were so complex that at least ten books were published between 1830 and 1880 to provide guidance to lawyers, journalists, and those in the theatrical profession who were trying to decipher them. In most nineteenth-century European countries, changes in censorship regulations accompanied almost every important change in regime, ruler, or domestic policy orientation: in France, for example, prior censorship of caricature was eliminated in 1814, restored in 1820, abandoned once again in 1830, reestablished in 1835, abolished once more in 1848, reimposed in 1852, terminated again in 1870, reinstated yet again in 1871, and finally abolished for good (at least in peacetime) in 1881. What the French caricature journal *L'Eclipse* observed on September 20, 1874, with regard to caricature censorship could apply equally well to other countries and other media: "One could, one day, write an exact history of the liberty which we enjoy during this era by writing a history of our caricatures."[24]

Metternich once defined censorship as the "right to hinder the manifestation of ideas which disturb the peace of the state, its interest and its good order." A late nineteenth-century Berlin court expressed essentially this same thought, which surely spoke to the primary motivation behind the censorship throughout the century and throughout Europe, when, without any apparent sense of irony, it upheld the legality of banning plays that could undermine "confidence in the administration of law," including "the consideration that the audience may be inwardly misled to views that endanger public well-being and order," such as "the disturbance caused by the thought that the existing political order does not grant the individual citizen his rights." Such hopelessly vague formulations were reflected in almost all nineteenth-century European censorship regulations; indeed, given their general purpose of silencing political opposition and the impossibility of defining in advance all possibly threatening ideas, regulations of enormous ambiguity were *required* so that they could be applied at will in response to the needs of the regime and the events of the day. As a Swedish parliamentary committee that drafted that country's 1812 press law (which authorized the government to ban any periodicals that, among other offenses, were "detrimental to public safety") accurately stated, vagueness was needed as "there are modes of writing, using allusions as well as allegories and irony, which cannot possibly be anticipated in any detail in the provisions of an act."[25]

Perhaps the single most all-encompassingly vague regulation was the 1822 Spanish press law, which banned writings that "spread rules or doctrines or which refer to acts dedicated to exciting to rebellion or to disturbing the public peace, even though they may be disguised as allegories of imaginary persons or countries, or of pastimes or as dreams or fictions, or anything similar," not to mention material that "made vulnerable the reputation of individuals, even though they are not named, or indicated by anagrams, allegories or in any other form." But in spirit this law was typical both of regulations providing for prior censorship and of those authorizing post-publication prosecutions where various media were freed from advance censorship. To give another example, the Austrian press decree of 1852 ordered the post-publication confiscation of printed matter that displayed an "orientation that was hostile to the throne, the monarchy, the unity and integrity of the empire, monarchical principles, religion, public morals, or the overall foundations of the state's society, or of an orientation that was incompatible with the maintenance of public law and order." Austrian restrictions on the peddling of printed matter late in the century declared the purpose of such rules was to "strengthen morality, the love of one's country and proliferate general education" and therefore all materials that might create "an unfavorable influence upon the people's morals, patriotism or education" should be excluded.[26]

Such laws and regulations could not, of course, be enforced with any consistency in any event, but their inherent vagueness was magnified because censors generally were not provided with more specific guidelines, while always fearing that, if they let something slip through that their superiors took offense at, their jobs or even their freedom, might be jeopardized. In Austria in 1823, when the leading playwright Franz Grillparzer's drama *King Ottokar* was blocked by the censorship for two years (reportedly until the empress personally intervened), the censor responded when Grillparzer asked what the problem was, "Nothing at all, but I thought to myself 'One can never tell'." Jacques-Louis Florent, who served three successive French regimes as a theater censor, testified at an 1849 legislative inquiry that the censors "never received any special instructions" and therefore:

> We have no other guide than our conscience. In seeing a scabrous passage, we would ask ourselves, "Would we take our wife and daughters to a theater to hear such things?" . . . In seeing passages with a political or social significance we asked ourselves, "does that aim at causing the different classes to rise up against each other, to excite poor against the rich, to excite to disorder?" We asked ourselves in principle if it was possible to allow ridicule on the stage of the institutions of the country, and especially those who maintain order most effectively . . . and expose them [i.e., the police and militia] to the laughter and mockery of the crowd. We had no trouble in answering no. . . . As for details and allusions, we forebade that which seemed to us to threaten public tranquillity and the nation's institutions.[27]

Many censors became frustrated by their lack of specific guidelines as well as the mounting numbers of texts that they had to examine and sometimes by their own lack of sympathy for their task. The liberal Russian censor A. V. Nikitenko, who was twice imprisoned in the guardhouse for censorship "oversights," pleaded in 1842 with the secret police chief to tell Tsar Nicholas I "how difficult" it was to serve as a censor as "we really do not know what is demanded of us" and "are never safe and can never fulfill our obligations." In his diary, Nikitenko characterized the Russian censorship as filled with "abuses and senselessness" because it depended on the "interpretation of ignoramuses and malevolent individuals who are ready to see a crime in every idea." His fellow censor, the well-known poet Fedor Tiutchev, compared the censorship to "curing a toothache by smashing the teeth with one's fist"; during the 1820s the Hessian censor Jacob Grimm (already famous as one of the Grimm brothers and later to be dismissed with his brother from the University of Göttingen in 1837 in a cause célèbre political firing) confessed to a friend that "in a way befitting the nature of the task, I am not quite scrupulous in my handling of it." The ever-increasing and crushing censorship workload, which seems to have been one reason why prior censorship was abandoned by 1850 in most European countries, was another burden for the censors. The Russian censor Apollon Maikov, a famous poet, censored 223 books totaling over 100,000 pages in four languages during a fourteen-month period; one Russian censorship official lamented that "there was no end to the writing and recopying," which reached such "incredible dimensions" that the "poor clerks got calluses on their hands from this Sisyphean labor day and night."[28]

Although both during the nineteenth century and in subsequent scholarly examinations most of the attention paid to nineteenth-century European restrictions on expression have focused on prior censorship of the press, many press constraints took other forms, and, as already noted, many other media than the press were restricted. While every major European country enforced prior press censorship during part of the nineteenth century (except Great Britain, which never enforced this means of press restriction after 1695), such controls ended in France as early as 1822, terminated in most of central Europe by about 1850, and ended in Russia in 1905. However, the abolition of prior press censorship did not mean expression was henceforth unconstrained in Europe. Even aside from the continued enforcement of prior censorship of caricature and (especially) theater (and later film) in many countries, every country that abolished prior press censorship replaced it with extensive and vague legal authorization of post-publication punishment, as in the just-quoted 1823 Spanish and 1852 Austrian press regulations. Moreover, in most European countries, post-publication proceedings often (if not always) were effected either via purely administrative measures that could not be challenged in the courts and/or via judges who were administratively appointed and could convict and penalize without consulting juries.

The issue of whether or not juries should judge press prosecutions became a tremendously contentious one in some countries—as Professors Shubert and Lenman document in their respective chapters on Spain and Germany—because juries were far less likely to convict than judges. Juries acquitted in 70 percent or more of press prosecutions in France between 1831 and 1833 and during the 1850s in Piedmont (Italy), but during the 1852–66 period when French press prosecutions were tried solely by judges, the government gained a conviction rate of 80 percent. In 1837 the Barcelona newspaper *El Vapor* proclaimed a toast to "the jury and only the jury, the safeguard of the press and shield against excesses of power"; fifty years later Munich's police director referred to the jury as the "highest palladium of press freedom."[29]

With or without juries and/or judges, post-publication press prosecutions were massive in scale across Europe after the ending of prior censorship: in Germany, under the formally liberal 1874 press law, over 3,800 press prosecutions were brought by 1890, the notorious Anti-Socialist Law (1878–90) was used to administratively suppress over 100 periodicals and over 1,000 other publications, and hundreds of prosecutions against socialist papers continued until 1914; in Austria, there were over 2,000 prosecutions and confiscations of newspapers between 1877 and 1880 alone; in Italy, over 100 newspapers were arbitrarily suppressed during a period of political turmoil in 1898; in Russia, during the five years following the ending of prior press censorship in 1905 there were nearly 1,300 newspaper suppressions (of which over 1,000 were administratively imposed compared to less than 225 by the courts), hundreds of journalists were jailed, and almost 4,400 penalties were imposed on the press (compared to only eighty-two during the previous five years); in France there were well over 3,000 press prosecutions and scores of newspapers were suppressed during the sixty years after the abolition of press censorship in 1822.[30]

The practical effect of the constant threat of post-publication prosecution was to force journalists (and, where applicable, theater directors) to become their own censors; indeed, as French press historian Irene Collins has aptly pointed out, laws without any trace of prior "censorship could sometimes be more oppressive than those which set up an elaborate system of preliminary inspection" because under prior censorship regimes newspapers and theaters could safely proceed once their material had been approved, whereas under regimes of strict post-publication repression they risked huge financial losses and the possible loss of their own freedom if their products were prosecuted, seized, or halted after their costs were already undertaken. As one editor remarked about the notorious system of administrative warnings utilized by French Emperor Napoleon III between 1852 and 1868, journalists were effectively forced by such systems to "assume the responsibility for their own castration." Theater directors sometimes even expressed a *preference* for prior censorship because the cost of suppression once they had undertaken the costs of hiring actors, holding rehearsals, building sets, and publicizing plays was so high.[31]

Whereas prior censorship and post-publication prosecutions focused on specific objectionable material, nineteenth-century European governments also utilized a variety of other restraints that did not focus on particular content, but rather sought to ensure that "unreliable" people would be unlikely to produce or consume various media at all. Most governments at various times required newspaper publishers and theater directors to obtain authorization to operate. This licensing requirement was often supplemented by the mandatory deposit of a heavy monetary "security" or "caution" bond and, in the case of newspapers, by a special tax on the sale of all copies. The licensing requirement (which often applied to printers, booksellers, and hawkers as well) was used to attempt to screen out potential "subversives." Theater licensing requirements, effective in Britain until 1843, in France until 1864, in Germany until 1870, and in Russia until 1882, clearly had considerable effect in restricting the number of theaters that operated, as is clear from the explosion of theaters that invariably followed once such requirements were lifted.

Security bonds and licensing requirements for newspapers similarly restricted the number of newspapers that were able to publish in many countries and helped to limit their owners to members of the "respectable classes," while newspaper taxes often had a significant impact in pricing newspapers out of the reach of ordinary citizens. In short, security bonds—required during at least part of the century in Austria, Hungary, Greece, Spain, Britain, France, and Russia—made it difficult for the poor to own newspapers and press taxes made it hard for the lower classes to buy them. Although security bonds were supposedly intended to guarantee payment of fines if newspapers violated press laws, they were frequently so costly that they ensured that only the wealthy could operate newspapers (and theaters in some countries): the 1852 Spanish press decree openly declared that its purpose in especially increasing the cost of security bonds for newspapers of "small size and cheapness" was to provide protection against these "most harmful newspapers" that "reach the less well-off classes with the strong intent of spreading subversive doctrines among the masses" and were greater threats to the press laws than those of larger size, whose editors were termed unlikely to breach "the limits of moderation and decorum." When the security bond in France was increased in 1848, forcing the closure of *Le Peuple Constituant*, its final issue headlined, "One needs gold, a lot of gold, to enjoy the right to speak. We are not rich enough. Silence to the poor!" The role of security bonds, along with nonjuried trials in press cases, was so significant that the ban on these practices in the 1831 Belgian constitution immediately made that document a model for liberals throughout Europe: "The press is free. Censorship may never be reestablished and no surety bond may be exacted from writers, editors or printers. . . . Jury trial is required in all criminal cases and in all hearings of political and press offenses."[32]

Press taxes were at times applied to newspapers in Austria, Belgium, France, Germany, Great Britain, and the Netherlands. Their undisguised purpose was, as the preamble to the 1819 newspaper stamp-tax bill in Britain forthrightly explained, to "restrain the small publications which issue from the Press in great numbers and at a low price," and their effect, as an 1851 British parliamentary committee noted, was to make prohibitive the cost of newspapers that would be "suitable to the means and the wants of the laboring classes." In France during the 1820s and in Germany during the 1870s these taxes swallowed up over 25 percent or more of total newspaper revenues and forced significant increases in price. In Austria, taxes doubled the price of newspapers before their 1899 repeal. Newspaper taxes were popularly referred to as "taxes on knowledge" in Britain and until their final repeal there in 1861 became the center of furious debates, which four-time Prime Minister William Gladstone recalled as the "severest parliamentary struggle in which I have ever been engaged."[33]

THE RESPONSE TO CENSORSHIP: HATRED, SELF-CENSORSHIP, AND DEFIANCE

Journalists and artists who were forced to submit to prior censorship or endure the constant uncertainty of potential post-presentation/publication prosecutions for their efforts not surprisingly hated these restrictions. This hatred was only reinforced because many of them—and many ordinary citizens, especially political liberals and working-class leaders—viewed the press and other media, if left unconstrained, as having extraordinary potential to expand the mind and improve the human condition. An 1841 poem by a British striker termed the press "that engine to enlarge the slave," and asked, "Can it refuse when truth and justice crave?" In 1840 a French orator told a huge crowd gathered in Strasbourg to dedicate a statue to Gutenberg that press freedom was the salvation of the poor:

> Until now the rulers have crushed the people under the weight of their cannons; now from the powerful cylinders of the press machines escape night and day millions of sheets which cross rivers, fortresses, customs controls, mountains and seas, and which assault ignorance and despotism with the intelligence projectiles of the press. Yes, ideas, like pacific armies, will advance on the fields of battle of the future; it is by the propaganda of ideas, by liberty of the press that you will conquer!

Irish-born dramatist Richard Brinsley Sheridan declared, "Against venal Lords, Commons or juries, against despotism of any kind or in any shape—let me but array a free press and the liberties of England will stand unshaken." German liberal leader and journalist Karl von Rotteck likewise declared in 1820 that a free press "assures certain victory for truth and justice, without force, solely through the divine judgment of unfettered public opinion, through the directing authority of human reason." When the French newspaper *L'Égalité* was suppressed in 1850, its final headline proclaimed, "Long live freedom of the press, which kills tyrants."[34]

The press and the cause of press liberty became virtually worship words to many nineteenth-century Europeans. French liberal historian Jules Michelet termed the press the "holy ark" of modern times, which fulfilled a "sacred mission," and declared in 1847 that an unfettered press could bring about a "moral union" of French society:

> Is not the press the universal intermediary? What a sight, when from the post office one watches newspapers leave by the thousand, these representatives of diverse opinions, who will carry until the distant frontiers the traditions of the parties, the voices of polemic, harmonizing nevertheless in a certain unity of language and of ideas! . . . Who does not believe that the national soul is going to circulate now by all the means of this great mechanism?

The usually hard-bitten Karl Marx dissolved into similar mystical raptures, writing in 1842 (before being hounded from Germany, France, and Belgium for his writings):

> A free press is the omnipresent open eye of the spirit of the people, the embodied confidence of a people in itself, the articulate bond that ties the individual to the state and the world, the incorporated culture which transfigures material struggles into intellectual struggles and idealizes its raw material shape. . . . It is universal,

omnipresent, omniscient. It is the ideal world, which constantly gushes from the real one and streams back to it ever richer and animated anew.

Even the repressively oriented German Confederation Diet's Federal Press Commission admitted in 1847 that "present-day Germany perceives in the mere words press freedom a strange enchantment, about whose success and impact one should harbor no illusions."[35]

Although fears of the authorities in nineteenth-century Europe were always most focused on the lower classes, during the period before 1850 few truly working class-oriented publications existed (except in England). Therefore, in practice the overwhelming majority of censorship struggles involved conflicts between the authorities and the middle classes. These elements, including the business and professional classes, such as merchants, journalists, lawyers, doctors, and teachers, generally felt that the monarchical-aristocratic elites who dominated political life before 1850 failed to adequately recognize their importance and contributions to society. Just as important, among potential dissidents they alone generally had the education, money, and leisure required to engage in organized opposition. Since the press was virtually their only potential outlet for expression, before 1850 demands for freedom of the press and an end to censorship became one of the major rallying cries of middle-class liberals. (After 1850, as the "respectable" press became increasingly tolerated and the middle classes increasingly co-opted into the ruling circles, it remained a constant demand of still oft-persecuted socialist and working-class movements.) Cries for liberty of the press, led by middle-class elements, played major roles in revolutionary upheavals in 1830 in France, Belgium, and Germany, in 1848 across central Europe, and in 1905 in Russia (which in both economic and political development lagged well behind Western Europe). Even when quarrels over press freedom did not reach revolutionary proportions, they often provided a key symbolic issue that focused demands (again generally led by the middle classes before 1850 and by the organized working classes thereafter) for democratization, whose resolution sometimes helped pave the way for more general reforms.

Swedish King Karl Johan's repressive press policy was severely discredited and ultimately abandoned partly due to the 1834 case of Captain Anders Lindeberg, editor of the *Stockholms Posten*, who was sentenced under a medieval treason law to decapitation for implying that the king should be deposed. Public reaction was so severe that the king reduced the sentence to three years in jail (Lindeberg insisted on his right to lose his head and after he subsequently refused to accept the king's desperate issuance of a general amnesty to "all political prisoners awaiting execution"—which applied only to him—the regime finally locked him out while he was walking in the prison courtyard). In Denmark, King Frederik VI's response that "we alone know" what was good for the people, after almost 600 Danes petitioned during the 1830s to protest his plans to further restrict the press, furnished the opposition with what one historian has termed a ready-made "symbol of inane autocracy" and led to the formation of the Society for the Proper Use of Freedom of the Press. The Society, which quickly attracted 5,000 members, became a leading focus for democratization in Denmark, playing a significant role in organizing the public pressure that led to a series of reforms during the late 1840s that established press freedom and peacefully transformed the country from one of the leading autocracies of Europe into a fledgling democracy. Similarly, during the 1870s Greek politician Charilaos Tricoupis was transformed into a martyr and liberal hero after he was jailed and then acquitted of sedition for a newspaper article that blamed King George I for that country's political troubles, especially for his refusal to recognize the principle of parliamentary responsibility. Tricoupis subsequently agreed at the king's request to form a ministry after the king agreed to abide thereafter by parliamentary principles.[36]

While press restrictions continued, journalists and artists constrained by them complained bitterly and suffered severely from the need to compromise their expression and from quite reasonable fears for their personal safety accompanying every word they wrote, every illustration they drew, and every play they performed. Historian Elizabeth McKay has captured extremely well the subtle way such fears shaped their behavior: "Just as a speaker with an imperfect knowledge of a foreign language restricts his conversations whenever possible to areas in which his vocabulary is adequate and adapts the expression of his thoughts to fit with his linguistic capacities, so many authors writing under the restrictions of . . . censorship, of necessity, and almost instinctively, began to exercise self-censorship."[37]

An entire book could easily be composed of complaints from those who were constrained by restrictions on their expressive freedom in nineteenth-century Europe, but they all essentially relate McKay's insight, varying only in degrees of eloquence and anger. For example, Russian author Alexander Pushkin, whose literary masterpieces were repeatedly mutilated or banned, moaned in a letter to his wife, "Only the devil could have thought of having me born in Russia with a mind and talent." Russian literary critic Vissarion Belinsky complained that under Tsar Nicolas I all liberal ideas were forbidden, "for example that two plus two equals four and that winter is cold and summer hot"; he lamented, "Nature sentenced me to bark like a dog and howl like a jackal, but circumstances order me to mew like a cat and swish my tail like a fox." French writer Maxime du Camp complained that during the regime of Napoleon III "you had to turn your pen around seven times between your fingers, since before the courts you could sin by thought, by word, by action or by omission." British writer H. G. Wells told a 1909 parliamentary inquiry that censorship had "always been one of the reasons I have not ventured into play writing." French author Emile

Zola echoed this thought, writing that censorship "has the inhibiting effect of a scarecrow; it paralyzes the evolution of dramatic art" as "everyone know the plays he shouldn't write, those which couldn't be performed, and no one writes them." The exiled Moravian priest Karl Postl asked, concerning conditions in the land of Metternich, "What would have become of Shakespeare had he been doomed to live or write in Austria?" Greek poet Alexander Soutsos declared, "The press is free so long as you don't bother / The authorities, / The judges, our Ministers and their friends, / The press is free so long as you don't write." The great German poet and journalist Heinrich Heine wrote of the "mental bitterness . . . created by the need to censor every thought that I think immediately in my head; writing while the censor's sword hangs over one's head by a thread—it's enough to drive one mad." Heine, whose works were banned in his native land both in the 1830s and the 1930s, prophesied in words now inscribed on a memorial at the Nazi concentration camp at Dachau, "Where books are burned, there in the end will men be burned too (*dort wo man Bücher verbrennt, verbrennt man auch am Ende Menschen*)."[38]

Some of the bitterest complaints came from authors and artists whose plays and caricatures remained subject to prior censorship after the printed word was freed, especially since (with a few exceptions, as in some of the German states) censorship decisions were arbitrary administrative rulings that could not be challenged in court. Thus, seventy-one British playwrights attacked theatrical censorship in a 1907 statement that demanded that their "art be placed on the same footing as every other art" rather than be subjected to "a single official who judges without a public hearing and against whose dictum there is no appeal" with the power to "cast a slur on the good name and destroy the means of livelihood" of dramatists and destroy their work "at a pen's stroke." French art historian and writer Edmond de Goncourt also complained about theater censorship, declaring in 1892, "Speech is free, newspapers are free, the book is free, only the theater is not. Why this anomaly under a Republic that has liberty for its motto?" The French caricature journal *Le Grelot* predicted on June 15, 1880, "When future generations learn that the preliminary censorship, abolished for the printed word in 1830, still existed for drawings in 1880 . . . they will surely consider us a remarkable race of hydrocephalics [i.e., people with brain damage]." The same journal lamented on March 17, 1872, that the "[drawing] crayon knows only one regime, one of arbitrariness," since "one drawing is refused, another is accepted according to whether a bureaucrat has had a bad lunch; whether he lost his cane or found his lost dog or his barber cut him; whether his wife is angry or a creditor gave him a bill."[39]

Nineteenth-century European writers and artists went far beyond mere verbal protest about restrictions on their freedom of expression: they also, often with the encouragement and participation of significant segments of the population, actively sought to subvert, defy, and evade these constraints. The means by which restrictions could be fought were extremely varied, as Victor Hugo's testimony before an 1849 French legislative inquiry into theater censorship spelled out:

> The offenses which one can commit [against censorship] in the theater are of all sorts. There are those which an author can commit voluntarily in writing in a play something against the law. . . . There are also the offenses of the actor; those which he can commit in adding to words by gestures or inflections of voice [not indicated in the script and thus not subject to prior censorship] a reprehensible sense not meant by the author. There are the offenses of the director who arranges a display of nudity on the stage; then the offenses of the decorator who exposes certain seditious or dangerous emblems mixed in with the decor; those of the costumer, then those of the hairdresser. . . . Finally there are the offenses of the public, an applause which accentuates a verse, a whistle which goes beyond what the actor or author intended.[40]

The means by which censorship restrictions were confronted constituted two categories: (1) direct defiance, such as smuggling books and newspapers into a country where they were forbidden or publishing or performing material not submitted to the censors where it was required, or submitted but rejected, or which violated other regulations; and (2) indirect evasions, a large variety of techniques that technically complied with restrictions while subverting their intent, like the "gestures" of actors and applause of the audience referred to by Hugo, and the use of so-called "Aesopian language" to express political views under the guise of something else.

Direct defiance of media restrictions, despite the severe risks involved that led to the suppression of hundreds of newspapers and the jailing of thousands of journalists, was extremely widespread, even in the most repressive regimes. Russian censorship officials reported during the period from 1858 to 1862 that "there are no books which you could not get in St. Petersburg if you wanted them," that banned books had an "added attraction in the eyes of the readers due to their secret fame and splendor of forbidden fruit," and that "Russia is flooded with these publications" that "pass from hand to hand with a great ease of circulation." In 1843 Austrian officials discovered 400 illegal volumes at one Viennese bookshop, while Russian officials uncovered almost 6,000 illegal books during 1849 raids on three bookshops in St. Petersburg, Dorpat, and Riga. Many of the most famous newspapers and publications of nineteenth-century Europe, such as Italian nationalist Giuseppe Mazzini's newspaper *Young Italy*, Victor Hugo's famous attack on Napoleon III entitled *Napoleon le Petit*, and the socialist newspapers of the exiled Russian radicals Aleksandr Herzen and Vladimir Lenin were smuggled into their target nations from abroad; during the 1878–90 period when socialist newspapers were outlawed in

Germany the Social Democratic Party's newspaper *Sozialdemokrat* was smuggled into that country by the thousands by a sophisticated operation run from Switzerland.[41]

The means by which media restrictions were legally evaded while technically complying with them were as varied as the mind can imagine. The use of blank space to replace censored words or caricatures was extremely common, as was the perfectly legal printing of extensive textual descriptions of censored drawings and theatrical scripts in states where prior censorship of plays and illustrations remained in effect after the printed word was liberated. Another common means of legally evading censorship restrictions was the use of what might be termed "dummy" newspaper names and editors. The first technique, known in Russia as "genealogy," was the practice of reopening a suppressed newspaper with the same staff under another name. For example, during the 1830s Swedish opposition leader Lars Johan Hierta's suppressed newspaper *Aftonbladet* was repeatedly resurrected as the "New," "Third," "Fourth" *Aftonbladet* and so on, until the regime finally gave up—and in general ceased harassing the opposition press—at the twenty-third *Aftonbladet.* Of course, such maneuvering required a somewhat tolerant regime to succeed: in Russia, after the Bolshevik newspaper *Pravda* (Truth) reconstituted itself eight times after 1912 under such names as *Workers' Truth* and *Proletarian Truth*, the regime shut it down for good on July 21, 1914, by arresting its entire staff and smashing its presses.[42]

In many countries, newspapers hired "dummy" editors to finesse the requirement that they name a "responsible editor" who could be prosecuted for any unsigned articles: newspapers responded by hiring "editors" who played no editorial role and thus could go to jail without disrupting their work. Thus, when the Danish socialist press was harassed during the 1880s, a house painter agreed to serve as the "responsible editor" of *Social-Demokraten* for ten crowns per week, plus a weekly bonus of five crowns while jailed, on the condition that no jail term exceed thirteen weeks. At one point, the *Frankfurter Zeitung* in Germany had five "responsible editors" jailed simultaneously, while *Pravda* employed forty "surrogate" editors, many of whom, the police reported, were "unintelligent" and often "absolutely illiterate" people who did "not take part in the work of the paper." The *Pravda* office frequently posted the sign, "No editors needed."[43]

Another virtually universal means of evading censorship was "Aesopian language," that is, critical commentary on the current political regime in veiled form. "Aesopian language" was perhaps most developed in Russia (where this term was coined). Historian Bertram Wolfe notes:

> Since direct political criticism was prohibited all literature tended to become a criticism of Russian life, and literary criticism but another form of social criticism. . . .

If the censor forebade explicit statement, he was skillfully eluded by indirection—by innocent seeming tales of other lands or times, by complicated parables, animal fables, double meanings, overtones, by investing apparently trivial events with the pent-up energies possessing the writer, so that the reader became compelled to dwell upon them until their hidden meanings became manifest. Men found means of conveying a criticism of the regime through a statistical monograph on German agriculture, through the study of a sovereign four centuries dead, the review of a Norwegian play, the analysis of some evil in the Prussian or some virtue in the British state.[44]

Russian writers became so skilled in such approaches that late nineteenth-century police chief V. K. Pleve (later minister of the interior, assassinated in 1904) asked the Populist socialist writer N. K. Mikhailovsky, "Why do you want freedom of the press when even without it you are a master of saying between the lines all that you wish to say?" The mid-century Czech journalist Karl Havlicek became famous for his articles about British mistreatment of Ireland, which everyone knew were really about Austrian denial of Czech national rights; the Serbian satirist Radoje Domanovic was equally renowned for his tales of the mythical land of "Stradija," where the police spared voters from troubling themselves to cast votes in free elections and government ministers played musical chairs. The young German historian (1927 Nobel Peace Prize recipient) Ludwig Quidde created a sensation when it was realized that his 1894 article, "Caligula: A Study of Roman Caesarean Madness," was clearly about Kaiser (Caesar) Wilhelm II, down to exact descriptions of the foibles and delusions of grandeur both shared. The article sold 150,000 copies as a pamphlet, and although the government did not prosecute Quidde in fear of further underlining the parallel, he was later jailed for three months for criticizing the Kaiser at a public meeting, which the authorities made clear was in retaliation for the Caligula article.[45]

Although "Aesopian language" unquestionably allowed skilled writers to frequently evade censorship restrictions and no doubt sharpened the authorial pen and the public mind, the need to use such linguistic maneuvers carried a cost: Karl Marx, whose newspaper *Rheinische Zeitung* was suppressed in Prussia in 1843 for pursuing a "tendency" to "stir up discontent," wrote a friend that the regime had given him "back my freedom," as he had become tired of having to "fight with needles instead of clubs" and "tired of hypocrisy, stupidity, raw authority, and our cringing, bowing, back turning and word picking." Similarly, an 1859 Russian journal demanded, "When, my God, will it be possible, in keeping with the demands of conscience, not to use cunning, not to fabricate allegorical phrases, but to speak one's opinion directly and simply in public?" The censor who passed this article was demoted and the journal was suppressed.[46]

THE IMPACT AND SIGNIFICANCE OF NINETEENTH-CENTURY EUROPEAN POLITICAL CENSORSHIP

Reaching global conclusions about the impact and significance of political censorship in nineteenth-century Europe is not only difficult but verges on the impossible. One problem is that the nature of restrictions varied considerably from country to country and, even within the same country, often from time to time and sometimes (as Professors Davis and Lenman demonstrate in their respective chapters on Italy and Germany) from region to region. But the greater difficulty arises in trying to meaningfully measure and isolate the impact of censorship, especially as restrictions on expression were part and parcel of a whole range of politically repressive controls in nineteenth-century Europe, such as severe limitations on voting rights, freedom of association and assembly, the freedom to form trade unions and strike, and so on.[47] And finally, the evidence about the impact of censorship is extraordinarily mixed: in some ways it was unquestionably highly effective, yet no country was able to even approach completely suppressing dissident ideas for a prolonged period of time or to indefinitely hold back the tides of change.

To elaborate on this last point first, the evidence just summarized about resistance to censorship makes clear that even the most repressive states, as Professors Höbelt and Ruud elaborate in their respective chapters on Austria and Russia, were never fully able to contain opposition media. Three fundamental reasons largely explain this. First, the sheer cleverness and persistence of writers and artists eventually always enabled them to find cracks in the censorship dams; as Prince V. F. Odoevsky, a drafter of the 1828 Russian censorship law, concluded, "No police can stop all the stratagems" of "talented writers." Second, the rising tide of print increasingly overwhelmed the censors. Even in Russia, which remained throughout the century the European repressive regime par excellence, in 1914 there were only about 100 officials charged with censorship responsibilities who were expected to cope with over 30,000 books and over 3,000 periodicals (compared to only 1,000 periodicals as recently as 1900) published in more than fifty languages.[48]

Third, as societies modernized and became more literate and politically aware, media restrictions increasingly backfired, discrediting the repressive regimes and increasing the interest and demand for the persecuted material. Thus, Swiss historian and journalist Jean Sismondi noted in 1847 that London and Parisian booksellers agreed that the primary demand for books was "in the countries where they are prohibited." As early as 1733 a popular British dramatist, James Branton, made the same point in verse, asking, "Can statutes keep the British press in awe/When that sells best, that's most against the law?" The German journalist and playwright Gustav Freytag, recalling the pre-1848 censorship in a book published in 1870, wrote:

> The most vehement complaints against the censorship have given but an incomplete reflection of the misery, dejection and bitterness with which this tyrannical, insolent and heavy-handed governess imbued the soul of the people. She made the author a rebel and the reader vindictive. No foe to the monarchy could have invented a better means to set people against their ruler. . . . Every word an author wrote on any question of the day was attended by a feeling of humiliation. . . . He had daily the temptation ironically and with dagger-point concealed to stab where he dare not fight with open words. . . . In a similar way millions of German readers grew accustomed to reading between the lines and to amplify the text in an obnoxious sense.

These three factors in combination can significantly explain the extraordinary 1913 admission of the Munich police chief who wrote to his superior, "The power of the press is these days so great that this important factor in public life cannot be left out of account even by the state authorities. In the long run no official agency can maintain a negative or hostile attitude towards it."[49]

Yet, viewed from another perspective, the significance and impact of nineteenth-century European political censorship appear to be overwhelmingly evident: measured by the tens of thousands of censorship bans, prosecutions, fines, jail terms, and suppressions, nothing is more clear than that the various restrictions on the press, drawings, songs, theater, and cinema substantially interfered with the free flow of opinions and expression of thousands of journalists, dramatists, caricaturists, and other artists and limited the choices of tens of millions of Europeans. There can be little doubt, for example, that the insipid quality of much of the nineteenth-century European stage throughout the century, as well as that of most pre-1850 European journalism, was substantially due to censorship. Thus, historians of the German stage have written that theater was "rarely inspired" as censorship "contributed to mediocrity by discouraging anything considered potentially offensive or dangerous," and that especially after the suppression of the 1848 revolutions "plays presented had to be so inoffensive as to become almost mindless." With regard to the press, historian Frederick Artz notes that an English traveler's comments about the Spanish press in 1820 could have been equally said of that of Austria and Italy: they contained nothing but weather reports and "accounts of miracles wrought by different Virgins, lives of holy friars and sainted nuns, romances of marvelous conversions, libels against Jews, heretics and Freemasons, and histories of apparitions." The great Czech historian Frantisek Palacky complained in 1830, "I do not know how it will end when we cannot write about anything except cook-books and prayer-books, fairy-tales and charades," and the Saxon journalist Robert Blum similarly lamented in the 1840s, "We must write pure nonsense or not be published at all." British observer William Howitt wrote in 1844 that the German press published nothing about "all those great questions which involve the political progress and development of a people," as "over all the heads of such journals hangs the iron pen of the censor and fills every writer with terror."[50]

Statistical data that compare levels of repressive media actions across countries are extremely scarce, but those available confirm the overwhelming impressionist evidence that among the major countries conditions were harshest in Russia and most tolerant in England, with France, Italy, Spain, Germany, and Austria occupying an intermediate position. For example, during the entire decade of the 1890s, only twenty-two plays were banned in Britain, but 157 were forbidden in Berlin alone; the yet far harsher censorship in Russia is suggested by the fact that in 1903 alone 249 plays were banned. Other data indicate that British censors banned entirely less than 1 percent of all plays between 1852 and 1912, while in France about 2.5 percent were entirely forbidden and another 18 percent suffered enforced modification between 1835 and 1847, and in Russia in 1866–67 about 10 percent of new plays submitted were entirely rejected and another 13 percent were forcibly modified; in 1865–66 in Russia, only 20 percent of all nonperiodical publications that were subject to prior censorship completely escaped modifications or bans.[51]

The relatively few statistical studies available concerning the motivation of repressive media actions confirm that maintenance of the current political order was the foremost goal (thus, in most countries, where working-class movements were perceived as the major threat as modernization progressed, they also became the leading censorship targets, but in Austria, as Professor Höbelt demonstrates in his chapter, the leading threat, and therefore the prime censorship victim, was ethnic nationalism). According to an analysis of over 200 French censorship and prosecutorial decisions involving plays, newspapers, and novels undertaken by four different regimes between 1815 and 1870, about 55 percent of such actions were based on perceived challenges to existing political/social authority; of almost 500 plays censored in France between 1835 and 1847, political motivations were foremost in 48 percent of the instances (with religious concerns accounting for 20 percent and moral considerations for the remaining 32 percent); and an analysis of articles censored in 1846–47 in the radical German newspaper *Trier'sche Zeitung* suggests that political motivations, such as attacks on the government, the censorship and the army, and inciting the poor against the rich, were foremost 80 percent of the time.[52]

When the German press was temporarily freed by the 1848 revolutions, the *Dortmunder Anzeiger* confirmed William Howitt's just-quoted 1844 observation about prior journalistic conditions, declaring on March 25 that "the citizens of Dortmund must now demand that their *Anzeiger* no longer provide them merely with advice on the subject of buying butter or herrings, but also advice on how they might act in the best interest of the town and the Fatherland." The newspaper explosion of the freed press of 1848 (along with similar developments in the wake of the 1830 Revolution in France, the 1868 and 1881 French press liberalizations, and the 1905 Revolution in Russia) provides an unusual example of a "factual counterfactual" example in history, demonstrating quite clearly how things might have turned out differently in the absence of censorship. Everywhere in 1848 demands for an end to press controls were foremost in the minds of those in the streets; everywhere they were among the first concessions made; and everywhere the result was an unprecedented eruption of journalistic energy. Throughout the Austrian Empire, the number of newspapers increased between 1847 and 1848 from seventy-nine (only nineteen of which were permitted to discuss political affairs) to 388 (306 of which discussed politics), and the number of Czech-language newspapers jumped from thirteen to fifty-two; in all of central Europe, the German-language press exploded from less than 950 in 1847 to about 1,700 two years later, including, in the Prussian Rhineland, a doubling of daily and weekly newspapers from thirty-six to seventy; in both Rome and Venice about 100 new newspapers began publishing. In Paris, an estimated 450 newspapers (some of them only one page and many of them ephemeral) were established and the total combined daily press run skyrocketed from 50,000 to 400,000. A contemporary Paris brochure described a profusion of "giant newspapers, dwarf newspapers, wise newspapers, foolish newspapers . . . elegantly-dressed newspapers, poorly-dressed newspapers . . . large, fat newspapers, consumptive newspapers." Press historian Irene Collins adds that "every color of paper was used: the *Chandelle démocratique* appeared in scarlet, the *Sanguinaire* in pink, the *Sorcière républicaine* in white with yellow stripes, and the *Souveraineté du peuple* in green, while the *Guillotine* startled the public with red ink on white paper."[53]

There were similar massive expansions in the number of theaters whenever licensing requirements ended—for example, in Germany the 1870 abolition of licensing led to the immediate founding of about ninety new theaters. The same phenomenon can be demonstrated when newspaper taxes were lifted and the press was made more affordable to common people: in the Netherlands, for example, the number of daily papers immediately jumped from nine to fourteen when newspaper taxes were lifted in 1869; in Britain after newspaper taxes were lowered from fourpence to one penny per newspaper in 1836, total annual sales doubled from 25.5 million to over 53 million within two years, and when the last of the taxes was abolished in 1855, six provincial dailies began operations on a single day in July 1855, while before then only a handful of dailies had been able to establish themselves outside London.[54]

Ultimately, any attempt to summarize, in a sentence or even a paragraph, the mass of sometimes contradictory information about the effectiveness and importance of nineteenth-century European political censorship across various media, countries, and time periods is doomed to futility, above all because censorship's effects simply cannot be isolated from other contemporaneous developments. But, in the end, there is no need to search for a magic summarizing conclusion about censorship's overall impact because we can reach one major conclusion that is both irrefutable and of great importance: the study of censorship offers an extraordinarily sensitive and often deep insight into the minds of the authorities, including how their hopes, fears, and overall strategies differed from time to time and place to place. In the words of French legislator Robert Mitchell to the Chamber of Deputies in 1880, addressing specifically the caricature censorship, but equally applicable to other types of media and other types of regulation:

> Drawings which displease the government are always forbidden. Those which have gained official favor are displayed in the windows of all the bookstores, are sold in all the kiosks. This provides a valuable indicator for the attentive observer, curious for precise information on the tastes, preferences, sentiments, hates and intentions of those who have control and care over our destinies. In studying refused drawings and authorized drawings, we know exactly what the government fears and what it encourages, we have a clear revelation of its intimate thoughts.[55]

NOTES

1. Alex Hall, *Scandal, Sensation and Social Democracy: The SPD Press and Wilhelmine Germany* (Cambridge, England, 1977), 13; *World Press Review*, May 1998, 14.

2. John Merriman, "Contested Freedoms in the French Revolutions, 1830–1871," in Isser Woloch, ed., *Revolution and the Meanings of Freedom in the Nineteenth-Century* (Stanford, Calif., 1996), 187; Gary Thurston, *The Popular Theatre Movement in Russia, 1862–1919* (Evanston, Ill., 1998), 166.

3. Theodore Hamerow, *The Birth of a New Europe: State and Society in the Nineteenth Century* (Chapel Hill, N.C., 1983) includes an excellent collection of statistical material.

4. Ibid., 135; Andrew Janos, *The Politics of Backwardness in Hungary, 1825–1945* (Princeton, N.J., 1982), 162–63.

5. Charles Ruud, *Fighting Words: Imperial Censorship and the Russian Press, 1804–1906* (hereafter Ruud, *Fighting*) (Toronto, 1982), 58; Irene Collins, *The Age of Progress: A Survey of European History, 1789–1870* (London, 1964), 278; B. J. Hovde, *The Scandinavian Countries, 1720–1865: The Rise of the Middle Classes* (Boston, 1843), II, 600; Gerald Brenan, *The Spanish Labyrinth: An Account of the Social and Political Background to the Spanish Civil War* (Cambridge, England, 1964), 56.

6. Roger Price, *The French Second Republic: A Social History* (Ithaca, N.Y., 1972), 254; J. McClelland, *Autocrats and Academics: Education, Culture and Society in Tsarist Russia* (Chicago, 1979), 116–17.

7. Ruud, *Fighting*, 69; James Allen, *Popular French Romanticism: Authors, Readers and Books in the 19th Century* (Syracuse, N.Y., 1981), 153; James Retallak, "From Pariah to Professional? The Journalist in German Society and Politics,

from the Late Enlightenment to the Rise of Hitler," *German Studies Review*, 16 (1993), 182; James Sheehan, *German History, 1770–1866* (Oxford, 1989), 215.

8. J. L. Talmon, *Romanticism and Revolt: Europe 1815–1848* (New York, 1967), 35; Donald Emerson, *Metternich and the Political Police* (The Hague, 1968, 116); Frederick Artz, *Reaction and Revolution, 1814–1832* (New York, 1963), 67; Raymond Carr, *Spain, 1808–1939* (Oxford, 1966), 240; Nancy Nolte, "Government and Theater in Restoration Europe," *Consortium on Revolutionary Proceedings 1985* (Athens, Ga., 1986), 435; Daniel Rader, *The Journalists and the July Revolution in France* (The Hague, 1973), 221–22, 14; Sedlnitzy quotation cited in footnote 22, Chapter 6 in this volume; Vincent Godefroy, *The Dramatic Genius of Verdi* (New York, 1977), II, 50.

9. *Archives Parlementaires de 1787 à 1860* (hereafter *AP*) (Paris, 1898), vol. 98, 258, (Paris, 1876), vol. 33, 330.

10. Mary Townsend, *Forbidden Laughter: Popular Humor and the Limits of Repression in Nineteenth-Century Prussia* (Ann Arbor, Mich., 1992), 180–81; Archives Nationales, Paris (henceforth AN), F^{18} 2342; *Journal Officiel de la République Française* (hereafter *JO*), June 8, 1880, 6212–13.

11. W. E. Yates, *Theatre in Vienna: A Critical History, 1776–1995* (Cambridge, England, 1996), 25; Donald Kimbell, *Verdi in the Age of Italian Risorgimento* (Cambridge, England, 1981), 25.

12. Yates, 26; Odile Krakovitch, *Les Pièces de Théâtre soumises a La Censure (1800–1830)* (Paris, 1982); Albert Delpit, "La Liberté des théâtres et les café-concerts," *Revue des deux mondes* (February 1, 1878), 623.

13. Odile Krakovitch, "La mise en pièces des théâtres: la censure des spectacles au XIXe siècle," in *Maintien de l'ordre et polices en France et en Europe au XIXe siècle* (1987), 294; Laurence Senelick, ed., *National Theater in Northern and Eastern Europe, 1746–1900* (Cambridge, England, 1991), 303.

14. Annie Prassoloff, "Y a-t-il une censure musicale?" in Franck Hochleitner, "La Censure à l'Opéra de Paris aux Débuts de la IIIe République," in Pascal Orly, ed., *La Censure en France a l'ère démocratique: 1848–* (Paris, 1997), 223–24.

15. Paul Leglise, *Histoire de la politique du cinema française* (Paris, 1970), 30–32; Marcel LaPierre, *Les Cent Visages du Cinéma* (Paris, 1948), 269.

16. John House, "Manet's *Maximilian*: Censorship and the Salon," in Elizabeth Childs, ed., *Suspended License: Censorship and the Visual Arts* (Seattle, Wash., 1997), 187.

17. J. Legge, *Rhyme and Revolution in Germany: A Study in German History, Life, Literature and Character, 1813–1850* (New York, 1918), 173; Jeffrey Brooks, *When Russians Learned to Read: Literacy and Popular Literature, 1861–1917* (Princeton, N.J., 1985), 299–301; Arlen Blium, "Censorship of Public Reading in Russia, 1870–1950," *Libraries and Culture*, 33 (1988), 18, 19; Albert Resis, "*Das Kapital* Comes to Russia," *Slavic Review*, 19 (1970), 221; Caspar Ferenczi, "Freedom of the Press under the Old Regime, 1905–1914," in *Civil Rights in Imperial Russia*, Olga Crisp and Linda Emondson, eds. (Oxford, 1989), 200, 201.

18. Elizabeth McKay, *Franz Schubert's Music for the Theatre* (Tutzing, 1991), 32; Norbert Bachleitner, "The Politics of the Book Trade in Nineteenth-Century Austria," *Austrian History Yearbook* 27 (1997), 109; AN, F^{18} 2342; Townsend, 179.

19. E. A. Swift, "Fighting the Germs of Disorder: The Censorship of Russian Popular Theater, 1888–1917," *Russian History*, 18 (1991), 31.

20. Odile Krakovitch, *Hugo Censuré: La liberté au théâtre au xixe siècle* (hereafter Krakovitch, *Hugo*) (1985), 131, 140; Claude Schumacher, ed., *Naturalism and Symbolism in European Theater, 1851–1918* (Cambridge, England, 1996), Document 46.

21. Laurence Fontaine, *History of Pedlars in Europe* (New York, 1986), 169–70; Bachleitner, 109.

22. Blium, 19.

23. Maryse Maget-Dodominici, "La 'Loi de Justice et d'Amour' ou la Liberté de la Presse," *Revue Suisse d'Histoire*, 40 (1990), 1–3; Rader, 9; Legge, 176; John Hohenburg, *Free Press/Free People: The Best Cause* (New York, 1971), 106.

24. Henry Schulte, *The Spanish Press* (Urbana, Ill., 1968); Peter Kenez, *The Birth of the Propaganda State* (Cambridge, England, 1985), 22; Anthony Smith, *The Newspaper: An International History* (London, 1979), 110; Irene Collins, *The Government and the Newspaper Press in France, 1814–1881* (hereafter Collins, *Government*) (Oxford, 1959), 129, 150, 188–89; F. W. J. Hemmings, *Theatre and State in France, 1760–1905* (Cambridge: England, 1994), 260–70; Robert Justin Goldstein, *Censorship of Political Caricature in Nineteenth-Century France* (Kent, Ohio, 1989).

25. McKay, 29; Roy Pascal, *From Naturalism to Expressionism: German Literature and Society, 1880–1918* (New York, 1973), 266; Torbjörn Vallinder, "The Swedish Jury System in Press Cases," *Journal of Legal History*, 8 (1987), 199.

26. Schulte, 197; Bachleitner, 105, 110.

27. W. E. Yates, *Grillparzer* (Cambridge, England, 1972), 12; Alberic Cahuet, *La Liberté du Théâtre en France et a l'Etranger* (Paris, 1902), 205–7.

28. Sidney Monas, *The Third Section: Police and Society in Russia under Nicholas I* (Cambridge, Mass., 1961), 180–81; Marianna Choldin, *A Fence Around the Empire: Russian Censorship of Western Ideas Under the Tsars* (Durham, N.C., 1985), 39, 57, 73, 94; Frederik Ohles, *Germany's Rude Awakening: Censorship in the Land of the Brothers Grimm* (Kent, Ohio, 1992), 52.

29. For the quotations, see footnotes 26 and 22, respectively, in chapters on Spain and Germany in this volume.

30. See, generally, Charles Ruud, "Limits on the 'Freed' Press of 18th- and 19th-Century Europe," *Journalism Quarterly*, 56 (1979), 521–530; and, for specific figures: Ruud, *Fighting*, 15; Hall, 14; Charles Gulick, *Austria from Habsburg to Hitler* (Berkeley, Calif., 1948), I, 22; Denis Smith, *Italy: A Modern History* (Ann Arbor, Mich., 1959); Balmuth, 136; Louise McReynolds, *The News Under Russia's Old Regime* (Princeton, N.J., 1991), Appendix B; Merriman, 194; Collins, *Government*, 79, 178.

31. Ibid., xi; Roger Bellet, *Presse et Journalism sous le Second Empire* (1967), 25.

32. Spanish quotation is cited in footnote 15 in Chapter 5 in this volume; Clyde Thogmartin, *The National Daily Press of France* (Birmingham, Ala., 1998), 58: Hohenburg, 92–93.

33. Rader, 19; Bruce Garver, *The Young Czech Party, 1874–1901* (New Haven, Conn., 1978), 47; Smith, *Newspaper*, 122.

34. Richard Stourac and Kathleen McCreery, *Theatre as a Weapon: Workers'*

Theatre in the Soviet Union, Germany and Britain, 1917–1934 (London, 1986), 191; James Cuno, "Philipon et Desloges," *Cahiers de l'Institut d'Histoire de la Presse et de l'Opinion*, 7 (1983), 152; A. Aspinall, "The Social Status of Journalists at the Beginning of the Nineteenth Century," *Review of English Studies*, 21 (1945), 217; Lenore O'Boyle, "The Image of the Journalist in France, Germany and England, 1815–1848," *Comparative Studies in Society and History*, 10 (1968), 308; John Merriman, *The Agony of the Republic: The Repression of the Left in Revolutionary France, 1848–1951* (New Haven, Conn., 1978), 39.

35. Stephen Kippur, *Jules Michelet* (Albany, N.Y., 1981), 116, 119; Saul Padover, *Karl Marx on Freedom of the Press and Censorship* (New York, 1974), xiv; Press Commission quotation cited in footnote 17 in Chapter 2 in this volume.

36. Hovde, II, 524–25, 541–42; Svend Thorsen, *Newspapers in Denmark* (Copenhagen, 1953), 7–8; Richard Clogg, *A Short History of Greece* (Cambridge, England, 1979), 86.

37. McKay, 35.

38. Monas, 244; Herbert Boman, *Vissarion Belinski* (New York, 1969), 50; P. Spencer, "Censorship by Imprisonment in France, 1830–1847," *Romanic Review*, 47 (1956), 27; Lamar Beman, *Selected Articles on Censorship of the Theatre and of Moving Pictures* (New York, 1931), 254; Andrés Spies, *Opera, State and Society in the Third Republic, 1875–1914* (New York, 1998), 129; W. E. Yates, "Cultural Life in Early Nineteenth-Century Austria," *Forum for Modern Language Studies*, 13 (1977), 108; Manolis Paraschos, "The Modern Greek Press," *Modern Greek Studies Yearbook*, 7 (1991), 27; Heine quote cited in footnote 15 in Chapter 2 in this volume; Choldin, 5.

39. Schumacher, Document 175; Krakovitch, *Hugo*, 245.

40. Ibid., 84.

41. Choldin, 63, 85.

42. Hovde, 524; Angus Roxburgh, *Pravda: Inside the Soviet News Machine* (New York, 1987), 17.

43. Thorsen, 27; Roxburgh, 18; Whitman Bassow, "The Pre-Revolutionary *Pravda* and Tsarist Censorship," *American Slavic and East European Review*, 13 (1954), 60.

44. Bertram Wolfe, *Three Who Made a Revolution* (New York, 1964), 36.

45. Hugh Seton-Watson, *The Russian Empire, 1801–1917* (Oxford, 1976), 481; Alex Hall, "The Kaiser, the Wilhelmine State and Lèse-Majesté," *German Life and Letters*, 27 (1974), 104–05.

46. Padover, xxi; Ruud, *Fighting*, 110.

47. See, generally, Robert Justin Goldstein, *Political Repression in Nineteenth-Century Europe* (London, 1983); and the introductory chapter to Goldstein, *Political Censorship of the Arts and the Press in Nineteenth-Century Europe* (London, 1989).

48. Ruud, *Fighting*, 56; Ferenczi, 198–200.

49. Eugene and Pauline Anderson, *Political Institutions and Social Change in Continental Europe in the Nineteenth Century* (Berkeley, 1967), 265; Smith, 59; Legge, 177; Robin Lenman, "Control of the Visual Image in Imperial Germany," in John McCarthy and Werner von der Ohe (eds.), *Zensur und Kultur/Censorship and Culture* (Tübingen, 1995), 115.

50. Oscar Brockett, *History of the Theatre* (Boston, 1977), 369; Marvin Carlson,

The German Stage in the Nineteenth Century (Metuchen, N.J., 1972), 121; Frederick Artz, *Reaction and Revolution, 1814–1832* (New York, 1934), 134–35; J. Zacek, "Metternich's Censors: The Case of Palacky," in P. Brock and H. Skillings, *The Czech Renascence of the Nineteenth Century* (Toronto, 1970), 99; E. Newman, *Restoration Radical: Robert Blum and the Challenge of German Democracy* (Boston, 1974), 46; O'Boyle, 305.

51. Gary Stark, "Trials and Tribulations: Authors' Responses to Censorship in Imperial Germany, 1885–1914," *German Studies*, 12 (1989), 449; Richard Findlater, *Banned! A Review of Theatrical Censorship in Britain* (London, 1967), 73; Daniel Balmuth, *Censorship in Russia, 1865–1905* (Washington, D.C. 1979), 42.

52. James Allen, *In the Public Eye: A History of Reading in Modern France, 1800–1940* (Princeton, N.J., 1991), 94; Odile Krakovitch, *Hugo*, 286; Jonathan Sperber, *Rhineland Radicals: The Democratic Movement and the Revolution of 1848–1849* (Princeton, N.J., 1991), 125.

53. Wolfram Siemann, *The German Revolution of 1848–49* (New York, 1998), 112–13; Jonathan Sperber, *The European Revolutions of 1848–1851* (Cambridge, England, 1994), 151–52; Charles Ledre, *La Presse à l'Assault de La Monarchie, 1815–1848* (Paris, 1960), 216; Collins, *Government*, 102.

54. Schumacher, Document 45; Maarten Schneider, *Netherlands Press Today* (Leiden, 1951), 10; Joel Weiner, *The War of the Unstamped: The Movement to Repeal the British Newspaper Tax, 1830–1836* (Ithaca, N.Y., 1969), 260; Lucy Brown, *Victorian News and Newspapers* (Oxford, 1985), 33; A. Wadsworth, "Newspaper Circulation, 1800–1954," *Transactions of the Manchester Statistical Society* (1954–55), 18–20.

55. *JO*, June 8, 1880, 6214.

2

Germany

Robin Lenman

> A revolutionary must be capable of anything. He must excel as much in the destruction of negative values as in the construction of positive ones. When you students assume the right to cast intellectual filth into the flames, you must also accept the duty to clear the way for a truly German spirit in place of this garbage. And for this reason you do well, at this midnight hour, to consign the evil spirit of the past to the flames.[1]

This speech by Nazi Propaganda Minister Josef Goebbels on the Berlin Opernplatz on the night of May 10 to 11, 1933, accompanied the Berlin students' public burning of thousands of books defined as degenerate, unpatriotic, treasonable, or otherwise inimical to Germany's emerging "race community." Newsreel pictures of this event are among the most powerful images of cultural control by a modern state. Less dramatically implemented was the highly comprehensive censorship of the former German Democratic Republic (East Germany), abolished only in January 1990. But official regulation of words and images has not been confined to recent and nondemocratic German states. The culturally liberal Weimar Republic passed laws sanctioning film censorship (1920) and protecting young people against exploitative pulp fiction (1926). Almost 200 years ago, the Carlsbad Decrees of 1819 established one of nineteenth-century Europe's most far-reaching systems of literary censorship, which remained in operation until the revolutions of 1848. In short, censorship has always been closely linked with broader German history, and never more intricately so than in the century following the Napoleonic Wars.

German history between 1815 and 1914 can best be summarized under three main headings: progress toward national unity; the development of liberal democratic political and legal institutions; and industrialization. The German Confederation, founded after the defeat of Napoleon and dissolved following the Austro-Prussian War of 1866, was not designed, despite its incorporation of the centralized system of political repression associated with Austrian Chancellor Prince Metternich, as the prototype of a unitary German state; indeed, one of Metternich's principal aims was the suppression of nationalism. The Confederation's thirty-nine member-states (from 1817) varied enormously in size—9.3 million Prussians at one extreme, 5,000 inhabitants of the Duchy of Liechtenstein at the other—economic resources, ethnic and confessional composition, and political structure. Differences in historical experience and dynastic allegiance further increased the diversity with which Germany's minority of committed nationalists had to grapple during the first few decades of the period. But the full complexity of the "national question" became clear during the upheavals of 1848–49, when liberals attempted, heroically but vainly, to create a single German constitution and state. When it eventually did occur, with the formation of the German Empire in 1871, unification (but without Austria) was the result of a power-political compromise, deeply regretted by many, that reflected Prussian political interests at least as much as German-nationalist aspirations. Moreover, diversity continued to be a fundamental feature of the new Empire. By 1914, a widespread sense of common identity probably had emerged, albeit coexisting with strong individual-state and regional loyalties. Politically and militarily, Prussian hegemony was a reality that, from the outset, no one could ignore. Cultural diversity persisted, however, and in important legal and administrative respects Germany remained fragmented until at least World War I.

Two other characteristics of the Second Reich, both originating before 1871, fostered a sense on the part of many Germans that they were living in a deeply divided society. The first was the clash between Germany's dominant liberal-Protestant political culture and its large Catholic minority, about one-third of the population. Many liberals perceived Catholics as an antinational element within the new Empire, and, more or less accurately, as inimical to the progressive secular society with which they themselves identified. The second, still more worrying split was between what can broadly be described as "bourgeois society" and Germany's rapidly growing industrial proletariat, much of it (though still only a minority in 1914) organized in trade unions affiliated to the Social Democratic Party (SPD). Neither intense persecution under German Chancellor Otto von Bismarck (1878–90), followed by continual state harassment after his departure, nor politically motivated welfare legislation could prevent the expansion of the

SPD, which in 1912 became the largest party in the Imperial Parliament (Reichstag), and developed a vast organization with scores of newspapers, hundreds of branches, and hundreds of thousands of members. Although by then its leaders' outlook was considerably more moderate than the party's general image and rhetoric suggested, the movement's very existence was regarded by the Empire's elites and by millions of ordinary Germans as a menace to the established order.

Like national unification, the development of liberal-democratic institutions in Germany was a process that continued throughout the century under discussion and, despite considerable achievements, was still incomplete in 1914. Broadly speaking, it was the affair of the liberal-Protestant middle class, though with significant input, respectively toward the beginning and end of the period, from progressive aristocrats and moderate Socialists. Liberals' democratic credentials were modest by twentieth-century standards, since they mostly opposed both mass suffrage and female participation in politics. However, they were identified with a number of interconnected aims essential to the creation of a modern democratic society. The first was the creation of a liberal legal culture, with the abolition of feudal jurisdictions, the consolidation of the rule of law, and the establishment of an independent judiciary capable of curbing arbitrary state power. The second was constitutionalism: the formulation of explicit and binding ground-rules governing the relationship between sovereigns, ministers, and representative bodies, and the establishment of parliamentary government. Finally, they demanded freedom of expression as the indispensable prerequisite for rational debate and constructive political action.

From this perspective, nineteenth-century Germany appears a battleground on which liberal parliamentarians, publicists, and lawyers fought for concessions from monarchs and bureaucrats determined to defend the prerogatives of the neo-absolutist state. For a brief period in 1848–49, liberals' most cherished objectives seemed to be within reach—only to recede again (though not entirely) in the subsequent years of reaction. In Prussia, after a period of brief and illusory participation in government (the so-called New Era, 1858–61), liberals' inability, in the 1860s, to assert parliamentary control over the executive, and especially the army, foreshadowed the problems of the Empire: chancellors responsible to the Emperor, not the Reichstag; soldiers sworn to obey monarchs, not politicians; and constitutional progress in the smaller states of the south and southwest, but not in Prussia or the Reich. However, once castigated for their failure to complete a democratic revolution, German liberals have been more kindly treated by recent historians, who have highlighted their substantive gains by 1914: the indispensability of Parliament at national and individual state levels; Germany's culture of obedience to law; and hard-won, still imperfect, but increasingly effective safeguards for freedom of expression.

In the background, finally, was one of Europe's most dynamic industrial revolutions, with Germany's transformation from a fragmented assortment of mainly rural economies before 1850 to an economic superpower by 1914. By then, Germany was not only overtaking Britain in coal and iron production, but had established a position of world leadership in the science-based, capital-intensive industries of the Second Industrial Revolution: chemicals, pharmaceuticals, optics, and electrotechnology. The price of economic modernization and the wealth and power it generated, however, was a vast change in the structure of society, with the creation of a huge working class living in terrible urban conditions and a mass movement (the SPD) of profound and sustained political protest.

Within this larger framework the history of censorship was complex, impinging on practically every means of expression, new and old: books and newspapers, cartoons, popular prints, photographs, theatrical and cinematic performances, and, to a degree, works of fine art. How far, in the interests of stability, the state should extend its traditional supervision of popular culture to that of an increasingly literate and mobilized mass society that was in the process of being reshaped by a communications and transportation revolution was a major political issue of the late nineteenth and early twentieth centuries. The production, distribution, and reception of verbal and visual messages were hugely altered by the industrialization of printing, the creation of dense transport and telegraphic networks, and the emergence of near-total adult literacy. Large-scale migration and urbanization further transformed the arena within which ideas were disseminated and controlled. The practice of censorship was further complicated by the political and legal diversity already mentioned. The instruments of control developed and changed as the century progressed: whereas "preventive" (i.e., pre-publication) censorship of printed words and images was effectively abandoned in 1848, it remained in force for the theater and other forms of live performance until 1918, and won a new lease on life with the coming of the cinema. Meanwhile, post-1848 "press products" were subject to forms of "repressive" (i.e., post-publication) control that had the effect, far more than the old preventive system, of placing publishers, editors, and distributors in the role of censors. Even under the comparatively liberal Reich Press Law of 1874, scope for official interference with the press was substantial, though varying in its application according to divergences of legal procedure in different parts of the Empire and—a perennial feature of control systems, not just in Germany—in relation to the different publics (educated men of property versus women, young people and the "lower orders") addressed by different media. Thus, cheap prints and pulp novels remained (controversially) vulnerable to police-state measures like colportage bans and the use of ill-defined criminal sanctions against "misdemeanors," while works of art and quality newspapers became increasingly immune to attack. Social Democrats, whose freedom of organization, movement, and expression had been radically curtailed by the Anti-Socialist Law of 1878–90, continued to be treated with exceptional severity by the police and the courts until the outbreak of World War I.

CONTROL OF PRINTED MEDIA UNTIL 1848

Censorship Regulations

Control of the printed word in German-speaking Central Europe had a history almost as long as that of printing itself. In Mainz, Johann Gutenberg's home city, Germany's first censorship mechanisms were established by the archbishop in 1486. In the sixteenth century, particularly in the reigns of Emperors Charles V and Maximilian II, the secular authorities also became involved in censorship, and by the late 1560s an Imperial Book Commission was established in Frankfurt-on-Main. Until the middle of the eighteenth century, the authorities were primarily concerned with religious literature. But news-sheets were suppressed as early as 1567; an Imperial Edict of 1715 warned against writings attacking the Holy Roman Empire; and after 1750 political censorship became predominant.

By the late eighteenth century the growth of reading and the emergence of a "public sphere" in which contemporary issues were being discussed encouraged demands for freedom of thought and communication. Most significant of all, perhaps, at a time when most jurists continued to defend censorship, was the view of the principal architect of the Prussian Legal Code (*Allgemeines Landrecht* [ALG]) of 1794, Carl Gottlieb Suarez, who described the institution as an attack on "one of the first and natural rights of human beings."[2] Nonetheless, incautious political commentators continued to risk heavy penalties: in 1777, for example, Christian Schubart received a ten-year prison sentence for insulting the Duke of Württemberg in his *Deutsche Chronik*. In Bavaria, Elector Max Joseph III set up a ten-man censorship college in 1769 primarily to suppress clerical attacks on his fiscal and other reforms, and the unpopularity of his successor Karl Theodor led to a tightening of the system in 1791. Against the background of the French Revolution, the list of authors whose works were banned, by the 1790s, with varying degrees of comprehensiveness in different parts of Germany, included Montaigne, Montesquieu, Rousseau, and Voltaire. German writers in the Bavarian index of forbidden books included Johann Wolfgang von Goethe, Immanuel Kant, Heinrich von Kleist, and Friedrich Schiller.

After the intensification of censorship resulting from the French Revolution, a somewhat more relaxed atmosphere returned at the very end of the eighteenth century. In Bavaria, for example, Karl Theodor abolished the College of Censors in favor of a system weighted more toward judicial (or "repressive") control. However, the Napoleonic invasion of Germany brought new upheavals, with the end of the Holy Roman Empire in 1806 entailing the abrogation of all imperial laws and institutions, including the censorship mechanisms in place since the sixteenth century. Although Napoleon did not attempt to impose a uniform system of formal press control on occupied Germany, French pressure increased after 1808 and demands for the suppression of hostile publications seem generally to have been followed with alacrity. (The notorious execution, in August 1806, of the Nuremberg bookseller Johann Philipp Palm for disseminating anti-French propaganda was carried out by the French military authorities on the Emperor's orders.)

At the Congress of Vienna held to redraw the map of Europe following Napoleon's defeat, Article 18 (d) of the Federal Acts of June 8, 1815, committed the Federal Diet to formulate, at its very first meeting (this proved to be wildly unrealistic), common press and copyright legislation for all the member-states of the new German Confederation. As pressure for legislative action mounted after 1815, the Diet faced three main options. At one extreme was the traditional "preventive" system requiring pre-publication censorship of all new writings, plus police powers to ban and confiscate material already in circulation. Its principal advocate, from the outset, was Austrian Chancellor Metternich, who regarded press freedom as "the scourge of the world."[3] At the opposite pole, adherents of the principles established in Britain and in revolutionary America and France rejected prior censorship, arguing that the press should be limited only by the ordinary laws protecting public order, morality, and the rights of individuals, to be enforced by the courts. An intermediate position distinguished between periodicals and "political" writings on the one hand and nonpolitical books on the other, maintaining censorship for the former but leaving the latter to the courts. This was the principle enshrined in the Press Edict appended to the Bavarian Constitution of May 26, 1818.

The Bavarian Constitution was the latest in a series of relatively liberal documents produced in the states recently under French influence, including Nassau (1814), Frankfurt (1816), and Württemberg (1817), all of which guaranteed press freedom in various forms. Meanwhile, behind the scenes, Metternich, alarmed by the spread of constitutionalism in Germany, was waiting for a pretext to impose his own reactionary program on the Confederation; this was supplied by the nationalist agitation that culminated in the assassination of the conservative publicist August von Kotzebue on March 23, 1819. Essential for the realization of Metternich's strategy was agreement between Austria and Prussia, where reform had been giving way to reaction since 1815, as symbolized by the banning of Joseph Görres's progressive paper, the *Rheinische Merkur*, in January 1816. Such accord was reached at a meeting between Metternich and Prussian Prime Minister Hardenberg on August 1, 1819, and endorsed later that month by the delegates of ten German states assembled at Carlsbad in an atmosphere of intense crisis. The resulting package of reactionary measures (known as the Carlsbad Decrees) was then passed unanimously by the Frankfurt Diet on September 20. In the winter and spring of 1819–20, a conference called by Metternich in Vienna drafted a series of conservative amendments to the 1815 Federal Acts that, among other safety mechanisms, provided for federal intervention to restore law and order in individual member-states and—crucially, in view of developments since 1814—invalidated any constitutional provisions that might prevent a ruler from honoring his commitments to the Confederation. These so-called Vienna Final Acts, passed by the Diet in July 1820, had the effect, in historian James Sheehan's words, of turning the Confederation into "a kind of counterrevolutionary holding company through which Metternich could coordinate governmental action against his political enemies."[4]

The first of the Carlsbad Decrees imposed strict controls on German universities. Academics who expressed subversive or immoral opinions—a pairing often encountered in censorship-related regulations—could be excluded from all institutions of higher learning. Students, too, could be banned from the entire system, and those involved with forbidden organizations like the nationalist fellowships (*Burschenschaften*) could also be denied public employment, a draconian sanction at a time when, as the writer Karl Gutzkow recalled of his student days, "Any kind of job that had some state connection was what people were after, and only that. Any independent activity, in which one relied on one's own resources, was regarded as adventurous and dubious."[5] The third decree established a central seven-man Investigation Commission with far-reaching powers to conduct inquiries, commandeer documents, and arrest and interrogate suspects in order to expose "revolutionary machinations and demagogic connections" throughout the Confederation.

Most notorious, however, was the long and detailed Press Law.[6] Its first paragraph imposed prior censorship on all periodicals, as well as books of fewer than 320 pages; laws permitting judicial ("repressive") control of such publications were suspended (§3). Although works longer than 320 pages could be dealt with according to individual state rules, a publication that gave offense to another member-state had to be prosecuted (§1). Any government that objected to a short book or periodical approved in another state could request repressive action there or, if satisfaction was not forthcoming, appeal to the Diet for a federal ban; and the Diet could also act on its own initiative, including the total suppression, without appeal, of any offending periodical (§§5, 6). The editor of any paper banned by federal decree was forbidden to exercise a similar function for five years (§7). These "provisional" measures were originally valid for five years, but they were extended indefinitely, at Austria's request, in August 1824. The wording of the Press Law, particularly the imposition of a "solemn undertaking" on member-states to implement it with maximum vigilance, while avoiding "mutual complaints and unpleasant discussions" as far as possible (§5), shows that Metternich—realistically, as we shall see—anticipated friction and lack of uniformity in its application. In principle, nevertheless, the Carlsbad "system" embodied a degree of censorship centralization and effectiveness hitherto unprecedented in Germany, so long as Austria and Prussia remained steadfast. Even if the Catholic publicist Görres described the Press Law in October 1819 as ludicrous, adding that its creators could "more easily fill a sieve with fleas than lock up the realm of ideas in their pen,"[7] its implications for writers and publishers were daunting.

Although the 1819 law effectively suspended the press legislation of individual member-states, it had to be promulgated separately in each of them, and its implementation relied mainly on their officials. But before sampling the varied practice of censorship across Germany, it is necessary to summarize the further repressive measures enacted centrally between 1819 and the early 1840s, which, to varying degrees, affected the conditions in which literature was created and disseminated. Despite some disturbances (many of them involving students), the 1820s were relatively calm, and the Federal Investigation Commission actually closed its doors in 1828. But a new era began after the July 1830 revolution in France. Its most visible repercussions in Germany, against a background of serious unrest in many places, included the creation of constitutions in Brunswick, Hesse-Cassel, and Saxony, and the passage of a libertarian press law in Baden. In the volatile atmosphere of the Bavarian Palatinate, the founding of Johann Georg August Wirth's soon widely supported "German Patriotic Association for the Support of a Free Press" was followed by an impressive national-democratic demonstration at Hambach in May 1832. These events were accompanied by an upsurge of political journalism, especially in Baden and other constitutional states.

Metternich and his allies responded by further strengthening and centralizing the Carlsbad "system." In October 1830 the Diet enjoined strict censorship of accounts of revolutionary disturbances in response to reporting like that of Heinrich Heine from Paris. The so-called Six Articles of June 1832 reminded governments of Article 59 of the Vienna Final Acts banning the toleration or reporting of inflammatory parliamentary speeches. The Ten Articles issued a month later imposed controls on German-language publications appearing abroad and banned political speech-making at popular gatherings and the flaunting of flags, cockades, and trees of liberty. Petitions against these restrictions were also banned. Also in July 1832, the Baden Government was compelled to suspend the new press law, and its leading proponents, Karl von Rotteck and Karl Theodor Welcker, were put on a list of wanted subversives (in the Palatinate, Wirth and his associates were subsequently imprisoned after a Bavarian military clampdown). In 1833 a new federal investigating body was set up, which in its nine-year life span examined more than 2,000 suspects. Further antipress measures—which remained secret for nearly a decade—

agreed at a conference in Vienna in early 1834 dealt with matters such as licensing, the circulation of foreign-language newspapers, and the reporting of trials, and included a commitment to reduce the overall number of journals. Finally, in December 1835, and remaining in force for seven years, there came the notorious ban on the "Young German" writers Heine, Gutzkow, Heinrich Laube, Ludolf Wienbarg, and Theodor Mundt.

But beneath the veneer of uniformity established by Austria and Prussia at the federal level, the control practices of the individual states varied greatly. Influences on the priorities, rigor, and effectiveness of different censorship regimes included history, geography, political interests, confessional and demographic structure, and level of cultural development. Hamburg, for example, as historian Margarete Kramer has shown, already had a censorship system in 1819 well attuned to the needs of the city-state's secretive plutocratic oligarchy. Only four newspapers were licensed to discuss public affairs at all, and were vetted by a senator without appeal. Between 1819 and 1848 censorship aimed to restrict political discussion to as few people as possible and to further the city's wider political and commercial interests. Thus, demands for bans were slavishly implemented when they came from powerful neighboring Prussia or from Hamburg's potential ally and protector Austria, whereas complaints from smaller states were taken less seriously.

In Saxony, an initially fairly lax system of control was tightened by a new censorship decree of October 13, 1836, that increased the scope of state agencies at the expense of municipal ones. Ironically, this measure may originally have been designed to protect the fiscally lucrative Leipzig book-publishing and distribution industry from possible federal intervention. But it proved all too convenient later when the Saxon government became increasingly repressive, partly in response to pressure from Austria and Prussia, but also on its own initiative, after the appointment of the anti-liberal von Könneritz ministry in 1843. Police action against works already censored elsewhere intensified, sealed consignments of literature in transit via Leipzig wholesalers were threatened with interference, and in 1844 Saxony imposed the most literary bans after Austria and Prussia. By contrast, the tiny duchy of Saxe-Altenburg became a favorite location for "ghost" publishing operations because of its government's decidedly greater interest in taxing the book trade rather than implementing the Carlsbad Decrees.

In a fascinating recent study, historian Frederik Ohles has drawn a detailed picture of censorship in politically reactionary, confessionally diverse, and culturally and economically underdeveloped Hesse-Cassel. The state's proximity both to Prussia and the Federal Diet in Frankfurt, sexual scandals at court, and the dynasty's general unpopularity were important elements in the scenario. In 1831, after a period of considerable turbulence, the situation was complicated by the grant of a constitution that guaranteed press freedom—albeit within the framework of both federal law and future Hessian legislation—"in its full extent" (§37).[8] Because it subsequently proved impossible to obtain a press law, the rest of the pre-1848 period was dominated by a protracted conflict, involving the courts, the censors, reactionary ministers like Ludwig Hassenpflug, and liberal constitutionalists such as Professor Sylvester Jordan, over the legal status and practical implications of this provision. Ohles vividly describes the censors' operations, with relatively few Hessian publications to vet, yet obliged to process countless requests for bans from outside, and their often futile attempts to intercept subversive material as it seeped over the borders in peddlers' bags or hidden in consignments of ordinary merchandise. The overall impression is of a system at once pervasive and cumbersome; with communications often so slow that booksellers had time to "forget" the purchasers (usually "mysterious strangers") of banned items, and police clearly at times prepared to exculpate "citizens above suspicion" found in possession of subversive literature.

Some suspects boldly resisted state harassment and sought redress from the courts. The Marburg publisher Noa Elwert kept the censors at bay with voluminous complaints penned in illegible handwriting, and was always astonished to learn that illegal texts, including the second edition of Georg Büchner's inflammatory *Hessischer Landbote*, had been run off his presses without his knowledge. If such cases have a certain Ruritanian charm, however, the picture was otherwise grim. The courts sooner or later sided with the state; recalcitrant booksellers were stripped of their livelihoods; and Jordan not only lost his Marburg chair but suffered years of Kafkaesque interrogation, house arrest, and imprisonment. (Büchner had to flee precipitately from neighboring Hesse-Darmstadt in February 1835; his fellow democrat Ludwig Weidig committed suicide after two years in prison.) Yet in Hesse as, probably, elsewhere by the 1840s, politically aware citizens still seem to have found access to the growing flood of literature being published in central Europe.

Prussia's size, military strength, and political orientation made it an indispensable ally for Metternich throughout the 1819–48 period. The size of its reading public made Prussian censorship policy a central factor in the calculations of publishers and booksellers throughout Germany and abroad. Moreover, Prussia could exert strong pressure on both its neighbors and the Diet: the initiative for the 1835 Young Germany ban, for example, came from Berlin. And Prussian internal problems, including Polish nationalism in the eastern provinces, liberal constitutionalism in the Rhineland, and periods of intense conflict with the Catholic Church, presented its censors with challenges comparable only to those in Austria.

The Prussian Censorship Decree of October 18, 1819, was even more comprehensively rigorous than Metternich's Federal Press Law. Article 1 of the 1819 decree subjected all publications, regardless of length, to censorship, which, however, would "not hinder any serious and modest investigation of truth, impose undue constraints on writers, or limit the free operation of the book trade" (§2). Censorship was to be exercised by provincial governors on the advice of censors grouped into political, academic/educational, and theological categories and ultimately responsible to appropriate ministries in Berlin (§§3, 4). Article 4 also gave local police the power to censor miscellaneous and ephemeral material appearing outside the provincial capitals: a deceptively offhand reference to a vast area of traditional police-state repression at the grass-roots level. A Supreme Censorship College was formed to handle appeals and generally monitor the system (§6), to vet newspaper editors (§10), and to scrutinize books in German published abroad. Even works printed outside Prussia and intended solely for non-Prussian readers had to be censored (§8). Printers and publishers were absolved of any further responsibility in respect of publications duly censored in Prussia, and could claim compensation (rarely obtained in practice) in the event of a subsequent federal ban. But an author—or, if he were out of reach, the publisher—could always be retrospectively punished if he was subsequently found to have bamboozled the censor with ambiguities or coded allusions (§13). Publishers and printers who ignored the censorship rules faced heavy fines and, on the third offense, a total embargo on their activities, as well as possible criminal sanctions in respect to offenses embodied in the uncensored texts; distributors of banned works also risked fines and an occupational ban (§16). Finally, periodicals dealing with religion, politics, or current affairs could only be published with ministerial permission, and could be summarily suppressed in the event of abuse (§17).

Although occasionally adjusted in detail—from 1824, for example, publishers had to pay for the privilege of censorship—the system thus created could hardly have been made more pervasive in principle, even if its actual impact was modified by friction between different control agencies and fluctuations in the political climate. In the 1830s and early 1840s, for example, the Berlin humorist Adolf Glassbrenner, though banned from editing newspapers, was able to produce satirical pamphlets and to launch the idler and street-corner philosopher Nante as a vastly popular comic character. The accession of Friedrich Wilhelm IV (an enthusiastic Nante reader) in 1840 inaugurated a brief period of liberal optimism, with a new Press Decree of December 24, 1841, permitting journalists "serious and moderate investigation of truth."[9] However, its restrictions, ambiguities, and contradictions were dissected with relentless sarcasm by Karl Marx, who in the summer of 1843 found himself fleeing to Paris after the suppression of his radical *Rheinische Zeitung*. The following year brought fifty-five Prussian press bans. Efforts to reorganize and streamline the censorship apparatus did not reduce its oppressiveness or, despite the creation of a Supreme Censorship Court, subject it to serious judicial restraint. One further gesture toward liberalization was a decree of May 28, 1842, lifting the censorship of political caricature imposed in 1823. But such censorship was reimposed eight months later, apparently because of a cartoon depicting the king as a tipsy Puss-in-Boots vainly attempting to follow in the footsteps of Frederick the Great.

The Practice and Impact of Pre-1848 Censorship

In 1831 Bavarian journalist Wirth described the censor as a "paid oppressor of the spirit, a servant of darkness . . . a miserable tool of brute force and arrogance . . . a declared enemy of all true and open opinions and expressions." Heine famously described "the German censors" with several lines of simulated cuts, leaving only the single word "fools."[10] But in reality (and leaving aside the fact that vast quantities of popular ephemera were summarily banned by police and other minor officials) most members of Germany's book and censorship commissions were neither fiends nor idiots. That the Prussian stipulation that censors be "men of scholarly education and proven integrity" was generally fulfilled in practice was accepted even by such opponents of the system as the liberal jurist Albert Friedrich Berner, who described Prussian censors as "trustworthy mediators between the government and the educated public" who included some of the "most celebrated and best men of their time."[11]

Censors' conditions of work varied from state to state and in different periods. In hard-line Prussia and Hesse-Cassel, for example, where in theory every publication had to be scrutinized, they were onerous from the start. But after 1830, as both political tensions and the quantity of suspect material increased, censors almost everywhere groaned under the burden: if only a pardoned criminal could be found to do the job, lamented the president of the Hamburg Censorship Commission in the early 1840s. Overwork, lack of resources, and penalties for mistakes sapped morale and health, all the more so as many censors were librarians, scholars, or administrative officials saddled with additional censorship responsibilities, often without much extra pay. And they were still vilified by Germany's proliferating literary professionals who, from their own precarious position in the marketplace, naturally depicted them as salaried stooges of government. Yet many censors clearly disapproved in principle of their tasks: in Cassel, Karl Bernhardi wrote secretly for opposition newspapers, while in 1845 the Hamburg censor Merck commented that it was impossible to justify an institution that curbed natural human rights. "Every day," he lamented, "the opposition to censorship of even the best and most loyal citizens grows; every day it sinks in public reputation and esteem as people become ever more convinced of its futility and uselessness."[12] Although government attitudes at this time continued to harden, such lack of commitment at the core of the system made an eventual change of strategy practically inevitable.

As every censor knew, total control of the printed word was impossible. This was particularly obvious after 1830, as the volume of publication mounted. The number of books published in Germany rose from over 7,000 in that year (compared to about 4,000 in 1800) to a pre-revolutionary peak of 13,664 in 1846. The sheer size of the book trade by the late 1840s, with individual Leipzig firms handling up to 10,000 packages per week, made surveillance ever more difficult. Periodical publishing also expanded: the Berlin Press Salon, founded in 1847, offered its patrons some 600 papers in fourteen languages. As far as prior censorship was concerned, the multiplicity of jurisdictions (sometimes even within states, as in Saxony even after 1836) and bureaucratic laxity in some places undoubtedly created loopholes. By the 1840s, for instance, press articles forbidden in Hamburg rapidly appeared, with scurrilous commentaries, in papers printed in neighboring Wandsbek or Itzehoe (in Danish-administered Holstein) for immediate "export" by rail back to the city, a grotesque situation that eventually forced the Hamburg censors into greater tolerance. At a more serious level, Rotteck and Welcker's liberal *Staats-Lexikon*, banned in Prussia, was published in Danish Altona, and the "Young Germany" publisher Julius Campe operated when necessary from Wandsbek (where, he reported, "For a dozen bottles the censor will do a lot")[13] or from Saxe-Altenburg. Writers, of course, could also use time-honored devices such as disguising political commentary as fable or ancient history, as in Gutzkow's depiction of Ludwig I of Bavaria in the guise of Nero.

However, for practical and economic reasons the advantage still lay with the state. The law governing Germany's largest market, Prussia, was framed to cover almost any contingency, and post-publication bans could be extremely costly for publishers. The prosecution of Gutzkow's controversial novel *Wally, the Skeptic* in 1835 effectively ruined its publisher Karl Löwenthal, even though he was formally acquitted. For writers it was neither satisfying nor profitable to produce coded texts for a few cognoscenti. Indeed, it was the very openness of the "Young German" authors that made them targets for suppression: the December 1835 ban explicitly accused them of attacking religion, morality, and the social order "in literary writings accessible to all classes of readers." Heine wrote later, "My crime was not the thought but the manner of writing, the style."[14]

From its victims' viewpoint, "pre-March" (1848) censorship, especially as refined and extended after 1830, was, for all its flaws, a formidable threat. Most vulnerable was the bookseller, who usually had to deposit a substantial sum for the privilege of trading, and was often the policeman's first port of call. Financial and other risks undoubtedly deterred many publishers, including major figures like Cotta, from touching politically sensitive material. Authors faced a battery of serious penalties: imprisonment (e.g., Gutzkow, Laube, Wirth); expulsion from their place of residence (Gutzkow and Wienbarg, both from Frankfurt); occupational bans (August Heinrich Hoffmann von Fallersleben lost his Breslau chair after publication of his second volume of *Unpolitical Songs*; Mundt's academic career was stymied because of his erotic and anticlerical novel *Madonna*); and exile (Ludwig Börne, Büchner, Friedrich Engels, Ferdinand Freiligrath, Heine, Georg Herwegh, Marx, Wirth). As Karl Heinzen wrote in 1846, "Germany has become, in literary emigrés as in emigrants generally, the richest country on earth." Most insidious was the subjective compulsion to trim and bowdlerize works as they developed. Heine, whose *Germany, A Winter's Tale* underwent just such a process, described "the mental bitterness . . . created by the need to censor every thought that I think immediately in my head; writing while the censor's sword hangs over one's head by a thread—it's enough to drive one mad."[15]

The 1848 Revolutions

The eventual abandonment of censorship in its classic Carlsbad form in 1848 had various antecedents. Especially after 1830, liberals increasingly opposed blanket controls on freedom of expression on legal and constitutional grounds. Particularly notable was the 1833 appeal of the Frankfurt authors of a *Protestation of German Citizens in Favor of Press Freedom* against a censorship ban and penalty imposed by a lower court, and their application to the Göttingen law faculty for an opinion on the legality of censorship. The result was a resounding appeals court ruling that—despite attempts to suppress it—publicly declared that freedom of expression under law was a fundamental right, affirmed in the Federal Final Acts and eight other German constitutions. "Censorship as a general and regular [control] measure," the jurists concluded, "could not be seriously defended."[16] Another important factor, in addition to the courage and resourcefulness of individual publishers, was the growing size, economic and fiscal value, and collective political determination of the publishing industry. This was reflected in a petition of the German Booksellers' Trade Association (founded in 1825) of May 3, 1842, to the Saxon government to induce the Federal Diet at least to limit censorship to the original 1819 norms, but preferably to allow press freedom under §18d of the Final Acts. Of course, neither economic and cultural considerations nor evidence of censorship's often counterproductive effects—well documented for states like Hamburg and Hesse-Cassel—turned conservatives into libertarians. But they underlined the need for more discreet and flexible methods of control. Realistically, the Federal Press Commission told the Diet in 1847, "Present-day Germany perceives in the mere words press freedom a *strange enchantment*, about whose success and impact one should harbor no illusions."[17]

In the tumult that swept Germany in February and March 1848, censorship was one of the first repressive institutions to fall. Appropriately, Baden led the way: on February 27 a mass meeting in Offenburg formulated demands, granted by the Grand Duke two days later, for press freedom and other basic rights. On March 3 the Federal Diet formally permitted Confederation members to abolish censorship, albeit with suitable safeguards against the abuse of freedom. In Cassel, soon after the outbreak of revolution on the 6th, the police director shouted to demonstrators clamoring for a free press, "Yes, just write, just write; everything you write will be printed!"[18] By the end of March, censorship had fallen across Germany, with a resultant nationwide vast upsurge of political and satirical publishing. In the Prussian capital of Berlin alone, according to press historian Ursula Koch, 135 new newspapers and journals, roughly 100 of them political, were launched between March 1848 and the end of 1849, plus about 2,000 pamphlets and countless single-sheet lithographed posters and flyers. The most durable of more than thirty new satirical papers in Berlin was Albert Hofmann and David Kalisch's bourgeois-democratic *Kladderadatsch*, which first appeared on May 7, 1848, and was to last until 1944.

Curbs on press freedom did not vanish entirely. In July, for example, an attack on Friedrich Wilhelm IV earned the Berlin journalist Albert Hopf a fortnight's imprisonment for *lèse-majesté*, and like similar events elsewhere, proved an ominous sign of counterrevolutionary stirrings. But, in the meantime, many states passed liberal press legislation, and potentially even more significant, the Frankfurt Parliament incorporated in the German Constitution of March 28, 1849, a set of fundamental rights that included (§143) exemplary guarantees of freedom of expression, prohibited censorship and other notorious constraints such as licensing, caution money, and postal restrictions, and offered the prospect of a national press law. Moreover, in common with both the Bavarian Press Law of June 4, 1848, and even the imposed Prussian Constitution of December, it stipulated the vital safeguard of trial by jury for press offenses. However, the tide of reaction flowing strongly by the end of 1848 was to make most of these gains for a time illusory.

FROM THE AFTERMATH OF REVOLUTION TO THE REICH PRESS LAW OF 1874

As historians like Wolfram Siemann have emphasized, the consolidation of political reaction after the final suppression of revolution in the spring and summer of 1849 was neither total nor immediate. It was widely recognized, for example, that pre-1848 rural feudalism would not be restored, and that constitutionalism, however restrictively framed, had come to stay. But fear of renewed revolution remained intense; in mid-1851 the notorious "Reaction Resolution" of the revived Federal Diet formally nullified the Fundamental Rights of the Frankfurt Constitution.

The next decade was characterized by the growth of bureaucratic and police power and, in some states, by extremely rigorous repression of political activity and debate. But over the longer 1849–74 period, other developments were transforming the nature and scope of communications. Between 1816 and 1846 the population of Germany had grown from under 25 million to over 35 million; by 1871 it reached over 40 million. More significant than the general increase was the massive growth of urbanization: Berlin's population, for example, doubled to 826,000 between 1850 and 1871 (and more than doubled again by 1900), a trend with vast implications for public order and the spread of ideas. Boosting urbanization was the contemporary transport revolution. Railway-building, described by economic historian Werner Sombart as "the greatest productive act not only of the nineteenth century but . . . in the whole of history,"[19] proceeded apace, with German rail mileage more than tripling from 1850 to 1870; and road and waterway networks also growing along with economic activity. Other means of communication expanded too: the postal system became increasingly integrated, efficient, and cheap, and by 1872 over 4,000 German telegraph offices were handling 12,165,954 telegrams, a form of communication first available for public use in Prussia in 1849. Although in the aftermath of the postrevolutionary crackdown, book production fell 15 percent below the 1848 level during the 1850s and did not recover fully until 1868, the basis of the late nineteenth-century literary boom was being created by changing regulations, technologies, and means of distribution. The relaxation of advertising restrictions in Prussia in 1850 pointed the way toward a mass press offering a mix of news, features, and fiction. The 1867 federal abolition of copyright restrictions on the classics made possible large book-price reductions, exploited most imaginatively by Leipzig's Reclam publishers, which rapidly sold 20,000 copies of its two-groschen edition of Goethe's *Faust*, and later sold its little paperback classics from slot machines. As popular literacy grew, door-to-door sales by peddlers of serial novels and other publications became a major means of distribution and, despite official harassment, remained so well into the twentieth century. In Berlin during the Franco-Prussian War street news vendors were tolerated for the first time since 1848.

After 1849 books and periodicals remained subject to a multitude of controls. Although pre-publication censorship was not reintroduced, the reasons for this were practical and political, not libertarian, and stemmed from long-standing awareness of the system's shortcomings. The new repressive measures of the 1850s, in fact, soon had booksellers and publishers harking back nostalgically to what they perceived as safer, more predictable conditions under prior censorship. As during 1819–48, the printed word in Germany remained subject, at least in theory, to two tiers of legislation, of which the "lower," individual-state one was much the more important in practice. The Federal "Reaction Resolution" of August 23, 1851, urging governments to suppress all "atheistic, socialist, communist" or antimonarchical periodicals, was followed by the oppressive Federal Press Law (BPG) of July 6, 1854. However, only Brunswick, Hesse (-Darmstadt), Oldenburg, and four small states actually introduced the BPG into their own territories; others, most notably Bavaria and Prussia, continued to apply their own preexisting press laws; and a third group, including Saxony, enacted new legislation after 1854. The most important state law was the May 12, 1851, Prussian statute (PrPG), the culmination of a series of increasingly restrictive ordinances and of an 1850 report by the Interior Minister to Friedrich Wilhelm IV that painted a lurid picture of subversive and atheistic press agitation. In May–June 1852 the PrPG was supplemented by measures abolishing trial by jury for press offenders, reestablishing newspaper taxes, and making confiscation more effective.

Although the different press laws varied both in detail and general severity, they centered mainly on post-publication, judicially imposed penalties for breaches of the criminal law. Because there was no national criminal code until 1870–71, sanctions derived from the individual state laws on *lèse-majesté*, blasphemy, obscenity, libel of state officials, and incitement. But a string of other instruments made the system still more onerous. First, publishers, newspaper editors, and booksellers had to obtain licenses, which were granted only to individuals of "good character" and could be withdrawn for misbehavior. In Prussia, during the diplomatic crisis accompanying the Crimean War, editors were summoned to the interior ministry and threatened with summary (administrative) license withdrawal if they caused embarrassment. Second, large sums of caution money, between 1,000 and 5,000 thalers (equivalent to 3,000 to 15,000 later marks) according to the population of the place of publication, were required from periodical publishers as pledges of good behavior and (as the reactionary Badenese minister von Blittersdorff had put it in 1842) to deter them from attacking "the rights of the possessing class."[20]

Third, an inspection copy of every periodical had to be submitted to the police as or just before distribution began. In Prussia, moreover, although the prosecuting authorities could in theory countermand confiscation orders, a ministerial rescript of November 25, 1851, instructed them to let the courts decide in every case, "since there is always some evidence for the culpability of confiscated publications."[21] Thus, editors often had to wait weeks for judicial rulings and the police could more easily cripple troublesome papers. Stamp duty and postal bans had a similar function. Finally, although the offenses that could be committed via the press were specified in the penal codes, the concept of responsibility in press cases was much broader than in general law enforcement. To reduce the possibility that anonymous or extraterritorial offenders might escape punishment, hierarchies of possible culprits were created, with the author at the top and publishers, newspaper editors, printers, and distributors further down. Each member of the hierarchy could exculpate himself by identifying the one above, but only if the latter were within reach of the law. In effect, this enlisted booksellers and printers as censors and meant that, given the volume of publication—even in 1849, more than 9,000 titles appeared—many people stood to be charged, at least with negligence, in relation to offenses of which they had no knowledge.

In October 1851, still fearful of revolution, the governments of Austria and Prussia requested the Diet to create a federal police authority. This scheme was blocked by Bavaria and other states that disliked the idea of federal agents operating on their territory, but already six months earlier an unofficial organization, the Police Association (*Polizeiverein* [PV]) had been organized at a high-level conference in Dresden, backed by Austria, Prussia, Saxony, and Hanover (eventually Bavaria, Württemberg, and Baden joined). As the documents assembled by Siemann indicate, the PV became at least as effective as any formal body, and probably more so than the central agencies of 1819–48. A decade of rail communication, commented a Saxon account of its origins in 1855, vastly facilitated the coordination of subversion: "This ever more elaborate centralization of forces hostile to the state, especially since the years 1848 and 1849, had to be countered by centralization of the institutions dedicated to defense of the state."[22]

The PV's objectives were threefold: the gathering and exchange of intelligence about subversive movements throughout the Confederation and abroad (it even employed agents in New York); the prevention of any national organizational activity by political parties; and the suppression of radical publications and the persecution of those responsible for them. Its operations were coordinated by rotating conferences—twenty in all between 1851 and 1866—held in the capitals of the member states, and by the circulation of reports listing matters of common concern. In 1853 Berlin alone produced thirty of these, comprising 558 items. The PV's activities were most intense during 1851 to 1853, when political anxieties were greatest; they diminished toward the end of the decade, with the start of the "New Era" period of reform in Prussia, the development of more pragmatic attitudes to opposition parties and the press, and growing tension between Prussia and Austria.

Although the initial impetus for the creation of the PV came from Berlin Police President Karl Ludwig Friedrich von Hinckeldey, one of its ablest representatives was the Hanover police chief, Wermuth, who combined energy and ruthlessness with considerable forensic skill. One highly successful action was the suppression in 1852 of an incriminated book, *Daylight Has Broken*, by the Bremen pastor and radical democrat Rudolph Dulon; seizure of the publisher's distribution list facilitated raids on outlets throughout Germany and enabled Wermuth to compile a register of all current booksellers. Another interesting case, involving dogged police investigation of a network of agitators and clandestine presses, was the campaign against the Brunswick radical journal *Blätter der Zeit*, edited by a succession of left-wing journalists and finally forced into liquidation in March 1855. In the background was the Duchy of Brunswick's tenacious adherence, despite enacting the BPG of 1854, to such liberal safeguards as jury trials and exclusively judicial proceedings against the press; Wermuth and his colleagues frequently bemoaned the independence of Brunswick judges and the political debates occasioned by press cases in open court. (The BPG, by contrast, permitted secret hearings.) Still, the fate of *Blätter der Zeit* shows that relative immunity in liberal states like Brunswick and Oldenburg could not outweigh bans and harassment elsewhere. Indeed, even before *Blätter der Zeit* disappeared, radical papers had been mown down practically everywhere. The PV, despite its built-in paranoia, rejoiced in an 1854 report: "A revolutionary press as it was to be found in 1848 and to a degree still in 1849 in Germany no longer exists; in the whole of Germany at this time there is not a single newspaper that would dare to preach open revolt."[23]

Especially vulnerable to state countermeasures was the satirical press that had sprung up during the "pre-March" and revolutionary years. For example, the anti-Prussian *Leuchtturm* founded in Leipzig in 1846, was suppressed in late 1849, and the Berlin humorist and democrat Albert Hopf served several prison terms between 1848 and 1852 and was forced by repeated expulsions from the capital to live as a homeless tramp. Papers like the Munich *Fliegenden Blätter*, founded in 1844, kept going by limiting themselves to harmless social satire. *Kladderadatsch*, during the eight-month state of siege that followed the reoccupation of Berlin by General Wrangel's troops in mid-November 1848, endured numerous bans and months of banishment from the city that reduced its circulation from nearly 7,000 to a mere 800. At the end of 1849 it published a cartoon of its emblematic Idler in a graveyard sadly contemplating monuments to many other caricature journals of 1848, including Hopf's *Berliner Krakehler*, either already defunct or about to be suppressed. *Kladderadatsch* itself, however, notwithstanding repeated clashes with the authorities, survived and eventually prospered, achieving national fame and a circulation of well over 20,000 by the mid-fifties. That this was possible despite intense police hostility was due partly to the paper's quality and its publisher Hofmann's determination, partly to editorial caution, but also, apparently, to the fact that Friedrich Wilhelm IV (like Bismarck) enjoyed reading it.

The end of the "New Era," and Bismarck's appointment as Prussian prime minister on October 8, 1862, with the task of implementing military reform with or without parliamentary backing, brought immediate confrontation with the liberal-dominated Chamber of Deputies and its journalistic allies. In Berlin alone, according to press historian Koch, four conservative newspapers with a circulation of 11,330 faced seven opposition ones with nearly 71,000 readers. Bismarck, who claimed to believe that the press was "largely in the hands of Jews and disaffected people," took up the challenge head-on; on October 26 *Kladderadatsch* depicted him as an autumn gale blasting the leaves from a (press) tree into the arms of waiting policemen. Although the draconian June 1, 1863, Press Decree, giving officials the power to ban papers simply for their general orientation, eventually had to be lifted (and was declared unconstitutional by the Chamber), the state continued to deploy its entire existing arsenal of administrative and judicial weapons. Press trials proliferated (there were 175 in 1864 alone); §101 of the Prussian Criminal Code, banning attacks on official institutions and measures, was stretched to cover almost any criticism; and some journalists spent as much time in prison or on the run as at their desks. By 1866 some sixty newspapers had been forced to close down. *Kladderadatsch* was confiscated about ten times in the sixties, but its growing support for Bismarck by 1864, and his practice of manipulating rather than intimidating influential papers, saved it from worse punishment. Even after Prussia's defeat of Austria in 1866 and the achievement of the government's domestic objectives, the position of Prussian journalists remained unenviable. "If any grievance is ripe for judgment," complained the liberal *Nationalzeitung* on November 13, 1869, "then it is the unworthy position created for the press by Prussian laws."[24]

FROM THE REICH PRESS LAW TO 1890

Section IV, §16 of the 1871 Constitution of the newly unified German empire created the prospect of Reich legislation to replace the twenty-seven press laws of the individual German states. However, it was not until February 1874 that a government press bill was presented to the Reichstag. This proved highly controversial, not least because it included a draconian clause—clearly aimed at socialism and political Catholicism—threatening up to two years' imprisonment for inflammatory printed attacks on such fundamental institutions as property, the family, military service, or what was elastically defined as "arrangements of civil society."[25] Although overwhelmingly rejected, this measure was to reappear in various guises over the next twenty years, demonstrating how profoundly Bismarck and other conservatives still distrusted the press. In its final form, however, the Reich Press Law (RPG) of May 7, 1874, was, despite some loopholes, a progressive piece of legislation; it was not finally superseded until 1966.[26] Its creation, in the teeth of strong official resistance, was a significant liberal achievement and, in conjunction with other legal, political, and commercial factors, facilitated the spectacular growth of the press over the next forty years.

First and foremost, the RPG was based on the "repressive" (as opposed to "preventive") principle. Moreover, publications could not be incriminated on the grounds of their general tendency, but only under the specific provisions of the 1871 German Criminal Code (RSGB). Second, those long-standing bugbears—some of them already abandoned by the individual states—caution money, licensing, and special press taxes, were finally outlawed, and a person's right to exercise any occupation connected with the press could not be removed either administratively or judicially. Administrative bans, in normal peacetime conditions, were permitted only in the case of foreign periodicals, and by the Reich Chancellor. Third, although the RPG stipulated that an inspection copy of every periodical had to be submitted at the place of publication (*Ausgabeort*, not a simple term, as we shall see) as distribution began, the speed of communication by this time, at least as regards major newspapers, was increasingly favoring the press. Even with police readers working round the clock, as in Berlin, the authorities could rarely hope to seize more than a small proportion of an incriminated edition: in an 1876 case involving the *Frankfurter Zeitung*, only 800 out of 20,000 copies were intercepted. Moreover, except in certain clearly defined circumstances, confiscation had to be ordered by the courts, not the police, with prosecution required within two weeks.

One serious shortcoming of the RPG from a liberal perspective, however, concerned the ever problematical issue of responsibility. Although RPG 20 required the nomination of a "responsible editor" (popularly known as the *Sitzredakteur*, or "jail editor") for every periodical, who would be automatically prosecuted for any offense, publishers, printers, and distributors might also be pursued for negligence, but could escape if they named the author (if he was within reach of the law) of an incriminated piece. But the authorities still remained free to hunt the author themselves and, if necessary, as in other criminal cases, to force witnesses—for example, a newspaper's employees—to testify on pain of fines or imprisonment. This possibility dated from 1850, and jarred increasingly with journalists' self-image as professionals with an ethical obligation to protect sources. But in 1874 Bismarck and most German governments were so determined to retain compulsion to testify (*Zeugniszwang*) in press cases that they successfully threatened to abort the whole bill if the Reichstag majority forced the issue. Only a year later, liberals' worst fears were confirmed by a prosecution of the *Frankfurter Zeitung* during which the paper's publisher, editors, printers, and even boilerman were subpoenaed no fewer than thirty-seven times, production was disrupted, and the five leading editors together spent seven and a half months in prison for their silence. Under Bismarck, aggressive use of compulsion to testify was not unusual, and all efforts to remedy the situation proved fruitless: *Zeugniszwang* for the press was not formally abolished until 1926. In the final years of the Empire, however, the increasing power and prestige of the press, and governments' sense that the practice tended to be counterproductive, meant that it was used ever more sparingly.

Trial by jury was not established as the national norm in serious press cases but was left to individual states' decisions. Baden, Bavaria, Brunswick, Oldenburg, and Württemberg held to the jury principle adopted in 1848, while elsewhere press offenders were dealt with by panels of professional judges or by mixed lay and judicial tribunals (*Schöffengerichte*). In conjunction with other procedural rules this legal diversity proved a major safeguard for journalists and satirists. Munich Police Director von Burchtorff's view that trial by jury was the "highest palladium of press freedom"[27] is certainly borne out by records of Munich press cases between 1875 and 1899, which reveal many acquittals and numerous prosecutions dropped due to poor prospects of success. Paradoxically, however, the value of the jury system is perhaps best illustrated by an 1884 press conviction. The defendant was the editor of the *Bayerische Vaterland*, Johann Baptist Sigl, a rabidly anti-Prussian, anti-Bismarckian, and anti-Semitic particularist, and the kind of "press bandit" officials loathed. His crude polemics landed him in prison for thirty-four months of his career, eleven of them for libeling Bismarck. The 1884 case followed politically embarrassing allegations such as that the Bavarian War Ministry was simply a relay station for orders from Berlin. Sigl's claims were comprehensively rebutted in court and on July 8, 1884, he was sentenced to nine months' imprisonment, but to obtain this verdict the Ministry of War had to explain its role and procedures at great length to an examining magistrate, and the prosecution was obliged to assemble a mass of evidence. Even so, Sigl was still acquitted on a minor charge, and the jury reached unanimity on only two of the seven questions put to it.

Without the safeguard of the jury, conditions for opposition journalists in the late 1870s and 1880s were unenviable. Between 1874 and 1877 alone, according to press historian Hans Wetzel, over 2,500 charges were leveled against the press. In July 1874, a fortnight after the RPG came into force, an allegedly "ultramontane"-inspired assassination attempt on Bismarck triggered a ferocious onslaught on Catholic papers with particularly massive use of the libel and incitement paragraphs of the RSGB. At one point in 1875 the Berlin *Germania* was charged on fifty-seven counts, and the same year the editors of both that paper and the *Westfälische Merkur* were sentenced to a year's imprisonment for printing a papal encyclical critical of Prussian legislation. The campaign was closely monitored by Bismarck and Wilhelm I, and in key areas like the Catholic Rhineland the police were enjoined to maximum vigilance on pain of disciplinary action. Compulsion to testify further increased the hazards for publishers and journalists, and judges refused to accept the plea, theoretically possible under RSGB 193, that a paper might be acting in the public interest. "A general right on the part of the daily press," ruled the Reich Appeal Court (*Reichsgericht*) in December 1881, "publicly to condemn supposed abuses, and to bring any event to the notice of the public even when it injures the honor of others, does not exist."[28]

By the beginning of the 1880s, as the anti-Catholic onslaught slackened, Germany was in the throes of another, even fiercer campaign of ideological persecution. The determination to combat Social Democracy underlay not only Bismarck's attempt to insert the perilous "fundamental values" paragraph into the RPG, but also an 1875 proposal (known later as the "little Anti-Socialist Law") to expand RSGB 110 and 130 on similar lines to facilitate suppression of "subversive" ideas. Although both efforts failed, two assassination attempts on Wilhelm I, followed by a panic election, finally brought Bismarck a Reichstag majority for the much more draconian and comprehensive Anti-Socialist Law (ASG) of October 21, 1878.[29] Although passed initially for two and a half years, it was renewed in 1881, 1884, and 1886 and did not finally lapse until 1890. The six paragraphs (ASG 11–15, 19) bearing directly on the press were an unequivocal throwback to the old police state, permitting summary and unlimited bans of "publications featuring social democratic, socialist or communist efforts to overthrow the existing social order in a manner endangering public peace, and especially the harmony of the different social classes" (ASG 11); additionally, it authorized the occupational disqualification of printers, booksellers, librarians, and others involved in the dissemination of illegal material (ASG 23). Although liberals hoped that the creation of a Reich Complaints Commission (ASG 26, 27) would curb excesses, that it was chaired by the Prussian interior minister and filled by senior Prussian officials and judges ensured that it functioned as a well-oiled mechanism for rejecting appeals, which it did in 97 percent of cases between 1878 and 1881 (later, for reasons of political expediency, it became more lenient).

Especially in conjunction with the use, in Berlin and other cities, of "minor state of siege" provisions, which permitted the summary expulsion of "undesirables" from their homes, the ASG had a devastating effect on the SPD's press and organization, and created an army of journalists and other activists in desperate need of support. According to a letter written by Socialist leader August Bebel in January, 1880, the "white terror" in Berlin featured surveillance "pushed to an enormous mass level," including "house-searches of everyone who is even remotely suspected of having anything to do with a banned paper or with people partial to them."[30] Within two months of the ASG's enactment, forty-seven out of fifty Socialist papers were banned, and attempts to relaunch journals under new names, even in nonpolitical form, generally proved fruitless. Over the whole 1878–90 period, 1,299 publications were banned, including 104 periodicals; amazingly, however, even given their ultracautious editorial policies, the satirical *Wahrer Jakob* and *Süddeutscher Postillon* somehow managed to survive the onslaught.

In September 1879 Bebel and his comrades founded an emigré journal, *Der Sozialdemokrat*, based initially in Zürich. Despite determined efforts by the Prussian authorities to infiltrate the *Sozialdemokrat* with spies and agents provocateur, its distribution chief, Julius Motteler—known as the "red postmaster"—was soon passing upwards of 3,600 copies to activists in Germany. Later, when plates rather than bundles of newspapers were sent across the frontier, the *Sozialdemokrat* could actually be printed in centers like Nuremberg undetected. The ASG's lapse in 1890 made life much easier for Socialists, but by no means inaugurated an era of untrammeled freedom of expression. In fact, the 1890–1914 period highlighted the perils of the ordinary criminal law, above all in the notoriously ill-defined areas of *lèse-majesté* and incitement, especially as prosecutors and judges remained generally far more alert to writings by Socialists than by their bourgeois counterparts. The two years before the war were a time of particularly fierce persecution: in the first half of 1913 alone no fewer than 104 SPD journalists were convicted, receiving a total of forty years in prison sentences and 11,000 marks in fines.

During the entire period from the passage of the RPG to Bismarck's resignation in March 1890, according to Wetzel, there were at least 3,287 press trials in Germany involving 5,975 separate offenses. Libel of private individuals, the Chancellor and other officials, and royalty accounted for 65.5 percent of the latter, with libel of Bismarck alone making up 16.7 percent and the proportion of libel prosecutions growing between 1874 and 1890.[31] Although about one-fifth of cases ended in acquittal, these figures confirm the impression that Bismarck's regime, despite the safeguards created by the RPG, weighed heavily on political journalists.

Yet Bismarck also played a key role in the nineteenth-century transition from primarily coercive state press policies to more flexible strategies of influence and manipulation. The Prussian Literary Bureau created in 1848, and attached from 1860 to the interior ministry, subsidized loyal papers and journalists and between 1863 and 1884 channeled officially slanted information to the local press via a weekly newsletter that soon reached a circulation of almost 30,000. In the 1860s and 1870s Bismarck also used various other channels, from the semiofficial *Norddeutsche Allgemeine Zeitung* to bribed "reptiles" in the independent press (in 1874, significantly, a vain attempt was made to include a ban on state subsidies to newspapers in the RPG). In the early 1880s Bismarck launched a new and extremely secret scheme that fed material from the interior ministry via a network of agents to 400 or so provincial papers with about 600,000 readers. In addition, the German Foreign Office retained tight control over Germany's main news agency, the semiofficial Wolff Telegraph Bureau, throughout the post-1870 period. Nevertheless, interdepartmental rivalries, shortage of funds, and the inability of any chancellor to create a unified system meant that civilian media management in the Bismarck and post-Bismarck era remained fairly rudimentary.

FREEDOM OF EXPRESSION AFTER BISMARCK, 1890–1914

Broadly speaking, the period between Bismarck's resignation and the outbreak of World War I was one in which the "bourgeois" press—conditions for Socialist papers were, as already noted, very different—enjoyed growing security, prosperity, and prestige. Once-dreaded sanctions like compulsion to testify slipped into abeyance, and journalists' status and organizational strength increased. "The power of the press," observed the Munich police president in March 1913, "is these days so great that this important factor in public life cannot be left out of account even by the state authorities. In the long run, no official agency can maintain a negative or hostile attitude towards it."[32] However, outspokenly radical journalists (even non-Socialists), satirists, and members of the literary avant-garde continued to face serious dangers from various sections of the RSGB, especially the paragraphs punishing *lèse-majesté* (95, 97, 99, 101, 103), blasphemy (166), obscenity (184), and, improbably, so-called "gross mischief" (360/11).

Lèse-majesté (*Majestätsbeleidigung*) was defined as "violation of the respect due to the ruler as the bearer of sovereignty"[33] and, except for incitement to high treason (RSGB 85), which carried a maximum sentence of ten years' hard labor, it was the gravest offense that could be committed simply by communicating an opinion. (The need for five separate paragraphs in the Code arose because of the Empire's plurality of monarchs, insults to whom had to be graded for the purposes of the law, with libel of one's own sovereign, or the Emperor, the most heinous.) It was also by no means a dead letter, especially in times of crisis. After one of the two 1878 assassination attempts on Wilhelm I, for example, a Brandenburg woman received eighteen months' imprisonment for remarking that "at least the Emperor is not poor; he can have himself cared for," and on a single day a Berlin court sentenced seven people to a total of twenty-two years and six months' jail for *lèse-majesté*. In 1878 as a whole there were 1,994 cases. In the politically and economically turbulent 1890s there were also many prosecutions: 597 persons were convicted in 1895, for example (395 of them in Prussia), while at the end of the decade, according to historian Alex Hall, one person was being convicted for every working day of the calendar.[34]

Many of the 1890s cases were by-products of Wilhelm II's "personal rule," since his erratic behavior and inflammatory speeches often provoked anger and ridicule which was seized on by zealous prosecutors. The prominent journalist Maximilian Harden was sentenced to six and a half months in a fortress at the beginning of 1899 and to another six the following year for criticizing the Emperor's bloodthirsty "Huns of Attila" speech to troops departing to quell the Boxer Rebellion in China. By this time, however, *lèse-majesté* was increasingly being perceived as a liability, not least because of the authorities' obligation to act on information received regardless of whether it was in the state's or the monarch's interest. Neither in Bavaria nor Prussia, moreover, could the sovereign halt proceedings and thus avoid the publicity of a trial. This was particularly awkward if a monarch or dynasty were especially vulnerable to attack: in Bavaria, where King Ludwig II's mysterious death in the Starnbergersee in June 1886 became the subject of endless lurid speculation, officials clearly stretched the rules to avoid action. This was the background for the RSGB amendment of February 1908 that made prosecution mandatory only in cases of deliberate malice. Socialists, of course, were malicious by definition—as the ultraconservative industrialist von Stumm-Halberg declared in the Reichstag, the very words "Social Democracy" were tantamount to *lèse-majesté*[35]—and persecution of them continued vigorously until the war.

Compared with the obvious danger of the *lèse-majesté* paragraphs, it is less clear how far freedom of expression was endangered by RSGB 166, which threatened up to three years' imprisonment for anyone who publicly blasphemed or abused the institutions or practices of a recognized religious faith. Legal theorists and judges tended to define §166 increasingly narrowly. Yet there was strong political support during the 1890s for treating as a form of criminal subversion attacks not only on religious doctrines but on Christian moral precepts. This was clearly demonstrated during the debates on the so-called Revolution Bill (*Umsturzvorlage*) that, with the Emperor's backing, was presented to the Reichstag in December 1894. Although the bill's immediate cause was a wave of anarchist outrages in Europe, it also reflected conservatives' long-standing desire to ban criticism of "fundamental institutions." The bill was eventually thrown out, yet the episode highlighted the attitude of some conservatives and Catholics toward intellectual freedom and helps to explain their repeated demands for more energetic use of RSGB 166.

One obvious target was the Naturalist avant-garde, which was influenced by a mixture of ideas derived from Emile Zola, Henrik Ibsen, Friedrich Nietzsche, and others who rejected orthodox religious beliefs and insisted on the primacy of science over metaphysics. The most notable use of RSGB 166 against the avant-garde was in Bavaria, where blasphemy became a political football between a hard-pressed liberal administration and an increasingly strong and militant clerical opposition. In general, thanks largely to the jury system, the danger to writers was indirect. One successful blasphemy prosecution, however, was that of Oskar Panizza, an eccentric psychiatrist-turned-author, in 1895 for *The Council of Love*, a scurrilously anti-Catholic dramatic satire on the origin of syphilis. The trial took place even though the play had been published in Switzerland and the authorities were unable to find any citizens who had taken offense (eventually two Leipzig policemen dutifully declared themselves outraged). Panizza, whose court demeanor was as recklessly provocative as his play, was jailed for a year in an ordinary prison: as cultural historian Peter Jelavich has noted, this was "the harshest sentence meted out to a writer during the Wilhelmine period."[36]

Although RSGB 184, which threatened up to six months' imprisonment for the sale, distribution, or display of obscene (*unzüchtig*) material, theoretically posed yet another threat to writers, statistics compiled by historian Gary Stark indicate that during 1882–92 the total "score" against serious writers in both Saxony and Prussia amounted to little more than a couple of bans on Zola translations, several fines against authors prosecuted in the widely publicized "Leipzig Realists" trial of 1890, and two obscenity convictions against the Viennese author Hermann Bahr.[37] Clearly, prosecutors were hampered by the rather restrictive judicial interpretation of *unzüchtig* to mean grossly offensive "in a sexual sense,"[38] and their problems were even greater in "jury" states. This was the background for a series of attempts during the 1890s to extend the RSGB to cover works of art and literature that, though not technically obscene, were regarded by conservative, clerical, and anti-Semitic politicians, morality pressure-groups, and Wilhelm II as criminally offensive and a significant cause of crime and immorality. But by 1900 opposition to the proposed measures—known collectively as the Lex Heinze—had developed into a remarkable mass movement, embracing both the "right" and the "left" of the cultural scene, including painters, authors, journalists, theater personalities, academics, and even businessmen. Along with a parliamentary alliance between liberals and Social Democrats, and the government's increasing battle-weariness, this extraparliamentary opposition finally resulted in a watered-down and relatively harmless new RSGB 184 simply prohibiting the sale of indecent material to juveniles.

Compared with the obvious hazards posed by the *lèse-majesté*, blasphemy and obscenity paragraphs to freedom of expression, Section 11 of RSGB 360, dating from the 1851 Prussian Criminal Code, which threatened up to a 150-mark fine or six weeks' imprisonment for anyone "who in an unseemly manner causes disturbing noise or who commits gross mischief (*grober Unfug*)" appeared harmless. In the Bismarckian period, however, it was interpreted increasingly elastically by the courts, and especially after 1890 became yet another means of harassing Socialists. Furthermore, since the 1870s, appeal courts in both Prussia and Bavaria had in principle approved its use against indecent, alarming, or inflammatory press articles. In Bavaria this proved a useful means of avoiding trial by jury, as gross mischief was a mere misdemeanor that could be dealt with either by a magistrate alone or by a *Schöffengericht*, and, although its penalties were comparatively trivial, they were an effective weapon against the backstreet scandal-sheets (so-called *Revolverblätter*) that officials most disliked. But two Bavarian episodes of the 1890s gave serious cause for alarm. In the first, following the killing of some peasants by troops in a dispute over forest rights in October 1894, RSGB 360/11 was used systematically to stifle press comment while circumventing the jury. In the second, in April 1898, journalist Harden was prosecuted and received a two-week prison sentence for a painfully explicit article about the condition of mad King Otto of Bavaria, thereby allowing the government to avoid the jury trial mandatory in press cases of *lèse-majesté*. This episode and the prolonged spate of consequent protests led the Reich Justice Office, in March 1902, to formally discourage the use of RSGB 360/11 unless there was a clear threat to public order. Nevertheless, it was too convenient to be abandoned altogether as a weapon against the press.

Because Harden was based in Berlin but prosecuted in Munich, the 1898 case also highlighted another hazard for journalists: so-called flying jurisdiction (*fliegender Gerichtsstand*), arising from paragraphs 7 and 8 of the Code of Criminal Procedure (SPO). These stipulated that a defendant could be tried either at his place of residence or—and in practice more usually—where the crime had been committed. As the prime characteristic of a press offense was distribution, the "scene of crime" could in theory be any place where an incriminated publication was offered for sale. During the debates on the SPO (in force from February 1, 1877) efforts were made to limit prosecution under SPO 7 to a publication's place of appearance (*Erscheinungsort*), an imprecise term generally taken to mean the main center of distribution or the publisher's place of business. The government blocked this, but it was more than a decade before the danger of flying jurisdiction became real. In 1892, however, the Reich Appeal Court ruled that the "scene of crime" jurisdiction for a publication was anywhere it was distributed regularly for gain, and that those responsible for it could therefore be tried wherever this occurred. Thus, for example, a Socialist editor in Munich or Stuttgart who attacked police brutality in Königsberg or the Ruhr could be dealt with in those places without benefit of trial by jury. Even in the event of acquittal, with costs being borne by the state, the disruption caused by editors having to travel hundreds of miles could be crippling for small papers. Eventually, pressure from jurists and the Reichstag became so great that in 1902 SPO 7 was amended to exclude all publications (i.e., not just periodicals) from "scene of crime" jurisdiction except in cases of private libel.

A peculiarity of the campaign against flying jurisdiction was that as, ultimately, with compulsion to testify, the vehemence of the protests seems to have been disproportionate to the hardship actually caused. Prussia had restricted the application of SPO 7 long before 1902; Wilhelm II had ordered that *lèse-majesté* prosecutions in his name should be tried at the place of publication; and most Bavarian cases apart from Harden's seem to have been trivial. However, it is essential to consider the tense political atmosphere of the 1890s, the real danger of new repressive legislation, and journalists' collective memory of state persecution under Bismarck. Moreover, prominent conservative and Catholic judges supported the Revolution Bill and the Lex Heinze, and fears about political pressure on the courts were real. Nevertheless, the overall impact of the criminal law on avant-garde writers and artists does not seem to have been huge. No doubt around 1890 fear of prosecution stimulated the "censor in the head" as it had half a century earlier, and made some publishers overcautious. But successful prosecutions of writers were rare (those who, like Paul Ernst, contributed to Socialist periodicals clearly ran higher risks) and probably counterproductive: three-quarters of the copies of the novels incriminated at the Leipzig Realists' trial, for example, were sold before confiscation could bite. Despite Wilhelm II's declared hostility and denunciations from clerical and other quarters, artists like Käthe Kollwitz, Max Klinger, and Max Slevogt faced nothing more serious than the loss of prizes or the draping or rehanging of their works. And persecution created useful publicity. Wilhelm Walloth, one of the Leipzig defendants, noted later that "nowadays authors can make it commercially only when they get involved in some scandalous political or sexual affair."[39] Retrospectively, 1900 seems to have been the high-water mark for state interference in the arts (apart from the theater)—in part, probably, because of the Lex Heinze furor's bruising effect on officials, but also because of a more general relaxation of political tension in the early years of the new century.

Although some forty new satirical papers were founded in Berlin between 1871 and 1890, reflecting the Reich capital's ever-increasing size and vitality, it was mainly in Munich, for legal and other reasons, that the new, more hard-hitting satirical journalism of the Wilhelmine period was based. (By the mid-1880s, at the latest, the veteran *Kladderadatsch* had become effectively a Bismarckian journal.) Its most famous example, the weekly *Simplicissimus*, first appeared on April 1, 1896, devised by the young publisher Albert Langen, who aimed to create an eye-catching, provocative product using the latest color printing technology. Within a few years, thanks to the efforts of brilliant collaborators including the cartoonists Thomas Theodor Heine, Olaf Gulbransson, Eduard Thöny, and Bruno Paul, *Simplicissimus* became one of Europe's leading humorous papers.

Its history provides a fascinating case study of the extent of press freedom in the pre-World War I era. In general, *Simplicissimus* demonstrated that aggressive pursuit of notoriety to boost sales could, in suitable conditions, succeed despite the best efforts of the authorities. But initially some painful lessons had to be learned. In 1898, when the paper was still being printed in Leipzig, ridicule of Wilhelm II's visit to Palestine brought sentences of six months' fortress confinement from the Saxon courts for Heine and the writer Frank Wedekind, and a large fine for Langen. As the paper's acting editor noted: "As long as we stay in Leipzig we always face the danger of being destroyed . . . it would not be difficult to lock us all up one after the other."[40] But prospects improved dramatically when a printer was found in Stuttgart, so that both branches of production took place in "jury" states. (Significantly, the Social Democratic *Wahrer Jakob* and *Süddeutscher Postillon* were based, respectively, in Stuttgart and Munich.) Subsequently a string of cases demonstrated not only the importance of trial by jury as a safeguard, but also the state's inability to destroy the paper even when convictions were obtained. Thus, in 1903 a cartoon satirizing the alleged obsequiousness of German diplomacy under Chancellor Bülow earned Heine and the responsible editor derisory fines and a mild judicial rebuke for gross mischief, while the seizure of only 1,341 copies out of an edition of 80,000 again illustrated the difficulty of making confiscation effective. (Equally futile were local police bans on street sales, since the attachment of red "*Kolportageverbot*" stickers boosted business in shops and kiosks). Even flagrantly provocative items sometimes had to be ignored, often due to the state's unwillingness to face juries. The latter, it is true, did occasionally convict: in 1905 a Stuttgart court sentenced the paper's editor, Ludwig Thoma, to six weeks' imprisonment for libeling a prominent (Protestant) morality crusader, and Gulbransson was jailed in 1910 for three months for attacking a Catholic bishop. But in January 1906, after publishing a raunchy polemic against moral bigotry, *Away with Love!!*, both were cleared of obscenity in one of the very few cases to come to trial in Munich.

Simplicissimus's virtual immunity was further enhanced by a bizarre seven-year legal wrangle between Bavaria and Württemberg. At issue was the definition of the term "place of appearance" (*Erscheinungsort*) in the amended SPO 7: was it Munich, where the paper's offices were, or Stuttgart, where it was printed and copies dispatched to the wholesaler? (A related, also vital question, since it affected the timing and effectiveness of any confiscation, was whether "distribution" began when consignments left the printer or when the paper actually went on sale a week later.) Once started, the dispute led to top-level conferences between Bavarian and Württemberg ministers and prosecutors, numerous court rulings, and lengthy and at times fantastically convoluted diplomatic correspondence. The Stuttgart authorities were unwilling to waste time and money on usually fruitless prosecutions of a paper that attacked authority figures throughout the Empire. So were those in Munich, who also needed an excuse to ignore *Simplicissimus*'s politically embarrassing vendetta against Bavaria's clerical parliamentary majority. Although Langen and Thoma had not set out to create this situation, they soon gleefully exploited it—for example, by shifting their distribution management to and fro between Munich and Stuttgart. Their happiest time was in the winter of 1907–08 when, because of diplomatic deadlock, the police were refusing to accept the inspection copy in Stuttgart while the Bavarian courts declined to prosecute Langen for not submitting it in Munich.

Ultimately a compromise was reached by which Stuttgart accepted routine responsibility for the paper, but the Munich police took out a subscription and agreed to act, under SPO 8, in cases involving the Bavarian dynasty or state. (Thus, in the summer of 1914 *Simplicissimus* was prosecuted for insulting King Ludwig III.) This slapstick episode graphically illustrates the difficulty of dealing with a large-circulation satirical journal in the fragmented legal conditions of Imperial Germany. If Thoma and *Simplicissimus* had withdrawn to Switzerland, commented the *Frankfurter Zeitung* in February 1906, "There are Stuttgart and Munich public prosecutors who would have bidden [them] a heartfelt adieu."[41]

Inevitably, in these circumstances the authorities were tempted to use other weapons reminiscent of the old police state. One was the so-called objective procedure under RSGB 42, which allowed a court to order the destruction of an "objectively" culpable publication even if punishment of those responsible was "not implementable" (*nicht ausführbar*). This phrase was interpreted by the Reich Appeal Court in 1889 to cover not only cases in which no one could be brought to trial, but also those in which the defendant was cleared (even by a jury) of subjective guilt! Thus, in 1906, despite the acquittal of Thoma and Gulbransson, *Away with Love!!* was declared obscene and remaining copies were pulped. (The same year, Wedekind's play *Pandora's Box* had to be destroyed, although both the author and the publisher, Bruno Cassirer, had been acquitted of obscenity.) Even if, as in this case, confiscation had been fairly ineffective, such action imposed a real penalty by preventing further commercial exploitation of a work. Much more damaging for papers like *Simplicissimus*, however, were bans from sale on state railway stations. As early as 1897, a Prussian railway ban allegedly cost *Simplicissimus* 5,000 copies a week in Berlin alone, and this embargo not only remained in force but was eventually imitated by several other German states (and even in tolerant Switzerland). In September 1909, despite earlier scruples, and demonstrably as an alternative to prosecution, even the Bavarians followed suit when *Simplicissimus* lampooned the Emperor, Prince Ludwig of Bavaria, and the Bavarian army. These bans, together with the paper's somewhat flagging quality, clearly help to explain *Simplicissimus*'s stagnating sales by 1914.

The fight against *Simplicissimus* took place against the background of a larger struggle against commercial pornography (and, shading into it in the public's perception, pulp fiction, so-called *Schund*, or trash), widely regarded as a threat to the morals of youth and, by extension, to the nation's vitality and defensive strength. By the 1900s vast quantities of more or less explicit erotica were in circulation, thanks to easy communications and modern reprographic technology. Demands for its suppression came from an increasingly vocal morality movement that by 1914 was winning converts among the moderate secular intelligentsia: thus, at a 1911 Munich obscenity trial liberal educator Georg Kerschensteiner declared, "If we do not find a means of barring all doors against such [erotic] works, we Germans will in a very short time go the same way that all nations with a lascivious art have gone: the way of destruction."[42]

Pornographic images and literature were combated by continual police seizures, inspection of the mails (under SPO 99), and, in Prussia, the establishment in 1895 of offices in Potsdam, Cologne, and Frankfurt-on-Main to monitor cross-border traffic. There was also an increasing number of prosecutions under both RSGB 184—more broadly interpreted since the late 1890s—and the newer §184a; RSGB 42 and 360/11 were also extensively used. However, past experience clearly inhibited further attempts to extend the Criminal Code itself. Indeed, even a modest proposal by the Imperial government in February 1914 to add a new §43a to the Reich Trade Regulations (RGO) prohibiting the display of material liable to corrupt youth in shops and public places provoked rumblings of complaint about a new Lex Heinze. The bill's progress was halted by the outbreak of war, and legislation to protect youth did not materialize until 1926.

One of the last jousts testing press freedom in prewar Germany involved the Munich Expressionist paper *Revolution*. A 1913 prosecution for both blasphemy and obscenity singled out from its variety of avant-garde conceits *The Hangman*, a poem by the later Dadaist Hugo Ball, that conveyed the feelings of an executioner about to dispatch a beautiful woman through phrases such as "the syphilis-dwarf pokes in pots of gall and glue." The outcome of the case, especially by contrast with the 1895 Panizza trial, demonstrated the growing difficulty of imposing legal norms on the avant-garde. The prosecutor eventually had to admit that Ball's poem was "so obscure and incomprehensible that it leaves room for every possible interpretation," and that during interrogation Ball, the editor and the publisher "revealed such eccentricity and confusion in their moral views that it must be seriously doubted whether they were even conscious of the immorality of their thought and speech."[43] The charges were dropped, and even an RSGB 42 application ultimately failed, proof that by this time press control could raise issues of politics, morality, and aesthetics that were extremely difficult to disentangle. Clearly, in the future publications like this either had to be tolerated or their authors silenced by rather different means.

STAGE AND SCREEN

In the nineteenth century the control mechanisms governing stage performances—a vast field ranging from classical drama and Wagnerian opera to back-street cabarets and boulevard variety shows—diverged increasingly from those regulating other means of communication. As already noted, prior censorship of the press practically disappeared after 1848, as did, eventually, other police-state weapons such as licensing and caution-money. But conditions in the theater remained different, at least in major states like Bavaria, Hesse, Prussia, and the kingdom of Saxony (in Baden, Brunswick, Hamburg, Saxe-Coburg-Gotha, Saxe-Meiningen, and Württemberg preventive controls had either never existed in their modern state-administered form or had been abandoned by 1870). Here a two-tier system prevailed, consisting of both licensing—except for court and municipal theaters—and censorship. During the first two-thirds of the century the former was regulated by individual-state legislation, but subsequently by the Reich Trade Regulations (RGO) of 1869, which successive amendments made increasingly restrictive. Thus, in 1880 RGO 32 was extended to include moral, artistic, and financial criteria for the refusal of licenses, and in 1896 the validity of licenses, originally nationwide, was limited to a particular enterprise and place. (Caution-money, though not provided for in the RGO, was usually also required.)

Censorship arrangements, by contrast, continued to vary from state to state. In Bavaria, for example, stage censorship dated from 1782, but its modern legal basis was RGO 147/1 in conjunction with Paragraph 32 of the 1871 Bavarian Police Code. In 1898, for example, the director of Munich's new German Theater was presented with minutely detailed conditions requiring that

> Every play or poem intended for performance, every act, part, prologue, epilogue and every addition thereto; in the case of musical productions, the libretto; of choreographic, mimed or three-dimensional representations an exact description of the subject-matter, is to be submitted—as a rule seven days before the intended performance—in two identical copies to the Royal Police Direction.

The police could ban, wholly or in part, any performance "on grounds of morality, propriety, or public peace," and permission already granted could be withdrawn. Policemen could attend rehearsals; actors were forbidden to improvise by penal clauses in their contracts, to be produced on demand; and the conditions could be extended or altered at any time.[44]

In Prussia, post-Napoleonic stage censorship (for nonroyal theaters) was established by an 1820 ministerial order that effectively transferred the task from book censors to the police. Though lifted in September 1848, controls thinly disguised as a permit system were reintroduced by Berlin Police President Hinckeldey in a decree of July 10, 1851, stipulating that "no public entertainment of any kind (ball, dance music, theater and the like) may be put on without the express permission of the Royal Police Presidency."[45] Its legal basis was the 1850 Police Administration Law and, originally, ALG 10, 11/17, obliging the police to uphold public order, morality, and safety. This basic regulation was later supplemented by various special royal and ministerial edicts relating to topics such as the representation of royal personages, attacks on court verdicts, and the treatment of biblical material.

A major anomaly of the censorship system was the special status of the court theaters, which in the first half of the nineteenth century had a monopoly or near-monopoly of opera and serious drama. Their repertoires and production guidelines were determined by aristocratic, court-appointed intendants, and, ultimately, by royal patrons. Sometimes the results were brilliant, but generally the court theaters reflected a narrow preoccupation with religion, morality, and dynastic authority as the pillars of a conservative social order. Part One of Goethe's *Faust* was mangled by intendants all over Germany during the 1829–39 period, for example, and Otto Devrient's pioneering production of the entire huge work in Weimar met the same fate as late as 1876. During the "Carlsbad" era and later, Schiller's libertarian dramas *The Robbers, Egmont, Don Carlos*, and, especially, *William Tell* were banned or bowdlerized; Rossini's *Tell* was tolerated in "pre-March" Berlin and Darmstadt only with heavy political alterations. In Dresden in 1861 Heinrich von Kleist's *Hermann's Battle* was banned by royal command halfway through its first performance! During the last century of the Hohenzollern monarchy most Prussian kings were keenly interested in the theater, mostly with negative consequences.

In addition to predictable moral prejudices—in 1903 Wilhelm II fired Royal Theater Intendant Bolko von Hochberg for staging Richard Strauss's "immoral" satirical opera *Conflagration*—they shared a veritable obsession with keeping even long-dead members of the dynasty off the stage. In 1828, for example, after only three performances, Kleist's *Prince of Homburg* was banned "forever" from the Berlin Royal Theater for offending the officer corps, as well as, on this score, Friedrich Wilhelm III himself. On the strength of Gutzkow's comedy *Pigtail and Sword* (successfully performed outside Prussia), Friedrich Wilhelm IV formalized the taboo with a cabinet order of April 20, 1844, making every stage representation of Hohenzollern family members subject to royal permission. This was anomalous in an intensely history-conscious age, and above all in relation to Frederick the Great, a national icon whose exploits were the subject of countless mid-nineteenth-century paintings and illustrations. Thus, in Giacomo Meyerbeer's *A Camp in Silesia*, a costume piece specially commissioned for the opening of the new Berlin opera house in 1844, the "Great King" was only to be heard playing his flute offstage. The ban was reiterated by Friedrich Wilhelm's successors; such royal decrees, of course, were binding on all theaters, not just the court ones. But the 1851 Hinckeldey Decree was essentially tailored to the proliferating and eventually dominant independent sector that was to characterize the second half of the century. By the eve of World War I, nineteen royal houses were ranged in Germany against 132 municipal theaters and more than 300 other enterprises, including traveling companies. It was in the commercial houses of cities such as Berlin and Munich, competing for the attention of a novelty-hungry public, that gritty modern dramas became part of the staple theatrical fare.

Despite periodic debates about theater censorship, there was no fundamental change in its operation between the 1870s and 1918. Both in court and Parliament it was often claimed to be incompatible with key documents such as the Bavarian Press Edict of 1848 or the Prussian Constitution of 1850, and therefore illegal. But mainstream legal opinion rejected this view, and efforts to create a uniform Reich Theater Law proved abortive, with the resulting deadlock leaving the mechanisms of control in their existing, legally fragmented form until the 1918 revolution. A key aspect of this diversity was the difference in appeal procedures between the major "censorship" states. In Bavaria, for example, licensing decisions were subject to judicial review, but complaints against censorship edicts could only be dealt with administratively, and rarely succeeded. But in Prussia and Saxony the censor's actions could be contested in court, and in some important instances were overturned.

Most nineteenth-century commercial entertainment was vetted according to routine considerations of public order and decency and the kinds of special decrees already noted. Aside from concerns to avoid slights to royalty, the drama censors appear to have been especially sensitive to plays that might be viewed as provoking class conflict or explicitly advocating socialist ideas. Naturalist drama also raised fundamental political and cultural issues, since it appeared to challenge the conservative notion, expressed by Prussian Interior Minister von Koller in 1895, that the serious theater was "an educational institution for the propagation of morals, a place for the advancement of historical memories, for the advancement, in short, of everything good and noble."[46] The 1890 Berlin police prohibition of Hermann Sudermann's Naturalist play about ambition and decadence, *Sodom's End*, the first cause célèbre in this area, led to a famous interview between Lessing Theater director Blumenthal and Police President von Richthofen, which was terminated by the latter with the classic words "We're agin the whole movement!" ("Die janze Richtung passt uns nicht!").[47] But a second case, centering on Otto Erich Hartleben's *Hanna Jagert* in 1892, demonstrated the value of the Prussian appeal system. With its heroine loosely modeled on a prominent female Socialist, and prostitution and free love among its themes, the play was inevitably banned in the tense atmosphere of the early 1890s. Yet the decision was subsequently reversed in 1892 by the Higher Administrative Court, which, though upholding the validity of the 1851 Hinckeldey decree, rejected police claims that *Hanna Jagert* threatened morality and order.

The major theatrical cause célèbre of the nineties centered on Gerhart Hauptmann's drama about the bloodily crushed Silesian revolt of 1844, *The Weavers*. The case for suppression was forcefully put by the provincial governor of Hanover, Rudolf von Bennigsen, who argued that the play's inflammatory depiction of exploitation and class conflict would encourage modern workers to believe that violence was their only means of redress. Yet, beginning with a ruling of the Prussian Higher Administrative Court of October 2, 1893, police bans were repeatedly overturned by judges, generally on the grounds that audiences at venues like Berlin's elegant German Theater were unlikely to be stirred to riot and mayhem. Extraordinary pressures were exerted to block *The Weavers'* progress. Wilhelm II demonstratively gave up his box at the German Theater and "discouraged" officers from patronizing it; the Prussian Interior Minister denounced the October 1893 ruling and praised provincial police authorities who ignored it; and the presiding judge apparently felt obliged to retire after a rebuke by the Emperor. Nevertheless, despite such resistance, *The Weavers* was publicly performed in Berlin, Breslau, Hanover, and several other Prussian cities by the turn of the century. In Saxony, a 1901 Leipzig ban was also reversed on appeal.

But another episode, which reached its climax in 1903, underlined the tenacity of stage censorship. At its center was the New Testament drama *Mary Magdalene* by the septuagenarian author—and later Nobel Prize winner—Paul Heyse (himself ironically not a Naturalist "wild man," but an antimodernist and erstwhile pillar of the "idealist" literary establishment). Although the play premiered without incident in Bremen in October 1901, permission to perform it at the Berlin Lessing Theater was twice refused in 1902. The ban was ultimately upheld by a 1903 Higher Administrative Court ruling that exposed the essentially political bedrock of the case by asserting that Heyse's drama constituted an attack on the Christian religion that, as part of the "public order" of the Prussian state, required protection under ALG 10, 11/17. As drama historian Andreas Pöllinger has argued, a major sticking point seems to have been the play's emphasis on the humanity of Christ and its suggestion of a possible love relationship between Him and Mary Magdalene.

In the meantime, the censorship issue had been taken up by the Goethe League movement: a loose federation of societies dedicated to the defense of artistic freedom formed during the anti-Lex Heinze campaign. The eventual result, in early 1903, was Imperial Germany's last set-piece debate on theater censorship at the national level (with a sequel in the Prussian Parliament), but although the issue was aired in all its legal and cultural aspects, nothing concrete was achieved. Heyse's play remained banned from the public stage in Prussia, though sales of the book briefly soared and performances continued to take place in other states.

In May 1903, notwithstanding these events, the Berlin authorities allowed a single closed performance of *Mary Magdalene* at the Lessing Theater before an invited audience, highlighting the fact that, even in Prussia (under §3 of the 1851 decree), private dramatic productions were subject neither to licensing nor censorship. This loophole in the system had already been famously exploited by the Berlin Free Stage (*Freie Bühne*), founded in March 1889 with the objective of mounting closed Sunday matinees of modern plays performed by professional actors. After debuting with Ibsen's *Ghosts*, the Free Stage followed up with the still more sensational premiere of Hauptmann's hard-hitting peasant drama *Before Dawn*; Hauptmann's *The Weavers* was performed there in 1893. Another society, the Free People's Stage (*Freie Volksbühne*), was founded in Berlin in July 1890 with the aim of offering mainly modern drama to working-class subscribers. Despite ideological disputes, the movement prospered, and by 1910 the club's offshoot, the New Free People's Stage, had some 48,000 members. The free stage movement was also imitated successfully outside Berlin: the Leipzig Literary Society premiered Wedekind's *Earth Spirit* in 1898.

In Munich, the University Dramatic Association (*Akademisch-Dramatischer Verein*), which produced works by leading German and foreign dramatists for more than a decade, was closed by the university in 1903 due to political pressure after a public outcry greeted the staging of three erotic dialogues from Arthur Schnitzler's banned *La Ronde*. But it was replaced almost immediately by the independent New Association, which pursued exactly the same agenda. Its major productions, moreover, took place in Munich's best theaters with the participation of first-class actors and directors, received wide press coverage, and in practice were accessible to any adult with a serious interest in drama. In February 1907, indeed, a second "closed" performance of Wedekind's puberty-drama *Spring Awakening* was disallowed on the grounds that the first had been held in the 730-seat Munich Playhouse; doubling this already substantial audience, the police claimed, would amount to the indirect abolition of censorship.

Munich soon afterwards became the scene of an interesting experiment: the Censorship Advisory Council (*Zensurbeirat*), a consultative body of unofficial experts that from 1908 attempted to resolve continuing bitter cultural conflicts between liberals and clericals. The council was conceived as a symbol of nonpartisan reasonableness, and as such included no members of the clergy, the morality organizations, or the Center Party or, equally, of the avant-garde. Instead invited to join were a conservative-liberal cross section of Munich's cultural elite, including, eventually, novelist Thomas Mann, who earlier had denounced the very idea of lay censorship advisors as a "disgraceful compromise." The council's prewar history was uneven. Its near-unanimous advice, accepted by the police, to allow Munich's first public performance of *Spring Awakening* in November 1908 caused predictable outrage, although the version permitted was heavily cut and had been widely staged elsewhere since its 1906 Berlin premiere. The next couple of years were comparatively uneventful, but in 1911 it became embroiled in a crisis occasioned mainly by a succession of Wedekind plays, resulting from Wedekind's determination to confront censorship and its supposed stooges on the council (not only on principle, but because Munich was his home base, and because only public stage productions yielded any serious income). The climax was a spectacular furor over *Lulu* in 1913, which led Mann to resign in despair over what he termed his attempt to "mediate politically between genius and order."[48] Ultimately, although there were further Wedekind storms in the summer of 1914, they were overshadowed by the outbreak of war, and the council continued to function in decent obscurity until November 1918.

Alongside the "serious" theater was the huge range of increasingly commercialized popular entertainments that developed as urbanization proceeded and leisure, even for the working class, expanded. Police archives, and the work of historians such as Lynn Abrams on popular culture in regions like the Ruhr, reveal close monitoring of spectacles ranging from fairground waxworks and peepshows to music-hall performances and song-and-dance routines in pubs and beer-halls (in 1883 a new provision, §33a, was added to the RGO requiring the licensing of performances in drinking establishments). Although most of the material involved had minimal political import, the thrust of this vast surveillance operation, together with the efforts of employers and voluntary organizations to "improve" and discipline the masses outside working hours, was essentially political in its aim to maintain an hierarchical and authoritarian society.

Political censorship proper embraced even the most trivial allusions to topical personalities and issues. In Munich, figures like British King Edward VII and Belgian King Leopold were unmentionable on stage (as was practically anything liable to give offense abroad), the feeblest jokes about Parliament were suppressed, and appearances by suspicious characters like the anarchist-bohemian Erich Mühsam were rigorously scrutinized. In November 1910 a song conveying the idea of the Emperor as a commercial traveler for "the firm of Germany & Co." was banned despite the fact that it had been in the entertainer's repertoire since 1893 and allegedly had been performed in theaters and officers' messes all over southern Germany. References to sensational events reflecting negatively on the Emperor or the court were absolutely taboo. Particularly interesting in relation to censorship were the "artistic" cabarets that flourished after 1900. One of the best was the Munich *Eleven Executioners*, which opened in April 1901 in the wake of the Lex Heinze episode and had several current or former *Simplicissimus* collaborators, including Wedekind and Thoma, among its early contributors. Another reason, clearly, for the brilliance of the group's early repertoire—hilarious dramatic parodies, Wedekind's erotic ballads, and jokes about half-witted princelings—was the fact that for six months its so-called executions successfully claimed to be censorship-free private functions. In due course, however, the *Executioners* was subjected to the whole rigmarole of licensing, script-vetting, and surveillance, with results that vividly underlined the difference between what could be done on stage and, sometimes by the very same people, in print.

It was against this background that control of a new mass medium, the cinema, evolved. Debuting in Germany in 1895, between 1900 and 1914 the number of cinemas in Germany grew to about 2,500; by then, average daily national cinema attendance reached about one and a half million. Strict regulation of the cinema was made inevitable both by its soaring popularity and, as in other countries, by widely held assumptions about its social effects: beliefs about the cinema closely resembled those about trashy literature, given that the plots, characters, and general luridness of early films owed an obvious debt to pulp fiction. But the impact of moving pictures, viewed collectively in the dark, was held to be far greater than that of print, especially on the women, youths, and uneducated people who dominated cinema audiences. Thus, psychiatrist Robert Gaupp told Tübingen citizens in 1912 that exposure to junk films could trigger sexual delinquency and excite the nervous systems of suggestible juveniles with criminal consequences; such views, often in connection with Germany's rising crime figures, were echoed with monotonous regularity by pundits, police chiefs, and ministers across the land.

In the meantime, the broad mass of cinemagoers continued to demand thrills and escapism, filmmakers supplied them, and the authorities endeavored to exert control. The mechanisms devised developed piecemeal, mainly on the basis of existing legislation. By 1914, although most states were operating more or less centralized systems, only Brunswick and Württemberg had passed special film censorship laws. Surprisingly, cinema regulation was deemed to be outside the scope of the RGO, so that, to the fury of theater- and pub-proprietors commercially threatened by the new medium, new picture-houses did not need licenses. More predictably, film was denied the protection of the Press Law, despite the definition of a press product in RPG 2 as including mechanically or chemically reproduced "writings and visual representations." Even more striking than the tortuous legal arguments used to justify this anomaly was the silence of the cultural establishment, usually so vociferous in defense of art, literature, and the theater. However, acceptance of film as a serious means of expression would have flouted the double standards routinely applied to high and popular culture.

In Prussia, a police ordinance of May 5, 1906, established compulsory film censorship in Berlin, and by 1913 decisions there had become binding, though with some scope for local variation, throughout the kingdom. In practice, moreover, Prussian rulings were increasingly also accepted in other states. The 1906 ordinance and its subsequent extensions went back, via the 1851 Hinckeldey decree, to the ALG. Extremely broad criteria were used to ban offending materials: thus, the depiction of criminal or immoral acts, scenes likely to incite religious or social conflict, or images liable to cause fear or repulsion, were forbidden. Although sex, crime, and vulgarity undoubtedly accounted for most prohibitions, there were explicitly political cases too. Thus, a film of the 1910 Portuguese Revolution was banned; soldiers in Halle were forbidden to watch newsreels of the funeral of Socialist leader Paul Singer; and in 1910 a film about Frederick the Great was forbidden (eventually throughout Germany) because, as the Berlin police president argued, it was "important that precisely among [lower-class people and juveniles] no film be shown that might leave a false impression about the personalities or actions of any member of our ruling dynasty or that might undermine popular loyalty toward the royal family."[49] As with the theater, appeals against Prussian bans were possible and occasionally, as in the case of a film of Dante's *Divine Comedy* in 1911, succeeded.

In Bavaria, the basis of censorship was §32 of the police code, which had originally been used to regulate such popular spectacles as waxworks and traveling menageries. In Munich, as cinemas proliferated—there were forty-one by 1914—random checks on programs were replaced by a system akin to that in Berlin, and a similar centralizing tendency was formalized with the 1912 creation of the Bavarian Film Censorship Office. However, the development of a nationwide distribution system and the fact that censorship criteria continued to vary from state to state—in Bavaria, for example, all films had to be suitable for children—increased pressure from the industry for more unified control. Demands for licensing and restrictions on the number of new establishments also gathered strength. But a bill to extend the RGO to cinemas, introduced by the Reich government early in 1914, was shelved on the outbreak of war, and it was not until May 1920, after extensive debates, that a Reich Film Law was finally promulgated.

The war's onset in mid-1914 had a far greater impact on German censorship than the mere postponing of the adoption of a national film censorship law: preventive press censorship, abolished since 1848, was reimposed, military authorities were empowered to summarily suppress publications and imprison journalists, and press regulations became so strict that many papers simply confined themselves to reproducing official communiqués or shut down entirely. Strict theater censorship similarly "purified" the stage of anything that, as one military censorship directive put it, might "unnecessarily" arouse the "feelings of the population" or cripple "its will to resist." Freedom of expression was restored only after the monarchy was overthrown by revolution in 1918, only to be crushed fifteen years later by the Hitler dictatorship, as evidenced by the book burnings at the Berlin Opernplatz referred to at the beginning of this chapter.

SOME FINAL THOUGHTS

So many issues are encapsulated in the history of German political censorship between 1815 and 1914 that it is impossible to summarize them all. But the most striking, and arguably the most distinctively German, was the historically conditioned cultural, legal, and administrative diversity of the states that combined to form the German Empire in 1871. Despite the centralizing efforts of authoritarian rulers during the lifetime of the German Confederation, and of liberal legislators in 1848–49 and after 1867, this diversity remained significant in all areas of communication control throughout the period. A second dominant theme was the profound distrust of freedom of expression on the part of Germany's powerful neo-absolutist bureaucracies, at all levels from lowly police officials to ministers. This manifested itself in governments' dogged rearguard actions against parliamentary efforts to extend press freedom and eliminate stage censorship; in the use of obscure devices such as "gross mischief," "objective procedure," and railway bans to circumvent the 1874 Press Law; and in the multitude of controls imposed on peddlers and popular entertainers at the grass-roots level. And, although it could be argued that by 1900 the position of the bourgeois press and literature was generally secure—certainly by comparison with the situation half a century before—this animus continued to be directed against Socialist utterances with great force until the war. A third, more modern feature of the German scene was the emergence since the late nineteenth century of broadly based morality organizations that, especially in conjunction with political clericalism, demanded repressive legislation and fiercer police action against cultural products they perceived as immoral, un-Christian, or un-German. To a certain extent, moreover, they were assisted by liberal distaste for mass culture and the democratization of press freedom.

By 1914 Germany was finally on the threshold of developments that would make state interference with freedom of expression both easier and, in the longer term, much more difficult. On the one hand, the growing cost, complexity, and centralization of filmmaking and, soon, broadcasting, offered control opportunities by means not only of censorship but, as in the Third Reich, by the exclusion of whole categories of people from the production process. On the other hand, 1914 wireless and telecommunications technology foreshadowed late twentieth-century satellite and computer links that governments have found increasingly hard to regulate. In the meantime, already during World War I, both censorship and official propaganda could be subverted by privately created photographic images and the letters written by millions of literate ordinary soldiers.

NOTES

1. J. Wulf (ed.), *Literatur und Dichtung im Dritten Reich: Eine Dokumentation* (Reinbek, 1966), 51.

2. U. Eisenhardt, "Wandlungen von Zweck und Methoden der Zensur im 18. und 19. Jahrhundert," in H. Göpfert and E. Weyrauch (eds.), *'Unmoralisch an sich . . . ': Zensur im 18.und 19. Jahrhundert* (Wiesbaden, 1988), 4.

3. E. Ziegler, *Literarische Zensur in Deutschland 1819–1848* (Munich, 1983), 119.

4. *German History, 1770–1866* (Oxford, 1989), 409.

5. E. Sagarra, *An Introduction to Nineteenth Century Germany* (Harlow, 1980), 276.

6. E. Huber (ed.), *Dokumente der deutschen Verfassungsgeschichte*, I (Stuttgart, 1961); Huber, *Dokumente*, I, 90–93.

7. A. Berner, *Lehrbuch des Pressrechtes* (Leipzig, 1876), 52.

8. W. Altmann (ed.), *Ausgewählte Urkunden zur deutschen Verfassungsgeschichte seit 1806* (Berlin, 1898), I, 91–92.

9. U. Koch, *Der Teufel in Berlin. Von der Märzrevolution bis zu Bismarcks Entlassung. Illustrierte Witzblätter einer Metropole 1848–1890* (Cologne, 1991), 47.

10. W. Hömberg, "Verhinderte Liberalisierung zwischen Juli-und Märzrevolution (1830–1848)," in H.-D. Fischer (ed.), *Deutsche Kommunikationskontrolle des 15. bis 20. Jahrhunderts* (Munich, 1982), 101; Heine, *Werke* (Frankfurt am Main, 1968), II, 212.

11. Hömberg, "Verhinderte Liberaeisierung," 101 (Censorship Decree of February 23, 1843); Berner, *Lehrbuch*, 6.

12. M. Kramer, *Die Zensur in Hamburg 1819 bis 1848* (Hamburg, 1975), 237–38.

13. W. Siemann, "Ideenschmuggel: Probleme der Meinungskontrolle und das Los deutscher Zensoren im 19. Jahrhundert," *Historische Zeitschrift*, 245 (1987), 87.

14. D. Breuer, *Geschichte der literarischen Zensur in Deutschland* (Heidelberg, 1982), 156; Ziegler, *Literarische Zensur*, 176.

15. Ibid., 169, 173.

16. Eisenhardt, "Wandlungen von Zweck und Methoden," 28.

17. J. Wilke, "Einleitung," in Wilke (ed.), *Pressefreiheit* (Darmstadt, 1984), 1.

18. F. Ohles, *Germany's Rude Awakening, Censorship in the Land of the Brothers Grimm* (Kent, Ohio, 1992), 164.

19. *Die deutsche Wirtschaft im 19. Jahrhundert* (Berlin, 1905), 280.

20. Eisenhardt, "Wandlungen von Zweck und Methoden," 16.

21. Koch, *Teufel in Berlin*, 132.

22. W. Siemann (ed.), *Der "Polizeiverein" deutscher Staaten: Eine Dokumentation zur Überwachung der Öffentlichkeit nach der Revolution von 1848/49* (Tübingen, 1983), nr. 4, 28.

23. Ibid., nr. 14, 57.

24. Koch, *Teufel in Berlin*, 164; Berner, *Lehrbuch*, 143.

25. E. Huber, *Deutsche Verfassungsgeschichte seit 1789* (Stuttgart, 1969), IV, 269.
26. Huber, *Dokumente*, II, 369–73.
27. R. Lenman, "Censorship and Society in Munich, 1890–1914" (Oxford Ph.D., 1975), 7.
28. H. Wetzel, "Kulturkampfgesetzgebung und Sozialistengesetz (1871/74–1890)," in Fischer, *Deutsche Kommunikationskontrolle*, 136.
29. Huber, *Dokumente*, ii, 364–67.
30. A. Bebel, *Aus meinem Leben* (Berlin, 1961), 722.
31. "Kulturkampfgesetzgebung," 140–41, 150.
32. Lenman, "Censorship and Society," 182.
33. Ibid., 14.
34. G. Craig, *Germany, 1866–1918* (Oxford, 1978), 145; Hall, "The Kaiser, the Wilhelmine State and *lèse-majesté*," 102–3.
35. Ibid., 105.
36. "The Censorship of Literary Naturalism, 1890–1895: Bavaria," *Central European History* 18 (1985), 357.
37. "The Censorship of Literary Naturalism, 1885–1895: Prussia and Saxony," *Central European History* 18 (1985), 329.
38. *Entscheidungen des Reichsgerichts in Strafsachen*, VII, 130, ruling of February 26, 1883.
39. Stark, "The Censorship of Literary Naturalism," 341 (modified).
40. Lenman, "Censorship," 85–86.
41. *Frankfurter Zeitung*, February 11, 1906.
42. Lenman, "Censorship," 167.
43. Ibid., 201.
44. Ibid., 214.
45. Breuer, *Geschichte der literarischen Zensur*, 185.
46. Schulz, "Naturalismus und Zensur," in H. Scheuer (ed.), *Naturalismus. Bürgerliche Dichtung und soziales Engagement* (Stuttgart, 1974), 105.
47. Ibid., 93.
48. Pöllinger, *Zensurprozess*, 148; Breuer, *Geschichte der literarischen Zensur*, 200.
49. G. Stark, "Cinema, Society and the State: Policing the Film Industry in Imperial Germany," in Stark and B. Lackner (eds.), *Essays on Culture and Society in Modern Germany* (College Station, Tex., 1982), 143.

BIBLIOGRAPHICAL ESSAY

First-rate general histories of modern Germany are plentiful. Particularly important are Thomas Nipperdey's monumental volumes, *Germany from Napoleon to Bismarck, 1800–1866* (Dublin, 1996) and, as yet untranslated, *Deutsche Geschichte, 1866–1918* (Munich, 1994–95). Also valuable are James Sheehan, *German History 1770–1866* (Oxford, 1989) and David Blackbourn, *Germany 1780–1918: The Long Nineteenth Century* (London, 1997).

For German censorship in general, Klaus Kanzog's article "Literarische Zensur," in the *Reallexikon der deutschen Literaturgeschichte*, iv (Berlin, 1984), cols. 998–1049, provides an indispensable overview. Another brief introduction is Dieter Breuer, *Geschichte der literarischen Zensur in Deutschland* (Heidelberg, 1982). An older but invaluable work by Heinrich Houben is the compendious *Verbotene Literatur von der klassischen Zeit bis zur Gegenwart: Ein historisch-kritisches Lexikon über verbotene Bücher, Zeitschriften Theaterstücke, Schriftsteller und Verleger* (Berlin, 1924–25). The standard collection of key documents is E. R. Huber (ed.), *Dokumente der deutschen Verfassungsgeschichte* (Stuttgart, 1961, 1964). Useful volumes of essays include Heinz-Dietrich Fischer (ed.), *Deutsche Kommunikationskontrolle des 15. bis 20. Jahrhunderts* (Munich, 1982); Jörgen Wilke (ed.), *Pressefreiheit* (Darmstadt, 1984); H. Göpfert and E. Weyrauch (eds.), *"Unmoralisch an sich . . .": Zensur im 18. und 19. Jahrhundert* (Wiesbaden, 1988); U. Daniel and W. Siemann (eds.), *Propaganda: Meinungskampf. Verfuhrung und politische Sinnstiftung 1789–1989* (Frankfurt am Main, 1994); and J. A. McCarthy and W. von der Ohe (eds.), *Zensur und Kultur/Censorship and Culture: Zwischen Weimarer Klassik und Weimarer Republik mit einem Ausblick bis heute* (Tübingen, 1995), with a valuable bibliography. A seminal essay is Wolfram Siemann, "Ideenschmuggel: probleme der Meinungskontrolle und das Los deutscher Zensoren im 19. Jahrhundert," *Historische Zeitschrift*, 245 (1987), 71–106. General studies on nineteenth-century German censorship in English are scarce, but there is some useful material scattered in Eda Sagarra, *Tradition and Revolution: German Literature and Society, 1830–1890* (New York, 1971).

On the early and mid-nineteenth century, see Margarete Kramer, *Die Zensur in Hamburg 1819 bis 1848* (Hamburg, 1975); Edda Ziegler, *Literarische Zensur in Deutschland, 1819–1848* (Munich, 1983), with a good selection of texts; J.-C. Hauschild and H. Vahl (eds.), *Verboten! Das Junge Deutschland 1835: Literatur und Zensur im Vormärz* (Düsseldorf, 1985); and Frederik Ohles' enthralling *Germany's Rude Awakening: Censorship in the Land of the Brothers Grimm* (Kent, Ohio, 1992). W. Siemann (ed.), *Der "Polizeiverein," deutscher Staaten. Eine Dokumentation zur Überwachung der Öffentlichkeit nach der Revolution von 1848/49* (Tübingen, 1983) is a fascinating selection of archival material on post-1848 reaction. A. F. Berner, *Lehrbuch des Pressrechtes* (Leipzig, 1876) is informative on the labyrinth of press legislation up to the RPG.

For developments after 1871, two excellent English-language studies are Robert Keyserlingk, *Media Manipulation: The Press and Bismarck in Imperial Germany* (Montreal, 1977); and, especially, Alex Hall, *Scandal, Sensation and Social Democracy: The SPD Press and Wilhelmine Germany, 1890–1914* (Cambridge, England, 1977). Roy Pascal, *From Naturalism to Expressionism: German Literature and Society, 1880–1918*, has a chapter with information on press and theatrical censorship. Robert Brooks, "*Lèse Majesté* in Germany," *The Bookman*, 40 (September 1914), 68–82, is excellent for the Wilhelmine period, as is Gary Stark's "Trials and Tribulations: Authors' Responses to Censorship in Imperial Germany, 1885–1914," *German Studies*, 12 (1989), 447–67, on the impact on censorship. On the press and literary background, see especially Reinhard Wittmann, *Buchmarkt und Lektüre im 18. und 19. Jahrhundert. Beiträge zum literarischen Leben 1750–1880* (Tübingen, 1982), and Kurt Koszyk's still authoritative *Deutsche Presse im 19. Jahrhundert* (Berlin, 1966).

On caricature, see especially William Coupe's meticulously annotated selection,

German Political Satires from the Reformation to the Second World War, 6 vols. (White Plains, N.Y., 1987) and Ursula Koch's excellent *Der Teufel in Berlin. Von der Märzrevolution bis zu Bismarck's Entlassung: Illustrierte politische Witzblätter einer Metropole. 1848–1890* (Cologne, 1991). Also useful are Mary Lee Townsend, *Forbidden Laughter: Popular Humor and the Limits of Repression in Nineteenth-Century Prussia* (Ann Arbor, Mich., 1992); Ann Taylor Allen, *Satire and Society in Wilhelmine Germany: Kladderadatsch and Simplicissimus* (Lexington, Ky., 1984); and Gisold Lammel, *Deutsche Karikaturen vom Mittelalter bis heute* (Stuttgart, 1995).

Studies of theater censorship are unfortunately scarce. But see Peter Jelavich, *Munich and Theatrical Modernism: Politics, Playwriting and Performance, 1890–1914* (Cambridge, Mass., 1985); Marvin Carlson, *The German Stage in the Nineteenth Century* (Metuchen, N.J., 1972); and Andreas Pöllinger, *Der Zensurprozess um Paul Heyses Drama "Maria von Magdala" (1901–1903): Ein Beispiel für die Theaterzensur im wilhelminischen Preussen* (Frankfurt on Main, 1989). On the Volksbühne and its evasion of the censors, see Cecil Davies, *Theatre for the People: The Story of the Volksbühne* (Austin, Tex., 1977). On pornography and popular literature, see especially Rudolf Schenda's classic *Volk ohne Buch: Studien zur Sozialgeschichte der populären Lesestoffe 1770–1910* (Munich, 1977); also R. A. Fullerton, "Creating a Mass Book Market in Germany: The Story of the 'Colporteur Novel' 1870–90," *Journal of Social History*, 10 (1977), 265–83; Gary Stark, "Pornography, Society and the Law in Imperial Germany," *Central European History*, 14 (1981), 200–29; and Ludwig Leiss, *Kunst im Konflikt. Kunst und Künstler im Widerstreit mit der "Obrigkeit"* (Berlin, 1971). Relevant to a number of themes in this period are several works by Robin Lenman: "Art, Society and the Law in Wilhelmine Germany: The Lex Heinze," *Oxford German Studies*, 8 (1973), 86–113; "Censorship and Society in Munich, 1890–1914, with Special Reference to *Simplicissimus* and the Plays of Frank Wedekind" (Oxford Ph.D., 1975); and *Die Kunst. Die Macht und das Geld. Zur Kulturgeschichte des kaiserlichen Deutschlands* (Frankfurt am Main, 1994).

Long eclipsed by developments in the 1920s, the early German cinema has recently attracted increasing scholarly attention. Specifically on censorship, see Gary Stark's outstanding essay "Cinema, Society and the State: Policing the Film Industry in Imperial Germany," in Stark and B. Lackner (eds.), *Essays on Culture and Society in Modern Germany* (College Station, Tex., 1982); and for the legal niceties, K. Zimmereiner, *Die Filmzensur* (Breslau, Kurtze, 1934). For general information on the early German cinema, see Thomas Elsaesser (ed.), *A Second Life: German Cinema's First Decades* (Amsterdam, 1996); Emilie Altenloh's pioneering study, *Zur Soziologie des Kino: Die Kino-Unternehmung und die sozialen Schichten ihrer Besucher* (Jena, 1914) is still essential reading.

3

Italy

John A. Davis

The history of political censorship in nineteenth-century Italy divides thematically as well as chronologically into two parts. Before unification in 1860 (until then Italy was divided into more than ten "independent" states that were mainly dependent on the Habsburg Empire), political censorship was endemic and intrusive and came to embody the most reactionary and despised features of the post-Napoleonic autocracies. When the Congress of Vienna (1814–15) returned the Italian rulers to their thrones after the collapse of Napoleon's empire, censorship came to play a central role in the politics of the Restoration (1815–48). Censorship was not new, but its importance was heightened by the governments' ideological crusade against the ideas associated with the French Revolution, which were blamed for having thrown Europe into turmoil and anarchy. The Restoration policies of cultural interdiction aimed to be comprehensive, even if in practice this could never be achieved. Nonetheless, censorship and autocracy became inseparable, and the faltering of the censorship regimes in the 1840s signaled a much deeper crisis of the Restoration autocracies.

The struggle for political change in the Italian states during the 1815–48 period was often primarily a struggle against censorship and the principal protagonists of the Risorgimento were all highly gifted journalists—nationalist leaders Giuseppe Mazzini, Camillo di Cavour, and Carlo Cattaneo being only the best known. The clandestine press eventually became what the nationalist writer Massimo d'Azeglio described in 1846 as "a conspiracy in open daylight." It was no accident that the decision of Pope Pius IX (1846–78) to relax censorship in Rome in 1847 marked the real starting point for the revolutions that a year later temporarily overwhelmed autocratic rule throughout Italy.

The failure of the 1848–49 revolutions meant that political censorship returned with a vengeance. The exception was the Kingdom of Sardinia, where the constitution (or *statuto*) granted by King Charles Albert on March 26, 1848, remained in force and guaranteed "a free press subject to the constraints of law." In 1861 the Piedmontese *Statuto* of 1848 became the constitution of the new unified Italian state and remained in force with few changes until the fascist seizure of power in the 1920s.

After 1860, therefore, the political context of censorship in Italy was quite different. This was not only because the new constitutional state guaranteed the basic freedoms of speech and citizenship. The creation of a unified constitutional monarchy under King Victor Emanuel II at least partly resolved the earlier conflicts between the Italian elites and their rulers, and established a degree of political consensus that was the premise for the development of a more open society and a more pluralistic political system. But political censorship did not become redundant, even if after 1860 its targets narrowed to focus on those who stood outside the liberal consensus. That consensus proved fragile, however, and the new state was confronted by sworn opponents of widely differing political colors. On one side, the Mazzinian democrats, republicans, anarchists, and later the socialists; on the other, the supporters of the former rulers, intransigent Catholics, many conservatives, and, by the turn of the century, the nationalists as well opposed the new regime. The highly restricted suffrage reflected the insecurity of the regime: only 2 percent of Italians were enfranchised in 1880 although this rose to 7 percent by 1900.

The hostility of the radicals toward the new state reflected disillusionment with its conservative political outcome, while that of the conservatives and clericals was rooted in the conflict with the Papacy that had been an inevitable outcome of unification and the attempts to free civil society of ecclesiastical controls. In 1861 Pope Pius IX anathematized the new state, seriously weakening its legitimacy in the eyes of many conservatives. Liberal Italy faced other serious challenges: violent rural unrest persisted and widened as urban and industrial workers began to mobilize, and the Italian Socialist Party, founded in 1892, quickly became Italy's first mass political party and, by 1900, the second largest socialist party in Europe.

Surrounded by real and supposed internal enemies, the political leaders, magistrates, and policemen of liberal Italy developed a siege mentality and continued to monitor and silence ideas deemed threatening to the political and social order. In moments of crisis, such as the convulsive internal conflicts that nearly overwhelmed constitutional government in Italy in the 1890s, the authorities did not hesitate to use measures that explicitly contravened supposedly guaranteed freedoms of information, association, speech, and thought. For that reason, defense of the rights of free speech and association was as much at the forefront of political conflict in Italy in the 1890s as it had been before unification. Despite the advent of more conciliatory policies after the turn of the century, Giovanni Giolitti's governments between 1901 and 1914 continued to exercise censorship widely and effectively.

The practice of political censorship in Italy before and after unification therefore poses different sets of questions. The liberal patriots of the *Risorgimento* (struggle for Italian unity) attributed the collapse of the censorship and autocracy before 1860 to the rise of progressive "public opinion," which more recent historians have linked to the rise of a new capitalist bourgeoisie. Yet this may be an oversimplification. Before 1848, challenges to censorship were weak and heavily qualified. There was nothing comparable to the popular campaigns in Britain and France for a free press, and despite what liberals might later claim, the political differences between the pre-unification Italian rulers and moderate reformers were always counterbalanced by a broader conservative consensus in the face of challenges to the social order and cultural or religious values. Indeed, in many cases the censorship regimes collapsed not because of pressure from without but because censorship began to appear dangerously counterproductive from the perspective of the rulers. This connects with the second set of questions, since the relative weakness of moderate "public opinion" may help explain why after unification the governments of liberal Italy continued to use political censorship systematically in ways that clearly violated constitutionally guaranteed liberties and perpetuated the practices of absolutism.

BEFORE UNIFICATION

Politics and Society

At the end of the eighteenth century, Italy was a jigsaw of dynastic states and principalities. Not all of these survived the political reorganization of the peninsula that followed the French Revolutionary invasions. French armies first invaded in 1796, precipitating the fall of the Ancien Regime rulers and the establishment of short-lived Italian republics. In 1799 the French withdrew and the republics collapsed, but after Napoleon's decisive victory over the Austrians in 1800 a more systematic reorganization and reform of the Italian states began. Between 1806 and 1814 all of Italy except the islands of Sicily and Sardinia came under French rule. Feudalism, where it persisted, was abolished, public finances were reorganized and centralized, autocratic administrative bureaucracies were established in place of the devolved systems of power-sharing between the rulers, the aristocracies, the Church, and the privileged corporations that had been typical of the former principalities.

When the Congress of Vienna restored the deposed Italian rulers, no matter how firmly they might set their faces against the French Revolution's political and ideological legacies, they showed little desire to dismantle the immensely powerful administrative bureaucracies that they had inherited. Despite outward appearances of continuity, the Restoration autocracies were quite different from their predecessors. The key innovation in the political organization of the post-Napoleonic Italian states was that Austria was now the power behind every Italian throne. Austrian viceroys ruled directly only in the newly created Kingdom of Lombardy-Venetia, but Austrian troops controlled the whole of northern and central Italy from the four fortresses of the so-called "Quadrilateral," and hence the entire peninsula. Military might was reinforced by tight networks of dynastic and diplomatic alliances. The Tuscan Grand Dukes were members of the Austrian imperial family, the rulers of the duchies of Parma and Modena were Austrian clients, and the popes looked to Vienna as their principal ally. Even the crowned heads of the largest dynastic states—the Bourbon monarchs of the Kingdom of the Two Sicilies (Naples and Sicily) and the rulers of the Kingdom of Sardinia (Piedmont and the island of Sardinia)—viewed Vienna as their principal protector.

During the Restoration, the vast majority of Italians were peasants who either worked small plots of leased land or sold their labor to the larger landowners. Even in the relatively prosperous regions of Lombardy and Piedmont, the conditions of the rural population were desperate. Only in the Austrian territories had there been any attempt to introduce elementary schooling; in the Papal States and the south the rulers remained firmly opposed to any form of popular education. Before unification Italy had few modern industries, yet large numbers of workers were employed in urban crafts, and water-driven technology and plentiful rural labor encouraged new industries to move to the countryside. The wealthiest Italian cities included a small number of commercial centers like Milan, the rest being royal or administrative centers like Turin, Florence, Rome, Naples, and Palermo. But despite the overwhelming importance of agriculture and the survival of traditional forms of farming until well into the twentieth century, Italy's rich patrimony of medium and large sized towns provided important opportunities for cultural change and innovation.

This was one reason why the Restoration proved precarious. Even before 1814, the autocratic character of Napoleonic government gave rise to demands for constitutional government, which during the Restoration became the principal agenda of Italian secret societies and liberals who took the Spanish constitution of 1812 as their model in the revolutions that occurred in Naples, Sicily, and Piedmont in 1820–21. The revolutions were crushed by Austrian troops, but the successful 1830 July Revolution in France touched off a second wave of insurrections in the Papal States, where the reimposition of ecclesiastical administration was bitterly resented. The insurrections of 1831 were again put down by Austrian troops, causing Mazzini to launch his organization (and newspaper) *Young Italy* in an attempt to give the revolutionary movement clearer objectives and organization. Mazzini tirelessly organized conspiracies and insurrections and, although these failed, they persuaded many moderate Italians that political reform was the only way of avoiding wider revolution.

The European revolutions of 1848 began in Sicily in January and spread rapidly up the Italian peninsula, reaching Lombardy in March when the revolution in Vienna and a popular uprising forced the Austrian army temporarily to abandon Milan. King Charles Albert of Piedmont made his bid for national Italian leadership and unity against Austria, but in July 1848 the Piedmontese army was defeated by the Austrians. The political initiative thereafter shifted to more radical leaders, but when in March 1849 Austrian armies returned in force. Charles Albert was again defeated and abdicated in favor of his son Victor Emanuel II. In the other Italian states, the failure of the revolutions ushered in another decade of bleak reaction, leaving Piedmont as the only constitutional monarchy, and making its capital, Turin, a haven for exiles from throughout Italy.

The changes in the European power system caused by the rise of Emperor Napoleon III in France and Austria's diplomatic isolation after the Crimean War (1854–56) finally made political change in Italy possible. In secret alliance with France, Piedmont again waged war on Austria in April 1859, and by the spring of 1860 a new state covering much, but not all, of northern Italy had been formed. This did not satisfy the Italian radicals and nationalists who wanted unification of all Italy as well as a more democratic political system. Their hopes were raised when Guiseppe Garibaldi and his "Thousand" volunteers sailed to Sicily in May to join a revolution there. The Bourbon Kingdom of the Two Sicilies disintegrated, but just as the radicals seemed poised to triumph, the liberal-monarchist Sardinian prime minister Cavour regained the political initiative and forestalled Garibaldi's advance on Rome. The process of political unification was nonetheless irreversible, and on March 17, 1861, Victor Emanuel II was proclaimed king of Italy (although Venice and Rome remained outside the new state until 1866 and 1870, respectively).

Censorship before the Restoration

Ever since the Counter-Reformation, censorship regulations had been enforced by both the ecclesiastical and the secular authorities throughout Italy. Only in the eighteenth century did the balance between ecclesiastical and secular censorship shift as the Italian princes began to assert their independence against ecclesiastical jurisdiction. Books that championed secular authority against the pretensions of the Church, like Pietro Giannone's *Istoria Civile del Regno di Napoli*, the works of Locke, Montesquieu,

Machiavelli, and Cesare Beccaria's essay on *Crime and Punishment* were quickly placed on the Papal Index, yet were tolerated and even encouraged by the secular censors. But the expansion of secular censorship did not always mean greater tolerance; in Naples Charles III's minister Tanucci imposed a two-year prison sentence for anyone possessing Voltaire's *Dictionary* and banned Fenélon's *Reflections on the Conscience of a King* because "We do not consider it advisable to place in the hands and mouths of the common people ideas that criticize our rulers."[1]

Following the French Revolution, Italian rulers sought closer alliance with the Church to combat the increasingly inflammatory ideas and news reaching Italy. When French armies invaded in 1796, the rulers fled and short-lived Italian Republics were established. Although the French government was even then reintroducing "preventive censorship" in France, the Italian "patriots" looked to the principles of the 1789 French Declaration of the Rights of Man, and during the three years of republican government Italy's first free press was born. Between 1796 and 1799, forty periodicals were launched in Milan alone, with another twenty in Genoa (where previously there had only been an official *Gazzetta*). In Paris, however, press freedoms were under attack, and in 1798 the ruling French Directory ordered the closure of all political clubs and the principal journals in Milan.

After the collapse of the Republics there would be no further opportunities for free speech in Italy until the 1820–21 revolutions. Napoleon's victory over Austria in 1800 led to a political resettlement of Italy very different from that of the 1790s. The French authorities in Milan subjected all publications to "preventive" police censorship, and Melzi d'Eril, the wealthy landowner nominated vice president of the Italian Republic by Napoleon, needed no encouragement to set up a *Magistratura di Revisione* (Court of Censors) to exercise "preventive censorship" over all "theatrical works and periodical publications whether national or foreign." The censors appointed by Melzi D'Eril included two who had formerly been employed by the Austrians: both kept their jobs after the post-Napoleonic Restoration.

When the Italian Republic was transformed into the Kingdom of Italy in 1805 preventive censorship was abolished, but any publication guilty of "disrespect to the government" remained liable to severe penalties. What this might mean was evident when the editor of the *Monitore* of Treviso was imprisoned for publishing an essay on pellagra, the debilitating disease endemic in rural Lombardy and the Veneto, of which presence the government refused to admit. Everywhere in Italy, political censorship became more effective, bureaucratic, and invasive, and only publications that were obsequiously subservient to the regime were permitted. The French also attempted to use the press as an arm of propaganda; thus, in 1805, Napoleon reprimanded his viceroy for the lack of good newspapers in Milan and instructed him to remedy this, "Providing of course that the publication of any work opposed to the government shall not be permitted."[2] The French authorities also encouraged the publication of "nonpolitical" journals dealing with scientific, literary, or artistic matters, and more generally with "useful knowledge," all of which were seen as reflections of the progressive character of the Napoleonic order.

The Restoration (1814–48)

After the Restoration of 1814, censorship would assume a central role in the politics of the legitimist rulers. The mentalities that informed Restoration censorship were eloquently set out in a report made later by the Minister of Police in Naples. Never, he claimed, had the state enjoyed wider or more effective powers of censorship, which he believed essential for its survival. The more "indulgent" policies of the past (i.e., the eighteenth century) had been the root cause of Italy's recent disasters:

> As a result of that indulgence, the fanaticism of innovation was spread by books. These were the source of the poison, which was presented in the guise of reform, regeneration, progress and freedom. It was in this way that the spirit of revolution brought desolation to our people, undid morality and destroyed religion. Everyone knows that there has never been, nor ever will be, any open attempt to subvert a legitimate government by force unless this has been prepared carefully over time. . . . [an aim that] has always been, and always will be, the purpose of books and printed writings, as to which there can be no shadow of a doubt since we all have before us the tearful memories of what has befallen us in recent years.[3]

Pope Gregory XVI's (1831–46) encyclical *Mirar Vos* (1832) reflected similar views, condemning both liberalism and "freedom of conscience" as "madness," and describing press freedom as "a detestable and execrable moral scourge."

Nevertheless, both the Austrian authorities in Milan and the Neapolitan Bourbons at first tried to imitate the French precedent of reaching out to intellectuals. The Austrians asked the poet Ugo Foscolo to edit a government journal designed to "encourage public opinion to support the Austrian system of government."[4] Foscolo refused, but the authorities actively promoted a number of "official" newspapers like the *Gazzetta di Milano*. They also continued to encourage the publication of journals devoted to science, letters, the arts, and "useful knowledge," provided they avoided any political comment or reference. Naples and Tuscany had important book-publishing industries, but Milan was the undisputed center of the book trade and publishing, producing 653 titles (the majority devotional texts) in 1816, compared to only 114 in the larger Kingdom of Naples.

Censorship was, however, a reality. The Austrian Department of Censorship had offices in Padua, Vicenza, Rovigo, Treviso, and Udine, as well as Milan, and all material for publication, together with all imported printed materials and all "papers bearing illustrations, geographical maps or allegories as well as music scores, pictures and figurative drawings" were subject to close inspection. The lists of banned books included more than 950 titles and were regularly updated and circulated to other government agencies. Among the prohibited works were those of Machiavelli, Enlightenment writers like Rousseau, Voltaire, Diderot, Condorcet, Beccaria, and Mirabeau, and contemporaries like the poets Vittorio Alfieri and Ugo Foscolo and the former republicans Vincenzo Cuoco, Mario Pagano, and Vincenzo Russo. The censors were particularly alert to antireligious or non-Catholic texts, especially translations of Protestant bibles carried by zealous foreign visitors. In 1821, 113 titles were seized or sequestrated in all of Lombardy, while in 1839 750 titles were seized by customs officials in Parma alone, which probably reflects both a heightened activity on the part of censors and a notable increase in the book trade.[5]

Austrian censorship was vigilant, but followed clearly established rules. Where censorship was more flexible, as in Tuscany, it was also often unpredictable and arbitrary. In 1821 the Swiss liberal Gian Pietro Vieusseux was allowed to found the *Antologia* in Florence, but the review was frequently subjected to unpredictable cuts and suspensions, even though it contained no explicit references to politics. However, its "liberal" reputation caused it to be banned in neighboring states and it finally fell victim to the alarms aroused by the July Revolution in France and the 1831 insurrections in Central Italy. Tuscany's relative tolerance in the 1820s was untypical, however, since the 1820–21 revolutions led most governments to adopt increasingly severe measures. On June 2, 1821, new laws were introduced in the Two Sicilies that subjected all printed materials, including books, printed invitations, all posters, leaflets, and even theater programs to preventive censorship. Under the terms of the Neapolitan Concordat of 1818, bishops already had the right to preventive censorship on all publications relating to morality and religion, and in 1821 the scope of ecclesiastical censorship was extended. In an attempt to prevent news of the July Revolution entering the Kingdom, an 1830 Neapolitan law subjected all imported books and even publications in transit to censorship.

Nowhere was the censorship regime more strict than in the Kingdom of Sardinia, with responsibility shared between the church and various secular officials. No publications other than official journals were permitted. Even these carried no news items except for proclamations, and reference to events in foreign countries was prohibited. Anything taken to imply criticism of the social order was also in jeopardy: in 1843 the Turin censors refused to allow an essay on cooking in the domestic science journal *L'Amico della Famiglia* on the grounds that instructions from a servant might conflict with the preferences of the master or mistress and cause household discord. Even a *History of Mathematics* was banned because it referred to Galileo, and libraries in Piedmont were prohibited from holding titles by writers such as Grotius, Montesquieu, Gibbon, and Pascal.

Francesco Predari, who moved from Milan to Turin in 1842 to launch the *Nuova Enciclopedia Popolare*, described Piedmont as a society still controlled by the Jesuits, with "the press . . . in the grip of the most arbitrary, capricious and uninformed Censorship exercised by the secular and ecclesiastical authorities, which rendered impossible not only any form of free manifestation of thought but even the exposition of the most orthodox doctrine should this fail to conform to the personal opinions of the ecclesiastical censor."[6] According to Predari, the Piedmontese censors insisted that terms like "political interests" had to be replaced by "civil interests"; "Italy" by "fatherland, nation or country"; "constitutional government" could not be used even in reference to Britain or France; the words "liberal," "liberalism," and "liberty" were completely banned in all forms; and "revolution" had always to be replaced by "upheavals," "anarchy," or "the rule of violence."

The censors paid particular attention to publications aimed at popular readers. Despite high levels of illiteracy among the rural population, in many parts of Italy there was a notable production of popular literature consisting mainly of devotional texts, almanacs, and horoscopes. Despite the conservative and highly moral tone of these initiatives, they were fiercely opposed in Piedmont by the church simply because they came from secular sources. But after the 1848–49 revolutions, the Tuscan censors too were warned to ensure that popular almanacs should contain nothing that might spread "ideas that threaten religion, 'public decency' or the social order." Drawings, designs, and illustrations—including those on snuff boxes and tobacco tins—were also subject to close attention because their messages reached well beyond the literate.

Padre Bernadini, the otherwise sensible and balanced Tuscan censor, intoned darkly against satire, which he considered to be "one of the most powerful means by which a political sect may seek to influence the semiliterate masses to become hostile to monarchic government."[7] But censors remained also keenly aware of social distinctions: Bernadini approved publication of a luxury version of the satires of Ariosto (despite the fact that these were on the Papal Index) as the edition was too costly to fall into the hands of any but the wealthy. The writings of the Florentine poet Giuseppe Giusti, the most biting satirist of his day, were banned in Tuscany, however, and Giusti was under constant police surveillance because of the "notoriety of his anti-monarchic opinions."[8]

Techniques and Contradictions of Censorship

Although censorship reigned in every Italian state, it was less easily circumvented than liberals later liked to pretend, partly because it was relatively easy for the authorities to control the points of production. In Milan, for example, despite the rapid expansion of the book trade during the Restoration period, few printers or publishers were willing to risk their livelihood by defying the authorities. An example from Tuscany demonstrates the same point. In 1822 Tuscan censor Bernadini informed the authorities in Livorno that he suspected that a book entitled *The Private Grief of Napoleon Bonaparte While on the Island of Elba* (which he described as "extremely dangerous") had been published illegally in the city. The city governor replied that this was impossible, for a number of technical reasons: the French language edition found by Bernadini had been printed using typeface that "does not exist in Livorno," and the Italian language edition was printed "on paper that is not known to any of our printers" and had "a loose binding with thick thread and is in an unwaxed cover" that was not typical of Livorno binderies. But the owners of the printshops had their own interests to bear in mind too. The governor noted:

> It seems impossible that the printing works owned by the Vignozzi brothers should have clandestinely printed this book. . . . [It] has made the Vignozzi very wealthy. But they run their affairs absolutely correctly and submit everything as they are required . . . to avoid anything that might prevent them carrying on their lucrative business. The only printer in Livorno who is suspect is Glauco Masi because of his political views, his frequent travels and his technical skill in this respect, and if an illegal edition promised a good financial return the printer Meucci might also be prepared to take a risk. Otherwise, none of the other printers in Livorno would ever get involved in the clandestine publication of material not authorized by the Censors.[9]

Poverty and high levels of illiteracy placed further limits on the circulation of printed material. High production costs were another major problem, as the fortunes of Mazzini's revolutionary broadsheet *Young Italy* illustrated. *Young Italy* was printed in Marseilles and copies of the journal were smuggled into Italy hidden with ingenuity in barrels of pumice stone, in containers with false bottoms, or in the clothing of seamen using destinations like Livorno where censorship and customs controls were lax. As a result, and despite the heavy penalties incurred for possessing banned materials, *Young Italy* found its way, in small numbers to be sure, even to the hands of Milanese artisans. Yet despite Mazzini's claim that "the periodical press is a potent force, indeed it is the only real force in modern times . . . being to the intellect what steam power is to industry,"[10] high production costs meant that only six issues of *Young Italy* were produced between 1832 and 1834. These constraints also limited legitimate publications aimed at more prosperous consumers, and even in the most advanced Italian states it was difficult to find a readership wide enough to cover costs. Paper and print were expensive, and books were additionally subject to a variety of taxes designed to limit readership and protect domestic printing and publishing industries. This meant that the technical innovations such as lithograph printing and the steam-powered press that had made possible the rise of the popular press elsewhere in Europe by the 1830s were slow to reach Italy.

The principal obstacles to the effective enforcement of censorship were political rather than technical, however, deriving from contradictions in the Restoration regimes. The most obvious was their political disunity: censorship criteria varied enormously among different states and censors. Thus, when considering whether or not to permit an edition of Filangieri's *Scienza della Legislazione*, which had been prohibited by the Austrian censors in 1821, the Tuscan censor Bernadini noted that although Filangieri's text defended "liberalism and representative forms of government" and that the "sentiments contained therein fully echo the party that challenges the authority of our Sovereigns," these ideas were not a threat in Tuscany, although they might disturb other Italian rulers.[11]

These differences were skillfully exploited by authors, who also knew how to lobby individual censors. In fact, the relations between writers and censors were often quite amicable. The liberal Catholic writer and journalist Cesare Cantù, for example, recalled that in the 1840s the Milanese censor Professor Ferdinando Bellisoni corrected all sorts of errors in the manuscript of his *Storia Universale*, particularly concerning important theological and doctrinal inaccuracies. When the Piedmontese aristocrat, artist, and politician Massimo d'Azeglio was ready to submit his romantic novel *Ettore Fieramosca* (which he had written "to give the Italians a bit of fire and persuade them to get the foreigners off their backs"), he too had to deal with Bellisoni, whom he described as "a good Christian gentleman, quite free of malice, an excellent person, somewhat fat, slow moving and a bit lazy—qualities, in other words, that are a real treasure in a censor!" To catch Bellisoni at the right moment, d'Azeglio made friends with his housekeeper and found out his likes and dislikes. Choosing a moment when he was in good spirits, "It pleased God that I should come away with the Imprimatur right through to the last page." But this did not always work: D'Azeglio recounted that when in 1846 he took his essay on *The Recent Events in the Romagna* to the censors in Turin, he was met by a "No as big and round as the mouth of a well." The Tuscan censor, padre Ferdinando Piccini, also refused the Imprimatur, but d'Azeglio had the pamphlet published in Tuscany anyway under a false place-name and with the censors' complicity.[12]

When Predari needed permission to publish his *Nuova Enciclopedia Popolare* in Piedmont he also carefully studied the inclinations of individual censors and officials. The chief censor, Domenico Promis, a mathematician and Keeper of the Royal Library, was a man of learning and crypto-liberal tendencies "so that all the writers of liberal tendencies did everything possible to ensure that their work would come before him." Predari succeeded in having Promis appointed as "civil censor" for the *Enciclopedia*, while the "ecclesiastical censor" was Padre Sciolla, whose fanatical hostility to the Jesuits enabled Predari to print an article on the Order that was "not especially reticent in speaking of their errors."[13]

Differing criteria of censorship gave rise to serious disputes between governments. It was in response to protests from the Papacy in 1833 that the Tuscan government closed Vieusseux's *Antologia* that year. An even greater scandal had occurred in 1832 when the Piedmontese authorities authorized publication of Silvio Pellico's memoir *Le Mie Prigioni*. Pellico had been accused in 1821 of planning a conspiracy, and served a long sentence in the terrible Spielberg prison in Moravia. His prison memoir was a pietist tract of religious introspection and repentance, but when it was published (with the full approval of the Piedmontese religious and secular censors) it was immediately seen as a tribute to the martyrs of Austrian rule. The Austrian government formally complained to Turin, banned the book in its own dominions, and requested that the censors who had approved its publication be punished. In 1849 Metternich would claim that although Pellico's book did not "contain a single word of truth . . . its effect was more terrible for Austria than a lost battle."[14]

Despite the alliance between throne and altar, censorship was the cause of constant tensions between the secular and religious authorities. Even in the most reactionary states, the works of intransigent champions of papal supremacy like Joseph de Maistre were banned. Except in the Austrian territories, where the state alone had exercised censorship since the eighteenth century, the most frequent disputes arose from demands that episcopal circulars and pastoral letters be subject to civil approval. In Tuscany, for example, the Bishop of Forlì was censured in 1831 for ordering prayers in all parishes for protection against the cholera that had recently reached Italy—an action the authorities deemed "an alarmist publicity."[15] In times of crisis, however, the rulers were quick to mend their differences with the church, and in 1851 the Tuscan government signed a new Concordat with Pius IX that abolished secular censorship of ecclesiastical publications.

Censorship and the Theater

Regulations governing the stage had been formulated since the Council of Trent (1545), and since theaters were accessible to wider audiences than the written word they were subject to stricter censorship. This was still the case in the eighteenth century: Pope Benedict XIV declared in 1748, "we are willing to tolerate theaters but with regret and they will be subject to the strictest control." A religious treatise warned that "the theater is an inheritance from paganism, a school of the language of passion and impurity and not just because of what is heard but above all for what is seen because the stage presents in a seductive and entertaining atmosphere all the pomps, pleasures and license of worldly things."[16]

The eighteenth century saw the rise of the court theaters where the rulers displayed themselves with their courtiers and made public their commitment to secular culture (although King Charles III of Naples claimed that he built the San Carlo theater in Naples mainly to keep a closer eye on his nobility). During the second half of the century many provincial towns also obtained permission to establish theaters, a trend that alarmed the authorities; in 1766 the Neapolitan minister Tanucci complained that whenever he gave permission for a new theater trouble always followed. The champions of the short-lived Republican regimes (1796–99) quickly proclaimed the political importance of the theater, as in Naples, where Republican Minister of the Interior Francesco Conforti argued that the theater provided "a form of public instruction of the greatest importance not only for the young but also for adults who have been subject to the stultifying effects of long lasting despotism. . . . Here instruction can be presented to the citizen in the guise of entertainment." But he also argued the need for close censorship: "since the theater can as easily portray vice as virtue . . . it should be the subject of rigorous scrutiny by the public authorities who must ensure that the people are not moved by sentiments other than patriotism, virtue and sound morality."[17]

Republican attempts to create a popular political theater did not survive. During the French occupation, the theaters became forums for celebrating Bonapartist triumphs and all that transpired both on the stage and in the audience was subject to minute censorship and control. After 1814 the emphasis was again on social exclusiveness, although even in the most reactionary states the theater survived if only as a rigidly regulated extension of courtly life. Theaters—and the gaming houses that were frequently attached to them—were a valuable source of revenue, but there were political motives too: the chief minister of Lombardy-Venetia argued that Milan's La Scala should be kept open even after the 1821 revolutions because "it attracts to a place open to observation during the hours of darkness a large part of the educated population."[18] In Rome the authorities also believed that the theater kept people's minds off mischief.

Control of the stage was more difficult than with the printed word, and the instructions to the Milanese censors warned that "theatrical performances can exercise the strongest impressions on those who watch them, are frequented by every sort of person and are organized by individuals who are eager to win applause and therefore inclined to bow to the tastes and opinions of the multitude without being scrupulous about how they may achieve this."[19] To guard against such dangers, theatrical productions were subject to multiple censorship. Written texts were subject to the press laws and any improvisation was strictly banned. Permission for performance had to be obtained from the police, and police agents were present at all performances to keep order and ensure that the approved script was strictly followed. Even after Pius IX relaxed controls on the press in Rome in 1847, the theater remained subject to prior censorship by the ecclesiastical authorities, by the police, and by local government officials. Forty-one copies of each script had to be submitted for approval, together with drawings of stagings and costumes. The censors were particularly sensitive to colors and would not permit any costumes that included any of "the colors of Italian demagoguery" (i.e., the tricolor green, red, and white) on stage.

In Tuscany, all plays were subject to prior censorship and no plays were permitted that dealt with "history or events concerning the Church." There could be no allusions to the Old Testament or to the Church in any form of dance sequence. In addition, the censors would ban any play that was based on "an evil theme that seeks to weaken respect for Religion or the Throne, that incites ideas contrary to either, or contains material of bad taste or represents crimes or terrible deeds like assassinations, premeditated murders, suicides brought on by despair, and similar subjects." The Tuscan censors were especially concerned that historical plays should not "cause offense to the conscience and principles of modern times" while "sentimental dramas which are generally translated from German or French" might be tolerated unless they portrayed "dangerous or over-heated passions" or if they incited depravity.[20] Such criteria were widely followed: the Neapolitan censors insisted, for example, that the heroine of Dumas's "La dame aux Camélias" should not be described as a courtesan to avoid offending the monarchy.

References to the recent past, and in particular to Napoleon, were another obsession. In 1822 the Florentine censors banned G. B. Niccolini's play *Nabucco* because it was seen as an allusion to the French emperor. The same author's *Sicilian Vespers* was permitted only under the title of *Joanna of Procida* (but that was subsequently banned too when the French ambassador complained that it was anti-French). When in 1844 the Tuscan police seized copies of Niccolini's play *Arnold of Brescia*, which had been published in Marseilles, the Tuscan censor reported with horror that "the theme of the play seems to be that the Holy Pontiff should not exercise temporal power in the Papal States, and in other places claims that the power of sovereignty rests only with the people and other such maxims of liberalism!" The Lombard censors banned Foscolo's play *Ajax* on the grounds that it "insinuates a spirit of freedom that is directed against Austria."[21] Ironically, the same play had been banned in the Napoleonic period because it was considered critical of Napoleon.

Direct censorship was only one of the means of controlling what appeared on the stage. In the court theaters, the rulers intervened in every aspect of performances, choosing subjects, reading and approving the libretti, and even selecting the staging and costumes. Since the opera impresarios were dependent on rulers' patronage, like publishers they were keen to avoid offense. Bearing out Michel Foucault's analysis of the interdependence of censorship and auto-censorship, theatrical producers, composers, and librettists generally endorsed the criteria of the censors and did their best to comply with them.

The constant and petty interference of the censors reflected the desire of the Restoration regimes to monopolize and regulate every form of public life. Censorship was most oppressive in those states where relations between church and state were closest—Piedmont before 1848, and until 1860 in the Papal States, the Duchy of Modena, and the Kingdom of the Two Sicilies. The censors in Rome, for example, refused to allow Bellini's *Norma* to be performed under that title because "norma" was a technical theological term. Where the rulers upheld the autonomy of secular power, notably in the Tuscan Grand Duchy but also in the Austrian territories, there was greater tolerance. But even there, the powers granted to the censors were enormous and subject to little control.

The theater has often been depicted as the birthplace of a new nationalist identity, although historian John Rosselli has argued that before the 1840s the Italian theaters and their audiences generally mirrored the aristocratic and reactionary values of the Restoration. Verdi's operas did mark an important turning point, however, that reflected new attitudes in the early 1840s and growing sympathy for the cause of Italian independence among the elites. The chorus of the Hebrew slaves in *Nabucco* and that of the Scottish exiles in *Macbeth* were greeted as symbols of Italy's slavery, even though Verdi dedicated both *Nabucco* (1842) and *I Lombardi* (1843) to the Austrian Emperor. But this may have been little more than expediency since Verdi was already frequenting the meeting places of the Milanese liberals who were to come to the forefront in the 1848 revolt against Austria.

Despite his popularity, throughout his early career Verdi was dogged by interference from the censors, who insisted on changes to plots, text, and titles, with the result that the same opera often played under quite different titles across Italy. Only in the Austrian territories was Verdi able to stand his ground. After the success of *Nabucco* his reputation as a composer was so great that the Milanese authorities treated him with special consideration because his works were sure to fill the theater. In Lombardy, he was also able to profit from the tensions between the secular and religious censors. On one occasion, the Archbishop of Milan, Count Gaisruck, protested that the libretto for *I Lombardi* contained "religious processions, churches, the Valley of Jehosophat and a baptism." If the chief of police refused to ban the opera, the Archbishop threatened to complain directly to the Emperor. But when Verdi and the producer declared that they would not go ahead with the production if the libretto was substantially changed, the police chief acquiesced and merely required that the words "Ave Maria" be changed to "salve Maria." But even Verdi was not always so fortunate and virtually all his productions were subjected to the same intrusive battles with the censors that in 1857 led him to withdraw *Un Ballo in Maschera* from La Scala just before opening night. For lesser writers, struggles to find audiences, patrons, and patronage encouraged a conformism that made censorship not only irrelevant, but unnecessary.[22]

It was not until 1848 that Verdi could openly declare his sympathies with the nationalists, first in Milan and then later in Rome where his new work *The Battle of Legnano* was presented in a fury of nationalist expectation after the declaration of the Republic. Not surprisingly, after 1849 the theater was subject to even tighter censorship and, except in Piedmont, its function as "the focus of the social life of the upper classes" went into deep decline.[23]

Censorship and the Crisis of Restoration Autocracy in the 1840s

Enthusiastic displays of nationalist sympathies during theatrical performances in the 1840s were the most public and, for the authorities, the most alarming evidence of the weakening of the censorship regime. But this has to be seen in the context of a broader crisis of Restoration autocracy in the years immediately preceding the 1848 revolutions. As in the former Soviet satellite states in Eastern and Central Europe in the 1980s, the crumbling of censorship in the 1840s was a critical sign of the internal collapse of the Restoration order. An emergent "public" opinion played a part in this process, but many of the initiatives, however confused and contradictory, came from the governments of rulers like Charles Albert of Piedmont, Leopold II of Tuscany, and even Pius IX.

By the 1840s the premises of Restoration autocracy were becoming increasingly contradictory, and the refusal to countenance any form of change was beginning to threaten the rulers' own interests. Without economic development, dynastic independence could not be maintained. Censorship might silence, but it could not remove the realities of the new industrial age. The issues of poverty, public health, science, and crime that were being debated throughout Europe were realities in Italy also. But economic growth meant greater commercial freedom, which fostered greater circulation of information, developments incompatible with the preservation of autocracy and censorship. The steps away from the triple alliance of throne, altar, and Austrian bayonets were faltering and uncertain, however, hedged around by fears that the revolutions of 1848 would prove well founded.

The first step was taken in 1839 when Tuscany gave permission for the first Congress of Italian Scientists to be held at Pisa. Subsequently, similar Congresses were held annually in different Italian states down to 1846. But Leopold II's decision to permit a gathering of experts to debate carefully formulated technical and scientific questions was not accompanied by any relaxation of censorship. Participants were nominated by the host governments, required passports and certificates of good conduct from them, and were subject to careful vetting on their arrival. All sessions of the Congresses were monitored by police agents and spies, who made daily and detailed reports on the proceedings.

Nonetheless, open discussion of public affairs marked an unprecedented change in the policies of the Restoration rulers. As historian K. R. Greenfield demonstrates in his study of pre-1848 Lombard journalism, political economists had long pointed, without explicit political references, to the disparities between the economic, social, and cultural conditions of Italy and other European countries. The subtext of the information carried by journals like Cattaneo's *Annali Universali di Statistica* (1832–36) and the *Politecnico* (1839–44) was that without independence the Italian states could not participate in the broader march toward "progress," which was seen to be the inevitable and irresistible characteristic of the century. Silvana Patriarca has recently argued that the same message was also present in statistical studies that conveyed images of alternatives to contemporary economic and social realities. If statistical tables could not catch the public ear in the same way as the operas of Verdi or the poetry of Foscolo or Alfieri, they did reveal growing interest in political discussion and more open and informed government in Italian intellectual circles.

Growing interest in the new problems that were facing nineteenth-century European societies—from public health to poverty and crime—made the Restoration interdiction of all forms of public debate and the attempt to maintain closed monopolies over all forms of information increasingly difficult to enforce, much less justify. Leopold II's decision to convene the Congress of Scientists in 1839 was motivated primarily by the terrible cholera epidemics that had swept through Italy in the previous year. Austrian censorship also became more selective, and by the early 1840s Milanese journals like the *Politecnico* were discussing issues—railways, free trade, education—that were still strictly off-limits elsewhere. In Piedmont, by contrast, Cavour's famous essay of 1846 that argued the case for a pan-Italian railway had to be published in Paris. But the appearance in Turin in the same year of Giuseppe Pomba's *Mondo Illustrato* signaled a more liberal policy. Pomba's periodical was a finely illustrated lithographed magazine modeled on the London *Penny Magazine* and the Paris *Magasin Universel*, providing its readers with political information and commentary enlivened with striking colored illustrations. Its price was sufficient to keep it from the hands of the masses, yet the government's decision to permit it, along with Predari's *Nuova Enciclopedia Popolare* and *Antologia Italiana*, showed that Piedmont was moving in a different direction from the Austrian government, which in 1844 suspended Cattaneo's *Politecnico*.

Yet, as Greenfield notes, intellectual debates did not translate easily into political action. Indeed when the 1848 revolution erupted, Cattaneo and the other Milanese intellectuals found themselves in a small minority with little support from the wealthy Lombard commercial bourgeoisie. Nor was it the moderate liberal press that precipitated the crisis of the autocracies in the 1840s, but rather the shapeless and largely unstudied clandestine and popular satirical press that grew from almost nowhere. In contrast, there was little spontaneity about the birth of the moderate press. The fact that its principal focus was Piedmont, which until the very eve of the Revolution retained a stifling apparatus of censorship, reveals very clearly that the new "public opinion" was to a certain extent also created by the rulers.

The Politics of Collusion and Confusion: Censorship in the Italian Vormärz

The hesitant opening of new spaces for public debate in the early 1840s was inspired by sections of the elites seeking rapprochement rather than conflict with the legitimist rulers. The backdrop lay in the fears of revolution that were beginning to haunt Europe as the "Hungry Forties" brought famine, economic recession, unemployment, and social and political unrest to the entire Continent. In Italy, these fears persuaded moderates to appeal to the rulers to implement moderate reforms and seek greater independence from Austria and the Church.

The opening round came with the 1843 publication of Vincenzo Gioberti's lengthy tract *On the Primacy of the Italians*. Although not the first breach of the rule of silence, it was the first such publication to receive tacit approval from the authorities, for reasons easily understood. Italy, Gioberti argued, would only regain its former political and cultural greatness if its rulers became free of foreign control, which he believed possible without political revolution and through the moral leadership of the Papacy. An alternative came from the venerated Piedmontese nobleman Count Cesare Balbo, whose 1844 *Speranze d'Italia* (Italy's Hopes) also insisted that independence was the premise for Italy's regeneration, but argued that only a secular prince could successfully and peacefully negotiate Austria's withdrawal from Lombardy-Venetia. Despite his deep religious conviction, Balbo championed the claim of the Piedmontese monarchy to lead a confederation of independent Italian rulers.

These initiatives were not private ones. Gioberti's *Primacy* was published in Brussels, but with the approval of the Piedmontese authorities, and it circulated widely in Italy because the Tuscan authorities refused to intervene. The same was true of Balbo's treatise, which the author had originally submitted in 1843 for King Charles Albert's approval and ultimately published in Paris upon the advice of chief Piedmontese censor Promis after the king advised Balbo that the treatise could not be published in Piedmont because of delicate relations with Austria. Following the French edition of 1844, further editions were printed across the Swiss frontier at Capolago and flooded into Piedmont. The Austrian government immediately protested and the governor of Lombardy informed the Emperor that the book was especially dangerous because its views seemed now to be shared by "His royal Highness the King of Sardinia."[24] The Piedmontese government did not ban Balbo's text, although the Tuscan government was unable to ignore Austrian pressure. Both examples show how censorship exposed the Italian rulers to humiliating foreign intervention that exposed their limited autonomy and forced them to become accomplices in evading their own censorship regulations. In Tuscany the censors openly encouraged printers of texts that might offend Austria or the Papacy to substitute "Italy" or "Paris" for the true place of publication, and generally turned a blind eye to books published illegally in the Grand-Duchy that did not carry a place-name.

Events were now gaining a momentum of their own. In 1844 two Venetian brothers, Emilio and Attilio Bandiera, launched a disastrous revolt in Calabria, which spurred other localized insurrections, especially in central Italy. Expectations were heightened in 1846 when Cardinal Giovanni Mastai Ferretti was elected as Pope Pius IX, since, after a long sequence of bleakly reactionary pontiffs, he was believed to be sympathetic to the cause of Italian independence and opposed increased Austrian power. When Pius granted an amnesty to political prisoners, reform agitation surged throughout the Papal States, which became inundated with clandestine publications that quickly found their way into neighboring Tuscany. This gave new immediacy to the moderate campaign; in a series of pamphlets Massimo d'Azeglio appealed to the revolutionaries in Central Italy to abandon insurrection and put their faith in the force of moral persuasion. D'Azeglio too could count on tacit official support, and his pamphlet *On Recent Events in Romagna*, which contained the famous reference to the "conspiracy in open daylight," was published in Tuscany (the place of publication given on the title page was simply Italy, 1846) and sold over 2,000 copies.

Censorship was now at the heart of a series of double games being played not only by moderates, reactionaries, and revolutionaries but also by influential figures within the autocratic regimes and—in the case of Piedmont and Tuscany—by the rulers themselves. In Turin, Predari played effectively on increasingly open political rifts within the government and royal court, and gained the support of influential conservatives who wanted the powers of the Church and the ultrareactionaries reduced. The politics of censorship became caught up in the struggles between different political factions at court, and when the reactionaries tried to block Predari's publications he appealed to more sympathetic ministers and also directly to the king. But when it suited them, the reactionaries broke the rules for their own ends, and it was widely suspected that the chief of police in Turin (the father of Cavour) distributed fly-sheets and satires hostile to the king in the autumn of 1847 to provoke disturbances that would discredit the moderates.

Other legitimist governments were also beginning to doubt the utility of censorship. In 1844 the Neapolitan council of ministers reviewed its present and past censorship policies, and the debate revealed how rivalry between different factions and ministries seriously compromised the whole operation. The Neapolitan minister of police requested that he be given additional censorship powers to combat growing political unrest, but this was opposed by the president of the Council of Ministers, the Marchese Ceva Grimaldi, who pointed out that "in the vast arsenal of our Provisions, especially those introduced after 1821, there is already the very strictest regulation, which would be quite adequate even if we were to make them more moderate." He argued that rather than introducing new measures the real problem was to effectively enforce existing laws, claiming that the Kingdom was "inundated with pernicious books . . . which our printers print publicly, so that as president of the Council of Ministers I have been able to buy openly from stalls in front of my own house" forbidden materials. He added this was because the police lacked the elementary skills needed to enforce existing regulations, a comment that provoked the minister of police to blame instead the laxity of the interior ministry's censors, who, he claimed, frequently approved the publication of books prohibited by the police, including a certain *Lettere di un Italiano* that was full of "patriotic, erotic and amorous expressions," as well as the novels of Wolter (sic!) Scott "many of which are redolent with a malicious anti-Catholicism." The debate revealed how interdepartmental rivalries compromised the enforcement of censorship in Naples, but Ceva Grimaldi voiced deeper doubts when he argued that censorship needed to become "commensurate with modern times, closer to the practice of other civil nations in Europe, so that it may lose much of its vexatious character."[25]

Even for the rulers, the utility of censorship was in doubt. It risked isolating them from moderate "public opinion" and prevented the emergence of a wider pro-government press. Its enforcement was not easily controlled and was increasingly subject to rivalry between individual censors and competing branches of administration. Even worse, censorship exposed the rulers to humiliating foreign interference. The problem was how to get rid of censorship without abandoning the whole edifice of autocratic government, a dilemma exacerbated by the relative weakness of "moderate" public opinion.

The Revolutions of 1848

Censorship played a central role in the dramatic events that culminated in the revolutions of 1848. At the center of the drama was Rome, where enthusiasm for Pius IX and expectations of wider reform rapidly led to a breakdown of government in the Papal States. In an attempt to stop the flood of clandestine pamphlets, in December 1846 the head of the Papal Police, Monsignor Pietro Marini, urged the government to relax censorship and attempt to create a pro-government press. In March 1847 the censorship laws were modified, and the *Contemporaneo* became the first political journal to be published legitimately in Italy since the 1821 revolutions. But Pius IX's reform was too limited to be effective. It did not abolish preventive censorship, but instead set up a Council of Censorship (*Consiglio di Censura*) that was responsible for ensuring that nothing could be published that might cause offense "to Religion, the Church and its Ministers, private families and citizens, foreign governments and sovereigns."[26] These measures proved useless against the clandestine press, and inadequate to support the moderate press: in May the *Contemporaneo* was closed down following complaints from the Austrian ambassador.

Events in Rome were closely followed throughout Italy, especially in neighboring Tuscany. In May 1847 Leopold II followed Pius IX's lead and relaxed censorship in the hope of encouraging development of a pro-government press. In the south, clandestine political tracts and books also increased, much to the alarm of the authorities, although Ferdinand II refused to relax censorship. In Piedmont, despite tumultuous public demonstrations in favor of press freedom in Genoa in September 1847, the government actually increased restrictions until Charles Albert's Letters Patent of October 30 took the first step toward legalizing the political press. The first moderate political journals—Cavour's *Risorgimento*, Giacomo Durando's *Opinione*, Valerio's *Concordia*, and Brofferio's *Messagero Torinese*—immediately began publication in Turin.

The collapse of censorship in central Italy in 1847 marked the start of the crisis, even though the revolutions proper began only in early 1848, when a revolt in Palermo forced King Ferdinand to grant a constitution and limited press freedom on January 29. Leopold II of Tuscany granted a constitution in February that declared that "the press shall be free, but subject to the controls of the law." The Piedmontese constitution of March 26 similarly declared that "the press shall be free, but a law will be drafted to repress abuses," and added that "no Bibles, Catechisms, liturgical or prayer books may be printed without the prior consent of the Bishops." Nonetheless, the Bishop of Pinerolo at once resigned to protest what he considered an intolerable infringement of the Church's jurisdiction.

Despite the previous history of strict censorship, a lively political press quickly emerged, including a mass of short-lived broadsheets, as well as a smaller number of periodicals that set high technical and artistic standards, using political satire and caricature to develop new political vocabularies and iconographies. The most prominent of these were the *Arlecchino* (Naples, March 1848–June 1849), the *Spirito Folletto* (Milan, May–July 1848),

Sior Antonio Rioba (Venice, July 1848–March 1849), the daily *Il Lampione* (Florence, July 1848–April 1849), and *Il Fischietto* (Turin, founded November 1848). Although these were moderate liberal publications, the Neapolitan *Arlecchino* was subject to frequent sequestration, closure, and fines before it was finally shut down. In all instances, the high cost of subscriptions limited circulation and only the Turin *Fischietto* survived the revolutions, with a circulation of about 2,500 by the early 1850s.

Violent clashes between political moderates and radicals soon raged around the limits that should be imposed on the new freedom of the press. In Rome, Carlo Ponzio argued that "censorship is even more necessary and useful in a representative government than in an absolutist state" and many moderates sought to silence the demagogic tones of the radical press. But moves in early 1849 to ban pro-papal journals like the *Costituzione Romano* were rejected by the Republican government on the grounds that this would infringe press freedom.

Once the revolutions were spent, censorship returned with a vengeance. When French troops entered Rome in July 1849, General Oudinot subjected all publications to military censorship. After Leopold II's return to Florence, pressure from Austria resulted in the banning of all political journals in September 1850. In Naples, after the royalist coup of May 15, 1848, the press was subject to the discretionary control of the police; in March 1849 new laws required the editors of journals to post 3,000 ducats surety, a prohibitive figure for any publication lacking full governmental support. In the Austrian territories, which remained under a state of siege until 1854, Imperial Patents of March 13, 1849, banned all political publications and introduced regulations that outlawed publishing anything that might incite or justify attempts "to break away by violence any part of the Empire, or to incite disobedience or rebellion." By an ordinance of July 6, 1851, the senior Austrian official in each province was empowered to suspend any publication that displayed "tendencies in any respect hostile to the throne, the integrity of the Empire, religion, proper behavior and other fundamental aspects of the State, or is in any way incompatible with the maintenance of public tranquillity and order."[27] A further law of March 7, 1852, introduced even tighter controls, set up new Commissions of Censors in every province, and transferred responsibility from the Council of Ministers to the police.

Piedmont in the 1850s

The Press. After 1849, censorship remained interred only in Piedmont, where Victor Emanuel II's government confirmed the freedoms guaranteed in the Constitution (February 24, 1852). The law on the freedom of the press was drafted by a commission headed by Federico Sclopis, whose introductory speech to the Chamber was a manifesto of the principles of moderate liberalism. Sclopis argued that greater freedom of public debate was the premise for a new and mutually beneficial relationship between government and enlightened public opinion:

> The aim of this Law is not only to open opportunities for scientific debate and make possible a wider communication of useful knowledge, but also to enable the Government to make use of the guidance which may only be derived from the considered, but nonetheless frank and respectful, discussion of all matters that relate to public administration. . . . It is proper, therefore, that the liberty of speech should be as broad as possible, provided always that this does not exceed the limits of discretion and of lawful respect for the Government.[28]

The purpose of the law was to establish freedom of speech, yet simultaneously set its limits. Based on the 1828 French press law, the Piedmontese law of March 26, 1848, declared that "the right to liberty ceases when this degenerates into mere license and becomes subject to evil-intentioned passions." Although it did not require editors to post bonds, it did require that all publications carry the name of the printer, place of publication and date, as well as the name of the "responsible director," who was liable for all material published and was obliged to inform the government of all changes in the nature of the journal or the printer. Although the law affirmed the right "to manifest ideas freely in the press," it banned publishing anything contrary to the 1838 Penal Code or that might "incite to commit crime, give offense to the Catholic religion or other religions acknowledged by the State, to public decency (*buoni costumi*), to the person of the King, the Royal Family, or members of the Diplomatic Corps." Any material that was "defamatory or injurious" was illegal, as were statements that "blamed the King for acts committed by his government" or that "challenged the inviolability of property rights," "openly advocated some alternative system of government" or "preached hatred between the different social orders or against the integrity of the family."[29] Enforcement was entrusted to a judge sitting with a jury composed of twelve enfranchised citizens, thus limiting the jury pool to the wealthiest 1 percent of the population.

Although hedged with conditions, the freedom to publish in Piedmont attracted frequent complaints from neighboring states and rulers during the 1850s. Prime Minister Cavour repeatedly brushed off these protests, claiming that tighter controls would jeopardize Piedmont's liberal reputation in Italy and risk making it like Spain, "liberal today, reactionary tomorrow."[30] But following Italian emigré Felice Orsini's unsuccessful attempt to assassinate French Emperor Napoleon III in Paris in January 1858, the French government demanded the immediate expulsion of radicals and extremists who had congregated mainly in Genoa, as well as the suppression of the republican newspapers *L'Italia del Popolo, Il Diritto, and L'Unione.* Cavour agreed to take action, but he told the French ambassador that "these measures are in some respects extra-legal" and that it would be preferable to rely on police action rather than suspend freedom of the press and of association. The republican paper *La Ragione* was prosecuted for defending the attack on the Emperor, but its editors were acquitted (January 1858), which provoked further French protest. The Piedmontese government then introduced new legislation that banned publicly defending acts of violence against foreign rulers, but this ran into fierce resistance in parliament.

Cavour was reluctant to bow to French demands for action against the Mazzinian *L'Italia del Popolo* because he believed that the radical press helped mobilize support for the moderate party, and also because the extremist press encouraged the French government to support more conservative solutions to the issue of Italian independence. Thus, Cavour argued that *L'Italia del Popolo* "does more good than harm. In fact, I would myself pay Mazzini to write for it."[31] After the Orsini incident, however, Cavour considered it politic to accede to French demands that the paper be suppressed, and in parliament he argued that the Republican press as a whole was opposed to the institutions of the state and hence constituted "a constant offense against our law." He also encouraged the Prefect of Genoa to deploy every means available against *L'Italia del Popolo* and the rest of the republican press, suggesting that he use a combination of police and judicial measures to force the printers out of business. Accordingly, *L'Italia del Popolo* was sequestered thirty-eight times in the first six months of 1858 and folded in August.

Cavour was also active in promoting a pro-government press. He supported *Il Fischietto*, which returned the favor with unstinting backing for Cavour. He also supported satirical journals like *Pasquino* that propagated the idea of Italian independence and was widely read in the Austrian territories as well as in Piedmont. Because the liberal revolution in Piedmont was dangerously hemmed in by the reactionary right and the extremist nationalists, Cavour used tactics such as backing "official candidates" in elections, using secret funds to create a pro-government press, and buying support from the foreign press. Although reductions in newspaper taxes (June 22, 1850) and postage rates for newspapers and periodicals (May 15, 1851) were intended to encourage and stimulate the development of a free press, the use of police powers and administrative means to curb the extremist press set dangerous precedents.

However, the legal guarantees now enjoyed by the press were not easily overridden even when the government wanted to circumvent them. Italian historian Rosario Romeo has calculated that over 70 percent of all prosecutions brought against the press in Piedmont in the 1850s ended in acquittals, one reason being that press offenses were the only criminal actions subject to jury trial. In 1857 Francesco Cota, a senior magistrate in Genoa and close confidant of Cavour, acknowledged that citizen juries were generally reluctant to convict. Cota pointed out that if he brought charges against the newspaper *Il Cattolico* for "inciting hatred between the Genoese and the Piedmontese" these would certainly be thrown out by a Genoese jury that would most likely share the paper's views. Worse, the defense lawyers would exploit the trial to give publicity to the paper and make inflammatory statements that would find a ready audience in the public galleries, and the acquittal would damage the government. But Cota also believed that there were better ways of harassing the editor of *Il Cattolico*. "I have other means to keep this paper in check. If the editor offends again I will place him under arrest, a measure that has always proved wonderfully effective in this city." Nonetheless, *Il Cattolico* survived, as did the Genoese opposition press more generally: in contrast to the fifteen of twenty-eight Turin newspapers and journals that were prosecuted and convicted, only five out of thirty-three press prosecutions in Genoa resulted in convictions.[32]

Despite these interventions and infringements, press freedom was firmly established in Piedmont in the 1850s and was certainly wider than in France, the Habsburg Empire, and the German states. When war with Austria broke out in 1859, press freedoms were temporarily suspended, but the Piedmontese press laws were subsequently restored and extended to the annexed territories and to the new Kingdom of Italy.

The Theater. The 1850s in Piedmont marked an important chapter in the history of Italian theater censorship. In the other states rigorous censorship virtually killed the theater for over a decade. Although this was not the case in Piedmont, the theater remained much more tightly controlled than the press. In April 1849 a General Directorate of the Theater was established in the interior ministry, with responsibility to ensure that censorship was "judicious, temperate and fully in harmony with our new political institutions." Many of the pre-1848 censors were retained, but a ministerial decree of 1852 set out new criteria for the theater, declaring, "Control over what appears on the stages of the theaters should be guided by moral rather than political criteria . . . a genuinely liberal government will win greater support by demonstrating that it is based on foundations that are too strong to be shaken by the radical aspirations of a play." It added that special attention should continue to be paid to "popular theaters and their repertory, from which we should seek to remove anything that might incite sympathy for crime and hatred for the punitive activities of the State."[33]

In practice, political concerns remained as important as moral considerations. The censors were energetic in banning foreign language (especially French) plays, while Piedmontese companies were encouraged to perform only Italian dramas. In 1856 controls tightened, and in 1857 the government circulated a list of 250 banned plays. Many of these were anticlerical, but works celebrating Garibaldi were also included. Cavour was especially insistent that children's theater and dialect puppet theaters should be particularly carefully censored. Foreign policy considerations were clearly important: in 1859, amid the Franco-Piedmont war against Austria, the censors banned all plays hostile toward France, and when news of the armistice with Austria reached Turin, dialect plays hostile or disrespectful toward Vienna were also forbidden. The censors were also keen to avoid upsetting religious sentiment: Niccolini's *Arnold of Brescia* was once again banned on the grounds that "it is not permissible to authorize works that set on the stage scenes that depict Popes, Priests and August, Sacred Holy Rites." Disturbances in the Turin theaters were frequent, and in an attempt to keep better order an inspector was assigned to each.

Stage censorship in Piedmont in the 1850s reflected a broader European tendency. The special attention devoted to dialect plays, puppet shows, and street theater indicates that the theater was perceived as transcending the literacy barrier and crossing the divide between elite and popular culture to reach outside the terrain dominated by the new liberal consensus. The new liberal order was not prepared to allow the theater the same freedoms as the press. But this reflected a deeper uncertainty. Representing a narrow and uncertain minority, the Piedmontese liberals needed to mobilize moderate opinion and to break the monopoly over information and communication enjoyed by the church and the reactionaries, yet their social and political apprehensions encouraged them to keep freedom discretionary when it came to political opponents and the less privileged classes. Despite the important political changes that occurred in Piedmont in the 1850s, there were still strong continuities with the past—and these would be carried forward into the new state that finally came into being after 1860.

LIBERAL ITALY (1860–1915)

The Political Background

Victor Emanuel II of Savoy was proclaimed king of Italy on March 17, 1861, but the life of the newly independent Italian kingdom proved difficult. Democrats and radicals were disillusioned by the triumph of the conservative Piedmontese constitutional monarchy. In 1862 Garibaldi attempted to help complete Italy's unification by militarily liberating Rome, but was blocked by the Italian army in Calabria. In the following months, southern Italy and Sicily were theaters for massive insurrections that the authorities attempted to disguise as brigandage. In 1866, after defeating Austria at the battle of Sadowa, Prussia brokered the cession of the Veneto to Italy. Another attempt by Garibaldi and the radicals to liberate Rome ended disastrously at Mentana in 1867, but Napoleon III's defeat at the battle of Sedan in 1870 during the Franco-Prussian War finally removed the Papacy's principal international guarantor and enabled Italian troops to enter the Eternal City (September 20, 1870) and complete Italian unification.

The Church's opposition to the new state had long been a source of tension and the Italian occupation of Rome made this rift irreparable. The new state was also under permanent censure from the nationalists who pressed for the liberation of the Italian-speaking lands that remained "unredeemed" under Austrian control (the Tyrol, Venezia-Giulia, Dalmatia). At a moment when many disillusioned Mazzinians and democrats were turning to anarchism, the uprising in France known as the Paris Commune (1871) threw an even darker shadow over the new state.

The civil war in the South earlier in the decade and the continuing challenges of the democrats had already caused plans for administrative decentralization to be abandoned after Cavour's death (1861). The administrative structure of the new state was based on the highly centralized French model, in which the central government was represented in each province by prefects who exercised wide powers over all local administration. Until 1874, government remained in the hands of Cavour's successors. Known as the Destra (right), this loose political alignment was composed overwhelmingly of men from Piedmont, Lombardy, Tuscany, and central Italy. In what contemporaries termed a "parliamentary revolution," the opposition Sinistra (left) alliance came to power in 1876 under Agostino Depretis. But this was more a shift in the regional representation of the government than a real change in policies, although it marked the entry of the southern gentry into national politics. In the next decade, Italian politics became synonymous with the loose cross-bench government majorities that Depretis created through the systematic and often cynical deployment of government patronage that became known as "trasformismo" (transformation).

The 1880s witnessed significant early industrial expansion, but the European-wide agricultural crisis hit Italy with devastating force and provoked the first waves of rural emigration from the North, as well as a series of strikes and riots in the Po Valley to which the government responded with great ferocity. In 1888 Italy's first Southern prime minister, Francesco Crispi, came to power. Italy had already followed the other continental European powers in abandoning free trade, but for Crispi protectionism was part of a wider program to remodel Italy along the authoritarian lines of Bismarck's Germany. Crispi's reforms were initially heralded as much-needed firm government, but his trade war with France provoked a crisis that began with the collapse of the urban real estate market and nearly brought down the Italian banking system. The result was massive unemployment and social unrest that developed into a political crisis that nearly overwhelmed parliamentary government. In 1894 Crispi responded to strikes in Sicily and the Lunigiana by declaring a state of emergency, and effectively made the recently founded Socialist Party (1892), anarchism, militant republicanism, Catholic critics of the government, and all other opposition to the government illegal.

The defeat of an Italian army at Adowa in Ethiopia in 1896 led to Crispi's fall, but under his successor, the Marchese Antonio Di Rudinì, the crisis worsened. New unrest in the spring and summer of 1898 panicked the government into using the army to crush strikes by factory workers in Milan. When a new government headed by General Luigi Pelloux introduced another package of emergency measures in 1899, the opposition parties in parliament adopted obstructionist tactics. At the moment when parliamentary government seemed on the point of collapsing, King Umberto I was assassinated by an anarchist. But rather than intensify the reaction, the political climate changed dramatically with the formation in 1901 of a new government committed to maintaining the constitution, headed by Giovanni Giolitti and Giuseppe Zanardelli. Giolitti, who would dominate Italian politics down to Italy's entry into the European war in 1915, switched from repression to conciliation, and tried to bring the socialists—now the largest mass party in Italy—into government. The backdrop to these political initiatives was the unprecedented expansion of the Italian economy between 1896 and 1906, which resulted in the consolidation of a new industrial base in the North.

Giolitti's strategy was to kill socialism with kindness, but the experiment in welfare legislation and consensus politics foundered when the economic boom turned into recession. As unemployment again rose after 1906, the reformist leaders of the Socialist Party were ousted and Giolitti's domestic policies came under concerted attack from both traditional liberals and the increasingly vocal nationalists who remained dissatisfied even after Italy invaded Libya in 1911. The Libyan War marked the collapse of the Giolittian enterprise, and, amid growing unrest, Giolitti's policies became increasingly confused. In June 1914 violent strikes in the Romagna aroused real fears that Italy was on the brink of revolution, while the outbreak of the European war in August further heightened these divisions as the government remained uncertain whether to intervene.

Censorship, 1860–1915

The Press. The history of political censorship in Italy did not cease with the creation of an independent constitutional monarchy. The Piedmontese *statuto* of 1848, now the Italian constitution, guaranteed freedom of thought, speech, mobility, and association, but these freedoms—as in other countries—were limited by subsequent legislation.

During the emergencies in the South after unification, and in response to violent protests in Emilia and Romagna against the reintroduction of the hated grist tax (*macinato*) in 1869, the authorities suspended civil liberties and imposed military law. Mazzinian and clerical publications were frequently seized or suspended. In the tense climate that followed the 1871 Paris Commune, these powers were deployed against a wide range of political "suspects." If the anarchists and (by the 1880s) the socialists were the principal targets, so were nationalists who opposed Italy's entry into the Triple Alliance with Prussia and Austria in 1882 and the anticlerical associations that organized demonstrations at the inauguration of the Giordano Bruno monument in Florence in 1889. No less closely observed was the intransigent clerical press, and during the crisis of the 1890s as many Catholic as republican and socialist associations and newspapers were shut down.

Conservative liberals were jealous to preserve constitutional guarantees of freedom of speech and association, but insisted that freedom should not be confused with license. The formula established by L. C. Farini in 1857 was endlessly repeated in subsequent debates on the limits of constitutional freedoms: "The principle of liberty must be the premise for all our laws: you must never adopt the system of prevention and must allow liberty in all things: you can make laws to repress and punish crimes, but never to prevent them."[34] Following this principle, the press laws abolished all forms of "preventive" or prior censorship, but established forms of "repressive censorship" (*censura repressiva*) that penalized material that "offends against, or instigates offense against religion, the person of the Sovereign and the ruling family, against representative institutions, the heads of foreign powers and diplomatic corps, or against other religious followings, public decency and property rights." The law required all publications to nominate a "responsible director" (*gerente responsabile*) who was legally liable for all material published and that all printed material carry the name and address of the printer and the date and place of publication.

The public security laws that governed policing seriously further limited the freedom of the press granted by the constitution and gave the police wide discretionary powers. No public meetings could be held or association formed without authorization from the police. In theory, police action required the assent of a local magistrate, but in practice the police had wide powers to act independently and could suspend, sequester, or require cuts in any publications, as well as detain or arrest the editors or owners of publications that were deemed any kind of threat to public order.

Opponents and critics of the government were nonetheless quick to take advantage of the new freedom to publish, and in the 1860s the number of political newspapers in Milan, Piedmont, Florence, and Naples expanded rapidly. But until the end of the century the reading public remained relatively limited. Only in the 1880s did a small number of papers begin to reach circulations of over 150,000. In the 1890s Italy still published only one newspaper per 17,000 inhabitants, whereas a decade earlier newspaper circulation in Switzerland, Belgium, France, and Germany was one for every 5,000 to 9,000 inhabitants; and only after 1900 did new dailies like the *Corriere della Sera*, the Turin *La Stampa*, and a growing number of newspapers with official party association begin to achieve truly mass circulation. Most newspapers were localized, municipal, and short-lived, and the narrowness of the market made it relatively easy for successive governments to create a "ministerial" press by using direct (although generally secret) subsidies and granting exclusive rights to carry official announcements. Few newspapers could survive without government support, while government or ministerial hostility could quickly prove ruinous. For example, when Crispi in 1894 instructed the prefect of Milan to boycott the *Gazzetta Piemontese* for criticizing the government, its circulation immediately fell from 25,000 to 7,000.

Despite the abolition of "preventive censorship," government officials continued to prevent distribution of republican, democratic, and clerical publications that were considered to be threats to public order or internal security. As early as 1862, Silvio Spaventa, principal secretary to the minister of the interior, openly supported the government's right to censor reactionary and seditious publications, and instructed the prefects to keep the government fully informed about the "periodical press" in each province. The prefects were required to establish permanent records of the number of newspapers and journals published in each province, along with the number of copies sold, their political sympathies, the names of their owners, editors, printers, and other information deemed relevant. In 1871 the interior minister further required the prefects to report on the "influence" exercised by each newspaper.

Anything that reflected the ideas of republicans, clericals, anarchists, and socialists was considered "subversive" or "dangerous." Since it was a criminal offense to publish anything that openly challenged "the established representative government," "the monarchy," or "the rights of property" there was little difficulty in bringing prosecutions. But because the outcome of jury trials was uncertain, following the precedent of Piedmont in the 1850s the authorities avoided the criminal courts and relied on the public security laws to suppress arbitrarily any offending material. Formal charges were rarely brought, but in the meantime the damage was already done and there was no redress.

With the advent of Crispi's government in 1888, monitoring of the press became ever more stringent and systematic. In 1890 the Director of Public Security instructed the prefects to send to Rome every day copies of all political publications or pamphlets in their provinces. To examine this huge volume of material, an Office for Political Affairs was created in the Interior Ministry under the authority of the Delegation for Public Security. This bureau's authority was extremely broad, including investigation of "the activities of all political parties, associations, the press, as well as the surveillance of suspect persons and foreigners."[35]

As the political situation in Italy worsened after 1890, forms of prior censorship were reintroduced. In May 1893 the prefects were instructed to submit all publications with socialist or anarchist sympathies to the public security police before publication, while Crispi's emergency laws of 1894 required that all publications carrying line drawings be submitted for approval to the police twelve hours before distribution. As part of the emergency measures introduced by General Pelloux in June 1899, the prefects were instructed to report on the nature of each publication, including whether it indulged in "propaganda hostile to the present constitution of the State" and whether it covered religion, electoral issues, and matters of public administration. In September 1899 Pelloux established new controls that effectively eliminated freedom of both publication and speech. All socialist, republican, anarchist, or clerical publications "that indulged in politics" were simply categorized as "subversive" and the prefects were instructed to also monitor all "papers presented at conferences, programs for public events, constitutions of associations, all single-issue publications, all publications celebrating anniversaries of particular individuals or movements, and all propaganda sheets." The latter were considered "especially dangerous, since they are cheap to buy and written in simple language and likely to fall into the hands of any modest workingman."[36]

In their efforts to muzzle the press, the authorities could count on loyal support from the judiciary. Even though jury courts were unreliable, the magistrates of liberal Italy generally interpreted the laws on the freedom of speech, thought, and expression in the most restrictive sense. When the Milan magistrates closed down the democratic paper *Fascio Operaio* in January 1886, they charged the editors, with no apparent sense of hyperbole, with being members of "an association of malefactors whose aim is to attack the powers of the State, to incite civil war, murder and mayhem."[37] The magistrates' tendency to deny constitutional guarantees to all self-declared opponents—or simply critics—of the liberal state was well illustrated in the upshot of a clamorous appeal by anarchists convicted of "acts of violence against property." In 1878 the Florence Cassation Court decided in favor of the anarchists, holding that none of the accused had actually carried out any such attacks, even though the lower court had ruled that by simply advocating anarchist principles the accused were guilty by intent. The Florentine ruling was then reversed by the higher Rome Cassation Court, which issued the notorious judgment that

> active participation in the [Socialist] International goes beyond the sphere of arid principles and enters the realm of deeds and as such is an act directed at subverting the basis of society. . . . To be an Internationalist is not in itself synonymous with being a suspect person, and indeed socialists may even be found amongst the ranks of University professors: but if that person is, say, a cobbler, it is imperative to discover whether his real intention is not to commit crimes against persons and property.[38]

In 1884 the Turin Cassation Court struck another blow against press freedom when it ruled that the editor in chief, as well as the director, were criminally liable for all material printed in their newspapers or journals. During the crisis of the 1890s the Justice Ministry kept reminding magistrates that it was their duty to keep the closest possible watch on subversive publications and to report to Rome at once "all publications of an anarchist or socialist nature or which in any way offer incitement to crime or public disorder." This repressive mentality was still evident when Giolitti's government passed new measures in 1906 to limit arbitrary "preventive" sequestration of publications by the magistrates. A circular from the Justice Ministry instructed royal procurators to increase their vigilance for "contraventions of the press laws" in view of the new freedom granted by parliament, and to ensure that all offenses be "brought swiftly to trial and that sentences be severe and exemplary."[39]

Despite the more open political climate that followed the formation of Giolitti's government, there seems to have been little real change in the mentality of the magistrates, public officials, or the police. Pelloux's September 1899 press instructions were never revoked, and Giolitti continued to subsidize pro-government papers from secret interior ministry funds. As opposition grew after 1906, his efforts to create a "ministerial press" increased; one official recalled that if editors were "paid and properly advised" they would "generally . . . sound a favorable note in the presentation of events" and especially "not transmit news items exaggerated by our opponents" or "transmit them in a muffled manner."[40]

In the North, the emergence of mass opposition parties and the establishment of modern mass circulation papers like the *Corriere della Sera* and *Il Secolo* in Milan, as well as the presence of a variety of different political and industrial interests, each with its own "house" press, made it more difficult to control the press by direct means, but a variety of indirect pressures and "sweeteners" could be used. In the provinces, and especially in the South, change was slower and the authorities continued to exercise considerable influence over what was published.

With the onset of the Libyan War in 1911, Giolitti did not hesitate to silence and suborn potential criticism or opposition through bribes and secret subsidies, while at the same time deploying Pelloux's measures of 1899 to outlaw publications that openly opposed the government or the war. The prefects were again required to send to Rome copies of all "subversive" publications, including the writings of socialists Filippo Turati, Andrea Costa, Enrico Ferri, Karl Marx, and Friedrich Engels, anarchists Prince Peter Kropotkin, Enrico Malatesta, and Amilcare Cipriani, and such famous authors as Leo Tolstoy, Maxim Gorky, Giosuè Carducci, and Gabriele D'Annunzio.

One of the manifestations of the rise of a mass press was the rapid growth of new satirical papers that developed a wide popular readership.

The first was *L'Asino*, which was founded in 1892 and immediately focused on the scandal that followed the collapse of the *Banca Romana*, which exposed a web of political and private corruption. Gabriele Galantara's caricatures in *L'Asino* portrayed Giolitti as a scheming crook, nicknamed "the cunning Palamidone" to point up the parallels with the contemporary Panama scandal in France. As the political situation in the 1890s grew more tense, *L'Asino* targeted successive prime ministers—Crispi, Di Rudinì, Pelloux—in its vivid and often crude satirical caricatures, and was frequently suspended and cut. After 1901 the paper switched its target to the Church and became the leading popular anticlerical paper in Italy, its principal targets being the reactionary Cardinal Sarto, who in 1903 became Pope Pius X, and his conservative Secretary of State Merry del Val.

L'Asino's fierce and often crude anticlerical campaign—which earned for it the privilege of being banned from Vatican City—was rooted in the political crisis that followed the violently antiliberal campaign orchestrated by the Vatican in opposition to a divorce bill presented to the Italian parliament in 1902, along with the first attempts to establish Catholic trade unions in opposition to those of the socialists. *L'Asino* deployed a striking armory of invective and calumny, lampooning the clergy as venal, gluttonous, rapacious, and lascivious. Galantara's caricatures of "Don Pepe" the crafty and carnal village priest, and numerous depictions of dissolute monks and nuns were part of a wider political campaign directed against the social and political influence of the priesthood. To reminders of the church's persecution of freethinkers and the horrors of the Inquisition, *L'Asino* added scathing attacks on financial interests closely associated with the Vatican.

L'Asino's satire was crude, but Galantara and his editors believed that this was the only way to reach a popular audience that hitherto had been captive to the clerical press. By 1904 it had reached a circulation of 60,000, and before 1912 rose to over 100,000. It suffered a number of private prosecutions, but less than *Avanti!*, the Socialist Party's official daily paper. *Avanti!*'s principal caricaturist was Giuseppe Scalarini, who produced nearly 4,000 cartoons and satirical drawings between 1911 to 1926, when three brutal beatings by the fascists forced him to retire. But his career was dogged by criminal convictions and exile. Two years after founding a satirical paper called the *Merlin Cocai* in Mantua, he was convicted in 1898 for publishing "anti-government drawings." In 1911, the year he joined *Avanti!*, Scalarini was convicted for publishing a drawing during the Libyan war that "made reference" to the 1896 Ethiopian disaster; he earned further convictions in 1914 for a drawing that denounced "police brutality" and in 1916, after Italy joined the war, for publishing "anti-militarist drawings." Scalarini's favorite caricatures included the capitalist depicted as a pig or shark, the "octopus of clericalism," the "cudgel of authority," and the "scissors of censorship."[41]

Theater. Liberal Italy adopted the regulations for theatrical performances that had been established in Piedmont in the 1850s, so the theater and all forms of public performance continued to be subject to a variety of controls. Plays came under the press laws, while all performances were also covered by the public security laws on public meetings and buildings. No play could be performed without prior approval of the script by the police or without the presence of a police officer.

By royal decree of January 14, 1864, the prefects were given responsibility for approving theatrical performances in their jurisdictions, although appeal to the ministry of the interior was allowed. In February 1864 Minister Silvio Spaventa reaffirmed the 1852 Piedomont theater censorship directives, while articles 32 and 35 of the 1865 Public Security Laws not only reaffirmed that all theatrical performances had to be approved in advance by local officials, but authorized such officials to forbid presentations "if some local circumstance leads them to believe that it would be inappropriate, or liable to cause commotion or disorder."[42]

In 1867 the government of Bettino Ricasoli made clear that political considerations would be just as important as "moral" ones in censoring plays by declaring that stage presentations should not contain anything "contrary to public morality and the sense of public decency, or anything that may tend to incite hatred between the social classes, or be offensive to Sovereigns, Parliament, the representatives of friendly Powers, or shows disrespect for law or public institutions or be liable to disturb public order, or gives offense to, or defames, the private lives of members of the Royal Family even by allusion." An 1874 regulation forbade actors to show disrespect to the army, while a 1879 law declared that all plays that "present deeds that may on account of their wickedness cause offense to public opinion will be subject to the attention of the magistrates" and should be banned.[43] Information on how these regulations were applied in practice is sketchy, however, since so much depended on the initiative of local magistrates and police chiefs.

In the years immediately after unification, virulent anticlericalism on the stage was a major problem for the authorities, especially in Rome and the former Papal States. The anticlericalism of plays like *The Mysteries of the Spanish Inquisition* and *The Nun of Cracow* was sufficiently crude that even the liberal press complained about "the disgraceful immorality of which the theaters have become a school, with performances that not only offend good taste but are downright obscene and through sensual excitement encourage young persons to abandon piety and give themselves over to vice, licentiousness and adultery."[44] In 1872 Pius IX protested in his Easter sermon against daily insults to the Church on the Roman stage, but Prime Minister Giovanni Lanza shortly afterward rejected a similar complaint in words that shed interesting light on the government's views of its own theater censorship: "Permit me, Your Eminence, to reject the harsh and unjust criticisms you make of the Italian government, which has done everything that is possible within the limits of the law to curb abuses in the theater, since I do not believe that there is any other civilized country in Europe that enforces censorship of the theater with greater severity than we do." According to Lanza, many plays that were permitted in France and Belgium—"countries that Your Eminence will surely not wish to rank amongst the barbarous or irreligious"—were prohibited in Italy. Acknowledging that it was not always easy to keep a close eye on what actually took place on their stage, the minister concluded that "Past experience provides ample evidence that even the most absolute censorship and the most arbitrary forms of prohibition are on their own of little avail when it comes to protecting morality and religion, encouraging good behavior and stamping out errors."[45]

The governments of liberal Italy relied heavily, if somewhat inconsistently, on theater censorship, but it was not until the end of the century that these policies began to attract criticism. When the revised public security laws presented to parliament in 1889 reaffirmed that "operas, dramas, choreographic representations and all forms of theatrical performance" required prior approval of the prefect, only one deputy protested. Prime Minister Crispi responded by strenuously defending the law and only agreed to change the wording to read, "The Prefect may prohibit any play or declamation for reasons of morality and public order."[46]

The 1889 public security laws continued what was a multitiered system of theatrical censorship: plays remained subject to the press laws and the laws regulating public performances, and might in addition be subject to censorship for infringing either the criminal law or public morality or both. Writing in the *Nuova Antologia* in 1912, V. E. Imperatori lamented that, especially in the provinces, theaters were subject to "capricious but constant censorship, which is not an insignificant illustration of the incomplete political unification of our country."[47] But without any apparent sense of self-contradiction, Imperatori also joined the clamor for stricter controls over popular theaters, claiming that the authorities consistently refused to take action even in cases of gross indecency.

The Cinema. The apprehensions aroused by forms of popular or mass culture were even greater when it came to the cinema. Because this medium lay outside the cultural world known and controlled by the elites, because it was new and foreign, and because it aroused all kinds of fears and speculations (not least because films were shown in the dark!), the application of rigid censorship to this new form of entertainment attracted remarkably wide support. The suspicions aroused by the new medium were eloquently articulated in an article in the *Corriere della Sera* in August 1910:

Since the time of the Huns there has been no invasion more formidable than that of the cinematograph. The theater, which is already under assault from the café-concerto, now languishes under the blows of the cinematograph. Our great tradition of history, legend, poetry and the glories of our art are now all prey to the manipulators of the moving-film and fifth-rate actors who celebrate on dim screens in darkened rooms this new triumph of vulgarity and the growing tyranny of bad taste.[48]

Demands for rigorous cinema censorship also came from the Parliamentary Commission on Juvenile Delinquency, whose existence reflected the concern over youth crime throughout western Europe in the decade before 1914. In 1910 Giolitti ordered the prefects to prohibit any film that "presented the police in ways likely to incite hatred," and in June 1913 parliament authorized the government's right to review all films prior to public showing. The return to "preventive" censorship in this case was justified by the need to prevent "pornography and the glorification of crime . . . as well as exhibitions that are contrary to public decency, public order, national dignity, or the prestige of public officials, or that present scenes of cruelty, licentiousness or other deeds that might become a school for crime." The law also prohibited "the representation of members of the Armed Forces and the Carabinieri in ridiculous or demeaning situations or engaging in actions that would bring discredit to their honor, decorum and prestige or undermine military discipline." A tax of ten *centesimi* per meter of film projected was additionally imposed with the explicit aim of pricing the cinema out of the reach of the young and the poor. Cinema censorship was entrusted to the interior ministry and the police; the list of banned subjects they produced included anything that might "lessen Italy's image and national honor."[49]

Censorship, Politics, and Society in Liberal Italy

The governments of liberal Italy continued to use routinely a variety of forms of censorship that seriously infringed constitutional freedoms and civil liberties. But how unusual was this? The chapters in this volume make clear that in all the western European democracies limits were imposed on freedom of speech beyond those designed solely to protect public morality and that individuals or groups who were considered to be a threat to the security of the state or the established order were often denied constitutional freedoms. However, the history of political censorship suggests that while liberal Italy had much in common with the most "open" European states of the second half of the nineteenth century, it retained political and administrative practices and mentalities that harked back to the traditions of absolutism and sought wherever possible to make civil and political freedoms discretionary. As the anarchist Francesco Saverio Merlino noted in the 1890s, in Italy the boundaries between what was and what was not legitimate were uniquely blurred. This was not simply a matter of the survival of antiliberal tendencies within the state bureaucracy, its judiciary, and police forces. Italy's most influential political leaders consistently employed a variety of direct and indirect means to silence political opponents and in moments of crisis did not hesitate to invoke emergency laws to suspend freedom of speech and political debate.

Indirect censorship was in many ways even more insidious and persistent than direct censorship. Fears that the government interfered systematically with the secrecy of the postal service, for example, were frequently expressed, and in 1877 Minister of the Interior Baron Nicotera was forced to resign when it became clear that he had violated the privacy of the telegraph service.[50] If Nicotera's resignation indicated the commitment of the Italian parliament to preserve constitutional rights, it also encouraged successive governments to resort to increasingly secretive methods in which espionage and censorship overlapped. Despite appeals in parliament for greater guarantees of secrecy, telegraph and telegram services were easily kept under surveillance because they were supplied by a single company; the police had access to all traffic, and the government retained the right to "revise" all dispatches from and to journalists.

A recent study of government attempts to cover up an outbreak of cholera in Naples in 1911 suggests that wiretapping and violations of the postal service were routine practice under Giolitti. The cover-up involved concerted action from central government down to local officials, who at every level employed intimidation, disinformation, and orchestrated concealment of the truth. Doctors who protested publicly were threatened and coerced. The editors of the leading newspapers were advised by government representatives that the cholera rumors were inflated and threatened Italy's national honor, while the provincial press was simply bought off. Private telegraph traffic was closely monitored and wires to newspapers that carried information about the epidemic were intercepted and destroyed.

These indirect measures of censorship became even more important as reactions grew to the government's heavy-handed attempts to silence its opponents. The League for the Defense of Democracy, founded in 1895 by a broad alliance of radicals, democrats, and progressive liberals in defense of civil and constitutional liberties, made its first priority "the unbending and uncompromising defense of the freedom of the press and thought." Nor were the governments' opponents easily cowed: in 1898, for example, *Avanti!* responded defiantly to government censorship by leaving censored columns blank and declaring on its title page that "our newspaper, Gentlemen of Order, is only a pallid expression of reality."[51] Repressive measures also affronted moderate liberals like the editor of the Turin daily *La Stampa* (soon to become one of Giolitti's principal supporters), who declared that if Pelloux's special laws had passed in 1899 "There would have been nothing left of the freedom of the press that exists in every other civilized country in the world, even in those states with authoritarian rulers and governments like Germany and Austria, so that you would have to go to some despotic regime like Russia to find laws that were similar or worse."[52]

Successive governments simply switched to more indirect and less visible methods, indicating that a deep hostility to more open forms of government permeated the liberal state. This was evident in virtually every sphere of public information and knowledge. Under the terms of the Casati Law, introduced while parliamentary powers were suspended during the war of 1859, the Ministry of Education exercised minute control over everything taught in schools and universities and had the right to approve all textbooks. The teaching of history was a matter of special concern and subject to especially close scrutiny. An 1894 royal decree required that only Italian history should be taught and laid down requirements for the texts to be used, the presentation of material, and even the maps that could be used. The texts approved for primary schools were reprinted without change and stressed the importance of obedience, thrift, and respect for authority and religion, and warned against involvement in any form of "collective organization." Such regulations were inspired partly by the need to create a new, secular school system and combat the influence of the clergy, but they also reflected what historian Raffaele Romanelli has termed the "impossible command," that is, the attempt by the state's leaders to impose liberal values and a sense of national identity from above.

Such controls were hardly exceptional in nineteenth-century Europe, but in Italy the principles of secrecy and control were perhaps more deeply engrained. Italy was the only major European power, for example, where press communiqués were not given; information was passed instead only to newspapers considered friendly to the government. Italy's laws on "official secrets" (*segreto di stato*) were also exceptionally wide, covering not only national and military security but all aspects of public administration and all public officials. While providing a powerful means for disciplining state employees, they also effectively undermined their public accountability and the public's right to information.

These were not simply institutional mentalities that survived from the absolutist past, but were more directly rooted in the political practice of liberal Italy. The system of political exchange known as "trasformismo," engineered from the time of Depretis, meant that political alliances were based on concealed private deals and trade-offs between individuals and interest groups. This was the political issue at stake in the scandal that followed the collapse of the *Banca Romana* in the early 1890s, which pointed to, without ever fully revealing, a web of political and private corruption in which two prime ministers (Giolitti and Crispi), and probably the monarchy as well, were implicated. The political system that developed in liberal Italy did not preclude moves toward more open government, but it did rely on forms of political brokerage that made secrecy a necessary instrument of government. Indeed, the experience of the Giolittian decade suggests that the greater the pressure for more open forms of government, the stronger the tendency to deploy overt and covert censorship and the greater the determination to limit and restrict flows of information.

Liberal Italy was nonetheless a pluralistic society in which the state was never the sole source of censorship. In this, as in everything else, the liberal state's principal rival was the Catholic Church. Between 1870 and 1929, 4,159 titles and 2,415 authors were added to the Index of prohibited books. Only a part of these were Italian, but they included virtually all the leading proponents of Italian liberalism, and later of socialism. Church censorship was exercised through a mixture of official and lay organizations that included direct instruction from the pulpit and confessional, rulings by diocesan committees, the recommendations drawn up for Young Catholic associations, and other religious congregations. Albeit informal, this censorship was not limited to questions of faith and values since both socialism and liberalism were central targets of popular Catholic literature. Although in the anticlerical climate of the time many saw Papal condemnation of their work as a welcome endorsement, publisher Carlo Treves asserted that "If mothers and priests declare war on a book, the impact on sales is disastrous."[53]

The Church took pro-active as well as repressive measures and was much quicker than the state to try to use the cinema as a means to reach mass audiences. For example, in 1910 a Catholic Cinematographic Federation was founded by two Milanese priests, and provided rooms and theaters for showing films that met the required standards of theme, content, and morality. Italy's first filmmaking enterprise, CINES, was founded in 1906 with the backing of a prominent group of Catholic financiers; between 1909 and 1915 it produced 1,525 films.[54]

The Catholic press and lay organizations also pressed their attack on liberalism by denouncing the state's laxity in matters of public morality, and lay organizations like the League against Blasphemy, the League for Public Decency, and the League against Alcoholism denounced moral disorder as symptoms of the corrupting materialism of liberal and socialist ideology. Despite repeated government instructions warning the prefects and police chiefs to be more active in censoring "obscene" publications, the number of antipornography associations, mostly Catholic in origin, increased rapidly in the 1890s.

The authorities were generally reluctant to act in cases of obscene art and literature, since prosecutions not only had a high failure rate but also often served only to promote the work in question. The unsuccessful prosecution of Umberto Notari, author of a salacious novel on prostitution entitled *Those Women* (Quelle Signore), turned the book into an unprecedented best-seller (209,000 copies) and made Notari a wealthy hero. The prosecution of *Mafarka, il Futurista* by the futurist Marinetti, on the grounds that it was an "outrage to public decency," also collapsed when the prefect of Milan reported that the state prosecutor's office had been unable to find any grounds for proceeding. In the south, however, the situation was different, and in 1902 the League against Pornography persuaded the authorities to bring a successful prosecution against *L'Asino*, indicating that even when it came to censorship Italy was still not truly united.

CONCLUSION

The continuing reliance on censorship after unification bears very directly on the nature of the state and the politics of liberal Italy. As the communist leader and intellectual Antonio Gramsci pointed out, political power in Italy and other western European parliamentary regimes at the beginning of the twentieth century was organized in ways that differed significantly from contemporary autocracies like Tsarist Russia or the pre-unification absolutist regimes. In the more open representative states, the power of the state was reinforced by the cultural authority and influence exercised within civil society by the elites. The elites participated directly in national politics and dominated political, cultural, and economic life at a more localized level. They controlled patronage, access to the professions, and determined standards of public taste.

The fact that political censorship did not give way to more informal types of censorship exercised by and within civil society indicates that the consensus between the state and elites in liberal Italy was relatively weak. This in turn suggests that "public opinion" continued to be relatively weak, or at least deeply divided, after as well as before unification. But if political censorship was a reality in Giolittian Italy, it was very different from the forms of censorship that would later be imposed by Mussolini's regime. The fascist state looked to establish an absolute monopoly over the supply of all information in ways that harked back to the totalitarian objectives of Restoration absolutism. Even if this totalitarian enterprise was never achieved in practice, the entries in the 1933 *Enciclopedia Treccani* on subjects like censorship, freedom of the press, or freedom of thought demonstrate how deeply the fascist regime rejected the juridical and constitutional premises of the liberal state. Mussolini's regime may in some respects have drawn on the practice and legislation of liberal Italy, but these were transposed to a political context that was fundamentally different. Before 1915 political censorship was a largely secretive, almost furtive, instrument for limiting the impact of mass politics and circumventing constitutional liberties. But by the 1920s those civil liberties no longer existed and the fascist regime ostentatiously vaunted its right to the total monopoly of information and thought—"nothing against the state, nothing outside the state, everything part of the state." Yet the practice of censorship in liberal Italy had contributed to that outcome by undermining civil liberties and convincing many opponents and critics of the deeply illiberal character of the "liberal" state.

NOTES

1. A. Rotondo, "La censura ecclesiastica e la cultura" in *Storia d'Italia: Documenti*, V, Part 2, eds. R. Romano and A. Tenenti (Turin, 1984), 492.
2. C. Capra, "Il giornalismo nell'età rivoluzionaria e napoleonica," in V. Castronovo and N. Tranfaglia, *La Stampa Italiana dal "500 all" 800* (Bari, 1976), 490.
3. Archivio di Stato (Napoli): Ministero di Polizia, Ministero Interno 1 Ripartimento, Diversi 1824–25, fascic 2912, Revisione dei libri, opuscoli, fogli volanti e periodici di attribuzione della polizia.
4. A. Galante Garrone, "I giornali della Restaurazione," in V. Castronovo and N. Tranfaglia, *La Stampa Italiana del Risorgimento* (Bari, 1976), 20.
5. G. Berti, *Censura e circolazione delle idee nel Veneto della Restaurazione* (Venice, 1989), 15–40.
6. F. Predari, *I primi vagiti della libertà in Piemonte* (Milan, 1861), 19.
7. A. De Robertis, *Studi sulla censura in Toscana* (Pisa, 1936), 212.
8. Ibid., 238.
9. F. Ghidetti, "Tipografi, stampatori e censura a Livorno dal 1815 al 1835," in *Risorgimento*, 61 (1989), 36.
10. Galante Garrone, 156.
11. De Robertis, 202.
12. Ibid., 361.
13. Predari, 23.
14. Ibid., 14.
15. Ibid., 55.
16. C. Di Stefano, *La censura teatrale in Italia* (1600–1962) (Cappelli, 1964), 25–26.
17. B. Croce, *I teatri di Napoli dal Rinascimento alla fine del secolo decimottavo* (Bari, 1947), 275.
18. John Rosselli, *The Opera Industry in Italy from Cimarosa to Verdi: The Role of the Impresario* (Cambridge, England, 1984), 82–83.
19. G. Berti, *Censura e circolazione delle idee nel Veneto della Restaurazione* (Venice, 1989), 9.
20. Di Stefano, 67–72.
21. Ibid, 51–83.
22. Mary Jane Phillips-Matz, *Verdi: A Biography* (Oxford, 1993), 131–33.
23. Rosselli, 169–70.
24. De Robertis, 323.
25. Archivio di Stato (Napoli): Ministero di Polizia, Ministero Interno 1 Ripartimento, Diversi 1824–25, fascic 2912, Revisione dei libri, opuscoli, fogli volanti e periodici di attribuzione della polizia.
26. G. Porizo, *Le origini della libertà di stampa in Italia*, 1846–1852 (Milan, 1980), 33.

27. F. Della Peruta, "Il giornalismo dal 1847 all'Unità," in V. Castronovo and N. Tranfaglia, *La Stampa Italiana del Risorgimento* (Bari, 1976), 519; Porizo, 380.

28. F. Predari, 453–57.

29. Ibid., 453.

30. R. Romeo, *Cavour e il suo tempo* (1854–1861), III (Bari, 1984), 399.

31. Ibid., 410.

32. Ibid., 423.

33. V. E. Imperatori, "Teatri e libertà: La censura in Italia nel secolo XIX," in *Nuova Antologia*, V series, 157 (1912), 318, 328.

34. E. Arbib, *Pensieri, sentenze e ricordi di uomini parlamentari* (Florence, 1901), 125.

35. F. Fiori, introduction to *Direzione Generale della Pubblica Sicurezza: La stampa italiana nelle serie F.* 1 (1894–1926) (Rome, 1995), 1.

36. Ibid., 13.

37. V. Castronovo, *La stampa italiana dall'Unità al Fascismo* (Bari, 1970), 130–35.

38. G. Amato, "La libertà personale," in P. Basile (ed.), *La Pubblica Sicurezza* (Milan, 1967), 121.

39. Castronovo, 180.

40. Frank M. Snowden, *Naples in the Time of the Cholera—1884–1911* (Cambridge, England, 1995), 347.

41. G. Camazzi, *La satira politica nell'Italia del Novecento* (Milan 1975), 2–5.

42. Imperatori, 319.

43. Ibid., 319.

44. V. Gorresio, *Risorgimento Scomunicato* (Florence, 1958), 171.

45. Ibid., 174.

46. Imperatori, 319.

47. Ibid.

48. V. Caldiron, "La censura in Italia dagli inizi del secolo al dopguerra," *Il Ponte* (November 1961), 150.

49. Ibid.

50. Richard Jensen, *Liberty and Order: The Theory and Practice of Italian Public Security Policy, 1848 to the Crisis of the 1890s* (New York, 1991), 51.

51. P. Spriano, "L'Informazione nell'Italian unità," in *Storia d'Italia: Documenti*, V, Part 2, eds. R. Romano and A. Tenenti (Turin, 1984), 1841.

52. Castronovo, 148.

53. S. Pivato, *Clericalismo e laicismo nella cultura popolare italiana* (Milan, 1990), 123.

54. Ibid., 49–52; B. Wanrooij, *Storia del Pudore: La Ouestione Sessuale in Italia, 1860–1940* (Venice, 1990), 43–46.

BIBLIOGRAPHICAL ESSAY

There is no general history of political censorship in either English or Italian, although the essential bibliography is Italian. For a general history of Italy in the period, the essays in G. Holmes (ed.) *The Illustrated Oxford History of Italy* (Oxford, 1997) and John A. Davis (ed.), *Italy, 1789–1900: Independence and Unifi-*

cation (Oxford, 2000) offer a good starting point, and for the period after 1860 can be supplemented by Denis Mack Smith, *Italy: A Modern History* (New Haven, Conn., 1996) and Martin Clark, *Italy 1870–1982* (London 1984). Adrian Lyttelton "The National Question in Italy," in M. Teich and R. Porter (eds.), *The National Question in Europe in Historical Context* (Cambridge, England, 1993) is an excellent guide to intellectual and cultural history, while K. R. Greenfield, *Economics and Liberalism in the Risorgimento: A Study of Nationalism in Lombardy 1814–48* (Baltimore, Md., 1965) is still the most extensive anglophone source on political journalism. Silvana Patriarca, *Numbers and Nationhood: Writing Statistics in Nineteenth Century Italy* (Cambridge, England, 1996) also touches on censorship, as does Roland Sarti, *Mazzini: A Life for the Religion of Politics* (Westport, Conn., 1997).

On the theater before unification, see David Kimbell, *Italian Opera* (Cambridge, England, 1991), and two books by John Rosselli: *Singers of the Italian Opera: The History of a Profession* (Cambridge, England, 1992); and *The Opera Industry in Italy from Cimarosa to Verdi: The Role of the Impresario* (Cambridge, England, 1984). On Verdi, see Julian Budden, *The Operas of Verdi from Oberto to Rigoletto* (New York, 1973); Mary Jane Phillips-Matz, *Verdi: A Biography* (Oxford, 1993); and W. H. Rubsamen, "Music and Politics in the Risorgimento," *Italian Quarterly*, 5 (1961), 100–20.

For the period after unification there are no studies in English that deal specifically with censorship. Both Richard Jensen, *Liberty and Order: The Theory and Practice of Italian Public Security Policy, 1848 to the Crisis of the 1890s* (New York, 1991) and John A. Davis, *Conflict and Control: Law and Order in Nineteenth-Century Italy* (London, 1988) deal with public order. Frank Snowden, *Naples in the Time of the Cholera, 1884–1911* (Cambridge, England, 1995) contains important information on measures used to control the press.

The Italian bibliography is immense and indispensable. Essential guides to press censorship include the following essays in the multivolume *Storia della Stampa Italiana*: G. Ricuperati, "Giornali e società nell'Italia dell'Antico Regime, 1668–1789," 1–353, and C. Capra, "Il giornalismo nell'età rivoluzionaria e napoleonica," 374–537, both in V. Castronovo and N. Tranfaglia, *La Stampa Italiana dal "500 all" 800* (Bari, 1976), A. Galante Garrone, "I giornali della Restaurazione," 3–225, and F. Della Peruta, "Il giornalismo dal 1847 all'Unità," 249–519, both in V. Castronovo and N. Tranfaglia, *La Stampa Italiana del Risorgimento* (Bari, 1976); V.Castronovo, *La stampa italiana dall'Unità al Fascismo* (Bari, 1970).

More detailed modern studies on censorship before 1860 include G. Porizo, *Le origini della libertà di stampa in Italia, 1846–1852* (Milan, 1980); G. Berti, *Censura e circolazione delle idee nel Veneto della Restaurazione* (Venice, 1989); G. Luseroni, *La stampa clandestina in Toscana (1846–47): I bollettini* (Florence, 1988); F. Ghidetti, "Tipografi, stampatori e censura a Livorno dal 1815 al 1835," in *Risorgimento*, 61 (1989), 25–50; C. Rotondi, "Periodici culturali a Firenze dalla Restaurazione alla fine del granducato," in *Rassegna Storica Toscana*, 29 (1983), 207–22; idem, "La legge toscana sulla stampa e i primi giornali politici," in *Rassegna Storica Toscana*, 28 (1982). The fundamental work on Cavour and censorship in Piedmont in the 1850s is R. Romeo, *Cavour e il suo tempo (1854–1861)*, III (Bari, 1984), while F. Predari, *I primi vagiti della libertà in Piemonte* (Milan, 1861) offers a detailed contemporary account of censorship in Piedmont.

On political censorship after 1860, the essential starting point is F. Fiori, "Per la storia del controllo governativo sulla stampa," *Rassegna Storica degli Archivi dello Stato*, 48 (1987), 9–102, and Fiori's introduction to *Direzione Generale della Pubblica Sicurezza: La stampa italiana nelle serie F.1 (1894–1926)* (Rome, 1995).

For the period before 1860, invaluable documentary collections include A. De Robertis, *Studi sulla censura in Toscana* (Pisa, 1936); "Cesare Balbo e la censura toscana," *Miscellanea di Studi Storici*, ed. A. Luzi (Florence, 1933) 321–29; F. Lemmi, *Censura e giornali negli stati sardi ai tempi di Carlo Alberto* (Turin, 1943); and A. Manno, *Anedotti documentati sulla censura in Piemonte dalla Restaurazione alla Costituzione* (Turin, 1907).

On journalists, see G. Ricuperati, "I giornalisti italiani fra potere e cultura dalle origini all'unità," in *Storia d'Italia: Annali* 4 (Turin, 1979), 1128–32; and M. Berengo, *Intelletuali e librai nella Milano della Restaurazione* (Turin, 1980). R. Maggio Serra, "Italia 1848–49, Immagini di attualità e di lotta tra storia ed arte," in *Le Rivoluzioni del 1848: L'Europa delle Immagini* (Turin, 1998) reviews the political press of 1848. On the theater, see B. Croce, *I teatri di Napoli dal Rinascimento alla fine del secolo decimottavo* (Bari, 1947); C. Di Stefano, *La censura teatrale in Italia (1600–1962)* (Cappelli, 1964); V. E. Imperatori, "Teatri e libertà: La censura in Italia nel secolo XIX," in *Nuova Antologia*, V series, 157 (1912), 315–25; and R.Tedeschi, "L'Opera Italiana," in *Storia d'Italia: Documenti*, V, Part 2, eds. R. Romano and A. Tenenti (Turin, 1984), 1144–72. In the latter source, restrictions on information are discussed in P. Spriano, "L'informazione nell'Italian unità," 1832–66; and the church and censorship are treated in A. Rotondo, "La censura ecclesiastica e la cultura," 1479–1503. Other important accounts of Church censorship are V. Gorresio, *Risorgimento Scomunicato* (Florence, 1958); B. P. F. Wanrooij, *Storia del Pudore: La Questione Sessuale in Italia, 1860–1940* (Venice, 1990); and S. Pivato, *Clericalismo e laicismo nella cultura popolare italiana* (Milan, 1990).

For literature, see N. Longo "La letteratura proibita" in *La Letteratura Italiana: Le Questioni*, ed. A. Asor Rosa (Turin, 1986), 965–99; and A. Fortuna, "Censura" in *Enciclopedia Einaudi*, II (Turin, 1977), 873–83. On political satire, see G. Carnazzi, *La satira politica nell'Italia del Novecento* (Milan 1975); G. Candeloro (Introduction to) *L'Asino è il Popolo: utile, paziente e bastonato* di Podrecca e Galantara (Milan, 1970); M De Micheli (ed.), *Scalarini: Disegni politici originali, 1911–48* (Varese, 1974); and V. Tedesco, *La stampa satirica in Italia, 1860–1914* (Milan, 1991). On the cinema before 1915 see the excellent essay by V. Caldiron, "La censura in Italia dagli inizi del secolo al dopoguerra," *Il Ponte*, 17 (1961), 1501–25.

4

France

Robert Justin Goldstein

France witnessed extraordinarily intense, bitter, and prolonged struggles over restrictions on freedom of expression during most of the nineteenth century. These contentious and virtually continuous disputes reflected the extraordinarily divisive nature of French politics, especially its inherently unstable combination of a highly politicized population (perhaps the most important legacy of the French Revolution) coexisting, until about 1880, with highly repressive regimes. As a result, ever-increasing demands of ever-larger segments of the population for more political liberty repeatedly clashed with the determination of almost all pre-1880 regimes to harshly suppress political dissent. What French liberal Benjamin Constant noted in 1815 was to prove true for the next sixty-five years: "All the constitutions which have been granted in France equally guarantee individual liberty, and under the shelter of these constitutions individual liberty has been ceaselessly violated."[1]

The continuing tension created by growing popular demands for more liberty combined with governmental inclinations to strictly limit political expression reflected the severe internal divisions that plagued the nation. French history created a country divided along many fault lines: clerical/anticlerical, commoners/nobles, rich/poor, urban/rural, monarchist/republican, Parisian/provincial, among others. Even within these fault lines, monarchists were divided between the followers of three different dynasties (Bourbonists, Orleanists, and Bonapartists); republicans between moderates, radicals, and socialists; and workers between skilled craftsmen, a small but burgeoning industrial proletariat, unskilled labor, and farmers of varying degrees of wealth. These sharp divisions led to repeated changes in regimes, invariably accompanied by major revisions in censorship policies, which therefore provide an extraordinarily revealing insight into the authorities' shifting thoughts and fears. As censorship historian Odile Krakovitch notes, French censorship archives provide "a marvelous witness to the preoccupations, mentalities, reflexes, struggles, fears, consciences and knowledge of people of the past century" and document a "strange ballet, with the appearances and disappearances of censorship, entering and leaving at more or less regular intervals. . . . France hated the censorship, but feared losing it. France's motto was liberty, but she was incapable of assuming it."[2]

Following Napoleon's defeat, France was ruled during the so-called Restoration (1814–30) by two members of the restored Bourbon dynasty, Louis XVIII (1814–24) and his brother Charles X (1824–30). Both made some attempts to reconcile the pre-revolutionary tradition of absolute monarchy with remnants of the revolutionary legacy—for example by accepting some constitutional restraints, including a regularly sitting elected legislature (albeit elected by only the wealthiest 0.3 percent of the population). But while Louis XVIII alternated between repression and concessions, Charles X increasingly inclined toward arbitrary rule, and his attempt to dissolve the legislature and emasculate the press provoked the 1830 July Revolution, which dethroned the Bourbons and enthroned a member of the cadet House of Orléans, King Louis-Philippe.

Although Louis-Philippe took power amid enormous hopes for major reforms from the working and middle classes who largely instigated the July Revolution, he quickly disillusioned them by barely expanding the suffrage, ignoring the poor, and increasingly resorting to repression and corruption to maintain his rule. Louis-Philippe, whose reign is known as the July Monarchy, was ultimately overthrown by the February revolution of 1848, which installed the Second Republic (1848–52), a regime based on universal male suffrage whose advent fostered renewed expectations of major reforms. Although political freedoms were originally dramatically expanded, worker unrest soon pushed elite politics in a conservative direction, which intensified after the election of Louis Napoleon Bonaparte (nephew of Napoleon I) as president in December 1848. After Louis Napoleon overthrew the regime in December 1851 and proclaimed himself Emperor Napoleon III a year later, political freedoms, which had been steadily whittled away after 1848, were almost completely extinguished during the Second Empire (1852–70).

Napoleon III was overthrown by a revolution in September 1870 after blundering into a disastrous war with Prussia. His removal was followed by a brief, but bloody civil war when a republican-worker revolt, the Paris Commune, erupted in March 1871 against the recently elected monarchist-oriented national government. Although the national government brutally crushed the Commune, it was bitterly divided between an internally fractured monarchist majority and a growing republican minority. The Third Republic (originally so-named because the monarchist majority could not agree on a new king) was transformed from a theoretical into a real republic by the 1877 elections. Subsequently, its highly repressive post-Commune policies were gradually replaced by landmark relaxations of press and other political restrictions, creating a genuinely liberal regime by the 1880s. Despite considerable turmoil and continuing bitter internal divisions, most clearly reflected by the 1890s Dreyfus Scandal, French liberties remained fundamentally secure during the remaining pre-World War I era.

CENSORSHIP MOTIVES

Although few French officials were as blunt as Napoleon, who declared, "If I allowed a free press, I would not be in power for another three months," governmental officials and conservatives generally regarded freedom of expression with hatred and fear. Vicomte de Bonald, a leader of French reactionaries during the 1820s, termed censorship a "sanitary precaution to protect society from the contagion of false doctrines, just like measures taken to prevent the spread of the plague," and shortly before the 1830 revolution Charles X's ministers declared that, by nature, the press had been at all times "only an instrument of disorder and sedition" and "a dissolving energy" that had prevented the establishment "of a stable and regular regime of government."[3]

If freedom of the *written* word alarmed French authorities, they feared even more the potential impact of *visual* and *aural* expression, such as that offered by caricature, theater, opera, songs, and cinema. This was so partly because sound and sight were viewed as having greater impact than print. And it was especially so because a large percentage of the particularly feared "dark masses" were illiterate—over a third of all adults could not read until after 1870—and thus "immune" to print, but they were not deaf or blind, and were viewed as highly susceptible to subversive imagery and sound. These fears were clearly articulated by French Minister of Justice Jean-Charles Persil in 1835, when he successfully urged legislators to reimpose prior censorship of theater and drawings (which had collapsed following the 1830 Revolution) on the grounds that these media were entirely different and far more dangerous than print, and therefore not covered by the 1830 constitutional charter's promises of the "right to publish" and that "censorship can never be reestablished":

> This ban on the reestablishment of the censorship only applies to the right to *publish* and have *printed one's opinions*; it is the [written] press which is placed under the guarantee of the Constitution, it is the free manifestation of *opinions* which

> cannot be repressed by preventive measures. But there the solicitude of the charter ends. It would clearly go beyond that goal if the charter were interpreted to accord the same protection to opinions converted into actions. Let an author be content to print his play, he will be subjected to no preventive measure; let the illustrator write his thought [in words], let him publish it in that form, and as in that manner he addresses only the *mind*, he will encounter no obstacle. It is in that sense that it was said that censorship could never be reestablished. But when opinions are converted into *acts* by the presentation of a play or the exhibit of a drawing, one addresses people gathered together, one speaks to their eyes. That is more than the expression of an opinion, that is a *deed, an action, a behavior*, with which . . . the charter is not concerned.[4]

That such views on the heightened dangers posed by sight and sound were widespread, rather than extreme or idiosyncratic, is clear from the fact that while prior press censorship ended in 1822, caricatures remained thus constrained until 1881, and the stage (including theater, opera, and even songs presented at cafés) was censored until 1906; even afterward censorship was imposed on the new cinema, which was viewed as yet more powerful, attractive, and affordable to the poor than print, drawings, songs, or theater.

Caricatures were seen as far more threatening than words because they were perceived as more visceral and more powerful in their impact. Thus, Minister of Commerce Charles Duchatel told legislators in 1835 that there was "no more direct provocation to crimes" and "nothing more dangerous than these infamous caricatures, these seditious designs" that "produce the most deadly effect." Moreover, caricature journals often attained sizable audiences, particularly among the feared lower classes: in 1869 a bureaucrat stationed in Rouen informed his superiors that while the "great Parisian newspapers" played a "role in the movement of public opinion," that "which dominates it especially" was the "illustrated [caricature] journals" which "sell many more examples and are read much more than the serious organs of the same opinion" and "by ridicule, by perfidious jesting and defamations" were "making war on our institutions and the men who personify them" and "succeeding among all classes." Caricature was also particularly feared because clever political drawings could be understood by the illiterate poor, precisely the elements of the population most feared as threats to the existing political order. The authorities' intense fears about caricature in general and especially its potential impact among the "unwashed masses" was summarized in an 1852 directive from the police minister to his subordinates:

> Among the means employed to shake and destroy the sentiments of reserve and morality so essential to conserve in the bosom of a well-ordered society, drawings are one of the most dangerous . . . because the worst page of a bad book requires time to read and a certain degree of intelligence to understand, while a drawing

offers a sort of personification of thought, it puts it in relief, it communicates it with movement and life, in a translation which everyone can understand.[5]

Theater, opera, and other forms of oral-visual presentations such as popular songs were viewed as even more threatening than caricatures (as evidenced by their longer submission to prior censorship) because they were presented to a collective audience, which might be stirred to immediate action when faced with subversive words or music. In 1849 even Baron Isidore Taylor, a playwright and then-president of the Society of Dramatic Authors, defended theater censorship, warning a state inquiry that the stage "produces, among all those watching, a sort of electric communication, even more seductive for the masses than a speech, and one thousand times more dangerous than the most vehement article in the daily press." Such sentiments undoubtedly reflected the indisputable fact that, especially before about 1850, theater disturbances were common, ranging from routine outbreaks of applause, hoots, and whistles to throwing food or even furniture, and occasionally escalating into full-scale riots that, especially in Paris, sometimes required police or military intervention with sabers or bayonets. As even an extremely hostile account of the "absurdity" and "tyranny" of the Restoration theater censorship concedes, spectators "jumped at each turn of verse to find allusions to the [Napoleonic] empire or to the Bourbons," with the result that the "theater was always ready to be transformed into a field of battle." Following an 1839 disturbance, author Théophile Gautier complained, "A theater auditorium ought not to be turned into a boxing ring; it's not nice at all to return home with a bloody nose and an eye all the colors of the rainbow." French theater censor Victor Hallays-Dabot even claimed—expressing a view that was severely exaggerated but nonetheless widely held—that several plays that provoked opposition demonstrations in the 1840s effectively provided "a sort of dress rehearsal" for the 1848 revolution.[6]

Such exaggerated fears reflected theater's quite extraordinary role in French public life, especially before about 1860. In an era in which large segments of the population were illiterate and in which radio, television, movies, and other modern forms of diversion were lacking, the theater was an uncontested focus of public interest and mass entertainment, the quickest road to fame and fortune for writers, the primary form of mass education before the establishment of publicly supported elementary schools in 1833 and the rise of a mass press after 1840, and the only public arena in which mass gatherings were authorized. Theater historian F. W. J. Hemmings writes that the nineteenth-century French theater provided "to a greater degree probably than for any other nation, a unique focus of collective interest" that engaged "the attention of every class of people throughout the length and breadth of the land" and as "the one and only purveyor of excitement, amusement and pathos that the mass of the population knew" offered "the one and only escape from their usually laborious and lackluster existence."[7]

At least until after 1840, when increasing literacy and urbanization, along with technological advances and modern advertising, reduced newspaper prices and produced the first mass press, the theater—if economically off-limits to the destitute (50 percent of the total population during the 1830s)—was far more affordable than newspapers. Around 1830, the daily circulation of the entire Parisian press was only 50,000, partly because newspapers could only be purchased by annual subscription, at costs averaging about 10 percent of a typical worker's annual salary. By contrast, in the popular Parisian "boulevard" theaters (so-called because many were located on the Boulevard du Temple), the cheapest seats cost less than a loaf of bread, and most regularly employed workers could afford to periodically attend. The French theater industry had extraordinary vitality and public appeal: during the nineteenth century, an astounding 32,000 new plays were produced; at mid-century more than 10,000 people were employed in the Parisian theater industry and over 32,000 seats were available each night in the capital; and during the 1880s about 500,000 Parisians attended the theater weekly. According to contemporary observer Pierre Giffard, "The population of Paris lives at the theater, of the theater and by the theater."[8]

One clear indication that the theater was especially feared for its accessibility to the poor is that frequently material that was approved by the censors for performance in the "legitimate" theaters patronized by the upper and middle classes was not allowed in "boulevard" theaters. As censorship historian Krakovitch summarizes, "The more modest and popular the theater, the harsher the censors' judgments and the more numerous the required modifications." For example, the censor's report for the 1822 play *Pauline Delorme* declared that its depiction of "theft, assassination, even arson, premeditated, openly carried out in a work whose characters come from the common people" should not be presented, especially to "those who habitually frequent the Boulevard theaters." Under Louis-Philippe, the censors asked with regard to Alexander Dumas's *Les Trois Mousquetaires*, proposed for presentation at a boulevard theater, "Would it not be troublesome for such a subject, already presented at the Odéon [one of the "respectable" theaters], to be presented at a stage especially frequented by the working class?" During Napoleon III's reign, a censor wrote about *King Lear* that "its boldness could only be presented in an essentially literary venue, before an elite public," as "before the public of the boulevard, it would be a spectacle whose philosophical import would not be understood but in which we fear only the degradation of royalty would be perceived."[9]

Censorship was designed above all to uphold the existing political and social order, and especially to protect the existing political regime. According to an analysis of over 200 censorship and prosecutorial decisions involving plays, newspapers, and novels undertaken by four different regimes between 1815 and 1870, about 55 percent of such actions were based on perceived challenges to existing political/social authority; in almost all other cases, challenge to the "moral order" was cited. Sensitivity to potentially "morally" objectionable material (i.e., pornography) and to "antireligious" views (which usually meant either generally anticlerical or specifically anti-Catholic opinions) varied considerably, but the censors' antennas were always especially attuned to political materials, and above all to direct political attacks on the regime in power.[10]

Napoleon expressed this attitude with great bluntness when he declared, with regard to public entertainment, "Let the people amuse themselves, let them dance, so long as they keep their noses out of government affairs." Similarly, officials during the Second Republic and the Second Empire directed the drama censors to eliminate "attacks against the principle of authority, against religion, the family, the courts, the army, in a word against the institutions upon which society rests," and especially to forbid "completely" all scenes "imprinted with a revolutionary spirit," as well as "all forms of factionalism, based on the principle that the theater must be a place of repose and of distraction and not an overt arena of political passions."[11]

Similarly politically attuned criteria were used to censor other media. Thus, the hero in Beaumarchais's text to Salieri's opera *Tarare* was changed from king to republican ruler to constitutional monarch as French regimes changed during the nineteenth century. The September 1835 press law, which the liberal poet Alphonse de Lamartine termed a "reign of terror for ideas," was typical of many nineteenth-century press regulations in its ban on "any attack against the principle or form" of the government, or even "expressing the wish, the hope or the threat of the destruction of the constitutional monarchical order [i.e., the Orléans dynasty and the monarchy of Louis-Philippe]." With regard to caricatures and drawings, in 1829 censors were informed, "that which belongs to the royal majesty and the august dynasty of the Bourbons" must be "spared from guilty attacks or allusions of whatever kind," and in 1879 they were directed to "refuse absolutely when a drawing is directed against the head of state," and to approve only "with the greatest circumspection" illustrations that targeted other state officials, religion, or the clergy.[12]

CENSORSHIP MECHANICS

French authorities devoted truly amazing amounts of time and energy to restricting expression: the 1881 press law replaced forty-two laws containing 325 separate clauses that had been passed during the previous seventy-five years by ten different regimes. By 1851 the press laws had become so complicated that two judges published a handbook to guide befuddled lawyers and journalists; restrictions on the stage were so massive and complex that they were the subject of over half-a-dozen manuals published between 1830 and 1880. Although no comprehensive list of prosecutions resulting from expression in nineteenth-century France exists, legal charges were brought in cases involving a minimum of 550 books, 300 pamphlets, and over 175 lithographs between 1814 and 1890; over 900 prosecutions were brought against the periodical press between 1830 and 1850; and during the 1877 electoral crisis an astounding 2,500 press prosecutions were initiated within six months.[13]

Whenever prior censorship was enforced, specialized censors implemented the regulations as they applied to different media. Although the censors, especially before 1830, were frequently well-known, educated men of letters, throughout the nineteenth century political reliability was the ultimate criterion for their appointment and retention. Since they generally lacked any formal regulations, support for their masters inevitably became their prime directive. Several censors had no difficulty serving both Napoleon I and his successor Louis XVIII; similarly, some of those who served King Louis-Philippe subsequently unhesitatingly took up their blue pencils for Napoleon III. Despite the scorn and bitterness often heaped on them, their posts were often highly sought, as they were viewed as well-paid, generally secure jobs with considerable power, not to mention a variety of fringe benefits, including free theater tickets, deference from actors and directors, and perhaps even "other signs of friendship on the part of actresses."[14]

The theater censorship for Paris (which regulated drama, operas, and drinking establishments that presented songs or other popular entertainment) was controlled by a board of (typically four or five) censors under the jurisdiction of the Bureau of Theaters, which was attached at various times to the ministries of state, interior, fine arts, and education (and, under Napoleon III, to the imperial household ministry). Other individuals acting under the censors' direction, known as theater examiners, frequently attended dress rehearsals and occasional performances in order, as one none-too-friendly account of the Restoration censorship put it, "to clean one last time the phrases clothed with the approval of the censors, to assure themselves that the actors conformed to these suppressions, to approve of the costumes, the actors and the extras, to measure with the eye the length of the dancers' skirts, to warn if they discovered that acts visibly hostile—anti-monarchical, revolutionary—could take birth from the combination of certain colors."[15] Caricature censorship was normally delegated to a bureau within the interior ministry for caricatures published in Paris (the relatively few caricatures published in the provinces, as well as dramas presented there, were censored by the local prefects). Adverse decisions by the drama or caricature censors could not be appealed to the courts, but usually could be administratively appealed to the head of the appropriate bureau or ministry; the minister himself frequently intervened with regard to highly politically sensitive drawings and plays, and if a dramatist had the right connections, it was sometimes possible to have his play personally considered by the monarch.

Considerable variation in the censorship's day-to-day operation occurred, depending on the medium involved, individual censor's personalities, and, sometimes, the author's renown (thus, Louis-Philippe's censors generally sought to avoid angering the esteemed author Alexander Dumas, sometimes approving plays by him that probably would have been banned if written by an unknown author, and on several occasions bribed him into withdrawing his plays). The theater censorship generally required submission of a script two weeks before the planned performance, while in recognition of the more timely nature of illustrations, the caricature censorship operated on a twenty-four-hour timetable. Both the theater and caricature censors could accept a proposal as submitted, forbid it entirely, or allow it with modifications. Although the caricature censors generally refused to provide written explanations of their decisions, the theater censors not only wrote written reports (until 1866), but often "negotiated" changes in scripts. However, since rehearsals and sets would already be well advanced by the time the censors acted, theater managers were virtually forced by potential financial disaster to ultimately accept the censors' demands.

In some celebrated cases, the stage censors suddenly reversed their original positions or were overruled by their superiors, leading to widespread rumors that personal connections or bribes, including the sexual favors of actresses, were involved. In perhaps the most notorious such case, Alexander Dumas *fils' La Dame aux Camélias*, the story of a courtesan, was banned in 1849 as offensive to public morality, but approved two years later after a friend of Dumas, the duc de Morny, was named to head the interior ministry. Morny simultaneously banned Balzac's *Meracadet*, a play satirizing speculators that had been approved by his predecessors, apparently reasoning, according to one historian, that financiers "who render the state no small service, have a right to be shielded from the darts of impertinent satirists; whereas no offense is given to any influential segment of the community by revealing that young men about town habitually frequent the houses of loose women."[16]

Until 1864, stage censorship was accompanied by the requirement that all theaters and theater directors receive licenses from the state. Under the licensing rules, in Paris only the handful of state-subsidized theaters such as the Comédie-Française and the Academie de Musique (the Opéra) could legally perform "legitimate" stage works such as "serious" comedies, tragedies, and opera, while the popular theaters could officially present only pantomimes, vaudevilles, melodramas, and short skits and songs that could not easily encompass serious political critiques (although in practice such restrictions were enforced with increasingly laxity after about 1830). For example, the Pantheon theater's 1834 license restricted it to "small comedies of manners and popular vaudeville, to the exclusion of all serious plays and especially of all political allusions." Theater directors also had to furnish security bonds; in 1846, for example, the director of the Vaudeville theater had to deposit 300,000 francs, the equivalent of $60,000 in contemporary American currency. Theoretically, the licensing and bond requirements simply guaranteed that theaters were reputable and had sufficient financial backing to meet their obligations to the state, the public, and their employees. In practice, they allowed the authorities to ensure that theater owners were politically reliable, as they had to be reasonably wealthy and their license applications had to be accompanied by letters from referees guaranteeing his (and until 1864 licensees were by law always male) morals, "public spiritedness," and "loyalty to the regime." Even after they were approved, theater owners remained subject to constant police surveillance.[17]

Similar licensing and/or security bond requirements were generally required until 1881 for booksellers, printers, and newspaper publishers, and were implemented with similar political motivations. The threat of withdrawing a printer's license often made it difficult for opposition journalists to find any outlets, while high security bonds ensured that only the wealthy owned newspapers. The true political purpose of security bonds was reflected in their constantly changing levels: as historian F. W. J. Hemmings notes, they fluctuated in "inverse ration to the liberality of the regime and also to the degree of security it felt it enjoyed." In 1822 legislator François Guizot, subsequently a dominant politician during the July Monarchy, declared that the "real purpose" of security bonds was to ensure that "one would not, without grave imprudence" hand the power to publish a newspaper over to "whomever wishes to use it."[18]

For most of the 1815–81 period, special taxes also applied to newspapers, resulting in often pricing them so high that the poor could not afford them. During the Restoration, press taxes swallowed up over 30 percent of total newspaper revenues, and during the July Monarchy the taxes were the single largest newspaper expense. Although formal prior censorship of the written press ended in 1822, until 1881, as discussed in detail below, a large variety of extremely vague laws continued to subject all written materials to potentially severe post-publication prosecutions.

THE HISTORY OF FRENCH POLITICAL CENSORSHIP, 1815–1914

The Background: Censorship Before 1815

As in other European countries, systematic censorship in France was spurred by the spread of the modern printing press in the late fifteenth century. A 1531 edict forbade the publication of all "false doctrines," while in 1535 King Francis I decreed death by hanging for anyone who printed anything whatsoever. Although this measure was quickly repealed, immense amounts of bureaucratic energy were devoted to developing intricate means of controlling expression during subsequent centuries. For example, beginning in 1545 the French government began issuing lists of forbidden books, and in 1561 Charles IX extended censorship to include even "cards and pictures," with those failing to comply subject to the lash for the first offense and to death for repeat violations. Embryonic attempts to regulate theatrical performances date to 1398, although systematic drama censorship began only under Louis XIV during the early eighteenth century.[19]

The eighteenth century proved to be a golden age of censorship, with the government issuing an astounding 3,000 edicts and ordinances to regulate all aspects of the printing and dramatic trades, thus creating a vast repressive net, which (even though it remained full of holes) swept up scores of prominent authors and dramatists. At least 1,000 books were forbidden between 1700 and 1750, and as the crush of printed matter increased geometrically with the spread of literacy, technical advances in the printing industry and the impact of Enlightenment doctrine (which stressed the importance of education and press freedom), the number of censors employed by the government increased from 73 to 178 between 1745 and 1789. Until just before the revolution, only one newspaper was licensed to publish political news, and strict limits were imposed on the number of authorized printers, in order to avoid, as a 1618 edict put it, "the abuses, disorders and confusion which occur daily as the result of the printing of an infinite number of scandalous, libelous and defamatory books." In 1694 two hapless print sellers were executed for publishing an engraving that pictured King Louis XIV enchained by his mistresses, while in 1757 King Louis XV decreed the death penalty for publication of materials tending to attack "religion, to trouble minds, to attack government authority or to trouble order or tranquillity."[20]

Although the death penalty was periodically imposed for press violations, lesser penalties, such as whipping, jailing, banishment, and the burning of condemned books and the closure of bookstores and printshops, were far more widespread: at least 385 separate titles were burned, often by the public hangman, during the eighteenth century, and almost 900 French authors, printers, and book- and printsellers, including Voltaire and Denis Diderot, editor of the famed *Encyclopedie*, were jailed in the Bastille alone between 1600 and 1756,. According to historian David Pottinger, "There were few authors, prominent or obscure, who did not spend at least 24 hours in jail." Nonetheless, forbidden material was regularly surreptitiously published in France and/or smuggled into the country from outside.[21]

On August 26, 1789, the French Revolution's famous Declaration of the Rights of Man pronounced that "all citizens can speak, write and publish freely," since the "free communication of thoughts and opinions is one of the most precious rights of man." This principle, and perhaps even more the effective collapse of royal authority, effectively terminated press censorship, with a resultant tidal wave of free expression: between 1789 and 1792 almost 600 newspapers began publishing, and the daily circulation of the Parisian press quintupled to 150,000. On January 13, 1791, theater censorship, including the requirement that all theaters be licensed and restrict their productions to approved genres, was abolished; the number of Parisian theaters, only ten in 1789, reached thirty-five by 1792. One observer lamented, "If this craze goes on, there will soon be one theater in every street, one dramatist in every house, one musician in every cellar and one actor in every garret."[22]

The post-1792 period witnessed a return to strict controls on freedom of expression as France was convulsed by continual internal strife and war with its neighbors. Major press crackdowns in 1791–94 and 1797 led to the suppression of forty-four Paris newspapers in the latter year alone; numerous journalists (almost 20 percent of those active in Paris), as well as at least two caricaturists, were executed during the 1793–94 Reign of Terror. Freedom of the stage also quickly eroded under these conditions; all references to monarchs and aristocrats soon disappeared from the theaters, to be replaced by pro-republican propaganda pieces. In 1794 theater censorship was officially reimposed.[23]

Although the Reign of Terror's end in 1794 was followed by a modest relaxation of censorship controls (punctuated by occasional severe crackdowns), Napoleon reintroduced the whole panoply of *ancien regime* restrictions after seizing power in 1799, while enforcing them with considerably more bureaucratic efficiency than the Bourbon kings had ever mustered. He reduced the Parisian press from seventy-two newspapers to four, closed two-thirds of the city's printshops, and reduced the number of Parisian theaters from thirty-three to eight. By 1810–11 he had reintroduced virtually all pre-1789 censorship controls, including licensing of printers, booksellers, and theaters, prior censorship of the written and illustrated press, and genre restrictions for theaters.

The Restoration, 1814–30

The restored Bourbon monarchy of 1814–30 largely continued that dynasty's past censorship practices. Although the June 4, 1814, constitution promulgated by Louis XVIII seemingly ended prior censorship with its pledge that citizens had the right to publish their opinions "while conforming to the laws that limit the abuse of this freedom," press censorship was maintained almost continuously until 1822, and thereafter a web of harsh press restrictions allowed the government to virtually prosecute newspapers at will. Theater censorship and licensing were continued, although prior censorship of caricature was allowed to lapse until the assassination of the heir to the throne in February 1820 was used as an excuse to reinstate it. Altogether, according to one clearly understated tally, the Restoration regime prosecuted the authors, publishers, editors, printers or distributors of at least 225 books, eighty-five pamphlets, thirty-five newspapers and other periodicals, and twenty-eight lithographs. Charges reflected political offenses in 45 percent of the cases, offense to morals in another 50 percent, and antireligious expression in the remaining instances. The government obtained convictions in well over 90 percent of the cases, but penalties directed against individuals were generally light, usually amounting to modest fines, generally without accompanying jail terms. However, the consequences for the publications involved were frequently severe, often involving suspension (if a newspaper was involved) for several months: for example, in 1823 the liberal newspaper *Le Courrier français* was suspended for tendency to cause a breach of the peace as a result of its criticism of French intervention to put down a liberal insurrection in Spain.[24]

As press historian Maryse Maget-Dedominici has pointed out, press regulations provoked "incessant debate" and "never ceased being the object of successive legislation" in Restoration France—more than a dozen press statutes were enacted in fifteen years—thereby reflecting the instability and bitterness of the era's politics. The opposition press was threatened by constantly changing press regulations, yet, as historian Alan Spitzer has summarized, if journalists never "enjoyed complete freedom from some sort of censorship or threat of prosecution for vaguely defined offenses . . . there was never a time, either, when it was absolutely impossible to publish material offensive to the royal authorities." Throughout the entire Restoration, however, the granting of licenses to printers and booksellers was strictly limited, and along with newspapers, songs, plays, caricatures, and even *cabinets de lecture* (rental reading rooms that made books and newspapers affordable to those too poor to purchase them), they were kept under intense surveillance and frequently prosecuted. At least twenty printers and booksellers lost their licenses for alleged legal infractions between 1821 and 1827. In 1826 the Paris police prefect warned his supervising minister that *cabinets de lecture* "tend to popularize the reading of works most likely to corrupt the heart and pervert the spirit," especially since they displayed a "marked preference" for "writings and periodicals of the revolutionary party" and thus functioned as "one of the laboratories in which the liberals work upon the public mind, and on which they place great hopes." In 1827 a supervisor of the book trade urged the minister of justice to require printers and booksellers to swear on being licensed that they would avoid selling books "which, though not illegal, are nonetheless pernicious in their effects on the lower classes." A royal prosecutor expressed similar fears in 1826 about the widespread circulation of small, cheap pamphlets, whose "format and price add to the danger" they posed by spreading among "all classes of society, to students, to children, to workers, and to domestics" the "most pernicious doctrines."[25]

The first Restoration press law, enacted provisionally in October 1814 and eventually extended until 1819, required licensing of newspapers and imposed prior censorship on newspapers and pamphlets and all other publications less than twenty pages in length, thus excluding lengthy books, which were viewed, as historian James Allen notes, as having a "smaller, more 'responsible' audience" and thus posing "less of a threat to the regime than newspapers." Government officials inspected all newspaper articles before publication and could threaten closure of the paper unless it struck objectionable articles. Press restrictions were reinforced by a November 1815 law that outlawed seditious cries or writings, including threats against the royal family as well as publication of any "news tending to alarm citizens in their support of legitimate authority and to shake their fidelity." Officials often administered such regulations with startling arbitrariness and bureaucratic fussiness. Thus, the authorization certificate for newspapers specified in detail what subjects could be discussed, down even to the publication of concert notices, and, on occasion, articles approved by the censors nonetheless led to police suspension or even criminal prosecution. In 1815–16 alone, the government shut down five newspapers and temporarily suspended another twenty.[26]

Although press censorship was briefly terminated in 1819 and then permanently abolished in 1822, throughout the Restoration press laws remained flexible enough to allow the government to prosecute and suppress publications virtually whenever it wished to. For example, the 1819 laws not only introduced a hefty security deposit of 10,000 francs ($2,000), but subjected to potential post-publication prosecution anyone who attacked "the person of the king, the succession to the throne" and members of the royal family, whether by "writings, printed matter, sketches, engravings, paintings or emblems." In March 1820, in response to the murder of the Duc de Berri, the heir to the throne, prior press censorship was temporarily reintroduced, and the Paris police prefect instructed his officers to ban songs and poetry that attacked "governmental and morality" from recitals in cafés.[27]

Although prior press censorship was abolished in 1822 over the government's opposition, during the intervening two years several newspapers shut down voluntarily or were suspended, and others were subjected to rigorous censorship. During one seven-month period in 1820, the censors suppressed over 40,000 lines, leading one journal to term the censorship the "bureau of castration." The 1822 press law removed juries from press cases (an innovation introduced only three years earlier), retained the requirement (abolished in 1819 but reintroduced in 1820) that newspapers be licensed, increased penalties for many of the offenses outlawed in the 1819 law, and added new offenses, including inciting to hatred and contempt of the government and the notorious provision that any periodical whose "spirit and tendency" were injurious to the public peace or the respect due to religion, the king, or the government could be prosecuted, suspended, and ultimately suppressed. Under this notorious "law of tendency," no specific material had to be specified; a series of articles, each individually legally inoffensive, could be cited as supporting a violation, with three convictions leading to permanent suppression. The 1822 law was followed by a wave of prosecutions, often for extremely trivial offenses, but in several notorious cases the royal courts refused to convict.[28]

In 1827 the government, already severely embarrassed by exposure of its recent attempts to silence opposition papers by simply buying them up, suffered a crushing moral defeat when, after an unprecedented storm of public opposition, it could not obtain legislative approval of a law (ironically known as the "law of justice and love" after an unfortunate characterization by a government minister) that proposed increased newspaper taxes and press fines and sought to hold newspaper publishers and printers, as well as editorial personnel, responsible for press infractions. One opponent declared that the proposed law amounted to declaring, "Printing is suppressed in France," while the royalist writer and diplomat François Cheateaubriand famously denounced it as a "vandal law" in a pamphlet that sold 300,000 copies.[29]

After liberal election victories in 1827, the government retreated somewhat in an 1828 law by ending newspaper licensing and removing the "tendency" provisions of the 1822 law, while still reserving press prosecutions for magistrates rather than juries. However, the reactionary ministry of Jules de Polignac (1829–30) unleashed a wave of about eighty press prosecutions within a year, many of which ended with acquittals or only produced martyrs (as had earlier occurred with the lengthy 1828 jail sentence given to the great liberal poet Pierre Béranger for his songs, which were memorized and sung by thousands throughout France). Following new liberal election victories in 1830, Charles X effectively attempted a coup d'état by decreeing dissolution of the new parliament, a reduced electorate, and renewed newspaper licensing, thereby touching off a successful popular revolution in July led by journalists and printers who bolted the doors of their printshops against police raids and distributed illegal calls for resistance. During the revolution Chateaubriand, who had become famous for his attacks on press repression, was carried on the shoulders of crowds who chanted, "Long live the champion of freedom of the press!"[30]

Before its demise in 1830, the restoration regime enforced theater censorship in a spirit of extraordinary pettiness and narrow-mindedness. As two specialists note, the drama censorship "furnished a kind of caricature of the state of the governmental soul, with its preoccupations and its fears" and resulted in a theater of "mediocrity" and "indisputable poverty." The

Paris newspaper *Le Globe* of December 7, 1824, complained that the theater censors had "done such a superb job that no trace of us will remain to satisfy the curiosity of our successors." Louis XVIII's censors forbade all theatrical allusions to Napoleon or even the sites of his great victories, as well as to virtually any events in French history between 1789 and 1815 and even to Enlightenment authors such as Rousseau and Voltaire. Ever sensitive to perceived attacks on the monarchy and the nobility, the censors especially frowned on any dramas treating royalty, even in the distant past and in foreign countries; they declared that "the monarchy has already lost too much of its remote magic without playwrights stripping it of the remnants of its dignity" and warned against plays "infested" with the "spirit of revolt" or the "dangerous taste of democracy." They even banned one play that had the son of a count marrying the daughter of a shopkeeper (it was suggested that the shopkeeper "get rich and become a great businessman" since then "at least, there would not be a misalliance").[31]

Although censorship of overtly political theater references was initially relaxed somewhat under Charles X, attacks on his close alliance with the Catholic Church soon led to a complete ban on any dramatic depiction of religious officials, rites, and costumes, as well as all references to suicide or depictions of death on stage, and the censoring of an entire religious vocabulary, including "mass," "religion," "Christian charity," and "Jesuit." The censors even insisted, in a 1827 comedy, that when a man expressed passion for his mistress that he offer "centuries" rather than "eternities" of celestial happiness in order to possess her "for a moment on earth." Rossini's 1826 opera *Le Siege de Corinthe*, a clearly supportive allusion to the contemporaneous Greek revolt against the Ottoman Empire, was approved only after six separate censors' reports, which resulted in the attenuation of some of its appeals to liberal sentiment: for, example, instead of "Liberty! All our sons will rise us in your name," "O fatherland!" had to be substituted for "Liberty!" The strict ban on Napoleonic references and a strong suspicion of all plays portraying former monarchs continued under Charles X; in 1829, shortly before the king was overthrown by a popular revolt, Victor Hugo's play *Marion de Lorme*, about the seventeenth-century King Louis XIII, was banned because, Hugo was informed by the interior minister, "people will see Charles X in it" and "this is not the time to expose the king to public laughter and insults."[32]

The Restoration caricature censorship (reinstituted in 1820 and extended in 1822 even while press censorship was abolished) struck at the same themes targeted in other media. Forbidden or highly restricted topics included drawings that ridiculed the monarchy, glorified Napoleon, or threatened French diplomatic relations with other countries. As a result, most caricatures focused on fads, fashions, and mild eroticism, although some caricaturists took to "coded" criticism of the regime by drawings scissors (a symbol of censorship), crustaceans, such as crayfish (which appear to walk backwards and thus symbolized reaction), or owls, moles, and other animals typifying gloom and reaction.

The Bonapartist monthly *Le Nain Jaune*, which pioneered the regular publication of caricatures, was suppressed in 1815 and, after moving to Brussels, was closed by the Belgian government in 1816 in apparent response to French diplomatic pressure. Several attempts to create successor journals, such as *L'Homme Gris* (1817–18), which regularly published grotesque depictions of the ruling orders, were similarly crushed. The Pellerin company of Epinal, well known for its publication of popular prints, was raided and its owner fined in 1816 for publishing pro-Napoleonic prints, and periodically throughout the Restoration sellers of a flourishing underground market in Napoleonic prints and other memorabilia were prosecuted. In 1828 the Pellerin company was repeatedly forbidden from publishing a depiction of Napoleon, especially because, the interior ministry declared, it might be "sold in large numbers because of its low cost." In 1829, after the Paris police prefect reported that portraits of Napoleon's son "are everywhere; on liquor bottles, engravings, even on the base of elegant lamps," the interior ministry demanded that an earlier decree forbidding "all images of Napoleon and his son" be especially enforced with regard to "the less enlightened classes." Subsequently, waves of prosecutions were brought for selling or producing depictions of Napoleon in a wide variety of forms, including engravings, medals, statues, snuffboxes, jewelry, and even canes with carved heads. In one of the last political prosecutions of the Restoration, an editor of the caricature journal *La Silhouette* was imprisoned for six months for publishing an unauthorized caricature alleged to offend "the person of the king" for portraying the pro-clerical Charles X's unmistakable face, complete with pouting lip and protruding teeth, in the guise of a Jesuit.[33]

The July Monarchy, 1830–48

Following the 1830 July Revolution, among the first acts of King Louis-Philippe were the annulment and amnestying of all press convictions and the proclamation of a constitutional charter declaring that "censorship can never be reestablished." This provision was generally interpreted as ending censorship of all media, including theater and caricature, as well as security bond and licensing requirements for newspapers and theaters. However, that the basic orientation of the ruling class had changed little was clearly indicated by the absurdly minute 1831 legislative expansion of the suffrage, which increased those enfranchised from 0.3 percent to 0.5 percent of the population. Rising urbanization and literacy rates combined with the hopes raised by the July revolution to massively increase public interest in news and politics, as was manifested by an explosion of newspapers, reading clubs, literary societies, libraries, and bookstores. Between 1830 and 1837, for example, the number of Paris dailies jumped from about ten to over seventy, and their combined daily circulation quadrupled from about 60,000 to over 275,000. Despite a rising tide of urban poverty, the regime turned a blind eye and deaf ear to the rising clamor for meaningful reform; the new king's attitude was symbolized by his response, shortly after the revolution, to one of his conservative ministers who chided him for joining crowds singing "The Marseillaise": "Do not concern yourself, Minister. I stopped saying the words long ago." In response to the desperate messages conveyed by a series of riots, strikes, insurrections, and repeated assassination attempts against the king during 1830–35, the regime answered primarily with mounting repression, including waves of political arrests and trials and increasingly elaborate legal restrictions on freedom of assembly, association, and expression.[34]

The new regime quickly initiated a massive crackdown on the press, bringing at least 530 prosecutions in Paris alone between 1830 and 1834, using legislation inherited from the Bourbons as well as its own ever-tightening restrictions. A November 29, 1830, law outlawed press attacks on the "royal authority," the "inviolability" of the king's person, the order of succession to the throne, and the authority of the legislature; a December 14, 1830, law reimposed, although at lower levels, the hated press security deposits and special taxes; and the law of February 16, 1834, required all streethawkers of writings and prints to obtain governmental permission to practice their trade. Although an October 1830 law made press offenses subject to jury trial (albeit by juries composed only of those enfranchised) and the government obtained a feeble 30 percent conviction rate, penalties were often far harsher than those of the Restoration: the over 100 convictions gained between 1830 and 1833 yielded punishments totaling over 100 years in prison and fines of over 350,000 francs. The leading republican opposition journal *Le Tribune* was subjected to a record 111 prosecutions, yielding, before it was finally battered into submission with its twentieth conviction in May 1835, penalties of forty-nine years and 157,000 francs. But the July monarchy was an equal opportunity oppressor: the small satirical journal *Les Cancans*, an organ of the legitimist (Bourbon) opposition, accumulated twelve years in prison sentences and 10,000 francs in fines. A number of the most-prosecuted journalists had special quarters reserved at St. Pelagie, the Paris prison for political offenders, as they sojourned there so frequently. Journalist Alexandre Saint-Cheron wrote in an 1832 French encyclopedia article that "nowhere else have government and press come into such open conflict, because nowhere else has journalism managed to become so completely representative of the entire society," while writer Maxime du Camp sardonically commented, "During the French Revolution, one cut journalists' heads; under Napoleon one silenced them; under the Restoration one jailed them; under the July Monarchy one ruined them financially."[35]

The 1830 collapse of caricature and drama censorship spawned an efflorescence of drawings and plays that could not have been produced during the Restoration: among the most popular themes were paeans to Napoleon, bitter attacks on the Catholic church and the fallen Bourbons, portrayals of class exploitation and social injustice, and increasingly embittered attacks on the new regime, in which money and business increasingly dominated politics, culture, and society. Political caricature first emerged as a truly mass medium during the July Monarchy, largely due to the adoption of lithography, which allowed artists to reproduce their work more quickly, accurately, easily, cheaply, and in larger numbers than via established engraving techniques. The master entrepreneur of French caricature, Charles Philipon, made his twin republican journals, *La Caricature* (1830–35) and *Le Charivari* (1832–1906), instruments of brilliant wit and artistry fused with bitter scorn directed against Louis-Philippe.

Philipon's entourage of caricaturists—accurately described by historian Howard Vincent as having "knives in their brains"—graphically and often brutally lambasted Louis-Philippe for numerous moral and legal crimes, but above all for his alleged betrayal of the liberal promises of the July Revolution, especially those related to liberty of expression, in an endless lust for power and money. Even the extremely hostile account of French historian Paul Thureau-Dangin concedes that Philipon "became one of the most dangerous adversaries of the new king" and that his caricatures had "such audacity, such importance, a power so destructive that history cannot neglect these illustrated papers, which from other points of view it would be tempted to scorn." Philipon's journals especially seriously damaged the king's prestige by repeatedly depicting him as a pear, a clever commentary both on the king's physical appearance and his alleged dimwittedness. The pear quickly became a ubiquitous form of popular imagery and graffiti that was scrawled all over the walls of Paris. The exiled German journalist and poet Heinrich Heine wrote in 1832 that Paris was festooned with "hundreds of caricatures" hanging "everywhere," featuring the pear as the "permanent standing joke of the people," that "the pear and always the pear, is to been seen in every caricature" and that the "glory from [the king's] head hath passed away and all men see in it is but a pear."[36]

Along with fame and notoriety, Philipon and his caricaturists ultimately won the bare-fisted hatred of the regime, which seized his journals and separate caricatures issued by his publisher dozens of times, leading to at least fifteen prosecutions, over half-a-dozen convictions, more than two years in jail terms, and fines totaling over 20,000 francs. Philipon, who was personally prosecuted six times, convicted thrice, fined over 4,000 francs, and jailed for a year, wrote that he "could not longer count the seizures, the arrest warrants, the trials, the struggles, the wounds, the attacks and harassment of all types, any more than could a [carriage] voyager count the jolts of his trip." One of Philipon's most talented artists, Honoré Daumier, was jailed for six months for the crime of arousing hatred and contempt of the king's government and offending the king's person by his 1831 drawing "Gargantua," which depicted Louis-Philippe sitting on a toilet-throne, consuming food and tribute from the poor while excreting boodle to his aristocratic supporters.[37]

Although the theater was freed from censorship in 1830—Victor Hugo wrote that "the plays that the Restoration censorship had buried alive broke out of the coffin and they scattered noisily over the theaters of Paris"—the regime quickly instituted a backdoor censorship by seizing on an obscure 1806 law that it claimed authorized the closure of any plays that posed the threat of public disorders. The 1806 law was invoked over twenty times between 1831 and 1835, almost always to ban politically sensitive plays, including dramas viewed as attacking the royal family, inciting to revolt, or alluding to censorship or sensitive foreign developments (although violently anticlerical plays and bitter social satires were left untouched). The 1806 law was most infamously invoked to shut down Hugo's *Le Roi s'amuse* (1832), which depicted the fifteenth-century French King François I in a highly unflattering light. Such closures—which were often imposed absent any demonstrated threat to the peace—threatened theaters with ruin, since the costs of hiring actors, rehearsals, publicity, costuming, and sets were already undertaken. As a result, theater owners increasingly succumbed after 1831 to growing pressures from the authorities to "voluntarily" submit advance scripts; in July 1834 the regime felt bold enough to put this "suggestion" in an official letter sent to theater directors: "You can avoid all problems by submitting your manuscripts in advance to the Fine Arts Ministry. Plays not submitted will be stopped, purely and simply, if by their contents they merit the application of the [1806] decree and you will only have yourself to blame for the loss resulting from the costs of staging a production which has become useless."[38]

Alarmed by the 70 percent jury acquittal rate and the growing boldness of written, drawn, and theatrical criticisms of the regime, Louis-Philippe seized upon a gruesome failed assassination attempt to quickly shepherd through a compliant legislature the notoriously repressive "September Laws" of 1835, which one historian has termed so drastic that they amounted to a "change of regime."[39] They reimposed prior theater and caricature censorship and the licensing requirement for theaters; increased the security deposit required of Paris dailies from 2,400 francs to the fantastic level of 100,000 francs; drastically increased fines, and created a vast new web of press violations, including "insulting" the king, holding him responsible for governmental acts, and "expressing the wish, the hope or the threat of the destruction of the constitutional monarchical order"; made it far easier to obtain press convictions by removing some cases from juries and reducing the required jury majority in all others; and banned newspaper accounts of press trials, the publication of the names of jury members, and public subscriptions to pay press fines, techniques that had been widely and effectively used to embarrass the regime and thwart press prosecutions. The September Laws led to the immediate closure of over thirty journals, including Philipon's *La Caricature*, and it largely (if not entirely) succeeded in stifling the press, caricature, and the theater for the next dozen years.

Altogether, between 1830 and 1847 the July Monarchy brought prosecutions against over 250 books, pamphlets, and caricatures and against about 750 newspapers and periodicals (of which about 225 were initiated after 1835). In 1841 a republican editor was sentenced to five years in jail for writing, after an assassination attempt on the king's son succeeded only in killing his horse, that the government was making too much of a fuss over the dead animal. According to an 1842 tally published in *Le Charivari*, during the previous twelve years press prosecutions yielded 500 years of jail terms and about one million francs in fines. Although the September Laws never completely silenced the opposition press, republican and legitimist journals were forced to moderate their general tenor and to replace open political criticism with allusions and cunning references. As Armand Carrel, editor of the *National*, wrote in 1836, "Newspapers are forced to censor themselves. They are resigned to it: you can't write all that you think and you can't publish even all that you write."[40]

The September Laws completely changed the rules regarding the stage by imposing prior censorship. Of a total of 8,300 plays submitted between 1835 and 1847, about 220 (less than 3 percent) were completely forbidden and changes were formally required to another 500 (about 6 percent); in a very large number of additional cases, the censors seem to have informally successfully demanded changes. In fifteen cases, most notoriously Balzac's *Vautrin*, plays that were originally approved were banned following their presentation. Along with official theaters, drinking and other popular establishments that presented informal entertainment were also subject to careful supervision. In Paris, where spontaneous singing of patriotic songs as an expression of political protest became frequent in the theaters after 1835, more than 500 *goguettes* (meeting places and bars that featured group singing) were closed in 1836. In 1847 the minister of the interior directed his officials to limit their authorizations of songs and music so that sponsoring establishments "will in the future present only romances or ditties" rather than parodies or political allusions.[41]

Political allusions to the current regime were cited as the reason for censorship modifications in 25 percent of censored dramas. Other types of political allusions accounted for another 20 percent, moral objections were cited in about one-third of the cases, and religious allusions accounted for the remaining 20 percent. Censors were especially alert for any criticisms of or suggestions of conspiracies against the king, the regime, and its functionaries, as well as against past kings (especially if these acts were presented in a favorable light or motivated by ideological beliefs, rather than by individual desires for power); they also banned works seen as directly inciting class conflict, advocating republicanism, or criticizing the concept of royalty, even if they centered on the French Revolution or the very 1830 Revolution that enthroned Louis-Philippe.[42]

A number of dramas that had been popular before 1835 were banned, notably including plays featuring or even vaguely referring to "Robert Macaire," a stage character whom the great actor Frédérick Lemaître had made famous as a means of satirizing the bourgeoisie, whose often unscrupulous ascendancy was so marked an aspect of the era. The regime could never decide whether stirring up nationalist sentiments associated with Napoleon would strengthen or undermine it: references to Napoleon were "temporarily" banned from the stage in 1835 and again in 1840, but generally tolerated in 1839 and after 1842 (reflecting the same ambiguity, the regime banned *living* relatives of Bonaparte from visiting France yet transferred Napoleon's *remains* from St. Helena to Paris in 1840 in a widely publicized reburial). Among the victims of moral and religious censorship after 1835 were scores of plays including material viewed as unacceptable to middle-class morality, including (especially in plays destined for the popular theaters) suicide, rape, prostitution, incest, nudity, illegitimacy, impotency, drunkenness, and, especially, adultery. Also banned were depictions of religious characters, settings, and insignia, including (especially following an unequivocal ministerial decree of 1844) virtually any scenes portraying convents, churches, cemeteries, tombs, and even the cross. Such bans caused especially severe problems for operas, which often heavily dealt with religious characters or themes: thus, Scribe's opera *La Favorite* was forbidden, since, the censors maintained, "one cannot tolerate in the theater an amorous priest who detests the vows he has taken, seducing a young girl, making her pregnant and clasping his child in his arms."[43]

Despite such bans, the July Monarchy's theater censorship was generally never quite as petty or pigheaded as the Restoration's, and especially with regard to socially conscious dramas, it never approached the sternness of the subsequent Second Empire. Even after 1835, numerous plays were allowed that focused on social injustice and indirectly challenged the entire foundations of society, of which perhaps the most notorious were Eugene Sue's *Les Mystères de Paris* and Felix Pyat's *Le Chiffonnier de Paris*. Referring to such plays, theater censor Hallys-Dabot complained in an 1862 book that even after 1835 "the popular theaters propagated an unhealthy and pernicious literature based exclusively on social antagonism against which the censorship unfortunately could not erect a strong enough barrier."[44]

The post-1835 caricature censorship was equally inconsistent and puzzling. Even though it theoretically only included illustrations, the censors also insisted on approving caricature captions: of the sixty-four drawings forbidden in 1840, nine were subsequently allowed after caption changes. In general, so long as caricatures did not directly attack governmental figures or impugn the legitimacy of the regime, such as depicting the deposed Bourbon dynasty or the Bonapartist pretender Louis Napoleon Bonaparte, the censors were quite tolerant. Presumably reflecting the authorities' greater fear of theater compared to drawings, *Robert Macaire* was banned from the stage yet was the central character in a fantastically popular series of Daumier caricatures published in *Le Charivari* between 1836 and 1842 that savagely lampooned the corruption and immorality of the bourgeoisie. Numerous other authorized caricatures in *Le Charivari* similarly portrayed symbolic social types in a manner that collectively depicted in a devastating manner the get-rich-quick enterpreneurialism and industrial abuses that characterized the times and inevitably, the government, which tolerated, encouraged, and was enmeshed in such behavior.[45]

During the entire 1835–48 period, the government banned about 430 drawings. This was less than 1 percent of all submitted caricatures, but no doubt newspapers and artists refrained from submitting drawings certain to be rejected. Philipon's printshop, run by his brother-in-law Gabriel Aubert, was kept under heavy police surveillance after 1835, and (although fifty caricatures submitted by Aubert were forbidden between 1835 and 1848) the police concluded that Aubert changed his ways, at least in the immediate aftermath of the September Laws. An 1836 police report declared, "Aubert seems to have understood the danger and, above all, the futility of the genre of political opposition which he pursued following the July Revolution. It has been replaced by portraits, anatomical studies, drawing manuals and flower designs."[46]

The Second Republic, 1848–52

In February 1848 Louis-Philippe was overthrown by a popular uprising partly provoked by the regime's incessant repression. As in 1830, one of the first acts of the succeeding (now republican) government was to free political prisoners and abolish most restrictions on the press and the theater, including abrogating the September Laws, along with newspaper taxes and security bonds. Subsequently, over 400 (often ephemeral) newspapers sprouted overnight. A batch of new caricature journals also sprang up, and the theater was similarly rejuvenated, as *Robert Macaire* and other banned works returned to the stage. However, as in 1830, the new regime soon embarked on a press crackdown, which was especially stoked by the "red scare" that followed the brutal suppression of a workers' insurrection in Paris in June 1848. Security deposits were reintroduced in August 1848; most press offenses spelled out in the 1819 and 1822 laws were reenacted with minor changes (such as banning attacks against republican institutions and the distribution of symbols intended to trouble the public peace); and in 1849 new offenses were added, including insulting the republican president and maliciously affirming erroneous facts likely to disturb the peace. Almost twenty newspapers were administratively suppressed in 1848–49. Many others were crushed by a ruthless campaign of judicial harassment between 1848 and 1851, during which at least 335 prosecutions were brought against 185 republican newspapers and more than fifty printers; one newspaper was prosecuted almost thirty times in twenty months. One editor complained in November 1850 that the regime had inaugurated a "clever and systematic war" against "everything energetic and independent in the press."[47]

Much of the press repression was especially directed against working-class-oriented publications. Thus, in urging passage of the July 1850 press law—which increased security deposits and reintroduced the newspaper tax, measures designed to make it difficult for poor people to publish or buy newspapers—the justice minister declared that it sought to control press elements that had "contested every principle and scorned every holy truth" while especially addressing "the least enlightened elements of the population." Laws and regulations adopted between 1849 and 1851 closely regulated popular entertainment and colporteurs, the itinerant sellers of books, prints, and pamphlets who peddled their materials in small towns and rural areas where they were otherwise unavailable. Thus, the regime ruthlessly banned any songs viewed as subversive from presentation at drinking establishments, which were required to obtain police permission for each song or drama they wished to present, with all permissions valid only for a particular time and day. In 1849 the minister of the interior instructed those supervising colporteurs to refuse to give the needed permission to work to those who "would sell subversive or malevolent" materials, to be interpreted as extending beyond material that had been officially condemned by the courts, since "immoral or seditious writings or emblems" might escape legal action" yet still "produce the most pernicious effects upon the minds of rural inhabitants" and "ignorant people" if they were "sold and distributed cheaply." In mid-1852 colporteurs were required, by a government decree issued without any legislative authority, to have every item they sold individually approved and stamped (a new "stamp bureau" was established to provide this free service). Over 3,100 colporteurs were convicted between 1849 and 1852 for defying or ignoring these regulations.[48]

At the government's request, the legislature provisionally reinstated theater censorship by a 352–194 vote on July 30, 1850. The resuscitated theater censors (most of whom had carried out the same task for the July Monarchy) were told by their superiors to "put an end to the moral disorder which reigned in the theater," and to remove "anti-religious propaganda, socialist theses," and "incitement to class antagonism." They were also explicitly directed to reexamine works allowed under the July Monarchy since "recent circumstances have given certain works an importance which they did not have before and which could not be presented today without danger." The theater censors proved especially sensitive to anything touching on class conflict: in 1851 a passage in George Sand's play *Moliere* was struck in which the hero toasted "the poor people of France, who pay the fiddlers for all the festivals and the trumpets for all the wars."[49]

The Second Empire, 1852–70

Whatever remained of freedom of expression was quickly destroyed after Napoleon's nephew, Louis Napoleon Bonaparte, who had been freely elected president of the Second Republic in December 1848, overthrew the regime in a coup d'état in December 1851. The coup triggered massive resistance in the countryside, suppressed with 25,000 arrests and over 500 killed, and in its immediate aftermath scores of newspapers were suspended or suppressed. Subsequently only fourteen Parisian dailies were permitted to survive, with the required security deposit more than doubled to 50,000 francs, while provincial dailies declined from 430 to 260 between 1851 and 1865, at least partly due to various forms of harassment. In a February 17, 1852, decree, Louis Napoleon reintroduced prior censorship of caricature, and in December 1852, as the newly self-crowned and declared Emperor Napoleon III, he indefinitely extended the revived theater censorship. Even "La Marseillaise" was forbidden between 1852 and 1870 (as it had been between 1815 and 1830); in 1870 a group of censors recommended that the ban continue because the song had become "the symbol of revolution" and the "war chant of demagogy" whose repeated public performance would cause "new and dangerous excitation."[50]

Louis Napoleon's February 17, 1852, press decree was perhaps as innovative and ingenious as it was repressive. Although the surviving press was not formally censored before publication, it was subjected to so many restraints, both administrative and judicial, that newspapers were effectively forced to censor themselves. All periodicals dealing in any way with "politics or social economy" were required to obtain licenses, which had to be renewed with each staff change; foreign publications could be imported into France only with official permission; and a long list of press offenses was defined, including the publication of false news and nonofficial accounts of legislative activity. Newspaper taxes were raised; all press prosecutions were denied jury trials (a procedure that had been reintroduced during the Second Republic) and any newspaper coverage aside from the final outcome; and one felony or two misdemeanor convictions automatically led to suppression of the implicated periodical. Any suspended or suppressed publication was banned from reappearing under any name whatsoever.

Most innovative and repressive of all, the decree established a system of administrative "warnings" that empowered the government to severely punish publications via purely administrative decisions not subject to court challenge. Warnings could be based on whatever criteria struck the government's fancy, and after three warnings the interior ministry was empowered to suspend a journal for two months. Finally, Louis Napoleon could suppress a journal at any time to protect the public safety. In a March 30, 1852, circular, the police minister instructed his subordinates that any periodicals that sought to "raise passions and revive bad instincts must encounter in the law insurmountable obstacles." Between 1852 and 1867, there were 150 judicial press prosecutions, often leading to fines and jail terms, while administrative measures were taken against 120 newspapers, resulting in a total of 338 administrative warnings, twenty-seven suspensions, and twelve suppressions. Between 1852 and 1861, twenty-six additional journals were suppressed solely for publishing "political" articles when they were not so authorized. At least 230 judicial prosecutions were also brought against books, pamphlets, and lithographs during the 1852–66 period. Compared to the 30 percent conviction rate obtained in juried press cases during the July Monarchy, the Second Empire gained a conviction rate of 80 percent between 1852 and 1866 by dispensing with juries. Requests for authorization to begin new political periodicals were almost routinely denied, since, as one petitioner was informed in 1856, the government had determined that "due to considerations of public order . . . the number of journals authorized to discuss politics and social economy should not be increased." Opposition journalism did not completely disappear, but it was largely reduced to such veiled criticisms as adverse reviews of books and plays by the Emperor's friends and backers.[51]

In effect, the writer Lucien Prévost-Paradol complained, the regime "established a vast and elastic series of subjects which cannot be discussed," and had placed the press in a position like that of "Gulliver between the hands of a giant" or that of a whimpering dog waiting for the slightest signal from its master. One newspaper editor complained that the law forced editors to "assume the responsibility for their own castration," while another lamented that press freedom was reduced to "the freedom to pay fines and to go to prison or to Belgium." Opposition legislator Jules Favre declared, "In France there is only one journalist and that is the Emperor," while journalist Philibert Audebrand declared that the regime seemed to regard with "horror the 26 letters of the alphabet."[52]

Administration of restrictions on plays and drawings was also extremely harsh during the Second Empire—considerably more so than during the July Monarchy, when a variety of social and political topics could at least be discussed, even if direct attacks on the regime were not tolerated. Censorship was especially strict during the period immediately following the December 1851 coup: according to an 1853 report, in 1852 the censors accepted outright only 246 out of 682 submitted plays, completely rejected fifty-nine and demanded changes in 323 (the remaining plays were still awaiting decisions). Numerous plays, especially with themes of social class conflict, that had been tolerated during the July Monarchy and the Second Republic were banned. The theater censors were also especially vigilant concerning dramas that displayed hostility to the imperial regime or the Catholic Church, as well as those that dealt with themes of conspiracy and revolt or that treated republican or democratic causes. As drama censorship historian Albert Cahuet notes, "As a general rule, the censorship did not allow criticism of the diverse branches of the imperial administration; and the more highly placed the target the better it was protected."[53]

Among the plays rejected were Glais-Bizoin's 1865 comedy *Le Vrai Courage*, forbidden because, the censors reported, it included "scenes in which the hateful recriminations of the socialists against law and order erupt in all their violence and brutality." *Robert Macaire* was again banished; an 1852 opera about a seventeenth-century rebellion was forbidden because any theme concerning revolt was viewed as dangerous; and in 1853 the comment that "the rich, in the design of God, are only the treasurers of the poor" was excised from a play that the censors denounced as a "violent diatribe" against the wealthy. A production of *Uncle Tom's Cabin* was allowed only on condition that the slave master be transformed into a mulatto and former slave himself, as this would make any analogy between "the Negro slaves and European workers disappear." In one famous case, the emperor personally approved Emile Augier's play *Les Lionnes pauvres* only after the author publicly declared that the censors' request that his adulterous heroine die of smallpox had led him to suggest it be retitled, "On the Usefulness of Cowpox."[54]

By 1857, Second Empire censors had forbidden at least 180 plays, including all of Hugo's works; moreover, a large percentage of authorized plays suffered enforced modifications (although there was a significant relaxation of the drama censorship after 1855, and in 1867 Hugo's dramas were again permitted). In one significant liberalization, in 1864 the government eliminated the licensing requirement, with its attendant restriction of repertoires, resulting in an immediate explosion in the number of theaters.

Physical changes that drastically affected the Paris theater under Napoleon III clearly reflected the regime's fear of mass disturbances among the poor. Most of the popular (and thus especially feared) theaters on the Boulevard du Temple were physically destroyed during the reconstruction of Paris during the 1860s. All remaining theaters were required to dispense with the notorious *parterre* (pit), where spectators of all classes were jammed together standing up or on often hideously overcrowded benches, to be replaced with assigned seats, with a resultant decrease in any sense of crowd collectivity and a considerable increase in prices that helped to drive the poor away from larger theaters into the smaller café-concerts (which one of Napoleon III's ministers described approvingly as "houses of tolerance ["maisons de tolerance," revealingly, a term also used for brothels] which shelter the people and prevent them from thinking about politics").[55]

Although the café-concerts generally featured far more frivolous material than was presented at the regular theaters, their appeal to the popular classes nonetheless made them subjects of strict surveillance. In December 1851 Louis Napoleon decreed that all popular drinking establishments, which often served as centers of working-class socializing and organization, could be closed at will; by 1855 their number had been reduced from 350,000 to 291,000 and the survivors were required to have all songs and sketches approved by the censors if they wished to present popular entertainment. Interior ministry figures for 1852, the year immediately following Napoleon III's coup, indicate that of over 600 songs submitted to the censors, almost 10 percent were completely forbidden and another 40 percent underwent enforced changes; during the entire Second Empire 800 songs out of around 6,000 submitted were banned.[56]

Colportage restrictions were also enforced with extreme severity during the Second Empire. An 1851 ministerial circular and reports by a government commission on colportage established in 1852 declared that this was required because colportage especially affected the "lower class press, far more important than the press which is intended to influence the upper classes" and indeed "completed the education of those who have left school," and because whereas before 1848 "eight million immoral books" had been "spread throughout our villages and our rural areas" by colporteurs, "eight million decent books" could introduce this audience to "a world of virtuous emotions and righteous ideas," inspiring in them religious devotion along with "love of their country and gratitude towards the monarch." In 1855 the colportage commission, which regularly distributed to local officials lists of approved and forbidden materials, described its function as like the "father of a family" who "chooses for his children reading material appropriate for their intelligence and their educational development." At one point, out of 3,649 books examined, the commission refused authorization to 556 (about 15 percent), including books by Hugo, Balzac, and Stendhal.[57]

Political considerations, especially the desire to prevent the lower class and rural population that overwhelmingly constituted the market for colporteurs from being exposed to "subversive" material, played a dominant role in the commission's decisions, with criticisms of the government, of Napoleon I and, frequently, material with any political implications whatsoever, likely to be forbidden. Thus, an 1854 book discussing French history was rejected because "if spread rapidly among the working classes, it could only have a deplorable influence;" Montesquieu's classic *Persian Letters* was rejected because it was "only written for educated people," whereas if it was placed "in the hands of everyone, most readers would focus on irreligious ideas"; and an 1865 book by the well-known clerical conservative Louis Veuillot was banned because although his argument "could be judged by educated people" it would be "poorly appreciated by the less educated" who might find their spirits "troubled." During the 1853–70 period, over 3,000 colporteurs were prosecuted, with a conviction rate of about 90 percent (prosecutions dropped sharply after 1858, probably reflecting the reduced need for such actions as a result of their success). By 1869, according the newspaper *Siècle*, colportage restrictions succeeded in creating a "virtually impassable customs frontier" between urban and rural France, with the latter deprived of "books, the food of thought" by a "whole series of laws concerning printing, bookselling and peddling." Similarly, an 1878 legislative inquiry declared that the Second Empire's colportage controls resulted in the capricious "torturing" and "dissection" of "French thought" and a "rationing of the intellectual and moral nourishment of the nation," all intended to "pervert public opinion solely to create an adulation of the Napoleonic dynasty."[58]

Napoleon III had been the target of a large number of stinging caricatures during the brief period of pictorial freedom during the Second Republic, and he was determined to squelch all illustrated criticism of himself, his regime, and the middle and upper classes that especially supported him. The caricature censorship that he reintroduced in 1852 was administered so strictly that during the next fifteen years there was an almost total absence of critical caricature in France. An uncensored version of *Le Charivari* published in Brussels as *Le Charivari Belge*, which featured bitter caricatures of the Emperor, was completely forbidden and one man was jailed for a month solely for bringing copies across the border. Hugo, a leading opposition figure who spent the entire Second Empire in exile, declared, concerning the regime's harsh censorship of illustrations, "The government feels itself to be hideous. It wants no portraits, especially no mirrors."[59]

According to clearly incomplete archival records, at least 676 illustrations were banned between 1854 and 1866, or an average of fifty-two per year, a rate almost 50 percent higher than the average of thirty-six annually forbidden between 1835 and 1847. No doubt many additional caricatures were never submitted or even drawn rather than face certain censorship. As even social or symbolic satires targeting the ruling classes were impossible (unlike during the July Monarchy), caricaturists overwhelmingly turned to mildly erotic portraits of women and light jests at the foibles, fads, and fashion of the day, such as air balloons and crinoline dresses. Only the cleverest artists, such as Daumier, were able to get some critical caricatures past the censors by, on the surface, drawing about foreign rulers and developments. For example, Daumier's series of twenty caricatures published between 1850 and 1860 in *Le Charivari* that ostensibly ridiculed the corrupt and brutal black Haitian Emperor Souloque (who had crowned himself in 1849 in an overt imitation of Napoleon I) almost certainly were directed against Napoleon III, but their exotic locale and racist stereotyping apparently convinced the censors that they were harmless.[60]

The Second Empire's final three years (the so-called liberal empire) witnessed an easing of the formal regulation of freedom of expression, but when this spawned an eruption of dissent, press prosecutions quickly skyrocketed. Under the May 11, 1868, press law, the government relinquished its licensing requirement for periodicals, as well as its right to administratively warn, suspend, or suppress them. However, press offenses were still excluded from jury trials, security deposits and press taxes were maintained along with a full battery of laws to prosecute the written press, and prior censorship of theater and caricature continued. Over 150 newspapers sprang up within a year, including Henri Rochefort's famous *La Lanterne*, which sold 120,000 copies of its first number, with the famous opening sentence, "The Empire contains 36 million subjects, not counting the subjects of discontent." Between 1867 and 1870, fifty new caricature journals were established, more than twice as many as during the previous fifteen years combined, leading one observer to note, "The rebirth of caricature announces the revival of the spirit." But while the number and circulation of periodicals exploded, almost 450 journalists (including Rochefort) were prosecuted within a twenty-four-month period (twice as many as during the previous fifteen years), yielding 340 convictions, ninety-two jail terms of at least a year, and fines totaling 120,000 francs. At least seven caricature journals were closed and half a dozen of their contributors were jailed.[61]

The Third Republic, 1870–1914

The Commune and Its Aftermath, 1870–77. With the revolutionary overthrow of the Second Empire in August 1870, amid the fiasco of the Franco-Prussian War, a provisional government quickly abolished most restrictions on freedom of the press (including security bonds, newspaper taxes, and restrictions on colportage), caricature, and the stage, and restored jury trials for remaining press offenses. However, between 1871 and 1877 the new regime was dominated by monarchists and conservative republicans haunted by memories of the 1871 Paris Commune, a working-class insurrection that was suppressed with the deaths of 25,000 Parisians—the vast majority of whom were slaughtered in cold blood—along with the imprisonment or exile of another 50,000 alleged Communards. In 1871, the monarchist-dominated legislature approved new press laws that restored security bonds, newspaper taxes, restrictions on colportage, and prior censorship of caricature, and contained numerous provisions designed to suppress the left-wing press. Theater censorship was reimposed by executive decree on March 18, 1871, and, after being maintained for three years as an emergency measure, was regularized by the legislature in 1874.

Fears of Commune-like working-class upheavals and of the growth of liberal republican sentiment were the driving forces behind the extremely harsh regulation of all media until the monarchists were defeated in the 1877 legislative elections. Military authorities frequently arbitrarily banned newspapers in the over forty departments (including Paris) where martial law was maintained for up to five years after 1871, and the prefects in other regions regularly banned street sales of any newspapers that displeased them under authority of the 1849 colportage law. During one seventeen-month period in 1873–74, twenty-eight newspapers were suppressed, twenty were suspended, and 163 were banned from street sales. One author was jailed for eight months for publishing a book in 1876 that called for amnesty for the jailed and exiled Communards. Prosecutions for colportage infractions, which had averaged about 100 per year between 1864 and 1870, soared to an average of almost 500 yearly between 1871 and 1875. The supervising minister declared, concerning the 1870–74 period, that censorship had "never been more severe" for the "repertoire of theaters and especially for those of café-concerts." All references to the Commune were excluded from the stage during the "monarchist republic" of 1871–77, and several dramas that had been allowed under the July Monarchy and the Second Empire were also forbidden. A February 1872 directive to the prefects warned them against lax theater censorship, especially with regard to political matters, and declared that while the "administration does not intend to proscribe political allusions in an absolute manner, it has the duty to forbid all works which strike at the political order and at morality as well as those which, owing to local circumstances, could cause disorder."[62]

In November 1872 café-concert proprietors were informed that all political allusions were "strictly forbidden;" of at least forty plays banned between 1870 and 1874, more than two dozen were intended for that venue, and in 1876 alone twenty café-concerts were closed in Paris (about 10 percent of all such establishments) for presenting unauthorized programs. Altogether, between 1870 and 1906 (when stage censorship was abolished), almost 9,000 songs out of over 90,000 submitted by café-concerts to the censors were forbidden, sometimes for "moral" offenses but very often for their political allusions. In December 1871 the military governor of Paris banned the sale or display of "all illustrations, photographs or emblems of a nature to trouble the public peace," including specifically pictures of "individuals prosecuted or condemned for their participation in the recent insurrection." This decree, which was interpreted to include virtually all images relating to the Commune, was subsequently extended throughout France and led to months of what press historian Fernand Drujon has characterized as "incessant searches and seizures" and an "almost incalculable" number of prosecutions, involving medals, statues, coins, pipes, cigarette cases, and even tapioca boxes. Caricatures in particular were subjected to minute scrutiny: during 1875 alone, a total of 225 drawings were forbidden. One of the leading victims of the censors, the caricature journal *L'Eclipse*, lamented on December 22, 1872, that despite three revolutions (1830, 1848, and 1870) that were supposed to have "crushed censorship," the "phoenix of arbitrariness has been reborn—not from its own cinders, but from the cinders it creates from books, drawings, our rights and our freedoms!"[63]

Censorship and repression of the press and other media reached previously unknown heights during the bitterly contested October, 1877 election for the lower legislative house. During 1877 almost 250 caricatures were banned, over 1,100 colporteurs were prosecuted, almost 3,000 provincial cafés were closed, and there were massive bans on street sales of opposition material and thousands of press prosecutions. Despite this reign of terror, liberal and moderate republicans won the 1877 elections and consolidated their control in 1879 by also winning the elections for the upper house. In 1878 the legislature enacted a press amnesty for political offenses committed in 1877, which reversed about 2,700 speech and press condemnations, including 846 jail sentences and 324,000 francs in fines.[64]

The Republican Republic, 1877–1914. Although the new regime (the so-called republican republic) quickly established a commission to draft a new press law, it also maintained theater and caricature censorship and continued to prosecute the written press, merely switching primary targets from the republican, socialist, and radical to the monarchist press. Thus, monarchist caricature journals were subjected to a blizzard of harassment and prosecutions: the most important of them, *Le Triboulet*, was prosecuted thirty-seven times between 1879 and 1881.[65]

In 1881, as republicans felt increasingly secure, and also increasingly embarrassed over implementing repressive statutes that they had long criticized, a landmark liberal press law wiped the statute books clear of almost all the vast existing web of press restrictions, including caricature censorship, newspaper taxes, security bonds, and the licensing of bookstores, printers, and colporteurs (in the latter case confirming laws passed earlier in 1878 and 1880). Remaining press offenses were, at least in comparison to the past, extremely limited and almost all subject to jury trial, although some were potentially repressive, such as the bans on insulting the president and defaming members of the government and the armed forces. In 1893–94, following a series of anarchist bombings and the assassination of President Sadi Carnot, new press restrictions (called by their opponents the "lois scélérates" [scoundrel laws]) banned inciting or apologizing for terrorism and the propagation of anarchist ideas (left undefined) "by any means whatever." But the French press was essentially free after 1881. A flood of new publications ensued: the number of French newspapers jumped from 3,800 to 6,000 between 1881 and 1892, and over 150 new caricature journals opened between 1879 and 1914.[66]

The relatively few press prosecutions of the 1881–1914 period were generally directed at militant anarchist or antimilitarist publications. For example, the revolutionary anarchist journal *Père Peinard* was convicted seven times between 1890 and 1892, leading to jail terms totaling almost eleven years, and in 1908 the editor and artist of the caricature journal *Les Hommes du jour* were each sentenced to a year in jail for portraying a French general as a bloody butcher for his role in the colonial subjugation of Morocco. Acting under extremely dubious authority, the government continued to claim the right to forbid street sales of particular journals; the graphically outstanding caricature journal *L'Assiette au beurre* (1901–12) was subjected to a number of such bans between 1901 and 1905, invariably for fear of offending lampooned foreign governments. In the most notorious such incident, the September 28, 1901, issue, devoted to attacks on British foreign policy, was banned from street sales for its depiction of English King Edward VII's face on the bare bottom of a woman; due to the enormous resultant controversy the journal reprinted the issue a dozen times, progressively covering up Edward's features and selling an unheard-of 250,000 copies.[67]

Despite the new press freedom, the continuing fears that French political elites retained of the "dark masses" was reflected in the maintenance of theater censorship until 1906, although its implementation gradually atrophied after 1875. During the next twenty-five years, fewer than sixty plays intended for the legitimate stage were banned, mostly on moral rather than political grounds, although several others were suppressed after their first performances. The range of acceptable political criticism on the stage broadened considerably compared to past regimes—for example, unflattering accounts of judges, police, soldiers, ministers, and parliamentary life became commonplace. However, as late as 1903 references to the Commune were banned from the stage, and other dramas viewed as exacerbating contemporary political conflicts were occasionally forbidden. For example, the left was offended when Emile Zola's *Germinal* was temporarily banned in 1885 for, as the censors put it, the play's "socialist tendency" and especially for depicting "troops firing at striking miners in revolt," while the right was outraged in 1891 when Victorien Sardou's *Thermidor* was closed on the grounds that it defamed the French Revolution by its depiction of the Reign of Terror.[68]

Rising opposition to drama censorship forced a parliamentary inquiry in 1891, and thereafter furious parliamentary debates regularly ensued. But as late as 1902 the minister of public instruction defended the censorship by telling legislators that "the power of the theater to offend is infinitely greater than that of the book." The legislature finally killed the theater censorship in 1906 via the stage door, so to speak, by refusing to further fund it, acting on a motion by legislator Henry Maret, who declared that "when one wishes to safeguard the advantages of liberty, one must also agree to suffer from its costs."[69]

Even after 1906, local officials were still empowered to stop any theatrical performances deemed immoral or prejudicial to public order. Moreover, even as the curtain fell on the stage censorship, local French authorities simultaneously, and with little challenge, began applying prior censorship to the wildly popular new medium of cinema. They cited as a legal basis an arcane 1790 law authorizing local officials to license "public spectacles" and also an 1884 law giving local police power to ban spectacles that could trouble public order, thereby creating what film historian Richard Abel has termed a "crazy quilt of standards and wild fluctuations in censorship practices" until a standardized and centralized national censorship system was implemented in 1916.[70]

Because the impact of film was considered far greater than that of the stage, whose importance had in any case considerably declined by 1906, and because the much cheaper movies had a far larger and more popular audience, the authorities apparently saw no contradiction in introducing film censorship shortly after terminating theater censorship. In the words of historian Odile Krakovitch, it was the "blossoming cinema which inherited the distrust and the fear, and then the censorship" formerly accorded the stage. The primary original impetus for film censorship appears to have been concern over depictions of sexual and criminal activity. Thus, following a series of local bans on depictions of executions and criminal activities, in 1909 and again in 1913 the French interior ministry instructed officials throughout the country to ban all "representations on the cinema screen of recent crimes" and executions as well as all "public film spectacles of this type, capable of provoking disruptions troubling to order and public tranquillity." But officials also early displayed concern over politically charged films: all films dealing with the Dreyfus Affair were banned after a documentary on the subject touched off riots in 1899 (a restriction lifted only in 1950!), and as international tensions increased on the eve of World War I, in 1913 local officials were urged to ban all portrayals of characters appearing in German uniform.[71]

THE IMPACT OF RESTRICTIONS ON FREEDOM OF EXPRESSION

Nineteenth-century French censorship unquestionably had a major impact on freedom of expression. Thousands of newspapers and other publications were prosecuted or otherwise suffered for their political views during the period, and, as demonstrated above, both the number and circulation of newspapers regularly varied in direct proportion to the harshness of press regulations. The same was true for the stage: following the abolition of theater licensing requirements in 1864, the number of Parisian stages increased from fewer than two dozen to forty-three by 1905. The caricature censors rejected thousands of drawings during the 1820–81 period and about twenty caricature journals were directly suppressed or indirectly forced to close as the result of government repression. Well over a score of caricaturists and their editors, directors, and printers were jailed, and virtually every prominent nineteenth-century French caricaturist was censored, if not prosecuted and imprisoned.[72]

Such gross measures cannot ascertain the effect that the censorship (or, after 1830, fears of post-publication prosecution of the written word) had on writers, dramatists, opera librettists, and caricaturists who did not even attempt to express their true feelings for fear of crossing the authorities. Thus, one journalist lamented that under Napoleon III:

> Obstacles and pitfalls on all sides beset the newspaper and those who wrote for it. Self-censored in the first instance, re-read and corrected with meticulous care by his editor, superintended in the last resort by the printer who was responsible before the law for everything that came off his press, stifled and hamstrung, attracting the thunderbolt and yet tied to the lightning-conductor, seated on the powder-barrel and condemned to strike the tinder-box, the journalist of 1860 was truly a victim tortured by the imperial regime.[73]

Caricature journals similarly lamented and denounced the censorship in the most virulent terms. During the 1870s, *Le Grelot*, a frequent victim of censorship, variously termed it a "worm-eaten and deadly institution," "deplorable, tyrannical and arbitrary," and the "last and odious vestige of customs of another age" that was "as useless for the country as a pair of braces for an elephant." Authors similarly lamented their fate: Alexander Dumas likened theater censors to "customs officers of thought," while Hugo compared the censorship to the Inquisition, terming it a "prison" for writers, which "like the other Holy Office," had its "secret judges, its masked executioners, its tortures and mutilations and its death penalty." When stage censorship was reimposed in 1850 after two years of dramatic freedom, Hugo declared, "It brought sobs to the depths of my heart." Gustave Flaubert, who was famously prosecuted during the Second Empire (on moral grounds) for his novel *Madame Bovary*, termed censorship "a monstrosity, something worse than homicide: attacking thought is a crime of soul destruction (*lèse-amé*)."[74]

Dramatists and caricaturists especially resented their continued subjection to prior censorship long after the written word was freed. Thus, Zola, who compared the drama censors to a "torturer," declared, "Books have been freed, periodicals have been freed. Why is the theater condemned to eternal servitude?" Similarly, the caricature journal *L'Eclipse* declared in 1872 that it was an

> absurd anomaly and a revolting injustice that a writer can vulgarize his thought today in a newspaper without any shackle and the recourse of the law against him can only occur after publication, while an artist, expressing the same idea, is subject to the control of an administrative agent who has the right to suppress that expression before it appears before the public and to condemn behind closed doors, affected only by his caprices, prejudices, and personal rancors, what would under written form probably be absolved in public by judges and jury.

The caricature journal *Le Don Quichotte* lamented in 1875 that the written press "would only be a vast whipped cream factory" if it were subject to the same controls that caricature endured.[75]

THE DEFENSE OF FREEDOM OF EXPRESSION AND RESISTANCE TO REPRESSION

Although French authorities were almost manic in their fears of the consequences of tolerating free expression, its advocates were, at least sometimes, seemingly just as convinced that complete freedom of expression would pave the path to paradise on earth. For example, Hugo termed the theater a "crucible of civilization" and "one of the branches of public instruction" that "forms the public soul" and, if subsidized and uncensored by the state, could reconcile class differences in France as "the rich and poor, the happy and unhappy, the Parisian and the provincial, the French and foreigners will meet each other every night [at the theater], mix their souls fraternally and share in the contemplation of great works of the human spirit."[76]

Advocates of freedom for the written word described similar enormous gains if their goal was attained. When the French newspaper *L'Egalité* was suppressed in 1850, its final headline proclaimed, "Long live freedom of the press, which kills tyrants." Liberal historian Jules Michelet, who was fired twice for political reasons from his teaching position at the College de France, termed the press the "holy ark" of modern times, which fulfilled a "sacred mission," and declared that a free press could bring about the "moral union" of French society, since it was "the universal intermediary" that would allow "the national soul" to circulate. He added, "What a sight, when from the post office, one watches newspapers leave by the thousands, these representatives of diverse opinions, which will carry until the distant frontiers the traditions of the parties, the voices of polemic, harmonizing nevertheless in a certain unity of language and of ideas!"[77]

Although the accessibility of the theater and caricature to the illiterate made them especially feared by the authorities, this same quality enhanced their virtue to their defenders. The prolific melodramatist Guilbert de Pixérécourt declared, "I write for those who cannot read," while the great caricaturist Daumier similarly proclaimed, "Caricatures are good for those who cannot read." Radical republican journalist Jules Valles, a leader of the opposition to Napoleon III, termed caricature a "weapon of the disarmed" that "makes a hole in the wood of idols."[78]

Opponents of nineteenth-century French censorship went far beyond words in fighting it: they also repeatedly defied or evaded it at the risk of suppression of their material, prosecutions, fines, and jail terms. The means by which press, caricature, and theatrical censorship restrictions could be evaded were too numerous and divergent to ever completely catalog, but they can be divided into two basic categories: (1) overt or outright defiance of the censorship regulations, such as publishing a caricature without submitting it for prior censorship approval; and (2) technical evasions, which complied with the letter of the law while subverting its spirit, such as publishing the written text of plays banned from the stage and highlighting censored material, an action that was perfectly legal during the period between 1822 and 1906 when the printed word was freed from prior constraints, but theater censorship continued.

Overt Defiance of Restrictions on Freedom of Expression

One of the most blatant means of outright defiance of censorship was the smuggling of banned publications into France from outside the country. Building on a long history of such methods developed during the prerevolutionary period, this was an extremely common and often highly sophisticated means of defying the censors. For example, during the regime of Napoleon III, opposition literature was smuggled into the country in hollowed-out lumps of coal, in hermetically sealed boxes dropped along the coast of Brittany, and occasionally even in plaster busts of the emperor himself (a technique revealed when one such bust "busted"). Other overt techniques of defiance included publishing material anonymously to avoid prosecution, failing to submit caricatures for censorship approval, and, during periods when prior censorship was not in effect, simply publishing written material and caricatures certain to violate press laws authorizing post-publication prosecutions.

The number of press prosecutions previously discussed suggests that the latter form of offense was extremely common, although, of course, it was always difficult to interpret the vague press laws and thus know for certain what would violate them. For example, during the 1830–35 period when there was no prior caricature censorship, but post-publication prosecutions were still possible for such vague offenses as "provoking hatred and contempt against the government of the King," *La Caricature* was seized about twenty times and was prosecuted on about ten occasions. But on numerous occasions when caricature censorship was in effect, journals simply published drawings without submitting them for approval. Thus, between 1878 and 1881, the right-wing caricature journal *Le Triboulet* carried out a campaign of bitter opposition against the fledging Third Republic through a long series of such "illegal" caricatures for which, as noted above, it was repeatedly harassed and prosecuted.[79]

Evasions and Circumvention of Restrictions on Freedom of Expression

The techniques of evading or circumventing censorship were both far more common and more inventive than those of outright defiance. One such technique was employing so-called "Aesopian language": the expression of political commentary in a form too indirect to violate the press laws, such as disguising political criticism as literary comment or making points about the current regime via superficially camouflaged remarks about another. For example, it was widely seen as more than coincidental that, during the waning days of Charles X, Prosper Mérimée published a "historical" study of the disastrous reign of the sixteenth-century King Charles IX. In perhaps the most famous example of such "Aesopian language" in a caricature journal, in 1867 *La Lune* published a drawing of Emperor Napoleon III in the guise of "Rocambole," the half-dandy, half-convict hero of a series of popular novels; although the drawing, by the leading caricaturist André Gill, seemingly fooled the censors, the emperor's likeness was widely recognized and the caricature thus highlighted his personality similarities to Rocambole. In true "Aesopian" style, caricature journals sometimes used animals as stand-ins for political figures. Thus, *Le Triboulet* announced on April 6, 1879, that since the censors made overt depiction of republican politicians impossible, henceforth "we will disguise them as pigs, donkeys, parakeets, geese"; on August 10, 1879, it published pictures of various animals, with captions along the lines of "[Minister of Public Instruction] Jules Ferry will not see his head in this."[80]

A variety of legal means of evading censorship restrictions involved technical compliance with their letter while undermining their intent. For example, newspapers that had to name "responsible editors" to be held accountable for press violations sometimes hired "editors" who could be jailed without distrupting their operations since they played no real editorial role. Theater censorship laws required the submission of all scripts proposed for public performance for the purpose of monetary gain, but their intent could be evaded by producing plays that were not formally open to the general public or did not charge admission. Toward the end of the nineteenth century, this form of censorship evasion was institutionalized in the form of the so-called "free [of censorship] theaters," where performances were open only to "members" who paid an annual subscription fee or purchased their tickets at another venue. The most famous such "free" theater, the subscription Théâtre Libre of Paris, flourished between 1887 and 1894, attracting over 50,000 subscribers and presenting sixty-two programs with 184 plays.[81]

Another legal means of evading theater censorship laws was the perfectly legal printing of censored plays, often accompanied by bitter denunciations of the censors. The Restoration press delighted in informing its readers exactly which lines had been deleted, sometimes by printing the original lines next to a censored version. When Népomucène Lemercier's play *La Demence de Charles VI* (The Madness of Charles VI), an unflattering portrayal of an insane fourteenth-century French king, was banned from the Odéon theater in 1820 on the personal orders of King Louis XVIII, even the royalist newspaper *Le Drapeu blanc* wrote a sympathetic account, adding that "curious readers" can "buy the play; it is published and sold at the Barba bookstore, Palais-Royal, stone gallery, behind the Théâtre-France, number 51."[82]

It was often quite easy for both audiences and actors to subvert the spirit of the theater censorship by subtle or not-so-subtle performance "alterations" to the approved text. For example, Balzac's play *Vautrin*, which had been cleared by the censors on its fourth revised submission, was banned in 1840 after only one performance because the famous actor Lemaître appeared in a wig that made him resemble King Louis-Philippe. During an 1849 Council of State inquiry into the theater censorship, the well-known actor Bocage recalled how he had subverted the censorship under Louis-Philippe by a simple dramatic pause: his response to a question as to whether his character was generous was, "As the King . . . of Spain." Similarly, café-concert performers imaginatively alluded to material forbidden by the censors "by a game of evocative words, repetitive or frankly absurd, by a comic 'visual code,' a gesture, a cry, a whistle, a game of body language, a mask, a costume or make-up."[83]

Even more frequent than such "alterations" to the approved text by actors were audience interventions by applause or hooting that unexpectedly underlined particular passages and attributed to them unintended political connotations. This form of audience intervention became so common that it was given the name of "making applications," characterized by historian Nicholas Harrison as "a creative act on the part of the audience, pressing words into a political service for which they had not been intended by the playwright." For example, the play *Edward in Scotland*, which dealt with an exiled ruler, was approved by both the Napoleonic and Restoration censors as inoffensive, but in performance was applauded under Bonaparte as a royalist piece sympathetic to the Bourbons and then subsequently hailed as a pro-Bonapartist piece during the Restoration. Under Louis-Philippe, the massive applause that greeted the phrase (referring to a king of Spain) "down with Philippe" in Lemercier's 1834 play *Pinto* led the authorities to close it.[84]

Because the theater censorship bureaucracy was not large enough to attend every performance to ensure that its instructions were obeyed, it was also extremely common for actors to gradually and surreptitiously restore banned material. Theater historian F. W. J. Hemmings notes that under Napoleon III "for the first few performances, the passages that had been blue-penciled would be obediently omitted" but subsequently "cuts would be imperceptibly restored by the players, or the authors would even add new matter that the censor had never seen." Although the censors sometimes tried to monitor performances more closely, at Paris's Porte Saint-Martin Theater when an inspector was sighted the actors would be signaled so that they could revert to the approved text.[85]

Those who sought to evade restrictions on the written word and on caricature also had a large arsenal of tricks. French publishers frequently evaded pre-1820 Restoration press laws that imposed prior censorship on all periodicals—defined as publications that appeared at regular intervals—by printing forbidden material in irregularly published issues, sometimes even with such titles as "censorship rejects." One such journal, *La Minerva française*, announced in its 1818 founding statement that it would publish thirty times in each three-month period, but at "indeterminate intervals," and promised that it could therefore evade the censorship and "if there will be less regularity in our appearance, there will be more frankness in our writing." *The Independent* was suspended three times in 1815, but simply resumed publication each time under a new name. Since the press laws usually required security bonds only from political journals, periodicals frequently attempted to evade payment by hiding political allusions under the guise of literary discussions or other matters. Since verbatim reports of court trials were exempt from prosecution, the *Gazette des Tribunaux* became a key and untouchable element of the Restoration opposition press by giving massive publicity to press prosecutions. One of the most effective techniques of legal resistance to censorship was to print blank spaces to indicate where the censors had deleted material (a technique eventually banned by the Restoration censors). For example, during the strict newspaper censorship regime of 1820–22, the August 9, 1821, issue of *Quotidienne* appeared with the signature of an author at the end of a completely blank column.[86]

The use of blank spaces—either for entire caricatures or only for the forbidden portions of a proposed drawing—was also a very common response of caricature journals, especially since last-minute bans often left them facing press deadlines with no alternative material. Caricature journals often supplemented their blank spaces with perfectly legal often-detailed written descriptions of the forbidden drawings, typically accompanied with a furious denunciation of the government's action. Thus, the June 23, 1872, *Le Grelot* replaced a forbidden caricature with a detailed description of the banned drawing, complete with an indication of exactly where each element of the design would have appeared. On March 3, 1872, the same journal reported a ban (by pro-Bonapartist censors) on a depiction of a dog raising its leg over a mass of discarded symbols representing the fallen regime of Napoleon III. "We have vainly searched the motive of this interdiction," *Le Grelot* solemnly remarked. "It is so difficult to understand the decisions of the censorship."

Both the written and illustrated press took full advantage of the post-1822 freedom of the word to publish frequent written denunciations of the censorship. Caricature journals also often published artistic attacks on the censorship (which, for reasons that are unclear, the censors generally seem to have approved). For example, on November 11, 1875, *Le Sifflet* published a drawing of two censors attempting to shred drawings with their huge scissors, but instead decapitating each other, over the caption, "Terrible Accident!!!" On May 26, 1878, André Gill published in his journal *La Lune Rousse* a drawing of a caricaturist with his arms and legs cut off and his drawing crayon tied behind his back over the caption, "product of the censors."

One of the most bizarre means of resistance to censorship, which sometimes blurred the boundaries between the legal and illegal, was the production of protest art and literature by jailed writers and artists. In general, nonviolent political prisoners were treated with notoriously laxity, especially in the case of those housed in the jocularly named "Pavilion of Princes" section of the Sainte-Pelagie prison in Paris. It was common for journalists expecting to be prosecuted to reserve their favorite cells there, and since they were allowed to pursue their vocations from jail, "It was a preposterous but normal procedure for prisoners to be brought before the courts and charged with fresh press offenses that had been committed while they were still in prison."[87]

Daumier reproduced on his cell wall the very caricature that had led to his imprisonment, while Philipon drew one pear (the symbol he had created to stigmatize King Louis-Philippe) on his wall for each of his days in captivity (indeed, according to a journal published in 1833 by Sainte-Pelagie prisoners, the prison walls were covered with graffiti depicting fruits that were "neither apples, nor cherries, nor peaches, nor apricots"). Charles Gilbert-Martin, the editor and caricaturist of *Le Don Quichotte*, gleefully reported in his memoirs that during his 1868 incarceration he had covered his prison walls with thinly disguised attacks on Napoleon III, but the prison director failed to understand them and delighted in showing them to visitors. Gilbert-Martin wrote that his "comrades, who were in on the secret, hurried to take turns in watching this piquant spectacle of a Bonapartist functionary enraptured by drawings against the Empire crayoned in a state establishment."[88]

SOME CONCLUDING WORDS

For most of the 1815–1914 era, French political censorship unquestionably dampened and retarded the discussion of public affairs and led to the suppression of, collectively, thousands of books, newspapers, caricatures, plays, and songs, and the fining and jailing of hundreds of their contributors and artists. But, just as clearly, at least partly because the censorship often proved porous or incompetent, it could not alone hold back the long-term tides of change, and even in the short run it could never entirely prevent either the circulation of "subversive" ideas or repeated tumults in the streets, which on many occasions threatened and thrice succeeded in toppling regimes (1830, 1848, and 1870). But accurately assessing the impact of the censorship as an independent factor is virtually impossible, because it was invariably intertwined with other forms of control, such as suffrage restrictions and limits on freedom of association, whose stringency typically directly varied with that of the censorship and whose aim was similarly to suppress the forces of change. Thus, whenever censorship was most stringent and effective, as during 1835–47, 1852–67, and 1871–77, it was only one constraining aspect of regimes of multifaceted repression, and although collectively such repression unquestionably substantially contributed to their temporary successes in blocking change, the separate contribution of political censorship simply cannot be assessed with any hope of precision.

If the success of political censorship in nineteenth-century France is difficult to evaluate, the frequent and marked failures of censorship, as pointed out in the discussion of the many ways in which it was defied or evaded, are clear and legion. But it must be stressed that widespread defiance and evasion of censorship only succeeded because there existed a large and receptive population for such efforts. Juries (which were restricted to that tiny percentage of the population wealthy enough to vote before 1848) acquitted in 70 percent of press prosecutions between 1831 and 1833, and in about half of all 1871–1913 prosecutions. The government's attempts to prosecute newspapers into financial ruin during the 1815–35 period were sometimes frustrated by the raising of public subscription funds to pay fines (a practice banned by the 1835 September Laws). When word got out that a publication was being seized or prosecuted, it usually touched off a mad scramble by citizens to try to purchase any remaining available copies, and the resulting court proceedings often led to massive publicity for the prosecuted play or publication. Alexander Dumas *fils* wrote of his experience with his originally banned play *La Dame aux Camélias* that the censorship was not such a bad thing, since all dramas were eventually authorized and a censorship controversy "makes brisker business for us than we could make with our unaided efforts." When the Bordeaux-based caricature journal *Don Quichotte* was repeatedly seized by police in 1877 as it was being distributed, hundreds of hopeful buyers regularly lined up in front of bookstores hoping to buy copies before the police arrived, forcing the stores to barricade their doors to avoid being overrun. Such experiences led the journal *Le Rappel* to declare in 1880 that unauthorized caricature prosecutions simply rendered "cheap advertisement; these journals obtain for [the fine of] 25 francs what they would not have had for a million, enormous publicity in all the journals of the world."[89]

If André Gill became famous for "outfoxing" the censors with caricatures such as his famous "Rocambole" portrait of Napoleon III, he succeeded only because many of his "readers" willingly devoted their time and imagination to deciphering his works. As caricature historian Émile Bayard notes, "Gill's caricature appeared inoffensive; but it was thus only more dangerous, because soon the crowd deciphered an idea which exploded in contempt of all sanction, all censorship."[90] According to *Le Trombinoscope* of April 1882, eventually the censors "got to the point of borrowing from the directory of the observatory the most powerful telescopes to scrutinize" Gill's drawings, while Gill himself, if lacking a subject, "said to himself, smiling, 'I'll make a simple clysopompe [an enema device] with no purpose, but the public will certainly find one.' Often he was wrong, the public found several."

NOTES

(Unless otherwise noted, all French-language books were published in Paris.)

1. Nicholas Harrison, "Colluding with the Censor: Theatre Censorship in France After the Revolution," *Romance Studies*, 25 (1995), 8–9.

2. Odile Krakovitch, "La mise en pièces des théâtres: la censure des spectacles au XIXe siècle" (hereafter Krakovitch, "Mise") in *Maintien de l'ordre et polices en France et en Europe au XIXe siècle* (1987), 299; Krakovitch, "Les Ciseaux d'Anastasie: Le Théâtre au XIXe Siècle" (hereafter Krakovitch, "Ciseaux") in *Censures: de la Bible aux l'armes d'eros* (1987), 56, 63.

3. Kenneth Olson, *The History Makers: The Press of Europe from Its Beginnings through 1965* (Baton Rouge, La., 1966), 156; Frederick Artz, *France under the Bourbon Restoration* (Cambridge, Mass., 1931), 84; Daniel Rader, *The Journalists and the July Revolution in France* (The Hague, 1973), 222.

4. *Archives Parlementaires de 1787 à 1860* (hereafter *AP*), 98 (1898), 257–58 (emphasis in original).

5. *AP*, 98 (1898), 741, 744; Claude Bellanger et al., *Histoire générale de la presse française* (1969), II, 352; Archives Nationales, Paris (hereafter AN), F^{18} 2342.

6. Odile Krakovitch, *Les Pièces de Théâtre soumises a La Censure (1800–1830)* (hereafter Krakovitch, *Pièces*) (1982), 14; Louis Allard, "La Censure Théâtrale Sous La Restauration," *Harvard Studies and Notes in Philology and Literature*, 14 (1932), 201; F. W. J. Hemmings, *The Theatre Industry in Nineteenth-Century France* (hereafter Hemmings, *Theatre Industry*) (Cambridge England, 1993), 113; Victor Hallays-Dabot, *Histoire de censure théatrâle en France* (hereafter Hallays-Dabot, *Histoire*) (1862), 320–21.

7. F. W. J. Hemmings, *Theatre and State in France, 1760–1905* (hereafter Hemmings, *Theatre and State)* (Cambridge, England, 1994), 1.

8. Hemmings, *Theater Industry*, 2; Harold Hobson, *French Theatre Since 1800* (London, 1978), 4–5; Hemmings, *Theater and State*, 1.

9. Odile Krakovitch, "Robert Macaire ou la Grande Peur des Censeurs," *Europe: Revue litteraire mensuelle* (1987), 55–56; Jean-Marie Thomasseau, "Le Melodrama et La Censure sous le Premier Empire et la Restauration," *Revue des sciences humaines*, 162 (1976), 179; Odile Krakovitch, *Hugo Censuré: la liberté au théâtre au XXe siècle* (hereafter Krakovitch, *Hugo*), (1985), 114; Harrison, 12.

10. James Allen, *In the Public Eye: A History of Reading in Modern France* (hereafter Allen, *Public*) (Princeton, N.J., 1991), 94.

11. Krakovitch, *Hugo*, 224–25, 227.

12. Paul Beik, *Louis Phillipe and the July Monarchy* (Princeton, N.J., 1965), 146–47; *AP*, 98 (1898), 257; AN, F^{18} 2342, F^{18} 2363.

13. Krakovitch, *Hugo*, 75.

14. Anthony Smith, *The Newspaper: An International History* (London, 1979), 110, Irene Collins, *The Government and the Newspaper Press in France, 1814–1881* (Oxford, 1959), 129, 178; Hemmings, *Theatre and State*, 260–70, 150, 178, 188–89; Jean-Pierre Aguet, "Remarques sur les Procès Intentes à la Presse Périodique Française sous la Monarchie de Juillet," *Cahiers Vilfredo Pareto*, 22–23 (1970), 67–68; Ted Margadant, *French Peasants in Revolt: The Insurrection of 1851* (Princeton, N.J., 1979), 214; John Merriman, *The Agony of the Republic: The Repression of the Left in Revolutionary France, 1848–1851* (hereafter Merriman, *Agony)* (New Haven, Conn., 1978), 31, 39; Stephen Atkins, "Repression and the Printing Press in Nineteenth-Century France," *Proceedings of the Annual Meeting of the Western Society for French History*, 12 (1984), 164–72.

15. Allard, 199–200.

16. F. W. J. Hemmings, *Culture and Society in France, 1848–1898* (hereafter Hemmings, *Culture*) (London, 1971), 48–49.

17. Krakovitch, "Mise," 289; Hemmings, *Theatre and State*, 163.

18. Hemmings, *Culture*, 53; Henri Avenal, *Histoire de la press française depuis 1789 jusqu'à nos jours* (1900), 262.

19. David Pottinger, *The French Book Trade in the Ancien Regime* (Cambridge, Mass., 1958), 56, 64; John Lough, *Writer and Public in France: From the Middle Ages to the Present Day* (Oxford, 1978), 75, 173.

20. Pottinger, 56, 64; Lough, 75, 174; René de Livois, *Histoire de la Presse Française*, I (Lausanne, 1965), 64; Robert Justin Goldstein, *Censorship of Political Caricature in Nineteenth-Century France* (hereafter Goldstein, *Censorship*) (Kent, Ohio, 1989), 90.

21. Pottinger, 77–79.

22. Hemmings, *Theatre and State*, 61.

23. Clyde Thogmartin, *The National Daily Press of France* (Birmingham, Ala., 1998), 39.

24. Stephen Atkins, "Restoration Policies Toward Books and Pamphlets, 1814–1830," *Proceedings of the Annual Meeting of the Western Society for French History*, 13 (1986), 153–62.

25. Maryse Maget-Dodominici, "La 'Loi de Justice et d'Amour' ou la Liberté de la Presse," *Revue Suisse d'Histoire*, 40 (1990), 1; Alan Spitzer, *The French Gen-*

eration of 1820 (Princeton, N.J., 1987), 255; Françoise Parent-Lardeur, *Les Cabinets de lecture: La lecture publique à Paris sous la Restauration* (1982), 165, 180; Isabelle de Conihout, "La Restauration: contrôle et liberté," in *Histoire de l'édition française*, II (1983), 539; Pierre Casselle, "Le régime législatif," in *Histoire de l'édition française*, III (1985), 48.

26. James Allen, *Popular French Romanticism: Authors, Readers and Books in the 19th Century* (Syracuse, N.Y., 1981), 184; Bellanger, II, 7, 57.

27. W. Scott Haine, *The World of the Paris Café* (Baltimore, Md., 1996), 26.

28. Avenal, 258; Bellanger, II, 7, 57.

29. De Livois, I, 195; Maget-Dodominici, 8.

30. Rader, 193, 251.

31. Claude Gevell and Jean Rabot, "La Censure Théâtrale sous la Restauration," *Revue de Paris*, 120 (1913), 339, 343, 351; Spitzer, 253; Thomasseau, 178, 180; Allard, p. 205; Krakovitch, *Hugo*, 36.

32. Allard, 208; Gevel and Rabot, 358; Anselm Gerhard, "La 'Libérté' inadmissible à l'Opéra," *Avant-Scene Opéra* (November 1989), 70–71; Jacqueline de Jomaron, *Le théâtre en France*, II (1989), 39.

33. Barbara Day-Hickman, *Napoleonic Art: Nationalism and the Spirit of Rebellion in France (1815–1848)* (Newark, Del., 1999), 34, 151; AN F^{18} 2342.

34. John Merriman, "Contested Freedoms in the French Revolutions, 1830–1871," in Isser Woloch, ed., *Revolution and the Meanings of Freedom in the Nineteenth Century* (Stanford, Calif., 1996), 179.

35. Aguet, 63–75; Jeremy Popkin, "Press and 'Counter-Discourse' in the Early July Monarchy," in Dean de la Motte and J. Przyblyski, *Making the News: Modernity and the Mass Press in Nineteenth-Century France* (Amherst, Mass., 1999), 17–18; De Livois, I, 218.

36. Howard Vincent, *Daumier and His World* (Evanston, Ill., 1968), 15; Paul Thureau-Dangin, *Histoire de la Monarchie de Juillet* (1888), 575–76; Heinrich Heine, *French Affairs* (London, 1893), 331, 412.

37. Goldstein, *Censorship*, 133.

38. Edward Hopkins, *Theater and State in France, 1789–1914* (Master's Thesis, University of Virginia, 1978), 29; Alberic Cahuet, *La Liberté du Théâtre en France et à l'Etranger* (1992), 203.

39. J. L. Talmon, *Romanticism and Revolt: Europe, 1815–1848* (New York, 1967), 74.

40. Aguet, 67–70; Paul Joblin, "Daumier's Orang-Outaniania," *Print Quarterly*, 10 (1993), 233, 244; Avenal, 362.

41. Krakovitch, *Hugo*, 88, 286–87; Concetta Condemi, *Les Cafés-Concerts* (1992), 24; Eva Kimminich, "Chansons étouffées: Recherche sur le café-concert au XIXe siècle," *Politix*, 14 (1991).

42. Krakovitch, *Hugo*, 155, 286–87.

43. Ibid., 130, 141, 153, 165.

44. Hallays-Dabot, *Histoire*, 319.

45. Michael Driskel, "Singing 'The Marseillaise' in 1840: The Case of Charlet's Censored Prints," *Art Bulletin*, 59 (1987), 603–25.

46. William Cleland, *Political Caricature During the July Monarchy* (Ph.D. dissertation, University of Washington, 1973), 200.

47. Merriman, *Agony*, 3, 36; Margadant, 214; Collins, 105, 109; Bellanger, II, 237.

48. Avenal, 432–33; Casselle, 50; Jean-Jacques Darmon, *Le Colportage de Librairie en France sous le Second Empire* (1972), 103, 105; Claire Pourrat, *Le colporteur et la mercière* (Paris, 1982), 254–55.

49. Victor Hallays-Dabot, *La Censure Dramatique et le Théâtre, 1850–1870* (hereafter Hallays-Dabot, *Censure*) (1871), 7; Cahuet, 217; Gay Manifold, *George Sand's Theatre Career* (Ann Arbor, Mich., 1985), 77.

50. Maurice Mauron, *La Marseillaise* (1968), 161–64.

51. Avenal, 449; Collins, 117–26; Caselle, 53; Patrick Laharie, *Contrôle de la Presse, de la Librairie et du Colportage sous le Second Empire* (1995), xx.

52. Roger Bellet, *Presse et Journalism sous le Second Empire* (1967), 5, 13–14, 25, 82; Bellanger, II, 252, 316; Phillip Spencer, "Censorship by Imprisonment in France, 1830–1870," *Romanic Review*, 47 (1956), 27.

53. Krakovitch, *Hugo*, 224; Cahuet, 225.

54. Neil Carruthers, "Theatrical Censorship in Paris from 1850 to 1905," *New Zealand Journal of French Studies*, 3 (1982), 22; Angela Pao, *The Orient of the Boulevards: Exoticism, Empire and Nineteenth-Century French Theater* (Philadelphia, 1998), 75; Krakovitch, *Hugo*, 241.

55. Harrison, 13.

56. Odile Krakovitch, "La Censure des Spectacles sous le Second Empire" (hereafter Krakovitch, "Censure") in Pascal Orly, ed., *La Censure en France a l'ère démocratique* (1997), 71–72.

57. Darmon, 108; Laurence Fontaine, *History of Pedlars in Europe* (Cambridge, England, 1986), 169; *Journal Officiel de la République Française* (hereafter *JO*) (1878), 4015–16, 4043; Lough, 285.

58. *JO* (1878), 4019, 4042, 4046, 4047, 4048; Fontaine, 169.

59. Philippe Jones, "La Libérté de la caricature en France au XIXe siècle," *Syntheses*, 4 (1960), 226.

60. Goldstein, *Censorship*, 180, 183; Elizabeth Childs, "The Secret Agents of Satire: Daumier, Censorship and the Image of the Exotic in Political Caricature, 1850–1860," *Proceedings of the Annual Meeting of the Western Society for French History*, 17 (1990), 334–45.

61. Casselle, 53; Goldstein, *Censorship*, 9, 185; Bellanger, II, 347; Bellet, 279; Philip Nord, *The Republican Moment: Struggles for Democracy in Nineteenth-Century France* (Cambridge, Mass., 1995), 130.

62. Avenal, 711; *JO* (1878), 4042; Krakovitch, *Hugo*, 249; Hopkins, 52.

63. Josette Parrain, "Censure, Théâtre, et Commune (1871–1914)," *Mouvement Social*, 79 (1972) 330; Krakovitch, *Hugo*, 249; Condemi, 39; Krakovitch, "Censure," 71–72, 77; Fernand Drujon, *Catalogue des ouvrages, écrits et dessins de toute nature poursuivis, supprimés ou condamnés depuis le 21 Octobre 1814 jusqu'au 31 Juillet 1879* (1879), xxix–xxxi; Goldstein, *Censorship*, 206.

64. Goldstein, *Censorship*, 206; *JO* (1878), 4042; Avenal, 749.

65. Philippe Jones, "La presse satirique illustré entre 1860 et 1890," *Etudes de Presse*, 8 (1956).

66. Jacques Lethève, *La caricature et la presse sous la IIIe Republique* (1961), 241–50; Georges Dupeux, *French Society, 1789–1970* (London, 1976), 158.

67. Goldstein, *Censorship*, 250–57; Raymond Bacollet, "Satire, censure et pro-

pagande, ou le destin de l'impudique Albion," *Le Collectionneur Français*, 174 (December 1980), 14–15; 176 (February 1981), 15–16.

68. Parrain, 338; Allen, *Public*, 102; Lawson Carter, *Zola and the Theater* (New Haven, Conn., 1963), 137.

69. Krakovitch, *Hugo*, 264.

70. Richard Abel, *French Cinema* (Princeton, N.J., 1984), 38.

71. Krakovitch, *Pièces*, 38; Jean Bancal, *La Censure Cinématographique* (1934), 79–81.

72. Goldstein, *Censorship*, 12, 23; Lough, 339.

73. Hemmings, *Culture*, 55.

74. *Le Grelot*, November 5, 1971, November 31, 1875, December 15, 1878, September 28, 1879; Allard, 198; Barry Daniels, *Revolution in the Theater: French Romantic Theories of Drama* (Westport, Conn., 1983), 193; Krakovitch, *Hugo*. 43, 69, 219; Roger Berthet, *Anastasie, Anastasie: Groupement de textes sur la censure* (Reims, 1992), 18.

75. Carter, 141; *L'Eclipse*, November 26, 1871; *Le Don Quichotte*, June 25, 1875.

76. Krakovitch, *Hugo*, 29, 216–17.

77. Merriman, *Agony*, 39; Stephen Kippur, *Jules Michelet* (Albany, N.Y., 1981), 116, 119.

78. Krakovitch, "Mise," 287; Goldstein, *Censorship*, 32.

79. Ibid., 133–41, 226–27.

80. Charles Fontane, *André Gill: Un maître de la caricature* (1927): I, 37; II, 224.

81. See Anna Miller, *The Independent Theater in Europe* (New York, 1931).

82. Barbara Cooper, "Censorship and the Double Portrait of Disorder in Lemercier's *La Démence de Charles VI*," *Orbis Litteratum*, 40 (1985), 300, 306.

83. Krakovitch, *Hugo*, 84–85, 87; Condemi, 57.

84. Harrison, 16; Krakovitch, *Hugo*, 55.

85. Hemmings, *Culture*, 50.

86. Avenal, 250; Charles Ledré, *La Presse a l'Assault de la Monarchie, 1815–1848* (1960), 18.

87. Spencer, 36.

88. Roger Passeron, *Daumier* (Secaucus, N.J., 1981), 68; *Le Don Quichotte*, July 16, 1887.

89. Roberts-Jones, 23; Bellanger, III, 155, 157, 246; Casselle, 53; Hemmings, *Culture*, 49; Goldstein, *Censorship*, 50.

90. Émile Bayard, *La caricature et les caricaturistes* (1990), 180, 183.

BIBLIOGRAPHICAL ESSAY

(Note: All French-language books were published in Paris.)

A good introduction to nineteenth-century French history is Roger Magraw, *France, 1815–1914: The Bourgeois Century* (Oxford, 1983). Studies that cover censorship of a variety of media in nineteenth-century France (as well as other time periods) include Louis Gabriet-Robinet, *La Censure* (1965); Maxime Drury, *La Censure* (1995); and Pascal Orly, ed., *La Censure en France a l'ère démocratique: 1848–* (1997). In English, information about a wide variety of media is included (by media rather than by country) in Robert Justin Goldstein, *Political Censorship of the Arts and the Press in Nineteenth-Century Europe* (New York, 1989). On resistance to censorship see, by the same author, "Fighting French Censorship, 1815–1881," *French Review*, 71 (1998), 785–96. There is brief coverage of press and theater censorship in John and Muriel Lough, *An Introduction to Nineteenth-Century France* (London, 1978) and in James Allen, *In the Public Eye: A History of Reading in Modern France, 1800–1940* (Princeton, N. J., 1991). Chapters related to limited aspects of press and caricature censorship are included in Dean de la Motte and Jeannene Przyblyski, *Making the News: Modernity and the Mass Press in Nineteenth-Century France* (Amherst, Mass., 1999).

Irene Collins, *The Government and the Newspaper Press in France, 1815–1881* (Oxford, 1959) is the leading press study. Sketchier but still helpful is Clyde Thogmartin, *The National Daily Press of France* (Birmingham, Ala., 1998). A useful specialized source is Daniel Rader, *The Journalists and the July Revolution in France* (The Hague, 1973). The standard French source for the press is the multivolume *Histoire générale de la press française*, Claude Bellanger et al., eds. (1969–72), and, for books, the multivolume *Histoire de l'édition française* (1982–84). Henri Avenal, *Histoire de la press française depuis 1789 jusqu'à nos jours* (1900) is still valuable, as are several specialized studies: Roger Bellet, *Presse et Journalism sous le Second Empire* (1967); Charles Ledré, *La Presse à l'Assault de la Monarchie, 1815–1848* (1960); Françoise Parent-Lardeur, *Les Cabinets de lecture* (1982); and Jean-Jacques Darmon, *Le Colportage de Librairie en France sous le Second Empire* (1972).

The only comprehensive source for caricature censorship is Robert Justin Goldstein, *Censorship of Political Caricature in Nineteenth-Century France* (Kent, Ohio, 1989), which is summarized in "The Debate over Censorship of Caricature in Nineteenth-Century France," *Art Journal*, 48 (Spring 1989), 9–15; and in "Censorship of Caricature in France, 1815–1914," *French History*, 3 (1989), 71–107. For the 1830s, see also Edwin Bechtel, *Freedom of the Press and L'Association Mensuelle: Philipon versus Louis-Philippe* (New York, 1952); Elise Kenney and John Merriman, *The Pear: French Graphic Arts in the Golden Age of Caricature* (South Hadley, Mass., 1991); and James Cuno, "The Business and Politics of Caricature: Charles Philipon and La Maison Aubert," *Gazette des Beaux-Arts* (1985), 95–112. For studies of leading caricaturists, see Roger Passeron, *Daumier* (Secaucus, N. J., 1981); Elizabeth Childs, "The Body Impolitic: Censorship and the Caricature of Honoré Daumier," in Childs, ed., *Suspended License: Censorship and the Visual Arts* (Seattle, Wash., 1997); and Robert Justin Goldstein, "André Gill and the Struggle Against Censorship of Caricature in France, 1867–1879," *Journalism History*, 21 (1995), 146–55. In French, for the post-1860 period see Philippe Robert-Jones, *De Daumier à Lautrec: Essai sur l'histoire de la caricature française entre 1860 et 1890* (1960); and Jacques Lethève, *La caricature et la presse sous la IIIe République* (1961). Charles Fontane, *André Gill: Un maître de la caricature* (1927) and Elisabeth and Michel Dixler's *L'Assiette au Beurre* are fine studies of, respectively, the most important caricaturist and the most outstanding caricature journal of the post-1860 period.

For theatrical (including opera) censorship, the leading work is Odile Krakovitch, *Hugo Censuré: La liberté au théâtre au XIXe siècle* (1985), summarized in "La mise en pièces des théâtres: la censure des spectacles au XIXe siècle," in *Maintien de l'ordre et polices en France et en Europe au XIXe siècle*, (1987), 58–67; and in "Les Ciseaux d'Anastasie: Le Théâtre au XIXe Siècle," in *Censures: de la Bible aux l'armes d'eros* (1987). Other indispensable French studies include Alberic Cahuet, *La Liberté du Théâtre en France et a l'Etranger* (1992); and two volumes by theater censor Victor Hallays-Dabot: *La Censure Dramatique et le Théâtre, 1850–1870* (1871) and *Histoire de censure théatrâle en France* (1862). In English, John McCormick, *Popular Theaters of Nineteenth-Century France* (London, 1993); and F. W. J. Hemmings, *Theatre and State in France, 1760–1905* (Cambridge, England, 1994) both have lengthy chapters on censorship. Concetta Condemi, *Les Cafés-Concerts* (1992) covers controls imposed on that venue. For film censorship, see Jean Bancal, *La Censure Cinématographique* (1934); and Neville Hunnings, *Film Censors and the Law* (London, 1967), 332–38.

5

Spain

Adrian Shubert

Spain's nineteenth-century political history was marked by instability, repeated military coups, and civil wars. The Napoleonic invasion set the stage for a war of independence that was also a civil war that pitted supporters of ancien regime absolutism against advocates of a constitutional monarchy. The emergency situation created by the invasion and then the forced abdication of Charles IV and Ferdinand VII led to the summoning of the Cortes, the long-dormant medieval assembly. This parliament, known as the Cortes of Cádiz, turned out to be dominated by liberals who created the Constitution of 1812, Spain's first written constitution and one of the most influential political documents of early nineteenth-century Europe. However, the constitution and the other revolutionary changes mandated by the Cortes, such as the abolition of the seigneurial system and the abolition of the Inquisition, were annulled by Ferdinand VII when he was restored to the throne in 1814 following the expulsion from Spain of Napoleon's armies.

Ferdinand sought to restore the absolutist monarchy of the eighteenth century, but even his highly repressive regime was unable to remove the opposition, especially among liberal army officers. There were a series of unsuccessful military uprisings, known as *pronunciamientos*, before the revolt led by Colonel Rafael de Reigo in January 1820 brought back the Constitution of 1812. This second constitutional experiment was short-lived; undermined by conflicts between moderates and radicals, the "Liberal triennium" was brought to an end in 1823 by a French invasion that again restored Ferdinand. The next ten years, until Ferdinand's death, was another period of absolutist reaction known as the "ominous decade." Ferdinand died without a male heir. Before his death he had revoked the Salic Law, the rule of the Bourbon family that prohibited women from inheriting the throne, so that his young daughter, Isabella, could succeed him. However, this did not prevent his brother, Carlos, from pressing his claim. This dynastic dispute became the occasion for the Carlist War—a civil war between absolutists, who backed Carlos, and liberals, who supported Isabella II—which lasted from 1833 to 1840.

Isabella II and the liberals won, but the liberals themselves remained divided. The struggles between Moderates and Progressives, successors to the moderates and radicals of the previous decade, produced severe political instability that continued well after the end of the war. Progressives advocated a wider franchise than the Moderates, although one still firmly tied to property qualifications; they were also more firmly committed to doctrinaire economic liberalism and were more vigorous in their attack on the power of the Church. Progressives also accepted the legitimacy of the tradition of revolution, which the Moderates did not. The Progressives came to power in 1836 and created a new constitution to replace the Royal Statute which, modeled on the French Constitution of 1814, had been granted by Ferdinand's widow, María Cristina, in 1834. An 1843 military revolt brought to power the Moderates, who created their own constitution in 1845. The Moderates used a highly restrictive suffrage, electoral fraud, and repression to remain in power until they were overthrown in July 1854 by a military revolt led by Progressive general and former regent Baldomero Espartero. Another coup ended this "liberal biennium" in the summer of 1856, before the new constitution could be approved. The Constitution of 1845 was brought back, but Spain was governed for a few years by the Liberal Union, a new party led by a former Progressive, General Leopoldo O'Donnell.

By the 1860s the Moderates were back, but their increasingly repressive rule provoked a series of military revolts that eventually produced the successful "Glorious" Revolution of 1868 and the abdication of Isabella II. The *Gloriosa* opened a period of extreme instability and renewed civil war known as the "revolutionary six years." A new constitution was proclaimed in 1869 and the following year, after a lengthy search, Amodeo of Savoy (Italy) was chosen to be the new king. But Amodeo abdicated in February 1873 and Spain became a republic for the first time. The new regime had to deal with a new Carlist uprising as well as revolts by extreme federalists in the south, who created short-lived autonomous cantons. A military revolt in December 1874 put the First Republic out of its misery and proclaimed Isabella's son the new monarch as Alfonso XII. The main concern of Antonio Cánovas del Castillo, the politician who dominated the "Restoration" (as the period after 1874 is known), was to create a stable parliamentary system on the British model. The new Constitution of 1876, which remained in force until 1923, was a conscious compromise designed to convince liberals to accept the new regime. When they did, Cánovas institutionalized the most cynical forms of electoral manipulation in order to achieve a so-called *turno pacifico* (peaceful alternation) in power between his Conservative Party and the Liberals, heirs to the Progressives of Isabella's reign. Cánovas also sought to bring to an end the frequent military revolts that had been so characteristic of Spain's political life since 1815, a feat he achieved at the price of turning the military ministries over to senior officers.

Despite this turbulent political history, Spain enjoyed significant economic growth during the nineteenth century. Agriculture expanded and landowners developed export-oriented crops, such as citrus fruits and, above all, wine. There was also industrial development, including the early industrialization of textiles in Catalonia, but throughout the nineteenth century Spanish industry remained concentrated on a few, limited foci, such as iron, steel, and shipbuilding in the Basque Provinces and coal in Asturias. Moreover, neither economic growth nor the institutional changes of the 1830s liberal revolution, including the disentailment and sale of Church and municipal lands, did much to alleviate tremendous social inequalities. This was especially true in the rural south, where an agricultural world polarized between the owners of large landed estates and a mass of underemployed landless laborers produced frequent explosions of violent protest.

The "social question," as it came to be called in the 1870s, was a constant preoccupation of Spanish elites and was reflected in both the censorship laws and the suffrage. Although the Constitution of 1812 had instituted universal male suffrage, subsequent constitutions reduced this drastically. Under the Constitution of 1837 the right to vote was limited to about 3 percent of the population; the Constitution of 1845 reduced this to only 1 percent. By the 1860s, eligible voters constituted 2.6 percent of the population, and in the early years of the Restoration the suffrage was enjoyed by 6 percent. In 1890 the Liberal government of Práxedes Sagasta introduced universal male suffrage and this remained in place for the remainder of the constitutional monarchy.

Cánovas's system worked well until the end of the century. Spain's humiliating defeat in the Spanish-American War of 1898, increasing industrialization and urbanization, and the consequent emergence of new political movements that refused to play by the rules of the Restoration—Socialists, Radicals, Republicans, Catalan Regionalists, and anarchists—produced renewed political instability. With the deaths of Cánovas, who was assassinated in 1897, and of Sagasta, his liberal counterpart, in 1903, the two ruling parties began to fragment. The system survived, although it relied on more blatant forms of electoral fraud and had to confront more serious threats. In Barcelona and across the rural south there was outright class warfare during the "bolshevik triennium" of 1917 to 1920. Although a 1923 military coup abolished constitutional government and installed the country's first real military dictatorship, it could not resolve Spain's political probems, and after a coalition of Republicans and Socialists won the municipal elections of April 1931, King Alfonso XIII abdicated and the Second Republic was proclaimed. The new regime, an unprecedented attempt to democratize political life and carry out pressing social reform, was killed in the summer of 1936 by a military revolt that initiated the Spanish Civil War.[1]

NINETEENTH-CENTURY CENSORSHIP: AN OVERVIEW

Censorship legislation during the nineteenth century was abundant, diverse, and contradictory, and thus faithfully mirrored the country's turbulent political history as censorship laws changed repeatedly and frequently along with governments and even regimes. There was only one constant: with the sole exception of the revolutionary interlude of 1868–74, there was always censorship of some kind. The Spanish story did not feature progressive lightening of the chains of censorship. Rather it was more the opposite: the freedom from censorship enshrined in the 1812 Constitution suffered repeated and increasingly serious amputations over the course of the century. In part this was the result of the prolonged struggle between liberalism and absolutism, which the liberals finally won during the 1833–40 Carlist War. But another, substantial, part was due to the liberals themselves, to the struggle between moderates and progressives, which was resolved only in 1876 with the Restoration settlement and its severe restrictions on freedom of expression.

Finally, there was the pressure exerted by two powerful institutions, the Church and the army, which felt there was too much freedom available in Spain, even when it was not especially extensive. One of the key elements of the 1830s liberal revolution was the assertion of state power over other institutions, especially the Catholic Church. The liberal redefinition of the Church's place was wide-ranging and included the abolition of the Inquisition and the assumption by the state of all censorship powers. The Church did not accept these changes happily, nor did it resign itself to a reduced position, but instead did everything possible to reclaim its role as the nation's moral arbiter. In the Spanish case—and in others—morality cannot be easily separated from politics when it comes to censorship. The very question of who had the legitimate right to censor was an eminently political one that went to the heart of the great political changes of the nineteenth century.

The liberal state and the Church eventually reached an understanding that was embodied in the Concordat of 1851. In return for the Church's recognizing the legitimacy of the sale of its lands and other concessions, the state recognized Catholicism as the official religion and promised that all education would conform to Catholic beliefs. In the years following the Concordat, Church authorities repeatedly appealed to government officials to ban works they considered offensive to the faith.[2]

Although military intervention in politics was a constant during the nineteenth century, it was only at the very end of the century that the army began to demand more thorough censorship. Smarting from the "Disaster" of the Spanish-American War, and facing a growing regionalist movement that it saw as a threat to the nation's integrity, the army became increasingly restive. When the government refused to censor Catalan regionalist publications that printed cartoons that military men considered offensive, officers took matters into their own hands.

The censors' concerns remained consistent throughout the century. There were three main targets, but in the eyes of contemporary authorities they were all closely connected. The first was attacks on the political system, including political figures and especially the monarch and the royal family. The second was religion. Even though the Church–state conflict was one of the central features of Spain's nineteenth-century history, Catholicism always remained a favored or state religion and the liberal state was never prepared to allow it to be treated with contempt. (This did not mean, however, that the two agreed on what should be censored or that the state did whatever the Church asked.) The third concern was morality, or what contemporaries called *las buenas costumbres* (good customs). These were the bedrock of the social order, and any cracks in its foundations were perceived as deeply threatening. As the royal order that renewed theater censorship in 1856 put it, "Once again plays of perverse social tendencies and deadly moral teaching have taken control of the Spanish theater" and it was the responsibility of the government to "exile from the stage those works which, by perverting customs, cause a deep wound by attacking the foundations on which society rests."[3]

Books and the Printed Press

Regulation under Absolutist Rule. Spanish censorship of published material dates to 1502, when Ferdinand and Isabella decreed that no book could be published without royal authorization. The Catholic Church had its own, separate censorship process, embodied in the Index of Printed Matter that was deemed unsuitable for the faithful to read. With the French Revolution, the long-standing constraints on the press became much more severe. In 1789 the government banned "satires, or things that attack the honor of individuals or groups, and direct allusions to the actions of the government and its officials," while the chief minister, the Count of Floridablanca, called on the Inquisition to attack all writing that contained revolutionary ideas "opposed to the subordination, obedience and reverence towards our venerated monarch, the Vicar of Jesus Christ."[4] The government also prohibited engravings that depicted events in France. Two years later, Charles IV prohibited all periodicals except the two official ones, the *Gaceta* and the *Mercurio*, as well as the semiofficial *Diario de Madrid*.

During the eighteenth century the press had been subject to censorship from a number of different authorities: the Crown, Council of Castile (analogous to the cabinet), the Council of the Indies (which handled the affairs of the American empire), the *audiencias* (royal courts), the bishops, and the Inquisition. After a number of attempts to establish better coordination, in April 1805 the Crown created a special office, the *Juez de Imprentas* (Print Judge), which was given exclusive authority over "all matters dealing with printing and book stores." The authorities were very concerned about foreign, especially French, books that were still entering the country. Their concerns, as expressed in a royal decree, again reflected the interconnectedness of religion, morality, and politics that was so characteristic of Spain during much of the nineteenth century: "The abuse of freedom of the press that has been and is still committed in many foreign countries, with grave harm to Religion, good customs, public tranquillity and the legitimate rights of Princes, demands efficient measures to prevent that such works and the evil they cause are introduced and spread through my dominions." Beyond these areas, censors were also to prohibit works that contained "infamous libels, satires against individuals or calumnies against any individual or corporation." The only type of publication that was left outside the responsibilities of the new official was granting permission for the publication of new newspapers, which was retained by the Crown "for just motives."[5]

Despite its comprehensiveness, the new system was not much more effective than its predecessors. Conflicts between jurisdictions remained, as the *juez de imprentas*, Abbot Juan Antonio Melón, had continual problems with the ecclesiastical authorities, the Vicar of Madrid, and the Inquisition, as well as with the Crown and the ministers. Melón sought to have novels banned because they "are not only a waste of time but excite the passions, putting the reader in an imaginary world and causing great corruption, especially among young women," but he received the noncommittal response that he could prohibit novels that might corrupt proper customs. Moreover, Melón was not given the budget to pay his censors and had to "be satisfied with sending works to be censored to those private individuals whose judgment he trusted." Melón himself was unable to collect his salary for three years.[6]

The French invasion and the popular rising against the French in May 1808 led to de facto freedom of the press as the press judge was overwhelmed by a flood of pamphlets and newspapers. On November 10, 1810, the Cortes of Cádiz sought to help rally opposition to the French by issuing a decree abolishing prior censorship and establishing freedom of the press, except for religious topics. The Cortes declared that "the ability of citizens to publish their political thoughts and ideas is not only a brake against the arbitrary actions of government but also a means to educate the nation at large and the only means of discovering true public opinion." The decree also established a Supreme Censorship Committee and similar provincial bodies to deal with infractions. The Supreme Committee had nine members, of whom five had to be clergy. In July 1813 the Cortes defined press abuses as consisting of "any printed work that conspires directly to incite the people to sedition." The principle of press liberty was formally proclaimed in Article 371 of the 1812 Constitution: "All Spaniards have the freedom of writing, printing and publishing their political ideas without the need of license, revision or any approval previous to publication, subject to restrictions and responsibility by law."[7]

Press freedom, along with the Constitution of 1812 and everything else that the Cortes of Cádiz had done, was abolished by Ferdinand VII immediately upon his restoration in May 1814. Ferdinand returned to the system that had existed before 1808, so that nothing could be published without prior government approval. In April 1815 he issued a decree again prohibiting all periodicals except the *Diario de Madrid* and the official *Gaceta*. He declared:

> Having seen that . . . instead of using freedom of the press for matters that serve the healthy education of the public or its honest entertainment, it is used in personal attacks that offend not only the people against whom they are directed but also the dignity and decorum of a circumspect nation . . . and totally convinced that the worst offenders are those writings known as periodicals, and some pamphlets provoked by them, I have decided to prohibit all of them that are published in [Madrid] and outside it.[8]

Even the possession of liberal periodicals published between 1808 and 1814 was outlawed and subjected to fine and excommunication. Such extreme measures had their effect: one British visitor described the Spanish press as full of weather reports and "accounts of miracles wrought by different Virgins, lives of holy friars and sainted nuns, romances of marvelous conversions, libels against Jews, heretics and Freemasons and histories of apparitions."[9]

The military rebellion of January 1820 led to the restoration of the Constitution of 1812 and the return of press freedom. On November 5, the Cortes passed a new press law that, while similar in general outline to its predecessor of 1810, was much more detailed, especially in defining types of outlawed material. These "criminal writings" included "attacks on the State or the actual Constitution of the monarchy," incitement to rebellion, direct encouragement to disobey the laws, obscenities, and libels against the personal honor or reputation of individuals. Punishments ranged from one month in prison and a fine of 500 *reales* (about $30) to six years in prison. The law's most significant innovation was the introduction of jury trials for press offenses, which had previously been decided by special judges.

French military intervention destroyed the constitutional regime in 1823. Ferdinand quickly abolished freedom of the press, as he had in 1814, and once more prohibited the publication of any newspapers except the *Gaceta* and the *Diario de Madrid*. There was some thawing toward the end of Ferdinand's reign: Mariano Jose de Larra's *El duende satírico del día* began publishing in 1828, and in July 1830 there was an attempt to create a set of general regulations for all published material. This included prior censorship of anything relating to religious topics and anything critical of "good customs, legal practices, and the form of government" as well as satires and insults against the authorities. The penalties varied in accordance with the "greater or lesser degree of malice of the author," and included the death penalty for *lèse-majesté*.[10]

The censorship system was highly inefficient, as the request by one Gregorio Morales Pantoja for permission to publish a translation of Sir Walter Scott's *Ivanhoe* in 1830 demonstrates. The manuscript was sent from one government office to the Council of Castile, which sent it to the Royal Academy of History, which returned it—and other books—with the comment that they did not "contain material relevant to this institution." The Council then sent it to the Ecclesiastical Vicar of Madrid, who twice refused to take responsibility for censoring anything. This, he claimed, was the role of the professional censor, not of the ordinary, individual Christian: "As a subject of Your Majesty, I would readily say that Ivanhoe should not be published, but any decision of mine would necessarily carry the lack of confidence proper for someone who does not consider his judgment infallible . . . the person who is not a censor by trade should state his principles and defer to superior judgment, which should reach a decision based on many opinions what cannot be decided by a single vote." In the end *Ivanhoe* was denied permission, largely because of its negative portrayal of Catholicism and the clergy.[11]

Press Regulation in Liberal Spain, 1833–75. Following Ferdinand's death in 1833, the very limited liberal regime of the Royal Statute recognized the freedom to publish about the sciences, arts, crafts, and administrative-economic matters without prior censorship, although periodicals dealing with religious or political questions were still subject to prior censorship. The law of July 1, 1834, created the "responsible editor" for periodicals. Taken from French legislation, this personage, who bore the legal liability for whatever the periodical might publish, would be a fixture in Spain for most of the rest of the century. Under the 1834 law, the responsible editor had to meet the extremely restrictive franchise qualifications that enfranchised less than 1 percent of the population. The law also demanded that publishers of all periodicals post a bond of 20,000 *reales* in Madrid and 10,000 in the provinces. This too would be a constant for most of the rest of the century. Policing of periodicals was done by specially designated press censors who, until 1836, also had responsibility for censoring the theater.

These measures remained in effect until the Progressives came to power in August 1836. Initially they repromulgated the 1820 press law, but soon enacted another press law on March 27, 1837 (even before finishing the new constitution), which was more restrictive than those of 1810 and 1820. It restored the jury, which had been abolished by Ferdinand in 1823, but retained the figure of a responsible editor, who had to be approved by the civil governor, and the deposit requirement (now raised to 40,000 *reales* for Madrid) that had been introduced in 1834. An October 1837 law added further restrictions: local authorities had to be given a copy of the periodical before it was distributed and they could prohibit its distribution if they viewed it as a threat to public order. The Constitution of 1837 formally established freedom of the press without prior censorship "subject to the laws." However, a Royal Order of June 5, 1839, expressed the government's concerns over the press's "pathetic and disastrous lack of self-control which kills liberty itself" and announced its intention to propose measures to "cut these [abuses] at the root, improving the current press law . . . but preserving unscathed the constitutional principle of the free publication" of ideas. The order required editors to deposit a copy of their paper two hours before distribution so that the authorities would have "adequate time to censure and suspend the paper prior to its distribution" instead of having to round up newspapers that had already been distributed.[12]

The ascension of the moderates in 1843 via a military coup opened a long period in which freedom of the press was even more tightly circumscribed. A decree of April 9, 1844, designed to control "the excesses of the periodical press due to the total ineffectiveness of the previous laws," increased the level of security bonds required of newspapers and severely restricted the membership of the juries that tried press cases by quadrupling the requireded income level. An 1845 decree completely abolished press juries and established a special new court for press offenses, while an 1847 decree prohibited discussion of "disagreements within the royal family," alleging that "the disrespect has gotten to the point that the press is trying to violate not only the sacred domestic hearth but even the very sanctuary of the royal palace."[13]

The major piece of press legislation during moderate rule was the decree of April 6, 1852, that sought to rationalize the regulations. The jury system was restored, but membership was limited to the hundred top taxpayers in Madrid and the thirty top taxpayers in each province. Novels published in serialized form in periodicals were made subject to prior censorship and the government retained the right to suppress any paper that "it considers a danger to the basic principles of society religion, the monarchy and the established form of government."[14] The financial requirements for responsible editors were reduced, but the level of security bonds was increased. Significantly, smaller format, cheaper publications had to pay much larger deposits than others: in Madrid, 160,000 *reales* instead of 120,000; in important provinces, 120,000 instead of 80,000; and elsewhere 60,000 rather than 40,000. The decree explained:

> As the most harmful newspapers are those that, because of their small size and cheapness, reach the less well-off classes with the strong intent of spreading subversive doctrines among the masses or carry the danger of taking the disadvantages of political struggle to this pacific and humble sphere, it has been necessary to increase the guarantees of such periodicals, demanding of their editors a greater deposit than that established for those which, because of their size, it is unlikely that their editors will violate the limits of moderation and decorum.[15]

The progressive government brought to power in the 1854 revolution replaced the moderate constitution of 1845 with the more liberal constitution of 1837, which had guaranteed freedom of the press "subject to the laws," restored the press law of March 1837, and reimbursed editors for all fines levied during the previous two years. However, following another coup, from 1856 to 1868 Spain had liberal union and moderate governments that imposed harsher press controls. The Nocedal Law of July 13, 1857, required that all newspaper articles be signed and that all papers have a director as well as a responsible editor. It again abolished press juries and gave the authorities wide discretion to suspend newspapers. The Cánovas Law of June 1864 reset the balance: it restored the jury and reduced the deposits, which had been significantly increased since the decree of 1852, from 300,000 to 100,000 *reales* in Madrid and from 200,000 to 60,000 elsewhere. However, it also referred all writings that "tend to attack the loyalty or discipline of the armed forces in some way that is not foreseen in military laws" to military courts.[16] The last measure taken by the moderates, the González Bravo Law of March 7, 1867, was the most restrictive since the death of Ferdinand, effectively restoring prior censorship by requiring that all periodicals be shown to the authorities two hours before distribution, and giving civil governors and mayors wide powers to ban papers. The law also created a new crime, "consummation," when prohibited material was distributed to more than ten people.

In the absence of any comprehensive studies, it is difficult to assess how effective press censorship was in nineteenth-century Spain. The laws that were in effect for most of the period certainly provided ready weapons against writers, editors, and publishers, and the authorities were not shy about using them. The press regulations of 1834 permitted the government to close papers virtually at will. After 1837 it was difficult for the authorities to take such drastic action but they could still target individual papers: in 1851, *La Patria* claimed that "there have been months when the government has confiscated twenty-one of our twenty-six issues." In Madrid alone there were 171 charges brought against newspapers between 1841 and 1844, and 158 more between 1854 and 1856. For the period 1864–66, there were 169 charges brought in Madrid.[17]

There are no statistics for actions taken against provincial newspapers, but unquestionably officials there were also prepared to act. The archives contain a wealth of materials concerning official harassment of the press. In one collection of references to archival material from the 1850s and 1860s, among many other reports are those on topics such as: "On the fine imposed on the editor of *El Seminario*, of Ciudad Rodrigo;" "the governor of Málaga reports on his suspension of *El Diario de Málaga*;" "Case brought by the owner of *El Norte de Castilla* in Valladolid protesting against the repeated fines imposed by the governor of the province"; "the governor of Lérida reports that he has lifted the suspension against the *Boletín Eclesíastico de Lérida*;" "the governor of Guipuzcoa reports having seized *El Ferrocarril del Norte* for writing about politics"; and "the editor of *El Nacional of Cádiz*, appeals against the fine of 500 *reales* imposed by the governor of the province."[18]

The extent to which provincial officials could—and did—harass papers they did not like has been described by Celso Almuiña Fernández. Some of their actions were within the law, albeit barely, while others were flagrantly illegal. The most outrageous was to use goon squads (*partidas de la porra*) organized by local political bosses to "make journalists and editors 'see reason,' " an approach used by the mayor of Valladolid as late as 1895.[19] Civil governors also used their authority over the post office to arrange for information to be delayed or go missing; they pressured printers so that they refused to print certain newspapers; and they could choke distribution by refusing permits to people who sold papers on the street or even to the *voceadores*, who announced that the paper was about to appear. Governors could also use fiscal pressure by arranging a large assessment, demanding that the tax be paid immediately, and closing a paper when the tax was not forthcoming.

The press also practiced self-censorship, especially during the numerous states of emergency in which normal constitutional guarantees were in abeyance. Thus, on January 4, 1866, *La Discusión* published the following announcement: "Yesterday a state of siege was declared in Madrid. . . . from now on complaints against the press will go to a military court. Thus, as of today and until the state of siege is lifted, we will cease to publish in-depth articles." Abraham Rincón argues that the decline in the number of complaints against the press in 1868 indicates that "both journalists and newspapers exercised a rigid self-censorship in order to avoid having the paper seized or suspended."[20]

The jury system introduced by the November 1820 press law turned out to be a significant obstacle to government assaults on the press, and as a result the jury had a particularly checkered history in press cases: along with press freedom itself, press juries were abolished in 1823, and thereafter were revived when the progressives were in power and abolished or put under tight constraints by the moderates. The jury was chosen by lot from among the pool of citizens defined by law: always limited to a small elite, the number of people eligible was greater under the progressives than under the moderates.

Juries had two tasks. The first was to decide whether a charge brought against a paper by the authorities had sufficient merit to require a trial; the second was to determine a verdict when trials were held. In practice, juries were much friendlier to the press than the government authorities and the press soon came to see the jury as a "great ally." Thus, in 1837 *El Vapor*, a Barcelona paper, denounced by the authorities for attacking the constitution and the throne, proclaimed a toast "To the jury and only the jury, that safeguard of the press and shield against the excesses of power."[21] Civil governors were "constantly complaining" to Madrid about the leniency of press juries and governments did what they could to assure the selection of favorable juries. In 1839 the civil governor of Madrid wrote that "the greatest stumbling block . . . is the jury. Your Excellency is aware of the constant tendency of juries in Madrid to absolve all kinds of writings, however seditious and subversive they may be." The following year he sent a secret report to the prime minister on a paper called *El Huracán*: "Why should we be surprised that it says what it says today when, having said that the Queen Regent is not sacred and inviolable it was absolved by a Jury? . . . Remember what I said in my report yesterday, that only force can make them respect the law; I repeat it today. There is no other remedy."[22]

The only available study of the jury system indicates that, in Madrid at least, juries clearly countered the enthusiasm of the authorities in attacking the press. Between 1841 and 1844, authorities presented 171 denunciations, but only seventy-eight were sent to trial, and between 1854 and 1856 only 87 of 158 denunciations were approved for trial. Juries were more likely to send cases to trial early in the life of a government; later on, and especially if the government's assault on the press became especially intense, juries were more likely to acquit.[23]

The liberal revolution took censorship power away from the Church and gave it to the state, but the Church repeatedly pressured lay authorities to use censorship on its behalf. The state's response was neither complete acceptance nor total rejection of the Church's demands, but one of judging each case on its merits within the law. For example, in 1851 the Bishop of Oviedo demanded that the government seize a number of irreligious and "immoral" works that were on sale: *The Spirit of the Laws*, Thiers's *History of the French Revolution*, and works by Bentham and Sue. The civil governor consulted with the university rector, who, after stating that the civil and ecclesiastical authorities should work together in such matters and that tougher laws were needed, recommended that the bookseller be given a warning. The Department of Public Instruction was more circumspect: the bishops had the right to complain to the government, but the government could not take actions not countenanced by the law. Pressure from the Church could sometimes lead the government to ban novels. In 1857 *Juan de Padilla* was prohibited after protests by the Vicar of Madrid about its "obscene and scandalous maxims and propositions." That same year, *Secretos, intrigas y misterios de los conventos*, a novel published in installments, was seized "at the excitation of the ecclesiastical authorities."[24]

The Church and its defenders did not rely solely on the—unreliable—repressive power of the state. Between 1844 and 1853 militant Catholics took advantage of the freedom of the press to put out a monthly periodical called, appropriately enough, *La Censura* to warn the faithful about dangerous books. *La Censura* consisted of reviews of a wide range of books that commented on their appropriateness for Catholic readers, including a section dedicated to "scandalous or lascivious books." From May 1845 it also included a list of books added to the Index, "so that our readers will not have to wait for news of the modern books that His Holiness feels appropriate to ban." After attacking a novel entitled *Juana la papesa*, which it described as "a cynical telling of the scandalous adventures of the supposed female Pope," the journal warned that "people of conscience are under the strictest obligation to *collect and destroy* this and other, similar books so that they do not fall into the hands of the young, who would not only develop the disgusting vice of lechery but would come to enjoy reading pestilent books, first those that are destructive and immoral, then those that are irreligious and impious."[25]

The Revolution of 1868 chased Isabella II from the throne and opened a period of broad press freedom. Shortly after the revolution, the Provisional Government decreed freedom of the press without prior censorship, did away with all special press crimes, abolished the special courts that tried them, and freed the press from having to post bonds. The 1869 constitution enshrined the "most absolute and unlimited freedom of emission of thought" by explicitly prohibiting restrictive legislation and the use of administrative techniques such as the responsible editor and monetary bonds. The government reduced the price of paper in an unprecedented effort to encourage the press, especially that aimed at the lower classes: "In Spain the newspaper is the book of the worker. . . . Spreading enlightenment in this way, giving the emission of thought in writing the widest sphere of action is the mission of a government that tries to achieve the greatest possible education of its people."[26]

Press Regulation During the Restoration, 1875–1914. The revolutionary interlude that began in 1868 came to an end in 1875 with the restoration of the Bourbons in the person of Isabella's son, Alfonso XII. Before a new constitution could be drafted, Prime Minister Cánovas del Castillo freely used censorship against his political enemies, whoever they were. The Catholic press, which vociferously opposed Cánovas's policy of limited religious toleration, was a favored target: the diocesan bulletin of Jaén, *El Siglo Futuro* and *La España Católica* (twice) were all suspended in 1875.

The Constitution of 1876 declared that "every Spaniard has the right to freely transmit his ideas and opinions, in speech and in writing, using the printing press or any other technique, without being subject to prior censorship." However, the Restoration regime distinguished between different types of publications and returned to the moderate approach of creating a special court for press crimes. The "systematic and important" press law of January 7, 1879, required publishers to post bond and to deposit copies of their papers two hours before distribution and prohibited the sale or announcing of newspapers in public places without government permission. It also established a series of press crimes, including attacking or ridiculing "the dogmas of the Religion of the State, its ministers or Christian morality . . . offending the person of the King, his acts and orders and other members of the royal family; directly attacking the form of government or its fundamental institutions . . . expressing doctrines contrary to the organization of the family and the right of property . . . provoking disobedience to the laws or the authorities." The law also confirmed special courts for press cases and special agents, the *Fiscales de imprenta*, empowered to seize any periodical that violated the law and to denounce it to the courts within twenty-four hours.[27]

Strikingly, books were exempt from these courts and offenses but their authors fell under the criminal code. The only requirement for the publication of a book was that the publisher's name appear. This was due to the clear distinction that the law drew among books, which were defined as nonperiodical publications with more than 200 pages, pamphlets, nonperiodicals with between eight and 200 pages, and leaflets, which had fewer than eight pages. There was a further distinction drawn between political and nonpolitical pamphlets, with the former subject to the press courts and the latter only to the penal code. The law did not define "political," however, which meant that the authorities could thus label any pamphlet they disliked. Overall, the law "attached little importance to non-political pamphlets" and "did not consider the book a dangerous object." The target was the political pamphlet, "which was treated the same as the press," a response to "the elevated production of political pamphlets which spread socialist, anarchist and generally leftist doctrines. . . . The pamphlet was cheap and . . . was the constant reading material of the working class."[28]

This law and the extremely restrictive approach it embodied was superseded by the 1883 *Ley de Policía de Imprenta* enacted by Sagasta's liberal government. With the exception of the Primo de Rivera dictatorship (1923–30), this remained in effect until the Civil War and marked the zenith of press freedom in liberal Spain. It eliminated the need for security bonds, abolished the distinction between political and nonpolitical pamphlets, did away with special press crimes and courts, and returned the press to regular civil law jurisdiction. The law also curtailed the ability of civil governors to act arbitrarily against the press; however, the 1884 Provincial Law restored their power to impose fines. The rise of anarchist "propaganda by the deed" in the 1890s led to an 1894 law that prohibited "provocation through the press, engravings or any other medium, to the perpetration of bombings or apologies for anarchism."[29] This was reinforced and strengthened two years later by a law that authorized the government to suppress anarchist papers and deport anyone who spread anarchist ideas through the press.

Theater

The theater was an area of special concern for Spanish authorities, both civil and ecclesiastical, since it was seen, in David Gies's words, as "a school for morals, a pulpit from which to teach and preach ethics as well as politics." Or, as Tomás Sancha, a lawyer who served as theater censor in 1836 and 1837, stated in his letter of resignation:

> Your Majesty is well aware of the powerful influence that the theater has on society, and so that that which should be a school of behavior does not become a house of prostitution, it is important that it remain under the responsibility of the municipal authorities, who are so interested in the preservation of order and public decorum, to assure that none of those plays which demoralize the public and corrupt social virtues, the true basis of the freedom of nations, be performed.[30]

The major piece of legislation regarding theaters, the 1849 Organic Decree for the Theaters of the Realm, shared this view, declaring censorship to be of "transcendent importance" because of the influence of the theater "on the morality, the politics, the education and on everything to do with private and public behavior." Even book publishers protesting against the censorship of novels were prepared to put the theater in another category: "Although it is undeniable that the abuse of cleverness in the writing of novels can be very harmful and warrants the vigilance of a wise and prudent government, there is no way that it can have as much influence in subverting good ideas and even less that it can cause as immediate damage as an ardent dramatic presentation."[31] Indeed, a number of writers—Ramón de Mesonero Romanos, Manuel Bréton de los Herreros, Andrés Borrego, and Ventura de la Vega—served on the Junta Consultative de Teatro that drafted the Organic Decree. This committee sought to establish fixed principles for theater censorship because the theater was so influential "in morality, education, politics and everything related to public and private customs." They even included in the Organic Decree an article that prohibited actors from using "gestures or actions that are offensive to morality."[32]

Throughout the eighteenth century, stage censorship was effected by both the Inquisition and the Council of Castile. Conflicts between these two bodies were frequent until 1789. Moreover, the effectiveness of the Inquisition's censorship is far from clear: booksellers continued to sell banned works; actors defied the Inquisition's prohibitions on performance, and local officials often refused to enforce prohibitions they feared might upset public order. The reaction against the French Revolution included the theater and, as a result, the number of plays censored increased markedly: from eighteen between 1707 and 1790 to twenty-five in 1790–1805.[33]

A new *Reglamento General* governing the theater in 1806 made censorship stronger still. The censor was to read all new plays and new versions of old ones to determine whether they contained "anything that goes against religion, the laws and custom." Between 1805 and 1819, forty plays were censored. The play *Orestes in Sciro* was banned in 1814 as "antipolitical, anti-social, subversive of public tranquillity and injurious to sovereigns, as it attacks the basic rights of many thrones" because it contained the line, "Power acquired by steel alone cannot be stable." During the "ominous decade" of 1823–33, theater censorship, historian David Gies writes, was "ubiquitous and explicit, aimed not only at new plays being written for the stage, but also at plays from the classical repertory which might allude to contemporary circumstances and reflect negatively on the king or any of his ministers."[34]

Theater censorship was not always a one-way street emanating outward from the capital. Local interests had a role to play and, as the experience of Córdoba, in southern Spain demonstrates, they did not always demand greater leniency from the Crown. The municipal government banned theater in 1694, and only in the 1770s, when the Count of Aranda, a government minister, compelled it to permit a theater company, was the ban lifted. However, in 1784 Charles III acceded to the city's request and banned theater again. Fifteen years later an aspiring impresario named Casimiro Montero petitioned Charles IV for permission to establish a theater company, but when Madrid consulted the municipal government the local authorities expressed opposition on the grounds of morality due to the fear that farmers would be "distracted from their labors [and] the attention owed to the subsistence of their families." The Crown chose to ignore these objections and granted Montero his license.[35]

Montero's triumph did not last long, and in 1801 the Crown acceded to local protests and reimposed the 1784 ban. The theater was reopened by the French during the War of Independence and kept open under the Cortes of Cádiz, but when Ferdinand VII returned to the throne in 1814 he closed it again, claiming to be responding to local demands. The theater was reopened in 1819 and remained open until 1824, when local opposition led the king to close it once more. This time, however, there was something new—and explicitly political—to their complaints: Montero was denounced as a revolutionary who allegedly had made the theater "a highly ominous place for the King, the Fatherland and the public peace." By the end of the 1820s the city government changed sides and requested that the theater be reopened, but now local authorities saw it as a weapon against the "vices which derive from the idleness of a youth which has no diversions at all." However, the Crown upheld the ban because the new impresario had been denounced as a revolutionary who had "purchased disentailed convent lands and . . . belonged to a secret society with contacts in Madrid." The Crown relented in January 1834, only days before the absolute monarchy disappeared forever.[36]

Between 1834 and 1836, theater censorship was controlled by one of the newly created press censors, but then a special theater censor was named. That same year, a Royal Order urged local authorities to keep an eye on performances of approved plays to ensure that "words spoken in the theaters of [Madrid], in the provinces never be burdened with accents or gestures that offend good customs or exalt the political passions of the spectators." A new *Junta de Censura* was created in 1840 for the theaters of the capital; in the provinces, local authorities were to choose their own censors from among residents "of known education, morality and experience." This system was riddled with inconsistencies, as plays allowed in Madrid might be prohibited elsewhere or plays locally approved by local censors might nonetheless be halted by the police or military. For example, in 1845 a popular and controversial play, *Españoles sobre todo* (Spaniards above all), was scheduled in the town of Valls when "the local commandant stopped it out of fear of disorder." A production of the play in Málaga was cancelled by the civil governor, and in Valencia the mayor arranged for policemen to be planted among the audience to dampen the enthusiasm the play had generated.[37]

This situation was adduced by Vicente de Lalama, the most important publisher of plays in mid-nineteenth-century Spain, as justification for compiling a comprehensive listing of all plays presented to the censors between 1849 and 1867. "Do we not regularly see that plays which have been prohibited are being performed? Why? Because there is no General Index to tell censors . . . which works have been approved or not or the corrections that had to be made." The availability of such a list would also assist provincial governors and local authorities in preventing traveling theater troupes from "changing the titles of plays in order to avoid the payment of royalties (derechos de representación)" and from presenting "gross and dirty farces in smaller towns."[38]

The authorities continued to worry about performance as well as text and about the absence of any fixed principles governing theater censorship. The 1849 Organic Decree for the Theaters of the Realm sought to make censorship more consistent and uniform by putting it into the hands of a five-man committee named by the Minister of the Interior. The decree also declared that "any actor who, with gestures or actions or words that are not in the written text, offends morality or does not show the respect due the audience, will be fined from two to fifteen days salary."[39]

The revolution of 1854 brought greater freedom for the theater but this, like the regime itself, was short-lived. A Royal Order of December 1856 restored theater censorship and in 1857 the *Junta de Censura* was replaced by an individual royal censor whose job was to "read all the plays presented for performance in Madrid and the provinces, and sign a pre-printed government form which either banned the play altogether, allowed it to be performed 'with changes made' or permitted its staging immediately." In the eleven years that this system lasted, censorship became increasingly harsh, as well as subject to the idiosyncrasies of one individual. By 1868 the situation was "more than arbitrary, it was chaotic." Jose Echegaray, who would win the Nobel Prize in 1904, wrote that "the difficulty is in writing plays that will please in a period of transition, when everything is topsy-turvy, when an entire society is shaking and does not know what it wants or where it is going."[40]

The Church frequently pressured the government to ban plays on religious grounds. In February 1858 the Ecclesiastical Vicar of Madrid requested that the government ban *Baltasar* because it "ridicules events from the Holy Bible." The play was sent to the theater censor, who reported that the play did not ridicule anything and could be performed. But resisting ecclesiastical demands was not a point of principle, and governments sometimes acceded, especially when plays included unflattering representations of religious beliefs, religious objects, or members of the clergy.

> "El moro por la fuerza" was banned because it made fun of a nun whose convent had been closed; likewise "Un Hypócrita" because the character Brother Diego was shown as immoral; "Abelard et Eloisa" should be prohibited because of the way it portrays two clerical characters." . . . "Una mujer con historia" was approved with the explicit condition that no religious objects may appear on stage.[41]

The portrayal of sacred figures was especially problematic, and in April 1856 the government issued an order prohibiting the portrayal of the Holy

Theater Censors' Decisions, 1851–66

	Approved	Changes	Rejected
1851	204	13	8
1852	145	1	1
1853	210	6	10
1854	308	5	4
1855	38	0	0
1856	53	0	0
1857	161	18	6
1858	215	38	41
1859	249	55	20
1860	227	41	18
1861	256	26	30
1862	357	0	29
1863	314	0	18
1864	284	1	8
1865	292	39	14
1866	295	68	17
Total	3608	311	224

Source: Vicente de Lalama, *Indice General por orden alfabético de cuantas obras dramaticas y lìricas han sido aprobados por las Junto de Censores y Censores de Ofico* (Madrid, 1867).

Trinity or the Holy Family in biblical plays. This was not enough for some bishops, especially those in Catalonia, who tried to have traditional and popular Christmas and Easter pageants stopped. The royal order was also the basis for the prohibition of "popular religious dramas," including dramatizations of the lives of the saints.

Theater censorship was quite comprehensive during the 1850s and 1860s, but the drama censors were far from consistent. The accompanying table, based on the comprehensive list of all plays submitted to the censors compiled by Vicente de Lalama, suggests the trends in censorship during the 1850s and 1860s. The years 1857 to 1866, immediately after the revolutionary *bienio* of 1854–56, stand out for their harshness compared to the rest of the period. The greater freedom of 1855–56 is clear from the small number of works that were actually given to the censors and from the fact that none were rejected or deemed to need changes. From 1860 to 1864 the censor was much more likely to reject plays outright than to demand changes, the opposite of the practice throughout the rest of the period. Overall, only 6.2 percent were rejected and 8.6 percent required changes; the vast majority passed through the censors' hands unscathed.

Plays were banned or altered for a wide range of reasons. Religion was a common one. Censor Ferrer del Río approved one play on condition that the author not have a Catholic woman marry a Jew, but he rejected another because "some of the characters are from the Bible and appear in situations that the poet has invented and which are not part of Scripture or the traditions with which I am familiar." Morality was another common problem. In 1861 del Río rejected *Dolores* due to the "immorality of having a man ask for the hand and be on the point of marrying a woman who is his daughter." "The Mayor's Hats" was rejected because of "various scandalous scenes and many lines so indecent that it is hard to believe that it could even be presented to the censor." *Homeopathic Love* was rejected because "the title indicates the extent to which the characters display few scruples in the amorous relations. There are many scandalous anecdotes and they say many vulgar things about marriage which cannot be eliminated without totally changing the nature of the play and reducing it to one third its length."[42]

Censors were equally zealous in defending the dignity of the Crown: *Princess Tellina and King Matarot* (1861) "ridicules the royal dignity in every single scene, even if this was not the author's intent" and was not allowed. The censor approved "The Consequences of Love" (1861), but only if "it is set in an earlier period because it offends historical truth to attribute illegitimate sons to Charles III and Charles IV." Dubious ideas about the social system were also grounds for censorship: "The Fairy of the Forest" (1861) was rejected because "it deals with the situation of the slaves and also locates the action in Cuba [then a Spanish colony], all of which strikes me as dangerous." *Ill-gotten Gains* (1857) was passed on condition that the author change "those sentences that refer to the wealth of the Duke of Osuna and the manner in which he acquired it."[43]

Some plays could touch a particularly sensitive nerve in an individual censor. This was what happened to *La última palabra* (The Last Word), a play about a young woman who is abandoned and forced to become a prostitute to help support her parents. Censor del Río wrote an unusually lengthy critique of the play, which reveals both a special concern of his and some of the dominant attitudes of the time:

> [The play] accuses Society of setting itself up as the judge of the virtue of the poor after having abandoned them. . . . There is no doubt that these matters should be fought against but with good morality as the starting point. . . . As far as I am concerned what is totally without justification is to attribute to Society sins which it has not committed. . . . what is totally inadmissible is that any Society in which public welfare and private charity exist to care for all types of misfortune; which sustains numerous establishments to help the needy; which maintains hospitals and creates asylums and offers home relief, be charged with abandoning the unfortunate. What is illicit, as well as harmful to good customs, is that excuses are offered for prostitution.[44]

Stage censorship provoked complaints about its slowness. For example, the director of Madrid's Teatro Francés complained in 1858 that to increase theater attendance "it is essential to change the productions frequently, but this is impossible because when the repertory is exhausted" new plays could not be performed "because they have yet to be authorized." In 1865 twenty Catalan dramatists petitioned the Minister of the Interior to permit the civil governor and the provincial censor to take responsibility for plays "written entirely in Catalan and which are to be produced where that language alone is spoken," since a Spanish speaker could not "accurately judge works written in Catalan" and might "permit things which translated literally are quite harmless but which for Catalans might be highly immoral, or vice versa," and also because "most of these productions are quite topical" and thus the delays involved in submitting plays to the Madrid censor meant that "once the moment has past they lose most of their effect."[45] The Catalans got a response nine years later, but it was not the one they wanted. On January 15, 1867, the minister of the interior issued a Royal Order banning all plays that were written "exclusively in dialect" on the grounds that they "contributed significantly to the spirit of autonomy" in those provinces where they were performed and thus destroyed "the most effective means through which the use of the national language is generalized."[46]

Opera and zarzuela, a Spanish form of operetta, also fell under theater censorship. Librettos had to be submitted to the censor just like play texts. Censor del Río rejected the opera *Los Pastorcillos* (The Little Shepherds) "because the plot deals with one of the mysteries of our holy religion and because the characters include the Holy Family." One author tried to get approval for a zarzuela whose manuscript included a number of blank pages, but the censor rejected the work because "this aim of filling the pages in after the work had passed censorship . . . is an intolerable abuse which would undermine the Censor's decision."[47]

The revolution of 1868 ushered in the period of greatest theatrical freedom from censorship. A royal decree of January 16, 1869, established "in its widest possible form, the freedom of the theater," but this, like the revolutionary regime itself, did not last long. The post-1875 Restoration revived many of the methods used against the theater by previous liberal regimes. Under regulations issued in 1886, producers were required to submit two copies of all plays to the civil governor or mayor, and police had to have twenty-four hours advance notice of all performances. A play could be banned either before it was performed or afterward. The regulations also forbade "that anyone be caricatured in any way. If the person involved or any member of the family complains, the authorities can forbid that character appearing on the stage."[48]

Governments were especially touchy about any satires. In 1904 the conservative government banned one song that attacked the prime minister and his party, but these efforts only made the refrain "hugely popular." Actors did not always respect such bans, but those who did not could find themselves jailed and fined. On one occasion, the civil governor of Madrid had an entire theater troupe fined for performing "pornographic songs," and on another, in 1907, he prohibited a play altogether and "sued the author, the chorus line, the impresario and the director for damages!"[49]

Images

Censorship was primarily concerned with the written word, but it did not totally ignore visual images, and most laws included them. As part of his attempt to seal Spain off from news of the French Revolution, Count Floridablanca prohibited books and "prints, boxes, fans, folders and other objects referring to the revolutions in France." But the borders could not be hermetically sealed and the government received reports from the Inquisition that banned materials were circulating, including one report from Bilbao about a Frenchman who sold "cheap fans with designs picturing the fall of the Bastille, Louis XVI 'restorer of liberty' and General Lafayette." In August 1790 the government imposed a ban on the entry of goods "containing paintings or expressions relative to the disorders in France." The variety of such goods was astounding: the 1790 ban was provoked by a Frenchman "who had been caught in the treacherous act of wearing a waistcoat on which was pictured a galloping horse with the word 'Liberté.' "[50]

The decree of 1805 that created the first special press court included the censorship of engravings in its mandate. The moderates, and especially their military strongman, Ramón María Narváez, were so concerned about visual images that they put restrictions on them in Article 3 of the Constitution of 1845: "No drawing, engraving, lithograph or medallion of any kind may be publicized, sold or exhibited to the public without the prior authorization of the [provincial] governor, subject to a fine of between 1,000 and 3,000 *reales* and loss of the [items], independent of the punishment deriving from the publication or exhibition of those objects."[51]

Spanish authorities did not ignore new technologies. The 1867 Gonzalez Bravo law included in its definition of printed matter "thoughts manifested by words fixed on any medium through printing, through lithographs, photography or any other medium." The 1879 press law also lent itself to the severe censorship of images: four days after the law was proclaimed, the minister of the interior issued instructions to provincial governors to prevent the "abuses committed against religion and morality as well as against important institutions" through lithographs, photographs, and engravings, by prohibiting such images, even in the form of "decorations of manufactured goods."[52]

These measures appear to have been effective in stifling political caricature. When an American embassy official in Madrid was asked about Spanish political caricature in 1875, he reported:

I have questioned many persons here in regard to Spanish caricature, but have always received the same reply, namely that pictorial caricature, political or other, has not existed in Spain until [the] 1868 [revolution which inaugurated the first Spanish republic]. I have searched book-stores and book-stalls, and find nothing; nor have the vendors been able to aid me. It is thought at our Legation there must have been caricature in Spain, from the writings of Spaniards being so full of satire and wit; but though the germ may have existed, I am inclined to think it was not developed until the dethronement of Isabel II and the proclamation of the Republic broke down the barriers to liberty, if not license, of the printing press.[53]

The Church was highly sensitive to the improper use of religious images. In 1853 the Bishop of Barcelona complained to the Civil Governor that he had heard about a store, allegedly run by a Frenchman, that was selling obscene prints "of the Infant Jesus between two extremely immoral and provocative nymphs and another of Saint John the Baptist with a nymph on either side [and] I believe that they sell many others of the same sort there." When the bishop lodged a similar complaint three years later the new civil governor promised to take action against the shopkeepers.[54]

At the end of the century, the press had to face a new enemy—the army—and it was satirical cartoons that most provoked the military's anger. The first incident came in 1895 when noncommissioned officers in Madrid protested against articles published in the newspaper *El Resumen* and attacked its offices. This led to demands from the captain general of Madrid that the Code of Military Justice be reformed so that libel and calumny in the press be put under military jurisdiction, but when the immediate crisis, including the collapse of the government, passed, nothing was done to assuage the army. By the turn of the century the situation had become much more volatile. In 1898 Spain suffered a humiliating defeat at the hands of the United States and lost the remnants of its once imposing global empire. This defeat, known in Spain simply as "the Disaster," triggered a profound loss of national self-confidence that was voiced by the great group of intellectuals known as the Generation of 1898. It also provided a major stimulus for new political movements, of which the most significant were Basque and Catalan nationalism. To a military already embarrassed by defeat, regional nationalism represented a threat to what they deemed the "integrity of the fatherland," and when the Catalan nationalist press began to criticize the army directly, officers had little patience.

On November 25, 1905, officers of the Barcelona garrison ransacked the offices of the nationalist newspaper *La Veu de Catalunya* and of the satirical paper *Cu-Cut!*, which had published a cartoon poking fun at the army. This was, according to historian Joaquin Romero Maura, the last of a long series of "pin-pricks" that included "a measure of deliberate baiting." Officers were further angered by the failure of the courts to impose stiff penalties for "statements or caricatures considered criminally offensive by the military." These included a cartoon in which a Spanish observer with the Russian army during the 1905 Russo-Japanese war was depicted as saying that the only thing he had learned was "What we already knew: how to lose battles"; another showed the Spanish foreign minister telling the German Kaiser that "Spain wants to be at peace with all nations," to which the Kaiser replied: "That's understandable, no one likes to get a whipping." The officers, who received the support of many leading generals and the Madrid garrison, demanded a new libel law and the strengthening of the Code of Military Justice to cover such "offenses." Under pressure from the high command, the legislature enacted the 1906 Law of Jurisdictions, which made offenses against the army subject to military courts.[55]

Moving pictures were first shown in Spain in May 1896, but film censorship was imposed only in November 1912 by Conservative Minister of the Interior Juan de la Cierva, whose career was marked by a series of efforts to moralize Spanish life. The rationale for the measure was similar to that of contemporary critics of television, especially with regard to the impact on children, who, it was argued, could be "easily influenced and predisposed to imitate the criminal and immoral acts depicted in movies." In language that recalled the theater censorship decrees of the 1830s and 1840s, the 1912 film censorship decree stated its preference for films that showed "normal and sane life [to] stimulate good actions and which exalt the love of country and of home and extol the heroism of sacrifice for the welfare of the community."[56]

To safeguard the public, the title and subject matter of all films "which have any pernicious tendency" had to be shown to the authorities beforehand. Children under ten years old were prohibited from attending evening shows alone. The private showing of "pornographic films" (left undefined) was prohibited and those responsible were to be prosecuted. Concerned that these provisions were not being properly enforced, the government issued a royal order on December 31, 1913, that required that all cinemas present the authorities with the titles and subject matter of "all the films they offer to the public . . . in case any of them had anything pernicious." Civil governors and mayors were authorized to appoint an advisory committee, with the members chosen by the local Committee for the Protection of Children, "to make the necessary selection." The censorship regulations upset filmmakers in Barcelona and led to a "tempest of protests" and the organizing of delegations that traveled to Madrid to futilely voice their anger. The regulations were first used in November 1913 when the civil governor of Barcelona banned a film entitled *La Posada Sangrienta* (The Bloody Inn). This measure was criticized in *El Cine* as excessive, especially since the movie contained "no love scenes" that might "make people blush." The magazine conceded that the film did present a series of horrific crimes, but only in the same naturalistic manner used by Zola and Ibsen and, in any case, the moral was a healthy one, that "the criminals cannot escape from justice and end up at the guillotine." In May 1914 censorship was again invoked in Barcelona to prohibit *Rocambole* on the grounds that it could provoke terrorist attacks.[57]

CENSORS AND RESISTANCE TO CENSORSHIP

Censors were drawn from a variety of professional groups. During periods of absolutist rule preceding the abolition of the Inquisition in 1835, the Church had a prominent role in censorship and many censors were clerics. According to a contemporary biographical sketch of the playwright Bretón de los Herreros, during the 1820s a certain Father Carrillo was "the scourge of the dramatists." On one occasion he "eliminated the word 'poor' wherever he found it in one of Sr. Bretón's plays"; on another he eliminated the sentence "I hate victory" because he "thought that it referred to his" Convento de la Victoria. But Father Carrillo was very fond of the work of the seventeenth-century author Tirso de Molina and let his works pass untouched: as a result "any old comedy was presented to him as [Tirso's] work and thus it was certain to be permitted."[58] Civil censorship was usually handled by government officials or by others appointed to serve as censors, a salaried job much sought after. According to Fermín Caballero, after 1834

> many subjects filled this difficult office because the slightest slip on some piece of writing that might anger the ministry was the occasion for changes. And there was no shortage of candidates, attracted by the job and the salary as a way of earning merit and a living. . . . Some were so eager not to anger the Government that they forgot the exclusive right they had to permit a work or not according to their knowledge and conscience and consulted with the Ministry to see if they were mistaken in letting works pass.[59]

Censors were often lawyers, but writers were also prominent, especially in theater censorship. From 1849 until 1857 the theater was censored by a board, and from 1857 until 1868 by a series of individual censors who received the handsome salary of 26,000 *reales* per year. In both cases, censorship was almost exclusively in the hands of writers. Some, such as Narciso Serra and Luis Eguilaz, were among the leading literary figures of their day, although they have been largely forgotten today. Others have retained a distinguished place in the Spanish literary canon: Leandro Fernández de Moratín, who was a censor for the Bonapartist regime, Juan Eugenio Hartzenbusch, and Gustavo Adolfo Bécquer. Ramón Franquelo, editor of the *Coreo de Andalucia*, was named theater censor in Málaga during the 1850s to replace another censor who resigned after coming under criticism for his handling of a zarzuela—the libretto of which had been written by Ramón Franquelo![60]

Writers could be tough censors, even when they themselves had suffered from censorship. Narciso Serra, who was theater censor from 1864 until 1868, went about his job "with surprising harshness," although he "tended to be more thoughtful of the plays under consideration than his predecessor, Ferrer del Río" who even banned a play because he disapproved of the list of characters. (Some of Serra's own plays had been criticized for being lewd.) Concerned lest the theater become the catalyst for "a discharge of passions . . . or a place of subversive demonstrations," Serra banned plays that he considered immoral or excessively political.[61]

Despite the harshness of the laws and the willingness of governments to enforce them, the effectiveness of censorship was frequently undermined by the vagaries and confusion in the process, as well as by the individual and collective efforts of writers, editors, and publishers to evade or protest government measures. They did not always accept censors' decisions, or even the existence of censorship, passively, and they found ways to get around those decisions and poke fun at the censors.

Probably the most frequent approach was to protest a censor's decision in the hope that the government would override it or seek another, more favorable opinion. This was usually done by individual authors whose work had been prohibited. Under Ferdinand VII's absolutist rule, authors could petition the king to overturn a censor's decision. Thus, in 1817 Angel Saavedra, a young but soon to be very famous poet, had an ode to the king rejected by a censor. His protest to Ferdinand led to the monarch's overruling the censor. Some of the censorship decisions by Narciso Serra "provoked outraged protests" and appeals. His prohibition of García Gutiérrez's *Juan Lorenzo* because of its "political tendencies" led the author, who had himself been a member of the Censorship Committee thirteen years earlier, to successfully request that the minister of the interior create a special panel to judge the play. The panel, which included two former censors, recommended that the play be produced, finding it "a highly enjoyable experience" that "lives up to the legitimate fame of the author and its tendencies are such that not a single member of the committee had the slightest concern about them." The dispute made "a great echo" in the press; the satirical paper *Gil Blas* went so far as to publish a dialogue between Serra and "Juan Lorenzo" in verse that imitated the censor's poetic style. When the play was finally performed it proved a critical failure.[62]

Appeals were not always successful. In August 1861 José María Díaz appealed the prohibition of his play *Light in the Shadow*. The three writers who did the reevaluation agreed with the censor that the play was unacceptable in its present form, but dissented from his opinion that it was totally unredeemable. Their twenty-seven-page decision is striking for the detail with which they examined the work and the thoroughness of their analysis of its moral tone. The play was about a young woman, Blanca, who agreed to live with a rich man in order to help support her father. Later she marries a politician and lives happily. The assessors criticized Blanca for not seeking out all the "licit means to help her father" and for not displaying "sufficient repugnance beforehand nor enough . . . repentance afterwards." She was "too happy" in Act One and "too resigned and not sufficiently afflicted" in Acts Three and Four; the reviewers "feared that the moral effect of this character will be dangerously repugnant at the beginning and dangerously seductive afterwards." Roberto, the seducer, was also problematic: he boasted of his lack of religious faith and "in a Catholic country which does not permit freedom of religion it clearly should not be permitted to be shown on stage, where every statement becomes a form of public education, characters who act impiously unless they are refuted immediately."[63]

One common technique to foil the censors was to resubmit a banned work under a different name. Thus, when Narciso Serra banned Pedro María Pardo's *A Poet's Fantasies*, because of the "immorality of the plot," Pardo presented the script again with a different title. The author of *The Bad Crop* tried the same trick, but del Río recognized it and rejected it again on appeal. This was also done with newspapers in the 1830s, as suppressed publications reappeared with the same staff under a different name. *El Boletín de Comercio* became *Eco de Comercio; El Universal* reappeared as *La Abeja*, and the *Diario Universal: Cartas españolas* became the *Revista española* that then joined with *El mensajero de la Cortes* to become *La Revista-Mensajero*. Perhaps the extreme case was that of the Valladolid paper *El Mirlo*, whose editor tried to outsmart the provincial governor by bringing out each issue under a different name so that technically it was not a periodical and thus not subject to the law.[64]

Newspaper editors could also have recourse to outright deceit. According to Carlos Rubio, who wrote for the Progressive paper *La Iberia* in the 1860s, when it was a favored target of the moderate government:

> When appeals to the courts failed, we would give the government one version of our paper and our subscribers another; that is we sent the censor the paper just as we wanted to publish it; he put on his glasses, studied it carefully and marked in red whatever he thought his masters would find offensive, and gave it back to us. We took out the material he had marked, but only in copies for the censor, the civil governor and some public establishments; to the rest of our subscribers we sent the paper as we had written it.[65]

In 1839 one provincial official complained that "the most exquisite and constant precautions are insufficient to guarantee that editors provide this office with the required copy two hours before so that we have time to examine it; nor can we know whether the paper has already been distributed to subscribers . . . before or at the very moment that we receive it."[66]

Aside from acts of individual resistance by journalists or newspapers, there were also occasional collective protests against the censorship. On October 31, 1842, the editors of eleven of the most important newspapers in Madrid signed an agreement to defend press freedom after the government named a commission to prepare a tougher press law. They announced the formation of a "uniting Association which has as its object the defense of the freedom of the press within the legal limits now extant and which conform to the Constitution" and that the association would defend "the guarantee of individual security and liberty established by the Constitution and the laws and [which are] violated and infringed in a large part of the Monarchy by the military and political agents of the government."[67] The government's response was to order the post office not to handle any newspapers other than official ones.

In November 1857 the Catalan publisher Rialp sent the government a petition from a number of Barcelona authors asking that novels be censored after they had been published rather than before to avoid "wasting time with a manuscript and then not be able to publish it." A few months later, a group of Barcelona publishers, writers, and journalists sent a petition to the minister of the interior requesting that the minister revoke "the instructions that have been given to the civil governors . . . requiring prior permission for the circulation of novels and reform them so that, without endangering morality and good customs, the interests of letters, the publishers and the book trade are protected." Their argument was not a principled statement against censorship, for they were happy enough to leave the theater under prior censorship; rather, their position was driven by economic self-interest, as the requirement to submit two complete copies of the manuscript before publication was extremely burdensome:

> The inconvenience of this practice and the damages that it causes can be seen in the shortage of original titles, since the law came into effect, and it cannot be otherwise. Publishing in Spain is only productive [profitable] if many titles are published, for each individual title does not sell enough copies to create an active interest, as is the case in other countries, where the joy of reading is more widespread. . . . If we add the not inconsiderable costs of double copies of the original . . . requiring considerable expense and running the risk of losing it entirely, it is natural that publishers are reluctant to acquire them. A consequence of all this is that writers languish in inaction, or contribute to diluting our customs by translating foreign books; *many take refuge in the burning sands of politics*.[68]

The press could itself be an effective weapon against censorship. Trials for press offenses gave other newspapers the occasion to attack the government to such an extent that in 1867 the law was amended to permit such trials to be held secretly. When negative remarks by the civil governor of Madrid about Benito Pérez Galdós's highly controversial anticlerical play *Electra* led to rumors that it might be banned, the government had to announce that "it had never considered the idea of suspending the play."[69]

Journalist Mariano José de Larra repeatedly directly challenged and ridiculed the censors, and, needless to say, consistently had problems with them, whatever the regime. In 1836 he criticized theater censors for finding political allusions everywhere: "The censor should understand that when we write about the theater, we are writing about the theater and nothing more; the satirist, the one who does harm to the Prime Minister is not the theater critic but the censor who alleges the allusions." Larra also used his knowledge of the censorship rules to evade them and discuss forbidden topics. In his review of the play *Numancia* he wrote:

> Another thing that the rules do not prohibit discussing is Mr. Luna: one can talk about this actor since he is not a matter of *religion, nor of the prerogatives of the throne, nor the constitution* . . . nor does his acting disrupt the public peace, nor violate any law, nor *disguise itself with allusions*, but rather with very bad costumes; nor is it licentious or against any custom, good or bad; nor is it *libelous or defamatory* nor do any of the many "no's" in the rules apply to it. Least of all is it *sovereign* or a foreign *government.*[70]

In March 1834 Larra published an edition of his newspaper, *El Siglo*, with blank spaces beneath the headlines, "On the amnesty," "Domestic Politics," and "On the Legislature"; he then published an article in another periodical in which he discussed the virtues of articles with no text. "A blank article can be interpreted in the most favorable ways; it is an article that favors all parties; it is soft wax that can be molded into whatever shape one wants." He added, on the subject of governments:

> Even without reading *El Siglo*, which you will probably not have read, however fond of reading you might be, you will know that it is not my intention to defend blank articles, and even less defend governments, of which I am quite afraid, thank you very much. . . . In spite of all its enlightenment and grandeur, the century is little, as are its men, and in times such as these prudent men should not *speak* and even less *keep quiet.*[71]

This more aggressive posture seems to have been particularly common when the objects of censorship were caricatures. One bullfight paper announced in bold type, "There was to be a caricature here but it was suppressed by order of the civil governor." Another periodical filled its unexpected blank space with a verse: "So that they don't lose control/ Calculating without good sense/Today's caricature/Is broken by Royal Order." The satirical *Gil Blas* habitually filled half a page with a description, in bold type, of the image that had been banned, for example:

The Civil Governor of the province has prohibited the caricature that was going to appear in this space and which showed him going through the streets at the head of the veteran Guard and coming across a boy with a whistle. Beneath the picture there was the following dialogue: "Who goes there?" "Spain." "Which regiment?" "The First Whistlers." This is the first time that Sr. Gutiérrez de la Vega has prevented his handsome likeness appearing for everyone to admire. Power also has its bitterness.[72]

La Filoxera covered an entire page with the following text, set out in the form of a death notice:

Perhaps you will have noticed by yourselves that this issue has appeared without a caricature. Don't worry about it because it has stayed in the Civil Governor's office. Count Heredia-Spinola's interest in the fine arts causes us this loss, for which we are indemnified by the satisfaction of having been taken before the governor. The caricatures are taken to him, like the women of the street, for prior examination and run the risk of not being to his pleasure. NOTE: . . . Another day, when unlike today we do not leave our physiognomy in the governor's office, we will explain at greater length.[73]

The Málaga-based satirical weekly *El País de la Olla* (The Nation of the Stewpot) had its caricatures banned twice in three years. The first time the editor ran a blank space with the text, "The Civil Governor has prohibited the publication of this week's caricature. Hail Cánovas, your rivals salute you." The second time the authorities seized the entire run of a number. The following week the editor responded by telling a story about a connoisseur of pornography who when asking for the illustrated edition of a book at a bookshop was indignantly told by the clerk, "We do not carry such disgusting things here." On one occasion the magazine printed a cartoon portraying a group of editors being assured by the minister of the interior that all was well, while behind them a giant claw was emerging from a copy of the Penal Code.[74]

Resistance and defiance were not the only responses. Much harder to measure, or even to detect, is the extent to which the fear of censorship inhibited writers and led them to censor themselves. According to one study, this was the practice of the noted essayist Ramón de Mesonero Romanos. Mesonero himself admitted that he "always tried to keep a convenient distance from politics and from the extraordinary circumstances of the country I wanted to consider and portray only in its normal, tranquil state." In his introduction to the 1851 edition of Mesonero's *Madrid Scenes*, Juan Eugenio Hartzenbusch noted that

whomever examines the articles published in 1832 and 1833 will see the reserve with which the author presented himself before the censorship, so as to avoid its terrible glance. . . . his prudent reticence allows the reader to understand how much more he would have said if the powers that be had not closed his lips. In his articles "Empleo-mania" and "Politico-mania" . . . he talks only of those who seek positions and not those who bestow them; of those who go crazy talking about politics and not about crazy politicians: that was the forbidden fruit, to touch it meant falling from grace and exposing oneself to death.[75]

CONCLUSION

Just as they proclaimed that sovereignty lay with the people and then proceeded to define the people as comprising between only 1 and 10 percent of the population, Spanish liberals constantly lauded and proclaimed freedom of expression and publication, only to restrict it through laws that imposed severe censorship. There were degrees of course, and censorship, like suffrage, was sensitive to political swings. But for all its complexity, the history of censorship in Spain during the nineteenth century is, above all, yet another symptom of the contradictions and limitations of Spanish liberalism, and of European liberalism as a whole.

NOTES

1. For further background see Raymond Carr, *Spain, 1808–1975* (Oxford, 1982) and Adrian Shubert, *A Social History of Modern Spain* (London, 1990).

2. On the Church, see W. Callahan, *Church, Society and Politics in Spain, 1750–1874* (Cambridge, Mass., 1984).

3. Rubio Jiménez, "La censura teatral en la época moderada, 1840–1868," *Segismundo: Revista Hispánica de Teatro*, 39–40 (1984), 203.

4. Ibid., 305.

5. On censorship of books and periodicals in the eighteenth century, see Richard Herr, *The Eighteenth Century Revolution in Spain* (Princeton, N.J., 1958), 201–8. The text of the decree is found in A. Rumeu de Armas, *Historia de la censura literaria gubernamentiva en España* (Madrid, 1940), 106–11.

6. Ibid., 112–20.

7. M. Cabrera et al., "Datos para un estudio cuantitativo de la prensa diaria madrileña," in *Prensa y sociedad en España, 1820–1936* (Madrid, 1983), 53–54. The complete text of the constitution in English can be found in A. Blaustein and J. Sigler, *Constitutions That Made History* (New York, 1988), 114–57.

8. M. Seoane, *Historia del periodismo en España* (Madrid, 1983), 83–84.

9. R. Goldstein, *Political Censorship of the Arts and the Press in Nineteenth-Century Europe* (London, 1989), 37–38.

10. F. Cendán Pazos, *Historia del derecho español de prensa e imprenta* (Madrid, 1974), 111–12.

11. A. González Palencia, *Walter Scott y la censura gubernativa* (Madrid, 1927).

12. Seoane, 175; Cendán Pazos, 124–25; C. Almuiña Fernández, *La Prensa Vallisoletana durante el Siglo XIX* (Valladolid, 1977), I, 210.

13. Cendán Pazos, 126; Seoane, 198.

14. Ibid.

15. Ibid., 199.

16. Cendán Pazos, 133.

17. H. Schulte, *The Spanish Press, 1470–1966* (Urbana, Ill., 1968), 186; Cabrera et al., 67–77.

18. L. Romero Tobar, "Sobre censura de periódicos en el siglo XIX" (hereafter Romera Tobar, "Sobre censura"), *Anuario de Historia Contemporánea*, 13 (1986), 119–60.

19. C. Almuiña Fernández, "Los gobernadores civiles y el control de la prensa decimonónica," in M. Tuñón de Lara, *La Prensa de los Siglos XIX y XX* (Bilbao, 1986), 173.

20. A. Rincón Moñoz de Morales, "El marco legal de la prensa en los años anteriores a la 'Gloriosa'," in *La Prensa en la Revolución Liberal* (Madrid, 1983), 135–36.

21. J. Valls, *Prensa y burguesía en el Siglo XIX español* (Madrid, 1987), 107–10.

22. L. Romero Tobar, *La Novela Popular Española del Siglo XX* (hereafter Romero Tobar, *Novela Popular*) (Madrid, 1976), 78; L. Romero Tobar, "Textos inéditos de escritores españoles relacionados con la censura gubernativa," in *Homenaje a D. Agustin Millares Carlo* (Las Palmas, 1975), 97.

23. Cabrera, 66–76.

24. B. Journeau, "Problèmes de Censure entre 1844 et l854," in C. Dumas, *Culture et Société en Espagne et en Amérique Latine au XIXe siècle* (Lille, 1980), 69–70; Romero Tobar, *Novela Popular*, 82–83.

25. *La Censura*, December 1846 (emphasis added).

26. Seoane, 267.

27. Cendán Pazos, 147–49.

28. Pascual, *Escritores y editores en la Restauración canovista, 1875–1923* (Madrid, 1994), 30–32.

29. Ibid., 150.

30. D. Gies, *The Theatre in Nineteenth-Century Spain* (Cambridge, England, 1994) 12; J. Rubio Jiménez, "La censura teatral en la época moderada, 1840–1868," *Segismundo*, 39–40 (1984), 197.

31. Gies, 201–2; I. Zavala, "La censura en la semiología del silencio, siglos XVIII y XIX," *Censura y literaturas peninsulares* (Amsterdam, 1987), 152.

32. Rubio Jiménez, 201–13.

33. Ibid., 284.

34. Ibid., 310; E. Cotarelo y Mari, *Bibliografía de la controversias sobre la licitud del teatro en España* (Madrid, 1904), 700; Gies, *The Theatre*, 11.

35. Michael Schinasi, "Theatre Repression in Córdoba, 1694–1834," in *Dieciocho* (1995), 159.

36. Ibid., 163–64.

37. Rubio Jiménez, 198, 200; Gies, 144.

38. Vicente de Lalama, *Indice General por orden alfabético de cuantas obras dramáticas y líricas han sido aprobadas por la Junta de Censores y Censores de Oficio* (Madrid, 1867), 1.

39. Gies, 201–2.

40. Ibid., 26.

41. Expediente 91, Legajo 11.388, Archivo Histórico Nacional (hereafter AHN), Madrid; Rubio Jiménez, 207–8.

42. Expediente 139, Legajo 11.396, AHN; Expediente 315, 324, 137, Legajo 11.396, AHN; Expediente 31, Legajo 11.392, AHN.

43. Expediente 325, 118 Legajo 11.396, AHN; Expediente 269, Legajo 11.396, AHN; Expediente 52, Legajo 11.396, AHN; Expediente 46, Legajo 11.392, AHN.

44. Expediente 35, Legajo 11.396, AHN.

45. Expediente 85, Legajo ll.388, AHN; Expediente 12, Legajo 11.391, AHN.

46. Lalama, *Indice General.*

47. Expediente 27, Legajo 11.391, AHN; Expediente 49, Legajo 11.392, AHN.

48. S. Arimón, *El código del teatro* (Madrid, no date), 85–86, 107.

49. N. Membrez, "The Bureaucratization of the Madrid Theatre," *Anales de la literature española contemporánea*, 17 (1992), 100, 118.

50. Herr, 247, 252, 254.

51. Valls, 124.

52. Cendán Pazos, 135; Almuiña Fernández, 259–60.

53. Goldstein, 89–90.

54. C. Martí, *L'Esglesia dins la Societat de Barcelona* (Barcelona, 1985), I, 197.

55. J. Romero Maura, *The Spanish Army* (Beverly Hills, Calif., 1976) 13, 15–17.

56. T. González Ballesteros, *Aspectos jurídicos de la censura cinematográfica en España* (Madrid, 1981), 351.

57. Ibid., 355; F. Mendez-Leite, *Historia del cine español* (Madrid, 1965), 98–101; *El Cine*, November, 15, 22, 1913, May 23, 1914.

58. N. Pastor Diaz, *Galería de españoles celebrés* (Madrid, 1842), III, 13–14.

59. Seoane, 141–42.

60. A. Guerola, *Memoria de mi administración en la provincia de Málaga* (Madrid, no date), 695–96.

61. Gies, 264–65.

62. Expediente 1, Legajo 11.391, AHN; Rubio Jiménez, 205; Carlos Cambronero, "Cosas de antaño," *Revista contemporánea*, 30 (December 1899), 603–5.

63. Expediente 12, Legajo 11.391, AHN.

64. Gies, 264; Expediente 195, Legajo 11.396, AHN; Seaone, II, 145–47; Romero Tobar, "Sobre censura," 133.

65. A. Rincón, "El marco legal de la prensa en los años anteriores a la 'Gloriosa,' " in *La Prensa en la Revolución Liberal* (Madrid, 1983), 136.

66. Romero Tobar, *Novela popular*, 78.

67. Schulte, 171.

68. Ibid., 65; I. Zavala, "La censura en la semiología del silencio, siglos XVIII y XIX," in *Censura y literaturas peninsulares* (Amsterdam, 1987), 152; Romero Tobar, *Novela popular*, 241–42 (emphasis added).

69. E. Inman Fox, " 'Electra' de Perez Galdós," in Fox, *Ideologia y politica en las letras de fin de siglo* (1989) (Madrid, 1988), 71.

70. A. Medina-Bocos Montarelo, "Larra y Mesonero," *in EPOS: Revista de Filologia* (1989), 195, 198.

71. M. J. de Larra, *Obras* (Madrid, 1960), I, 353.

72. *El Fandango*, September 15, 1845; *El Noventa y Tres*, November 22, 1870; *Gil Blas*, April 22, 1865.

73. *La Filoxera*, September 5, 1880.

74. F. Arcas Cubero, *El País de la Olla: La imagen de España en la prensa satírica malagueña de la Restauración* (Málaga, 1990), 120–22.

75. Medina-Bocos Montarelo, 187–89.

BIBLIOGRAPHICAL ESSAY

For general background, see R. Carr, *Spain, 1808–1975* (Oxford, 1982) and A. Shubert, *A Social History of Modern Spain* (London, 1991). There is very little on censorship in Spain available in English. The best source is H. Schulte, *The Spanish Press, 1470–1966* (Urbana, Ill., 1968), which provides fairly complete coverage of legislation, but is marred by an interpretative framework that sees Spain as suffering from a peculiarly authoritarian tradition in this respect. There is a brief overview, which goes through the Franco regime, in J. Green, *The Encyclopedia of Censorship* (New York, 1990), 294–302. Spain is also included in R. J. Goldstein's general study, *Political Censorship of the Arts and the Press in Nineteenth-Century Europe* (London, 1989). Richard Herr, *The Eighteenth Century Revolution in Spain* (Princeton, N.J., 1958), is good on censorship of books and periodicals in the eighteenth century.

Histories of Spanish literature generally ignore censorship, although David Gies's work on the theater, "Glorious Invalid: Spanish Theater in the Nineteenth Century," *Hispanic Review* (Spring 1993) and *The Theater in Nineteenth-Century Spain* (Cambridge, 1994) are exceptions. N. Membrez, "The Bureaucratization of the Madrid Theater: Government Censorship, Curfews and Taxation, 1868–1925," *Anales de la literatura española contemporánea*, 17 (1992), 99–123 and J. Rubio Jiménez, "An Attempt at an Approach to Censorship of Theater in Spain in the Moderate Era, 1840–1868," *Segismundo*, 18 (1984), 193–231, also contain some interesting material on theater censorship. The *Cu Cut!* incident of 1905 and its political aftermath is one of the most heavily studied episodes of censorship in this period. J. Romero Maura, *The Spanish Army and Catalonia: the "Cu-Cut" Incident and the Law of Jurisdictions* (Beverly Hills, Calif., 1976), provides an excellent account. It is also discussed in his *The Spanish Army and Catalonia* (Beverly Hills, Calif., 1976).

Naturally, there is more material in Spanish, but the coverage is fairly spotty. J. E. de Eguizábal, *Apuntes para una historia de la legislación española sobre la imprenta desde el año 1480 al presente* (Madrid, 1879) and A. Rumeu de Armas, *Historia de la censura literaria gubernamentiva en España* (Madrid, 1940) are older narrative accounts of censorship legislation. Rumeu de Armas is especially useful for including the texts of the laws. M. Seoane, *Historia del periodismo en España* (Madrid, 1983), is a more recent survey that focuses on the press, while F. Cendán Pazos, *Historia del derecho español de prensa e imprenta*, (Madrid, 1974), looks at both the press and book publishing. Celso Almuiña Fernández, *La Prensa Vallisoletana durante el Siglo XIX* (Valladolid, 1977), is a thorough study of the press in one province that pays much attention to censorship. The same author's article, "Los gobernadores civiles y el control de la prensa decimonónica," in M. Tuñón de Lara, ed., *La Prensa de los Siglos XIX y XX* (Bilbao, 1986), 162–82, provides an excellent analysis of the power provincial officials wielded over the press.

Press censorship has received the most attention. J. Marcuello Benedicto, "La libertad de imprenta y su marco legal en la España liberal," *Ayer*, 34 (1999) is a recent synthesis of legislation between 1812 and 1936. O. Pelayo Galindo and J. Pereira Castañares, "La prensa en tiempos de Fernando VII," *Cuadernos de Investigación Histórica*, 12, (1989), looks at the situation under Ferdinand VII. B. Journeau, "Problèmes de Censure entre 1844 et 1854," in C. Dumas, *Culture et Société en Espagne et en Amérique Latine au XIXe siècle* (Lille, 1980) examines the first decade of Moderate rule. M. Cabrera et al., "Datos para un estudio cuantitativo de la prensa diaria madrileña," in *Prensa y sociedad en España*, 1820–1936 (Madrid, 1975), discusses the press in Madrid during the 1860s, as does A. Rincón Moñoz de Morales, "El marco legal de la prensa en los años anteriores a la 'Gloriosa,' " in *La Prensa en la Revolución Liberal* (Madrid, 1983). L. Romero Tobar, "Sobre censura de periódicos en el Siglo XIX: algunos expedientes gubernativos de 1860 al 1865," *Anuario de Historia Contemporánea*, 13 (1986) and "Textos inéditos de escritores españoles relacionados con la censura gubernativa," in *Homenaje a D. Agustín Millares Carlo* (Las Palmas, 1975), provide some primary sources. F. Arcas Cubero, *El País de la Olla* (Málaga, 1990), describes the experience of one provincial periodical during the Restoration. J. Valls, *Prensa y burguesía en el Siglo XIX español* (Madrid, 1987) offers an overview. Larra's responses to censorship can be found in M. J. de Larra, *Obras* (Madrid, 1960), vol. 1, while A. Medina-Bocos Montebello, "Larra y Mesonero: Dos Actitudes ante la Censura de Prensa," in *EPOS: Revista de Philology* (1989), compares Larra's responses to those of Mesonero Romanos.

On theater censorship, M. del Río Barredo, "Censura Inquisitorial y teatro de 1707 a 1819," *Hispania Sacra* (1986), examines the role of the Inquisition in censoring theater in the eighteenth and early nineteenth centuries. On Quintana as a theater censor, see E. Cotarelo, "Quintana, Censor de Teatros," *Revista de Archivos, Bibliotecas y Museos* (1900). J. Rubio Jiménez, "La censura teatral en la época moderada: 1840–1868," *Segismundo, Revista Hispánica de Teatro*, 39–40 (1984), is an excellent study of the moderate period. For an analysis of the furor over Pérez Galdós's play *Electra*, see E. Inman Fox, " 'Electra' de Perez Galdós," in Fox, *Ideología y política en las letras de fin del siglo (1898)* (Madrid, 1988).

On the Inquisition as censor, see A. Marquéz, *Literatura e Inquisicion en España, 1478–1834* (Madrid, 1980) For an example of book censorship during the reign of Ferdinand VII and some of the problems involved, see A. González Palencia, *Walter Scott y la censura gubernativa* (Madrid, 1927). Most studies of Spanish cinema censorship focus on the Franco regime, but the early years are discussed in T. González Ballesteros, *Aspectos jurídicos de la censura cinematográfica en España* (Madrid, 1981) and F. Méndez-Leite, *Historia de cine español* (Madrid, 1965).

6

The Austrian Empire

Lothar Höbelt

There is a well-worn joke that Prussia was not a state with an army but an army in possession of a state. Something very similar might be said about Austria, if not quite in the same martial terms. Austria is not a state with a bureaucracy, but a bureaucracy that created a state. To some extent, of course, this holds true for all states, but for Austria more so than others. France would remain France, no matter what form of government it adopted. But it was the Austrian bureaucracy that created an integrated corporation out of a holding company of disparate fiefs and lands. The "Empire of Austria" was nothing but a label hastily created in 1804 when Napoleon's onslaught spelled the end of the Holy Roman Empire, whose crown the Habsburg dynasty had worn for centuries. The "Austria" of 1804 consisted of more than a dozen separate entities, with separate histories and cultures. Some had been part of the old Empire (and went on to belong to the German Confederation established in 1815); others, like Hungary and Galicia (part of Poland today), had not. What held this disparate collection of lands together was the dynasty and, increasingly, the bureaucracy that governed in its name.

Even in the terms of the old regime Austria had an executive bias. There was no all-Austrian parliament before 1848. There was a central bureaucracy that dealt with a dozen or so noble regional legislatures (diets) that had gradually lost most of their remaining powers since the Habsburgs had started experimenting with enlightened absolutism in the eighteenth century. That bureaucracy was set up after 1749 to administer all the Habsburg lands that belonged to the Holy Roman Empire—for example, present-day Austria, Slovenia, the Czech lands and Trieste (Italian today). After 1772 it branched out into Galicia and the Bukovina (now Ukrainian). It never—except for a brief period in the 1850s—extended into Hungary. Hungary had an old established constitution that the natives liked to compare to England's. Above all, Hungary had retained its system of local government by elected members of the "gentry," the untitled nobles. This is why, even during the heyday of Habsburg absolutism, Hungarians in some faraway counties could indulge in a tax revolt with near impunity. The nondefeat of the Hungarian nobles in the seventeenth century and the nonintegration of Hungary by the centralizing bureaucracy of the eighteenth century constituted a "decision by default" that could not be reversed in the nineteenth century. That is why even before Hungary and the rest of the Habsburg Empire finally parted ways as far as domestic politics were concerned after 1867, Hungary constituted a special case—one, moreover, that for linguistic and other reasons the present author feels unfit to address at any length.

The state bureaucracy as first established by Empress Maria Theresa (1740–80) was enlightened in origin and authoritarian in practice. There is a German rhyme that describes the situation very well: "Verfassung vergeht, Verwaltung besteht" (Constitutions come and go, administrations stay the same). Although resisting all demands for a constitution during the first half of the nineteenth century, Austria lived through a bewildering succession of constitutions afterward: the decentralizing October Diploma of 1860, the centralizing February Patent of 1861, and finally the December Constitution of 1867, which reflected the division of the monarchy into Austrian-German and Hungarian spheres of domination. Thus, from the 1860s onward, Austrians enjoyed a certain measure of constitutional freedoms. Yet Austria never experienced a revolution. The only exception to that rule was 1848, of course. But even then what happened was not one revolution, but several liberal and national revolutions that could easily be played off against each other. Instead, time and again the impetus for internal reform was provided by external defeats: at the hands of Prussia in the 1740s, Napoleon in 1809, his nephew Napoleon III in 1859, Bismarck in 1866. In a dynamic that probably reveals more about the true workings of history than revolutionary bathos, the regime grudgingly consented to co-opt parliamentary assemblies as junior partners and emergency accountants in order to prop up its credit ratings when it ran out of steam and legitimacy in the 1860s.

The bureaucracy that for a long time denied the middle classes their say in politics was in itself composed of middle-class career civil servants. Austria simply did not have a sufficiently large aristocratic upper crust to ensure that the officer corps remained the exclusive preserve of the nobility, as was the case in Prussia. If noble birth, a well-connected family, and inherited riches eased one's way in the world, there were notable examples of "careers open to talent." That mixed elite's traditional enemy was not the aristocracy, but the Catholic Church, which had dominated intellectual life since the Thirty Years War. The famous cartoonist Wilhelm Busch gave a tongue-in-cheek definition of liberalism: "Wo man am Tisch der Reichen praßt/ und den Heiligen Vater haßt" (Where one feasts at the table of the rich/ While denouncing the Pope). The litmus test of liberalism—apart from a tepid constitutionalism that distrusted democratic aspirations—was anticlericalism, a staunch opposition to the claims of the Church.[1]

The liberal bureaucrats' patron saint and hero was Emperor Joseph II (1780–90) who severely reduced the power of the Church in the 1780s; he suppressed all ecclesiastical institutions except those serving socially useful purposes (like nursing and education) and imposed close control of religious affairs. If ground ceded to the Church after the upheavals of the French Revolutionary period seemed to have underlined the case for a close alliance between throne and altar, it was not before 1855 that the Church came back into its own—and then only briefly: between 1868 and 1874, during the Austrian version of the Prussian "Kulturkampf" (the "cultural war" against the Church), it was again stripped of its powers over education. At the same time, the "Kulturkampf" served to rally an overwhelming proportion at least of the rural population behind the church and its standard-bearers in politics. This added another layer to the liberals' mistrust of full-blown democracy. In contrast to Wilhelmine Germany and to France after 1848, Austria adopted universal (male) suffrage only in 1896 (with votes weighted by class), and universal and *equal* (male) suffrage only in 1907. Until 1896 the lower legislative house represented an electorate defined by property and education that comprised only about a fifth of Austrian adult males. The upper house consisted of hereditary and life peers. The emperor (Francis Joseph, 1848–1916) possessed the power of absolute veto but used it sparingly.

Finally, or rather first of all: much more so than by the usual cleavages of class and interest groups, Austria was, at least potentially, torn by ethnic conflict. Germans—although predominant among the elites—made up only about 25% of its population; Slavic peoples composed slightly more than half; Hungarians about 20%; a smattering of Italians and Rumanians shared the balance. Conventional wisdom during the nineteenth century—with little regard for late twentieth-century notions of political correctness—classified these nations into so-called "historic nations" and others.[2] Germans, Italians, Poles, and Hungarians counted among the historic nations because they had once proven their state-building potential, even if hundreds of years earlier. In the mid-nineteenth century, Ukrainians, Slovaks, Rumanians, and South Slavs counted only as dimly perceived tribes about whom it was debated whether their idiom actually qualified as a language or merely as a dialect. Czechs were a borderline case: much of the Empire's late nineteenth-century domestic politics centered on whether they should be accorded status as one of the monarchy's "historic nations"—and, if so, what would happen to the "Sudeten" Germans who made up a third of Bohemia's population and were among the most active segments of Austrian society.

Such a conglomerate of ethnic groups produced equal complexity as far as political parties and domestic politics were concerned. Until 1879 the anticlerical, centralist German liberals held the upper hand in parliament; from 1879 to 1893 they were succeeded by a pro-clerical decentralist-oriented combination of Slavs and German Catholics. During the 1890s an almost all-inclusive coalition briefly held power. After 1897, cabinets reverted to a state of color-blindness and ruled by emergency decree, while parliament almost committed suicide by obstruction. That deadlock was produced by the infamous Language Ordinances of Count Casimir Badeni (prime minister, 1895–97), which sought to appease the Czechs, but mostly roused the ire of the Germans; when they were finally withdrawn, the Czechs retaliated in kind. The universal, equal male suffrage reform of 1907 presumably sought to leave such troubles behind, but did little to lessen ethnic conflicts. It merely extended the privilege of bringing parliamentary business to a standstill to the "nonhistoric" nations, which had by then started to come into their own. Whereas the German-Czech confrontation previously dominated political life, by 1914 they increasingly had to share the limelight with Poles and Ukrainians battling for supremacy in Galicia, or with Slovenes and Italians competing for attention in the Adriatic. Austrian political life presented a chaotic picture. Yet, if it were madness, there was method in it. What the multiplying of ethnic cleavages did was to broaden the scope for a subtle policy of divide and conquer on the part of the ruling bureaucratic structure. Only defeat in World War I finally brought that establishment down and marked the end of the Empire it had regarded as its own.[3]

CENSORSHIP OF PRESS AND BOOKS

Before the 1848 Revolution

The history of modern censorship starts with what many regard as a Golden Age, the reign of Emperor Joseph II. There was no doubt about the liberalizing trend of his decrees: as one historian notes, "The prevailing atmosphere was undeniably permissive." The result was the so-called flood of pamphlets, "as anyone with a bee in his bonnet hurried to let it buzz in public." In a famous paragraph, the Emperor even appeared to appreciate the benefits accruing to government from this intellectual ferment: "Criticisms, if they are not slanderous, are not to be prohibited, no matter who their targets might be, whether the humblest or the highest, including the sovereign, especially if the author appends his name as a guarantee of validity. For every lover of truth must rejoice to be told the truth, even if it is conveyed to him via the uncomfortable route of criticism."[4] That certainly sounds enlightened—except for the thorny problem of establishing exactly what the truth is (a dangerous loophole, that). Despite his tolerant rhetoric, Joseph II had no intention of allowing any participatory activity on the part of the citizens. On the contrary, he further reduced the few remaining powers of the only existing representative institutions (unrepresentative as they were). His was an enlightened absolutism, and, if more enlightened than his predecessors, he was also more absolutist (something the French kings never managed). The saying attributed to his role model Frederick the Great ("I have made a deal with my subjects: They grumble as they like and I rule as I like") could equally be said to sum up his attitude.

For Joseph the enemy stood on the right. Thus, if middle-class criticism was directed against the pretensions of the nobles and the church, Joseph would not mind. Even his brother and successor Leopold II (1790–92) secretly encouraged that sort of thing. Put another way, it was easy for him to tolerate a moderate form of free speech, because for the time being "public opinion" had the good sense to largely agree with him. In addition, as a utilitarian he must have realized the futility of much of the effort that went into censorship. When he tried to calm an enraged prince of the Church, Joseph argued that prohibitions only succeeded in making bad books interesting. (Whether that nonchalance would stand the test of the times if the going got rough was another matter.) He also established the principle that censorship only applied to the book trade. Private possession of noncirculating books was not penalized. In his view, censorship should be part of overall commercial policy, not an exclusively political concern: in a famous comparison that did not help his popularity with intellectuals, he likened the book trade to selling cheeses.[5]

Technically, what he did was to centralize censorship and take it out of the hands of the Church and the church-controlled universities. Indeed, as far as the Church was concerned, censorship of a sort was actually strengthened. "Significantly, censorship for the clergy actually became more rigorous, for now all religious publications—even the shortest prayers—were subject to approval by the secular authorities." Nonetheless, the 1781 censorship guidelines still required that books that systematically attacked or ridiculed religion be forbidden. Censors were also encouraged to treat harshly "everything that contains immoral scenes and pointless vulgarities that can never breed learning or enlightenment." Beyond that remained a (revised) index of forbidden books that included about 900 titles.[6] Joseph was comparatively egalitarian, however, because he did away with most of the intermediate categories between forbidden and permitted material. The category "erga schedam" (i.e., books that could only be bought with special permission) was restricted to religious instruction books for non-Catholics, who were for the first time tolerated during his reign. Laymen and non-officials were to be drafted to review incoming material (university professors doubled as censors until the very end of that institution). Special rules applied to imported books. Some could be tolerated but must not be reprinted, sometimes because they might offend somebody abroad. (The inescapable dilemma of states that practice censorship is that everybody holds them responsible for what is being produced—i.e., concludes that anything allowed carries a stamp of official approval.)

In February 1787 Joseph went one step further. In Vienna only, pre-publication censorship was lifted entirely. If a publication was subsequently found to be inadmissible, the publisher had to withdraw it and pay a fine for every outstanding copy. We are assured, though, that under Joseph II no one was ever prosecuted under that decree.[7] A harsh statutory policy coupled with a lenient enforcement policy left control in the hands of a tightly knit bureaucracy. In any case, this was one of the ordinances to be withdrawn on Joseph's deathbed. Joseph never held a very high opinion of newspapers, and in May 1789 he imposed a heavy newspaper tax—roughly equivalent to half their price—that effectively bankrupted most of them. (Another reason was that the official *Wiener Zeitung* continued to enjoy a legal monopoly of advertisements; other papers had to live off their sales until 1848.) As a result, the market was swamped with foreign newspapers or pirated translations that became objects of the greatest suspicion once the wars with France started in 1792.[8]

Joseph's honeymoon with the public ended long before his death. In 1787 the Emperor found himself drawn into an unpopular war against the Turks. Conservative discontent welled up, although it is still debated whether the clampdown that followed was a concession to conservatives or a measure against them. His successor Leopold II "combined timely concessions to tradition, maintenance of Joseph's reforms, and permissiveness towards the political aspirations of the unprivileged."[9] He decentralized censorship, returning it to the universities, the provincial authorities, and the Hofkanzlei (court chancellery), the surrogate ministry of the interior that had a certain aristocratic bias; this was seen as a sop to conservatives but might have developed a liberalizing potential in the long run. There was to be no long run, however. In the spring of 1792 Leopold suddenly died, six weeks before Revolutionary France declared war on Austria. Count Pergen, the chief of police affairs, who had been appointed by Joseph, dismissed by Leopold, and then recalled by Leopold's son and successor Francis II (1792–1835) at the end of 1792, finally managed to have censorship added to his brief in 1801. His one-time deputy, Count Saurau, continued to dominate domestic policy until 1830.[10]

As the struggle against rebellious conservatives was supplanted by an external war against French revolutionaries, Austria experienced a tightening of restrictions. For Leopold's son, the inexperienced Francis II, the enemy was no longer on the Right but to the west. Even so, the threat posed by the few isolated cells of supposed Austrian Jacobins has probably been exaggerated. Nevertheless, the regime believed in "better safe than sorry," so they gave no hostages to fortune. The tightening of press restrictions was codified in a comprehensive 1795 law that tried to close all the loopholes left open by a liberal interpretation of Joseph's ordinances. Several decrees ordered censors to devote their attention to all discussion of policy issues. Fines were not just threatened, but actually collected, and prison sentences imposed on those who could not pay. Partially due to wartime pressures, the list of treasonable offenses was enlarged and included clauses that could be stretched to mean almost anything.[11]

Fighting a losing war and in financial disarray, the government had far more to worry about than a few cells of discontented illuminati. In 1801 the court commission in charge of censorship was merged with the police and a reclassification of books undertaken that made the retrograde movement of intellectual life measurable. More than 2,500 books that had formerly been found inoffensive were now no longer deemed suitable. Thus, "large portions of booksellers stocks were reduced to waste paper at a single stroke."[12]

The French occupation of Vienna in 1809 provided an interlude of almost unrestricted freedom for the book trade (if less so for the theater). Austria's informal poet laureate, Franz Grillparzer—certainly the most loyal of citizens—like many others hastened to obtain a complete set of Goethe's works, available in Vienna for the first time. Even if there was another purge of bookshops after the French left, the more reflective mood engendered by defeat found expression in the 1810 censorship decree and the enactment of a Civil Code in 1811 that reflected an emphasis on individual rights. Circulating libraries, banned in 1798, were allowed to reopen under certain conditions, and the theoretically unlimited prison sentences that could be handed out for infringements of the 1795 press law were reduced. Political offenses now carried a maximum penalty of six months in prison, and that only for repeat offenders.[13]

The 1810 censorship law was even designed to compare favorably with a recent Napoleonic edict. It started lyrically and optimistically, "No ray of light, from whatever source shall henceforth remain unacknowledged or be deprived of its potential usefulness." But of course, it added, the minds of the immature must still be protected against seducers and cranks. Although highly paternalistic and smothering, the law reflected the didactic and utilitarian instincts of a good deal of enlightenment thinking. Unlike many modern authoritarian regimes, absolutist Austria did not favor "escapist" literature. Novels and light entertainment designed for the masses were discouraged: "Brochures, youth and popular entertainment must be treated with the full rigor of existing censorship laws." The 1810 decree's real purpose was to permit some freedom for scholarly work. But it took great pains to define and restrict the notion of what constituted a scholarly work: "Endless repetitions of well-known facts devoid of force of expression or argument" did not qualify for the promised greater leniency, only "those works that excel by new discoveries, conclusive and enlightening exposition and the exploration of new approaches."[14]

No massive breakthough for intellectual freedom could be expected with such rarefied guidelines. Indeed, the chief consequence, one that apparently caused a lot of resentment among intellectuals, was that censors acquired the right of pronouncing on the literary or scholarly merits of the manuscripts submitted and no longer just on questions of political expediency. As the poet Count Anton Auersperg (pseudonym of Anastasius Grün) once quipped, "It is comforting and edifying to be judged on your literary merits by a man who does not know how to spell his native tongue correctly."[15]

There was a theoretical right of appeal against the decisions of the censors, but as they were supposed to do their work anonymously and were not required to justify their decisions, in practice it was difficult and pointless to argue with them. Censorship was not restricted to books and periodicals. Paintings were unique works of art, but if their topic was deemed unsuitable, they could not be exhibited publicly. Also subject to censorship were all illustrations intended for publication, theatrical performances, songs, musical programs and handbills, lectures, sermons, posters, funeral notices, advertisements for balls and hunts, maps, house and business signs, badges, medals, cufflinks, tobacco boxes, and even graveyard headstone inscriptions. The great playwright Johann Nestroy termed the censorship a "crocodile lurking on the banks of the river of ideas and biting off the heads of the writers swimming in it," while the oft-censored dramatist Grillparzer lamented that the censorship made "invisible chains rattle on the hand and foot" of writers, that with it the only freedom of thought was the freedom to "keep our thoughts to ourselves." The aging composer Ludwig van Beethoven complained that the Austrian mania for regulation was so severe that "they are discussing a law about how high a bird can fly and how quickly hares may run."[16]

At least 5,000 separate book titles were forbidden in Austria between 1835 and 1848 (including 1,250 titles of English and French fiction); according to 1840s police statistics, about 20 percent of all submitted books were forbidden. The banned list, which has been compared to a "catalogue of masterpieces of European literature," included works by Rousseau, Spinoza, Heine, Lessing, Goethe, and Schiller. Yet not all books that were banned were banned equally: the different shades of gray that Joseph had all but abolished came back into fashion. This was a selective opening, elitist in the way it granted exceptions, that followed the general rule summarized by one historian as "the lower the social and educational status, the more information was to be withheld."[17] The censors placed each work in one of five categories, ranging from "Admittur" (unrestricted for all) to

"Damnatur" (forbidden to all), while the middle three categories contained various restrictions designed to limit circulation to the supposedly "safe" educated classes. For example, the "Transeat" category could be freely sold but not announced or reviewed in the papers, while books labeled "erga schedam" were available to a limited number of professionals such as governmental officials and scientists. Ranke's histories were among those works available to all bona-fide scholars but not to the public at large; in general collected works were treated less harshly than individual books on the theory that their high price would prevent unduly wide distribution.

One of the advantages of pre-publication censorship was that authors and publishers ran few risks. No stigma attached to having a manuscript rejected by the censor and even when their works were suppressed authors were not prosecuted. When he finally confessed to being the Anastasius Grün who had published his poems abroad without asking for official permission, Count Auersperg was fined a symbolic twenty-five florins. A less august person like the lawyer and dramatist Adolph Wiesner served eight days in prison for the same offense. Other writers might even be offered money to hush them up: in one famous case involving Grillparzer, the emperor offered to buy the rights of a play that might prove controversial. Obviously, a system that openly relied on exceptions had a certain degree of flexibility—and unpredictability. The authorities even reserved the right to reverse their judgment; permission to publish was valid only for one year, and second editions had to be resubmitted. A lot depended on who was actually in charge of the whole process. Baron Franz Haager, the author of the 1810 decree, died shortly after the Congress of Vienna; the police institution he had headed then became infamous under his successor, Count Joseph Sedlnitzky. The emperor himself was not above every now and then putting the blame for unpopular decisions on overeager officials (especially in cases involving his beloved theater). In fact, Police President Sedlnitzky was far from being an Austrian-style version of Napoleon's secret police chief, Fouché, and certainly no suitable role model for any of the secret police barons of this century intent on building up a state within the state, but a timid and conscientious civil servant, slow and pedantic, who in later life was well known for his interest in charities. It could even be argued that the secret police with its fabled network of informers functioned not so much as an instrument of repression but as an intelligence service, a sort of early warning system in an age not yet used to constant polling.[18]

A great deal of attention was devoted to imported books, which were handled by Foreign Minister Metternich's State Chancellery in tandem with the police. Due to Paris's dominant cultural position, French books figured prominently among those on the blacklist, yet it was the German books that appealed to a public on both sides of the Austrian border that were the most difficult to control. Despite the infamous 1819 Carlsbad Decrees that theoretically gave the German Confederation centralized censorship powers, standards in most German states were considerably more relaxed and loopholes could always be found. Metternich himself threatened influential dailies like Johann Cotta's widely read *Augsburger Allgemeine Zeitung* with circulation restrictions if they did not mind their manners, and in the mid-1840s perhaps only 25 percent of the approximately 10,000 titles available elsewhere in Germany were approved in Austria.[19]

In the case of the Poles, the independent city state of Cracow (until 1846 when it was annexed by Austria) was a thorn in the flesh. The potential danger from across the borders was presumably less of a worry in cases where co-nationals smarted under Czarist or Turkish rule. Austrian Germans sometimes thought they noticed a suspicious leniency on the part of the authorities toward the aspirations of the Czechs (who had nowhere to turn anyway). If there was some truth in that observation, it probably owed more to the elitist character of the people active in the Slavic revival of the early nineteenth century, who were typically well-connected landed magnates. The Hungarians were subjected to increasing scrutiny as nationalist feelings increasingly flowered there after 1830.[20]

Over time, the genuinely antirevolutionary intent and purpose of censorship probably increased, especially after the July Revolution of 1830 in France, which helped to trigger unrest in a number of German and Italian principalities. Thus, Metternich was quite content to manipulate the German princes with tales of fearful conspiracies around 1820, yet was genuinely consumed by such fears in later life. To associate his name with Austrian censorship is in one sense unfair, as he was responsible for foreign affairs only and gained an institutional foothold in domestic policy only after 1835 (even then his planned takeover failed). On the other hand, it is well deserved, as his celebrated feat was to ram a draconian censorship and association law (among them the Carlsbad Decrees, which are discussed in detail in the chapter on Germany in this volume) down the throats of the German Confederation in the aftermath of the 1819 assassination of the establishment author August von Kotzebue. The main target of that crackdown, which gave rise to a number of celebrated songs (e.g., "Die Gedanken sind frei"—Thoughts are Free), were the student fraternities, but a swipe at their teachers soon followed.[21]

Even before 1819, of course, Metternich and Police President Sedlnitzky certainly never shared the intended spirit of the 1810 reforms. Metternich held no high opinion of academics and once sighed: "If only we could have knowledge without scholars." Metternich's view of the press was even lower: he termed it a "scourge" and the "most urgent evil" of his time, which only served as "a party antagonistic to all existing governments." When the emerging middle classes were permitted to open their Juridical-Political Reading Club in Vienna against his objections shortly before 1848, Sedlnitzky prophesied, "People will read themselves into criminals."[22]

The authorities were certainly caught in a dialectical dilemma. As Beaumarchais once put it, "Great men are not afraid of small booklets, are they?" Put another way, censorship was a backhanded compliment, as banning a text acknowledged its potential danger and thus its importance. (Of course, that compliment would be devalued if the impression was created that it owed more to bureaucratic obscurantism or sheer sloth than to high-level policy decisions.) A regime that lived in denial of social tensions and real grievances had little choice but to blame popular discontent on the agitation of irresponsible demagogues—a "Catch 22" situation that is maybe not as alien to our world as we would like to think. Even the translations of Sir Walter Scott's novels (and, remember, he was a Tory!) were subject to all sorts of alterations. It was not enough for the right side to win in the end; the wicked ones (like the Puritan regicides in *Woodstock*) had to be denied expression altogether.[23]

On the other hand, the regime saw no need to politicize citizens (or rather subjects), not even those in favor of the government's agenda: As the famous Prussian slogan in 1806 had it: "Peace and quiet is the first duty of a citizen." The corollary was that neutrality counted in one's favor; the "Gutgesinnten" ("well disposed") included the indifferent and nonpolitical, in stark contrast to totalitarian movements that are liable to ask for total dedication and active commitment. The structural tension between the socially conservative but politically and intellectually increasingly open-minded aristocratic provincial assemblies and the initially reforming but heavy-handed and increasingly ossified bureaucracy that had pushed them into the background during the previous century remained the same. Only labels changed: Who were the "progressives" and who were the "reactionaries" now?

Francis II and Metternich were acutely aware that the bureaucratic monster they headed might develop a dynamic of its own, and sometimes wondered whether it could any longer be effectively controlled. As a result, whereas Joseph II had apparently believed himself capable of riding the tiger and valued efficiency above all else, Francis II experimented with a series of reforms designed to provide a sort of internal separation of powers. Unfortunately, the internal checks and balances set in place could, when combined with bureaucratic infighting, all too easily translate into deadlock. As far as censorship is concerned, part of the internal friction derived from sheer volume of work. The number of publications submitted for approval increased, but the number of censors did not. At no time did the central Court Censorship Commission employ more than two dozen censors and half of them were part time. Sedlnitzky's painstaking slowness and procrastination certainly did nothing to improve matters. Censorship accurately reflected an evil that became endemic throughout the state machinery after 1835, when Francis was succeeded by his epileptic son Ferdinand I (1835–48), who left ruling to an unhappy triumvirate adept at blocking each others' initiatives.[24]

Toward the end of the monarchy Austria was once described as a "tyranny tempered by incompetence." Ironically, one of the complaints of pre-1848 writers (few of them fire-breathing radicals, anyway) was the inefficiency of the censorship apparatus. Above all, the fact that censors worked according to guidelines and instructions known only to them made rational calculation in all matters connected with publishing difficult. In 1845 a number of the most respected writers futilely petitioned, not for an abolition, but for an overhaul of the censorship system that would make censors accountable. "Where there is no law, only the individual view of the censor, it can happen easily that even the permitted and harmless, nay, the useful is still banned. . . . The author is judged according to norms he is not acquainted with, and sentenced without being heard or given an opportunity to defend himself."[25]

In response, Metternich followed the classic strategy of Austrian bureaucrats: the silent deposition of the petition, he grandly opined, was the only answer consistent with the dignity of the government. Nevertheless, he privately, or for internal consumption, penned a few remarks: he tried to turn the tables on the petitioners and recover the moral high ground by insisting that the rules of censorship were solely based on moral laws, reason, and common sense—and surely the authors would not want those high principles to be replaced by the paragraphs of a positive law. He wrote, "Woe betide the author who has to look to the legal code for instruction about what morals, reason and the natural feeling for good and bad should tell him."[26]

What does seem to have become easier, with improved means of communication all around, was to obtain banned books from abroad. The "Chinese Wall" that shut off Austria from the rest of Europe, as German writer Ludwig Börne phrased it, was clearly beginning to crumble by the 1840s. As Count Franz Hartig, a close ally of Metternich, later wrote, "All foreign literary productions were easily obtained in private, so that a man of any literary pretensions would have been ashamed in society to acknowledge himself unacquainted with a forbidden book or journal that had excited observation. For instance, even in the presence of the highest officials, and in the most public places, it was customary to speak of the worst articles in the journal *Die Grenzboten*." (The well-known "green booklets" of *Die Grenzboten* were published in Leipzig by the exiled Ignaz Kuranda and widely smuggled across the frontier; they provided a forum for Austrian dissenters of all stripes.) In 1843 the police seized almost 400 forbidden volumes from one Viennese bookseller, and in March 1848, when the regime collapsed, booksellers were reportedly ready to sell any number of forbidden books out of their stock.[27]

The flood of illegal imports translated into a competitive disadvantage for Austrian writers and publishers: the number of printers in Vienna actually declined during the seventy years following Joseph II's death in 1790. If Stuttgart or Leipzig rather than Vienna dominated German publishing, censorship had something to do with it; the authors of the 1845 petition argued censorship cost Austria a million florins a year in lost trade. For the regime, the years before 1848 were the worst of both worlds: it was still considered obnoxious, but no longer feared, a "nuisance rather than tyranny."[28] A collapse of bond prices, sparked by Metternich's counterproductive counterrevolutionary fervor and fears of another round of revolutionary wars with France, helped deal the final blow to his by then rather ancien regime and ushered in 1848. As Kuranda noted in his *Grenzboten*, "Financial speculation recoups what the state denies to philosophical speculation."[29]

The Post-1848 Period

Two days after Metternich's fall on March 13, 1848, following a popular uprising in Vienna, two of the best-known writers of the period, the dramatist Eduard von Bauernfeld and the poet Count Anton Auersperg, personally persuaded their patron and colleague (and Metternich's rival) Minister of the Interior Count Anton Kolowrat to grant complete freedom of the press (with the result that the number of newspapers in the Empire jumped from seventy-nine to 388 in a single year). If it seems fanciful to blame the newly free press for the chaos that followed, as some of Metternich's disciples claimed, it certainly did nothing to abate the rising storm. (Stories were told that rural vintners misunderstood freedom of the press as a lifting of taxes on the products of the wine-press.) The April 1 provisional press law still retained some restrictions, however: publishers had to pay a deposit and the state reserved the right to have official rejoinders printed without further ado. In the face of popular objections, spearheaded by the student caucus, the offending law was immediately withdrawn. A new one that provided for trial by jury was finally hammered out in May after consultation with the writers' association. The first press case that went to court, on August 24, ended with the acquittal of the editor of a student paper, Oskar Falke. Austrians for a few months did indeed enjoy the blessings of a free press, even if conservatives scoffed that the disapproval of the censor's pen had been mild compared with the rough justice of mob rule, at least in Vienna: "Früher drohten Striche, jetzt drohen Stricke" (In the past you were threatened with cuts, now with the noose).[30]

The defeat of revolutionary Vienna in October spawned martial law and a few executions. But the victorious counterrevolution proved that its purpose was neo-absolutism rather than complete restoration. Young Emperor Francis Joseph (1848–1916) in many ways paralleled his upstart cousin, French Emperor Napoleon III, rather than his august ancestors, and his high-born but enterprising prime minister, Prince Felix zu Schwarzenberg, even co-opted turncoat liberals into the cabinet. Censorship was modernized: the aim was no longer to outlaw potential opposition papers outright, thus driving them underground, but to convert them into involuntary agents of government propaganda from fear of suppression and commercial ruin. Pre-publication censorship was not reintroduced, but papers had to put down a hefty security bond to publish, and could be suspended or prosecuted if they ignored official warnings or were deemed to violate the exceedingly vague provisions of the 1852 press decree, which banned all works "of an orientation that was hostile to the throne, the monarchy, the unity and integrity of the empire, monarchical principles, religion, public morals, or the overall foundations of the state's society, or of an orientation that was incompatible with maintenance of public law and order." Self-censorship in the shadow of Damocles's sword might be more effective than the cumbersome process of the pre-1848 period, especially as newspapers were finally allowed to carry advertisements and allowed to develop into worthwhile commercial enterprises (although the number of newspapers published in the Habsburg lands dropped to 128 by 1856, less than one-third of the 1848 peak, largely as a result of the renovated press controls, presumably increasing the market share of survivors; in Prague, where thirty-seven periodicals had sprung up in 1848 and many journalists were afterwards prosecuted, only eight periodicals were left by 1852.)[31]

To quote the journalist Kuranda, the preoccupation of journalists after 1848 was "the art of using language in a state that is neither censorship nor freedom of the press."[32] The authorities followed the principle that newspapers had to be given some leeway to be believed at all. As Kuranda put it, "How could they be believed if they said something in support of Austria, if they had never been allowed to say anything against it?" Toward the end of the 1850s neo-absolutist regime, someone made the paradoxical comment that the police were the journalists' only friend—because they happened to agree on anticlericalism. (With all its economic modernization, the regime had fatally undermined its reputation with the intellectuals by signing a concordat with Rome in 1855.)[33]

External defeat in both 1859 (France) and 1866 (Prussia) and the financial pressures that went with it finally acted as a catalyst for the transition to constitutional government. Journalists were among the first to profit, as the 1862 press law ended licensing requirements for publishers and referred all disputes to the courts (if not yet to trial by jury), rather than to the police or the administration. In cabinet, Foreign Secretary Count Rechberg tried to restore the old licensing system by a variation on the theme formerly used by Joseph II—only this time papers were not compared to cheeses but to poison dispensed by chemists who were strictly regulated accordingly. When debating whether journalists should sign their names, the conservative Liberal Baron Lasser pessimistically advised against it because these days "more courage was needed to come out in favor of rather than against the ministry."[34]

Maybe that perception was why Anton von Schmerling, prime minister in all but name from 1861 to 1865, insisted on a high level of immunity from criticism for the state and its servants, incidentally including priests. If any of them was libeled, the state prosecutor had to swing into action automatically. The lower legislative house initially rejected that clause, but finally gave way when Schmerling threatened that if they remained obdurate the old censorship law would simply remain in force unreformed. Vestiges of the old system survived, anyway: a journal could still be suspended after three warnings and until 1869 these infringements were not subject to trial by jury, but solely by a panel of judges. In the peculiarly Austrian concept of a so-called "objective trial," these judges could judge and condemn articles independently of the journalist who wrote them, who could not testify and was not charged with evil intentions. To make matters worse, the man in charge of the relevant department in the Ministry of Justice, Georg Lienbacher, was a maverick conservative distinctly unsympathetic to journalists.[35]

On the other hand, unlikely alliances formed in support of greater freedom of the press: Even Kuranda and F. L. Rieger, the leading newspaper owners of, respectively, the German centralists and the Czech States Rights faction, publicly joined forces in parliament. (A poetically gifted parliamentary colleague caught the spirit of that moment in a mocking poem, referring to Ovid's Golden Age where lions lie down with the lambs.)[36] The Czech States Rights party, which refused to accept the legitimacy of the all-Austrian parliament, as distinct from the Bohemian diet, labored under a specific difficulty, because it was a crime to disparage the Vienna parliament.

In 1867 the constitution was amended and a bill of rights added. In October 1868 the press law was further reformed to eliminate such arbitrariness as Lienbacher and his ilk practiced. Individual copies of newspapers could still be confiscated, but offending papers could no longer be forced to suspend publication for three months. Confiscation was a slap on the wrist that served to give offended state officials (and the party in power) some protection over and above the libel laws. In Salzburg, for example, the main opposition paper was confiscated ten times in the space of four years. In one case, the same version of a speech that was confiscated in Graz went unpunished in a Vienna paper. Newspaper owners still had to deposit a security bond, ranging from 1,000 to 8,000 florins, from which fines and trial costs were deducted.[37] These financial disincentives militated against small papers, but no longer prevented the big dailies from having their say. Partly to make confiscations easier, newspapers were still not allowed to be sold on the streets (and as late as 1890 only about 300 especially approved books could be sold by itinerant peddlers). On the other hand, after 1869 offending journalists could choose trial by jury. As a result, in many cases national solidarity in the face of a hostile bureaucracy meant prosecutors found it hard to obtain convictions. And even if sentenced, in a multinational empire where most conflicts could be traced to a background of ethnic strife, many of the leading politicians were proud to parade a record of convictions for political offenses.

Not all confiscated material was political in nature. Victorian values still held sway. A certain kind of erotic literature had to be sold under the counter. Toward the turn of the century someone went to the trouble of compiling a list of books that had been taken out of circulation.[38] Its pages list the diatribes of a combative bishop and an unauthorized photograph of Crown Prince Rudolph's death mask, alongside racy eighteenth century classics like Casanova and the Marquis de Sade, not to mention "Horny Anna," an artfully "simple girl" whose memoirs were published in Cincinnati, only to run foul of an Austrian court fourteen years later. Political literature such as Pan-German, Italian irredentist, anti-Semitic, and Social Democratic pamphlets made up the bulk of the rest.

Apart from minor press offenses like defamation of character, there were several categories of political offenses. One was *lèse-majesté*. Thus, speculation about the crown prince's suicide at Mayerling had to be conducted outside the columns of the Austrian press (just as forty years later the English had to learn about Wally Simpson from American papers). Other political offenses included incitement to resistance against the laws of the land and "disturbance of the peace," a term so loose that it included all those who could be accused of trying "to turn the inhabitants of the state into inimical factions" ("die Einwohner des Staates zu feindseligen Parteiungen gegeneinander auffordert"), thus arguably criminalizing the whole point of party politics. What could not be forbidden under any circumstances, however, was to reprint the pages of the official records of parliamentary assemblies. Passages likely to encourage "inimical factions" could therefore be placed beyond the reach of even the most suspicious state prosecutor provided they had been said in parliament. That way to beat the system was, strictly speaking, only available to Germans, however, since non-German speeches went unrecorded until 1917.[39]

Abetting high treason in print was punishable by ten to twenty years in prison. Treason law has often been used as a convenient excuse for a crackdown on fringe groups, but in the Habsburg monarchy, according to the letter of the law, there were quite a number of potential "traitors" who swam in the political mainstream, since this offense theoretically encompassed irredentist and secessionist tendencies of every stripe. In a multinational empire like Austria, any number of people, even pillars of local society, were suspected of at least toying with "high treason" at one time or another, and rightly so. To cite just one example, Emanuel Engel, leader of the Young Czech party that in his day included almost the entire political elite of his nation, was quoted as having privately said he would not mind serving as the Russian governor of Bohemia one day. Drinking to the health of the Prussian Hohenzollerns or the Italian House of Savoy (fellow monarchs as they were) was another borderline case. Under normal circumstances no untoward consequences would follow such indiscretions. But the safeguards of a liberal constitution were to no avail if the authorities declared a state of emergency, as they did in Galicia in 1864–65 or in Prague and the surrounding areas in 1868–69 and 1893–95. In such circumstances, papers could be suppressed for three months and treason trials were conducted in an atmosphere unlikely to lead to acquittals.

Ever watchful for any sign of treason, Austria for a few years had its own version of Germany's anti-Socialist laws that actually pre-dated the formation of a unified Social Democratic movement and was mainly directed against isolated pockets of anarchists. Compared with the disruptive potential of nationalism, socialism was a minor threat from the empire's point of view. Some die-hard conservatives even argued that every labor strike helped check "manchesterism" and the factory system, while liberals granted that the socialists were at least stalwart anticlericals, even if not to be trusted with the family silver. As a result, while they certainly suffered their share of court battles over the antics of overeager agitators, in the long run the socialists tended to be regarded as the lesser evil by the establishment.[40]

The overall picture of press freedom in the Austrian Empire remained extremely mixed right down to World War I. On the one hand formal press controls continued to ease, and the number of periodicals steadily increased: During the 1890s, security bonds and special newspaper taxes (which had doubled the price of newspapers) were abolished, and as such controls ended (newspaper licensing requirements having earlier been abolished in 1862) the number of periodicals published in the Empire jumped from 128 in 1856 to 345 in 1862, 1,300 in 1882 and 4,500 in 1912 (figures that, of course, reflected increased literacy and population as well as lessened press controls). But enough loopholes, such as those discussed above, remained in the press regulations to allow massive crackdowns during periods of tension and against selected, especially nationalist and working-class, targets. If the Czech press was especially targeted, this was in response to the continued rejection of the legitimacy of the 1867 constitution by Czech political parties, which withdrew into a sort of fundamentalist opposition for a dozen years: In 1868–69 Czech editors were given jail sentences totaling seventeen years. Even afterward, a Czech opposition paper like *Narodni Listy* was confiscated 330 times during the 1880s, and during the notorious 1893–95 period of emergency rule eight Prague newspapers were suppressed.[41]

During the prime ministership of Ernest Koerber (1900–5) there was a considerable easing of press restrictions, but the last peacetime minister of justice, Viktor von Hochenburger (1909–16), established a fearsome reputation as an avid confiscator. A cartoonist even "praised" his even-handedness in pressing for verdicts against newspapers from both the right and left: "No matter whether Czech or German, Hochenburger confiscates!" Cartoonists themselves were fairly safe after 1905 so long as they spared Emperor Franz Joseph. But before then caricature journals were occasionally confiscated, staff members of the democratically oriented (and rather stridently anti-Semitic) caricature journal *Kikeriki* were jailed on several occasions, and during the 1890s the authorities also banned posters advertising the great German caricature journal *Simplicissimus*.[42]

THEATER AND FILM CENSORSHIP

As discussed elsewhere in this book, the stage was treated even more gingerly than the printed word by the authorities. Reading was an essentially private pastime. Theater was a public spectacle—and probably a less elitist one than today. A politicized audience might be provoked into a mob and with inadequate means of riot control one never knew what might happen. Selective applause, even in performances of the safe classics, continued to provide an outlet for otherwise censored opposition sentiments well into the twentieth century. In any case, the target of theater censorship was less the text itself than the possible "interaction between audience and stage."

The paranoia of mid-nineteenth-theater censors gave rise to a great number of funny anecdotes that would become favored reading for the aging liberals of the "Gilded Age": among them was the director who told his devils to wear green trousers because red ones might be mistaken for those of Austrian generals. (It remained standard practice until the end of the monarchy to ban real-life uniforms from the stage, whether they were those of officers, ranking civil servants, or priests.) The plays of Shakespeare and other bards were sometimes altered out of recognition. Like Hollywood, Austrian censorship seemed to prefer happy endings, so Romeo, Juliet, and King Lear all had to survive. Because anything to do with royalty was a touchy business, even a rip-off on *King Lear* was frowned on because one simply did not make fun of kings. Schiller's *Don Carlos* had to be remodeled, not for the obvious reference to freedom of thought, but because a Habsburg prince was not supposed to fall in love with his stepmother, while in Mozart's *Don Giovanni* the line declaring that "freedom lives" had to be changed to "jollity lives"! Burgtheater actors took to referring to the censorship office as the "Intimidation, Cuts and Rejection Office" (Schreckens-, Streich-, und Verwerfungsstelle). As theater historian W. E. Yates notes, "The treatment of the German classics in particular made nonsense of the original intention that the Burgtheater should function as a national theater."[43]

In line with the overriding aim of preventing any sort of discord or unrest, it was completely forbidden to treat religious subjects or violent and shocking crimes, to satirize nationalities or classes of citizens, to in any way belittle the state or the monarchy or portray rebellion against the ruling house, or even to discuss political terms such as "constitution," "liberty," "equality," "tyrant," and "despotism." Thus, Schiller's *William Tell*, a portrayal of a medieval Swiss revolt against Habsburg rule, was performed at the Burgtheater in 1827 (a 1824 ballet on the subject was completely banned "for political reasons") only after the censors "adapted" it so that, in their words, "Austria and her former relations to Switzerland are not mentioned, and the democratic tendency, which one might ascribe to the original, disappears in favor of a merely domestic and generally human interest." Dramatists and actors were also strictly forbidden to refer to persons who were still alive; the prolific Viennese playwright and actor Johann Nestroy was prosecuted only once, for a snide impromptu about a well-known theater critic that prompted his incarceration for five days. The authorities were less sensitive to social criticism: rich and poor were allowed to have their differences on stage, and in the early stages of the industrial revolution the nouveaux riches provided an obvious target for jokes that gave satisfaction to both the poor and the exclusive set, such as Nestroy's sarcastic comment that "Ten Dukes and a Prince cannot rival the arrogance of a porter who has suddenly become a millionaire."[44]

If the censors in Naples insisted that Swedish King Gustavus III in Verdi's *Un Ballo in Maschera* had to be transformed into a governor of Boston in order to be assassinated (even though that was not a place where balls and masques held sway in the early modern period), it is even more baffling why in 1850 (when France was not even a monarchy) the Austrians took care to save the sixteenth-century French monarch Francis I's reputation in Victor Hugo's *Le Roi s'amuse* by moving the story to Mantua. On the other hand, all the really stirring stuff like the prisoners' chorus "Va, pensiero" in Verdi's *Nabucco*, which was first performed in Austrian-ruled prerevolutionary Milan in 1842, apparently went unnoticed. The same was true for Verdi's *Attila*, which premiered in Venice in 1846. Maybe the saving grace of the opera was, to quote an Anglo-Saxon critic, that "for any one not an Italian under Austrian occupation, Attila was easily the most sympathetic character." Perhaps music as a medium, if not the lyrics that went with it, presented insurmountable obstacles to censorship (perhaps partly because, at least formally, scores were considered manuscripts rather than printed works and thus not subject to censorship). Or Italian censors working for the Austrian authorities may have cheated on their masters; it has been claimed that censorship in Italy was "least serious in those two provinces [Lombardy and Venetia] which Austria actually occupied."[45]

Personal likes and dislikes played a large part in censorship decisions (inevitably, stories of actresses exercising their charms were current). In Vienna theater is (still) a cause célèbre, more intensely discussed than weightier policy issues. Francis II himself was no exception. He took a personal interest in it—and sometimes resorted to the game of pretending to be outraged or amused by the antics of his censorship department. He offered to buy Grillparzer's *Ein treuer Diener seines Herrn* to prevent its performance (maybe because it dealt with a Hungarian topic); on the other hand, he enabled *König Ottokar* to be performed over the objections of the censors.[46]

The big drawback for the stage was that, unlike the press, it was never freed from prior censorship while the empire lasted. In 1850 the theatrical censorship that had collapsed in 1848 was formally restored, with much the same guidelines: nothing could be presented that was directed against the dynasty, threatened law and order, offended public decency, religion, or morality, or intruded into individuals' private lives. Theater owners still needed a license that could be arbitrarily denied and the police sat in at the rehearsals to enforce censorship cuts. "The stage is excluded from that measure of freedom that is guaranteed by law to the other arts, science and literature."[47] (Of course, to pursue the parallel a bit further, there is some difficulty in confiscating performances after the event. Yet there is a certain make-believe quality about banning or excising passages that could easily be checked in any library.) It is worth noting, though, that when the subject came up for discussion during the 1890s, some theater directors opposed abolishing pre-censorship because they saw it as a safety valve that prevented their houses from being subjected to heavy fines and penalties after the event in case the authorities spotted some legal offense.

Theater censorship seems to have become considerably more tolerant after 1850 compared to the previous era, and it was fairly uncontroversial during most of the latter part of the nineteenth century. In a partial reversal of the original rather puritan enlightenment spirit, there was a tendency to tolerate risqué scenes in French style light comedies. What was frowned on was "the serious presentation of immorality"[48] that purported to deal with sexual matters and related questions of morality in a way that was didactically critical of the values and/or the hypocrisy of society.

Things became more turbulent from the 1890s onward: the number of theaters and productions multiplied. Naturalism with its "kitchen-sink realism," so at odds with the lofty ideals of the classics, challenged the dominant aesthetic sensibilities of the Romantic age. Moreover, on the wider stage of politics the rise of rival mass movements like Christian Socialism and Social Democracy led to a revival of a "Kulturkampf" atmosphere. One gets the impression that for Imperial statesmen theater censorship had almost become an embarrassment as soon as it was no longer a matter of defending a single, accepted standard of good taste against the hoi polloi, but of balancing between rival popular notions of standards of propriety. The censors no longer tried to impose their version of norms on society and actually made some effort to be responsive to changing moods in popular taste. In 1903 Prime Minister Koerber declared, "The stage should not on principle be closed to the discussion of any conflict" and appointed a censorship advisory board for regional governors that included even Karl Glossy, the foremost historian of pre-1848 censorship and an intimate of Vienna's former liberal mayor.[49]

The motivating factor behind early twentieth-century theater censorship was to prevent rowdy scenes in the audience, if not on stage. A play might be considered dangerous just because it was good and convincing and that much more likely to raise havoc. (The censor once declared an anticlerical play to be a true masterpiece: "But—and my heart aches I have to say that—perform it we cannot, either at the Burgtheater or elsewhere in Austria.") On the other hand, another play with an antimonarchical plot was considered tolerable just because it was considered so mediocre as to be useless in support of whatever its cause was.[50]

Generally speaking, at least in Vienna, with Mayor Karl Lueger's rise to power in 1897, censors seemed to become more responsive to Catholic objections. In part this meant that, just as aesthetic sensibilities became more broad-minded, political considerations interfered to prevent a more thoroughgoing permissiveness. But there are some indications that old-style liberals fought a successful rear-guard action outside Vienna.[51]

The police tended to be skeptical of plays with a strong element of social criticism and potential for popular agitation, the censors less so. Censors from Berlin and other German towns stayed in contact with their opposite numbers in Vienna to compare notes on the disruptive potential of particular plays, even if priorities were sometimes different. Anticlerical plots caused less of a stir in Protestant Berlin, while the Viennese were somewhat more relaxed about naturalistic portrayals of poverty and depravity. When Theodor Herzl handed in his *Unser Käthchen* in 1898 the police called him a utopian socialist, who "wants to find virtue only where poverty reigns. The educated better sort of people he consistently sees as morally rotten." On the other hand, the emperor himself is said to have confided to his "friend," the actress Katharina Schratt (who had asked him to intervene in favor of Schnitzler's *Professor Bernhardi*), that he would do his best, "but if it's banned because of the clericals, it will have to stay that way."[52]

At any rate, concern with not arousing strong emotions either one way or another led to a marked tendency to avoid topical plays that might strike an all-too responsive chord. If drama thrives by conflict, the harmonizing tendencies of the authorities who did their best to defuse issues whenever possible were indeed an artistic antithesis. The fate of Gerhart Hauptmann's social critique *Die Weber* (The Weavers) provides a good example of government strategies in controversial matters: the play was initially banned in both Berlin and Vienna (as well as in New York and Paris); in Budapest it was performed early on, but discontinued after a visit by the prime minister. When it was finally performed in Vienna, some ten years had passed and the play no longer caused a great stir. This is what the censors had both wanted and foreseen. As one of them put it, "It's actually a question of whether a movement is a hot-button issue or not, and today—when unfortunately ethnic questions have succeeded in pushing everything else into the background—it's possible to approach with less trepidation even such a revolutionary social drama like 'Die Weber' whose claim to greatness I cannot deny."[53] Thus, the sharpening of ethnic tensions had a liberalizing influence in formerly forbidden areas, especially as the one thing Pan-Germans and Young Czechs had in common was their fervent anticlericalism. If Prime Minister Koerber wanted to appeal to both of them (and to the Social Democrats to boot), a relaxation of controls on anticlerical sentiments was just the right means to do it.

The pillars of the throne, the military and the "bureaucretins" (to use literary critic Karl Kraus's phrase) still expected to be shielded from vitriolic criticism on stage (dueling being a favorite target in one case, corruption in the other). Maybe not surprisingly, in some cases the servants appeared more thin-skinned and petty-minded than the emperor himself. But it was easy for playwrights to transfer plots about the difficult metier of kingship into the legendary past or to convert them into timeless fairy tales, a device not possible in the case of institutions that by their very nature betrayed their nineteenth-century context and origins.

A certain backlash against Koerber's period of incipient liberalization has been detected after 1908. If so, that may have been due to the growing influence of the heir-apparent, the Archduke Franz Ferdinand, who had strong opinions and in cultural matters sided with the conservative Catholics. There was a certain authoritarian trend in government circles that became more marked in reaction to democratic developments. But there may be a simpler explanation. The censorship issue had become thoroughly integrated into the give-and-take of day-to-day politics. More democratic elections did not necessarily mean more liberal (in American terms, libertarian) results. The mass parties were conservative. Even liberals and anticlerical nationalists could no longer hope to win elections without clerical support, whereas the socialists were an opposition party. Administrations behaved accordingly.

The Burgtheater and the Opera in Vienna, with their special link to the court, fell into a category of their own. However, one should be cautious about attributing to political opportunism or aesthetic conservatism what may simply have been commercial prudence on the part of theater managers who preferred plays (and operas) that had already proved their crowd-drawing potential elsewhere. In 1881 responsibility for censorship was passed to the foreign office (whose brief included court affairs), where a perplexed successor to Metternich had to find a suitable subordinate for that delicate task. In the end his choice proved quite adept and—not unusual with diplomats—he recruited his wife as an unpaid extra, to whose judgment he deferred on matters of good taste: *mulier locuta, res finita* (the wife has spoken, the matter is closed). The harmonizing tendency became even more pronounced under this system, but still did not result in a complete ban on artistic avant-garde and innovation. Ever alert to the interests of its own field, the foreign office ensured that references to Serbia and Bulgaria were excised from performances of an early musical version of Shaw's *Arms and the Man* that happened to coincide with the Balkan crisis of 1908–9.[54]

The experiences of the early cinema that started around 1895 provide an interesting contrast to the theater. On the one hand, it was easier to control without sitting in on every performance. On the other hand, the rhythm of performances and the number of films soon outstripped police resources; by 1912 Vienna was home to 113 cinemas (more than today!). In the absence of centralized film censorship, provincial authorities imposed widely varying controls: there was no censorship at all in Hungary, but in Prague the governor's office was especially fierce in opposing moral decay. After 1910 Catholics increasingly lobbied for stricter controls to protect young minds from scenes of violence or indecency, and some provinces completely banned schoolchildren from the cinema. Although cinema owners favored a centralized mechanism of censorship, wishing to avoid the costs and delays of having their films checked by numerous provincial authorities, royal ordinances issued in September 1912 did not quite grant their wish, as local officials retained their ultimate decision-making powers. Theater owners, meanwhile, took great pleasure in the cinema's growing pains: if you had to endure censorship yourself, the last thing you wanted was a competitor who did not.[55]

CONCLUDING REMARKS

Censorship was a nuisance. So much is clear. Was it also effective or did it prove to be counterproductive at the end of the day? That is far more difficult to answer because it obviously involves some counterfactual arguments. There is a saying: Where news is lacking, rumors are rife. Thus, it is not enough for the powers that be to suppress hostile news and comments; they must also provide a plausible alternative. A tentative conclusion might be that Austrian bureaucrats were not particularly good at that task They succeeded in creating an atmosphere of healthy skepticism toward all official pronouncements. Austrians are supposed to be deferential toward authority. True enough. But they hardly ever believe in what authority says. In defense of these hapless rulers, it might be argued that they faced an uphill struggle because of Austria's peculiar ethnic mix. Official harassment might succeed in lessening the impact of merely critical voices. But when it was directed against fundamentalist causes like ethnic revivalist movements or the entrenched religious fervor of rural Catholics, it proved counterproductive indeed. Thus, nationalists of all stripes and conservative princes of the church were turned into involuntary martyrs of liberalism. As an instrument of tyranny, censorship can be a fairly blunt weapon. Liberals are supposed to dislike censorship. But even liberals are prone to persuade themselves that some greater good justifies some form of censorship. If it comes to the worst, they can always call it by another name. Austrian liberals certainly did so, even if their standards of political correctness differed from late twentieth-century notions on the same subject. Austria did not boast of any First Amendment, and it certainly shows.

NOTES

1. Pieter Judson, *Exclusive Revolutionaries: Liberal Politics, Social Experience and National Identity in the Austrian Empire, 1848–1914* (Ann Arbor, Mich., 1996).

2. Robert Kann, *The Multinational Empire: Nationalism and National Reform in the Habsburg Monarchy 1848–1918* (New York, 1950) still serves as a good introduction.

3. *The Last Years of Austria-Hungary*, ed. Marc Cornwall (Exeter, 1990); Lothar Höbelt, *Parliamentary Politics in a Multinational Setting: Late Imperial Austria* (Minneapolis, 1992), 92–96.

4. T. C. W. Blanning, *Joseph II* (hereafter Blanning, *Joseph*) (London, 1994), 161, 163.

5. Christine Mueller, *The Styrian Estates, 1740–1848* (New York, 1987), 115–47; Adolph Wiesner, *Denkwürdigkeiten der österreichischen Zensur* (Stuttgart, 1847), 172; Norbert Bachleitner, "The Politics of the Book Trade in Nineteenth-Century Austria" (hereafter Bachleitner, "Politics"), *Austrian History Yearbook*, 27 (1997), 97.

6. Blanning, *Joseph*, 162; Wiesner, 145; Franz Hadamovsky, "Ein Jahrhundert Literatur-und Theaterzensur," in *Die österreichische Literatur: Ihr Profil an der Wende vom 18. zum 19. Jahrhundert*, ed. Herbert Zeman (Graz, 1979), 296.

7. Wiesner, 185.

8. Johann Winckler, *Die periodische Presse Oesterreichs* (Vienna, 1875), 54.

9. Mueller, 120.

10. Paul Bernard, *From the Enlightenment to the Police State. The Public Life of Johann Anton Pergen* (Urbana, Ill., 1991); Viktor Bibl, *Der Zerfall Östereichs: Kaiser Franz und sein Erbe* (Vienna, 1922), I, 76; Hermann Leitner, *Der geheime Dienst der Polizei in seinen Anfängen zur Zeit des österreichischen Absolutismus* (Master's Thesis, University of Vienna, 1994).

11. T. C. W. Blanning, *The Origins of the French Revolutionary Wars* (London, 1986); Michael Hochedlinger, *Die Krise der österreichischen Außenpolitik 1787–1792* (Ph. D. dissertation, University of Vienna, 1997); Wiesner, 193–208; Julius Marx, *Die österreichische Zensur im Vormärz* (hereafter Marx, *Zensur*) (Vienna, 1959), 68–73.

12. Bachleitner, "Politics," 102.

13. Marx, *Zensur*, 27; Josef Mayr, *Wien Napoleon* (Vienna, 1940); Wiesner, 374.

14. Günther Kronenbitter, *Wort und Macht: Friedrich Gentz als politischer Schriftsteller* (Berlin, 1994), 160; Marx, *Zensur*, 73–76; Wiesner, 279.

15. Madeleine Rietra, *Jung Österreich: Dokumente und Materialien zur liberalen österreichischen Opposition, 1835–1848* (Amsterdam, 1980), 44.

16. Rietra, 85, 467; W. E. Yates, *Grillparzer* (Cambridge, England, 1972), 12; Johann Hüttner, "Theater Censorship in Metternich's Vienna," *Theatre Quarterly*, 37 (1980), 63; Robert Waissenberger, ed., *Vienna in the Biedermeier Era, 1815–1848* (New York, 1986), 84, 243; Hans Fischer and Erich Kock, *Ludwig van Beethoven* (New York, 1970), 146.

17. Stanley Pech, *The Czech Revolution of 1848* (Chapel Hill, N.C., 1969), 11; Hüttner, 63.

18. Bachleitner, "Politics," 102; Rietra, 43, 457–58; Julius Marx, "Die amtlichen Verbotslisten: Zur Geschichte der vormärzlichen Zensur in Österreich," *Mitteilungen des Österreichischen Staatsarchivs*, 9 (1956), 150–85, 11 (1958) 412–66; Kronenbitter, 154–58; Waissenberger, 38, 82, 230; Alice Hanson, *Musical Life in Beidermeier Vienna* (Cambridge, England, 1985), 40–41; Julius Marx, "Die Amtslaufbahn des Grafen Sedlnitzky bis 1817," *Jahrbüch für Landeskunde von Niederösterreich*, 27 (1938), 189–207; Bibl, I, 255.

19. Donald Emerson, *Metternich and the Political Police, 1815–1830* (The Hague, 1968), 147; Kronenbitter, 183; Bachleitner, "Politics," 102.

20. Heinrich v. Srbik, *Metternich: Der Staatsmann und der Mensch* (Vienna, 1925), I, 150–56, 482–90; R. John Rath, *The Provisional Regime in Lombardy-Venetia 1814–1815* (Austin, Tex., 1969), Chapters 4–7; Bibl, II, 58–59; Marx, *Zensur*, 41–43; Domokos Kosáry, *The Press During the Hungarian Revolution of 1848–49* (Boulder, Colo., 1986).

21. Veit Valentin, "Metternich Guilty," in *The Metternich Controversy*, ed. Enno Kraehe (New York, 1977), 127; Egon Radvany, *Metternich's Projects for Reform in Austria* (The Hague, 1971), 72–134; Eberhard Büssem, *Die Karlsbader Beschlüsse von 1819* (Hildesheim, 1974); Michael Gehler, "Entstehungs-, Organisierungs- und Wirkungsgeschichte der österreichischen studentischen Vereine (1815–48)," *Jahrbuch der Hambach Gesellschaft*, 4 (1992/3), 37–67; Kronenbitter, 167–175.

22. Alan Palmer, *Metternich* (Düsseldorf, 1977), 299; J. L. Talmon, *Romanticism and Revolt: Europe 1815–1848* (New York, 1967), 35; Emerson, 116; Srbik, I, 258, 292–94; II, 67.

23. Norbert Bachleitner, "Lesen wie ein Zensor: Zur österreichischen Zensur englischer und französischer Erzählliteratur im Vormärz," in *Zensur und Selbstzensur in der Literatur*, ed. Peter Brockmeier and Gerhard Kaiser (Würzburg, 1990, 107–25; idem., ". . . der so nachtheiligen Romanen-Lektüre ein Ende zu machen: Der historische Roman und die österreichische Zensur im Vormärz am Beispiel von Walter Scott's 'Woodstock,' " *Sprachkunst*, 22 (1991), 35–48.

24. Srbik, I, 456–64; Alan Sked, *The Decline and Fall of the Habsburg Empire, 1815–1918* (London, 1989), 46; Anna Benna, "Organisierung und Personalstand der Polizeihofstelle (1793–1848)," *Mitteilungen des Österreichischen Staatsarchivs*, 6 (1953), 197–239.

25. Rietra, 58–71.

26. Karl Glossy, *Literarische Geheimberichte aus dem Vormärz* (Vienna, 1912), 132–33; Srbik, II, 223–24.

27. Sked, 51; Bachleitner, "Politics," 104; Lothar Höbelt, " 'Die Freiheit und die Nationalität!' Ignaz Kuranda: Ein deutschböhmischer Literat, Publizist und Politiker (1811–1884)," in *Die deutschsprachige Literatur aus den böhmischen Ländern*, ed. Dietz-Rüdiger Moser and Herbert Zeman (Munich, 1999).

28. Bachleitner, "Politics," 99; A. J. P. Taylor, "Perceptive But Superficial Tinkerer," in *The Metternich Controversy*, 102.

29. *Die Grenzboten*, 1846, I, 2.

30. *Die Protokolle des österreichischen Ministerrates 1848–1867, Abteilung I: Die Ministerien des Revolutionsjahres 1848*, ed. Thomas Kletecka (Vienna, 1996), 251; Paul Molisch, "Die Wiener akademische Legion 1848," *Archiv für österreichische Geschichte* (1924), 3–205; Wolfgang Häusler, "Die österreichische Publizistik und ihre Probleme im Vormärz und im Revolutionsjahr 1848," in *Die Öffentliche Meinung in der Geschichte Österreichs* (Vienna, 1979), 64–88; Joseph v. Helfert, *Die Wiener Journalistik im Jahre 1848* (Vienna, 1877), 45–52, 144; Richard Charmatz, *Adolf Fischhof* (Stuttgart, 1910), 38–40; Lothar Höbelt, *1848. Österreich und die deutsche Revolution* (Vienna, 1998).

31. Winckler, 83–86; Bachleitner, "Politics," 105; James Retallak, "From Pariah to Professional? The Journalist in German Society and Politics, from the Late Enlightenment to the Rise of Hitler," *German Studies Review*, 16 (1993), 179; Frank Kaplan, "The Czech and Slovak Press: The First 100 Years," *Journalism Monographs*, 47 (1977).

32. *Ostdeutsche Post*, December 19, 1848.

33. *Das Tagebuch des Polizeiministers Kempen von 1848 bis 1859*, ed. Josef Mayr (Vienna, 1931).

34. *Die Protokolle des österreichischen Ministerrates 1848–1867, Abteilung V: Die Ministerien Erzherzog Rainer und Mensdorff*, II, ed. Stefan Malfer (Vienna, 1981), 392, 403.

35. Haus-, Hof- und Staatsarchiv Wien, Nachlaß Anton v. Schmerling 1, "Denkwürdigkeiten," fol. 603–5, 652–59; Winckler, 104–6; Walter Rogge, *Oesterreich von Vilagos bis zur Gegenwart* (Leipzig, 1873), II, 176; Heinrich Kanner, *Zur Preßreform in Österreich* (Vienna, 1897), 35–36; Friedrich Steinkellner, *Georg Lienbacher* (Salzburg, 1984), 21, 361.

36. Alexander von der Traun (Alexander Schindler), *Carte Blanche* (Leipzig, 1862).

37. Hanns Haas, "Salzburg in der Habsburgermonarchie," in *Geschichte Salzburgs: Stadt und Land*, II/2 (Salzburg, 1988), 760, 764; Karl Schwechler, *60 Jahre Grazer Volksblatt* (Graz, 1927), 17.

38. Anton Einsle, *Verzeichniss der in Oesterreich bis Ende 1895 verbotenen Druckschriften* (Vienna, 1896).

39. Lothar Höbelt, "Late Imperial Paradoxes: Old Austria's Last Parliament 1917–18," *Parliaments, Estates & Representation*, 16 (1996), 209.

40. Gernot D. Hasiba, "Das österreichische 'Sozialistengesetz' von 1886," *Geschichte und Gegenwart*, 8 (1989), 255–76; *Sozialistenprozesse: Politische Justiz in Österreich 1870–1936*, Karl Stadler, ed. (Vienna, 1986); Christine Eichinger, "Karikatur und Satire im Kampf um die Rechte des Proletariats," *Jahrbuch des Vereins für Geschichte der Stadt Wien*, 38 (1982), 139–70.

41. Charles Gulick, *Austria from Habsburg to Hitler* (Berkeley, Calif., 1948), I,

22; Bruce Garver, *The Young Czech Party, 1874–1901* (New Haven, Conn., 1978), 48, 135.

42. Karl Eder, *Der Liberalismus in Altösterreich* (Vienna, 1955), 226; Casimir Sichulski, *Der österreichische Reichsrat in der Karikatur* (Vienna, 1912), 19; John Grand-Carteret, *Les Moeurs et la Caricature en Allemagne, en Autriche et en Suisse* (Paris, 1885), 347–48.

43. Michael Walter, *"Die Oper ist ein Irrenhaus": Sozialgeschichte der Oper im 19. Jahrhundert* (Stuttgart, 1997), 297.

44. W. E. Yates, *Theater in Vienna: A Critical History, 1776–1995* (Cambridge, England, 1996), 26, 27, 34.

45. Ibid., 28; Hüttner, 66–67; Helmut Ahrens, *Bis zum Lorbeer versteig ich mich nich: Johann Nestroy—sein Leben* (Frankfurt, 1982); Marx, *Zensur*, 63–64.

46. George Martin, *Verdi: His Music, Life and Times* (London, 1965), 291, 225, 87, 137; Thomas Widrich, *Die Versprachlichung nationalistischer Mythen im Frühwerk von Giuseppe Verdi* (Master's Thesis, University of Vienna, 1991), 59; Birgit Pauls, *Giuseppe Verdi und das Risorgimento* (Berlin, 1996); Rietra, 87; Walter, 284.

47. Marx, *Zensur*, 28; Karl Glossy, *Kleiner Schriften* (Vienna, 1918), 112–37.

48. Djawid Borower, *Theater und Politik: Die Wiener Theaterzensur im politischen und sozialen Kontext der Jahre 1893 bis 1914* (Ph.D., University of Vienna, 1988), 36.

49. Ibid., 113.

50. Ibid., 43.

51. Ibid., 237, 289.

52. John Boyer, *Culture and Political Crisis in Vienna: Christian Socialism in Power, 1897–1918* (Chicago, 1995).

53. Borower, 258, 265.

54. Ibid., 280.

55. Ida Wickenhauser, *Die Geschichte und Organization der Filmzensur in Österreich, 1895–1918* (Ph.D. dissertation, University of Vienna, 1967).

BIBLIOGRAPHICAL ESSAY

Many good English introductions to the Habsburg Empire during the nineteenth century are available, including A. J. P. Taylor, *The Habsburg Monarchy, 1809–1918* (New York, 1955) and C. A. Macartney, *The Habsburg Empire, 1790–1918* (New York, 1969). For a much shorter account, see Jean Béranger, *A History of the Habsburg Empire, 1700–1918* (London, 1997). A good account for Hungary is Andrew Janos, *The Politics of Backwardness in Hungary, 1815–1945* (Princeton, N.J., 1982).

Material on nineteenth-century Austrian censorship in English is scarce. Perhaps the best account is Norbert Bachleitner, "The Politics of the Book Trade in Nineteenth-Century Austria," *Austrian History Yearbook* 27 (1997), 95–111. There is also considerable useful information in Robert Waissenberger, ed., *Vienna in the Biedermeier Era, 1815–1848* (New York, 1986) and in the chapter on "Metternich and Censorship" (27–37) in Elizabeth McKay, *Franz Schubert's Music for the Theatre* (Tutzing, 1991). Paul Bernard has provided an enlightening portrait of an ambivalent Enlightenment figure, Count Pergen, the man who ran the state police from Maria Theresa to Francis II, supplying an element of continuity between periods of supposed "liberalization" and "reaction": *From the Enlightenment to the Police State: The Public of Johann Anton Pergen* (Urbana, Ill., 1991). For Hungary and the Czech lands, see the rather sketchy accounts of Tamás Révész, "Freedom of the Press: Its Idea and Realization in Pre-1914 Hungary," *Hungarian Studies Review*, 20 (1993), 93–101; and Frank Kaplan, "The Czech and Slovak Press: The First 100 Years," *Journalism Monographs*, 47 (1977).

Two extremely useful sources on the theatrical censorship are W. E. Yates, *Theatre in Vienna: A Critical History, 1776–1995* (Cambridge, England, 1996), 25–48; and Johann Hüttner, "Theater Censorship in Metternich's Vienna," *Theatre Quarterly*, 37 (1980), 61–70. On musical censorship and the police, see the work by McKay cited above and also Alice Hanson, *Musical Life in Beidermeier Vienna* (Cambridge, England, 1985).

For German sources, as a starting point of how censorship actually operated during its most infamous period, Adolph Wiesner and his *Denkwürdigkeiten der österreichischen Zensur* (Stuttgart, 1847) provides a very fair and detached view from the receiving end. Stories and anecdotes about the inanities of pre-1848 censors can be lifted from Karl Glossy's works, such *Literarische Beheimberichte aus dem Vormärz* (Vienna, 1912) and *Wiener Studien und Dokumente* (Vienna, 1933), that provided Austria's turn of the century literary elites with a pleasant feeling of "You've never had it so good" and of evils overcome. Some of these clichés have been in their turn pricked by archivist Julius Marx, whose most accessible summary is *Die österreichische Zensur im Vormärz* (Vienna, 1959). It is more difficult to trace monographs on post-1848 censorship practices. Michael Walter includes a chapter on censorship in his thoughtful social history of nineteenth-century opera, *"Die Oper ist ein Irrenhaus": Sozialgeschichte der Oper im 19. Jahrhundert* (Stuttgart, 1997), although his focus is on France and Italy more than Austria. But most of the information has to be assembled from standard histories of politics or literature. Some of it is hidden away in unpublished dissertations and master's theses; for example, on theater, see David Borowers, *Theater und Politik* (Ph.D. dissertation, University of Vienna, 1988); and on cinema, Ida Wickenhauser, *Die Geschichte und Organization der Filmzensur in Österreich, 1895–1918* (Ph.D. dissertation, University of Vienna, 1967). The flow of secondary literature only starts once the flow of primary material ebbed again, that is, during World War I when censorship was reimposed with a vengeance for obvious reasons. Ideally, the forthcoming eighth volume of the *Geschichte der Habsburgermonarchie, 1848–1918*, eds. Adam Wandruszka and Peter Urbanitsch, to be published early in the next millennium, will cover the subject in greater depth.

7

Russia

Charles A. Ruud

Largely to counter the spread of disruptive Western ideas, Russia's rulers in the nineteenth and early twentieth centuries never protected free expression to the degree that became normal in Western Europe. But neither, with some exceptions, were they able to consistently enforce draconian limits on content in books, newspapers, journals, theatricals, and the like. Mixing strict and loose controls in the Russian system of censorship was rooted in the political and social systems of the country. All governing power flowed from the tsar (designated the emperor from the early eighteenth century), whose official title was Autocrat. The ruler presided over a vast territory by means of a notoriously cumbersome and arbitrary bureaucratic system and with the assistance of a conservative and dutiful Russian Orthodox Church. Much of the population consisted of largely illiterate peasants who were in a condition of chattel bondage until 1861. Whether enserfed or free, this vast peasant mass, with its history of anarchic revolts, posed a constantly worrisome problem of governance.

A small social layer of educated and cultivated persons—many of whom favored Western values and institutions for Russia—furnished writers and artists. They pressed against the limits imposed by the autocracy, but the tsar would not consider any basic change in his arbitrary, absolutist, and paternalistic power, and especially feared that disruptive Western ideas would penetrate the countryside and disrupt the historic and uniquely Russian alliance among tsar, nobility, Church, and people. Gradually, however, during the nineteenth century, the tsars yielded more latitude to writers, dramatists, and artists, as is explained in this chapter.

With respect to formal controls, preliminary (or pre-publication) censorship was officially established only in 1783; that system, borrowed from the West, remained intact until the censorship "reform" of 1865. Then came the shift to the monitoring of works already in the public arena by government agents no longer termed censors. Contrary to an implicit intent of the reform, however, the Imperial government never gave exclusive power to its judiciary to impose penalties to limit expression. To provide an overview of censorship practices in Tsarist Russia from 1815 to 1914, this study centers on the key players: (1) the high officials who made the rules that governed expression; (2) the censors and, after 1863, the members of press affairs committees who applied them; and (3) the writers and others subject to those rules who variously obeyed, challenged, manipulated, and disregarded them. The following concentrates on limits on printed works, the media of widest influence, that therefore stood first in importance to officials and subjects alike. State monitoring of nonprint media is detailed in separate sections. (All dates herein reflect the Julian calendar used in Russia until 1918, and must be increased by twelve days for the nineteenth century and thirteen days for the twentieth century to reach their modern equivalents.)

TSARIST LIMITS ON THE PRESS, 1815–1914

Developments before 1825

Catherine II (1762–96) was the first tsar to permit private ownership and use of Gutenberg's fifteenth-century invention of moveable type, through her January 1783 law "On Free Publishing," but at the same time she acted to preclude publications that might subvert the existing order. Besides requiring the registration of privately owned presses, Catherine initiated preliminary censorship by spelling out that "Free Publishing" applied only to writings that her police had read and found legal. Earlier tsars had entrusted censorship power to other institutions: Peter I (the Great, 1682–1725), for example, gave screening authority for all secular and religious works to the Ecclesiastical College and then the Holy Synod, both of them crown publishers and guardians of the official Russian Orthodox religion. Responding to Enlightenment ideas, Catherine ventured to allow privately operated presses because she expected the educated few who used them to have reason enough to respect her few rules—namely, that no published work counter "the laws of God and the state" or spread "clearly seditious" ideas.[1] When, despite the censorship, works nonetheless circulated that she found criminal, Catherine seized all copies and punished those responsible. Alarmed by the revolutionary "madness" in France that culminated in the 1792 execution of Louis XVI, Catherine ended her reign by disallowing private presses and setting up committees in Russia's five principal ports of entry to interdict dangerous printed works from abroad.

Although Catherine's son and erratic successor, Paul I (1796–1801), continued and even strengthened her restrictions on printed expression before he was assassinated, Paul's son Alexander I (1801–25) inaugurated a series of reforms designed to make the exercise of state power more rational, consistent, and predictable. One early result was Russia's first censorship statute (July 9, 1804), which reinstated private ownership of registered presses and divorced preliminary censorship from the police. Much like his grandmother, the new tsar forbade any printed work that contravened the laws of God, state, and moral conscience or that violated personal honor. Unlike her, he linked publishing with "the cause of education"—to use the words of his statute—and chose academics, not police, as censors. Even more liberal was his mandate that censors make "reasonable" judgments in the spirit of *glasnost* (openness).

With the invasion of Napoleon's armies in 1812, however, strict wartime censorship took effect and, despite Napoleon's final defeat in 1815, Alexander did not return to his earlier moderation of restrictions on the printed word, instead making a determined effort to spread the religious fervor that had seized him and many others in the war's dark days. By 1817 he had reoriented the ministry charged with censorship by assigning it to the new Ministry of Spiritual Affairs and Public Enlightenment, headed by Prince A. N. Golitsyn, the Russian Bible Society president and Alexander's close friend. As chief censor, Golitsyn encouraged the publishing of pietistic views and wide dissemination of the Bible. As overseers of the separate Ecclesiastical Censorship system that had previously screened all devotional publishing, high officials of the Russian Orthodox Church chafed not only at Golitsyn's preempting some of their authority but also at his conveying what seemed to be official approval for private interpretation of scripture. Not until 1824, the year before Alexander's death, however, did they bring sufficient pressure to bear on the Emperor to cause him to remove Golitsyn.

Nicholas I and Strict Censorship, 1825–55

Because his older brother Constantine had refused the crown, Nicholas I (1825–55) unexpectedly became emperor and at once confronted the liberal-reformist Decembrist uprising. Convinced that Western beliefs had misled the rebels and could cause broad unrest, the new tsar resolved to make Russian ideals dominate society through his strong, pervasive rule. Of key importance, he would justify autocracy—the ultimate paternalism—as inherently and historically right for Russia. To regiment expression, the emperor ordered the drafting of two new statutes to govern secular and religious publishing, created new committees to screen foreign works and keep theatricals in line, and set up special ministerial offices to oversee censorship as a whole.

In mid-1826 Nicholas issued the more important of his pending press laws, the one to govern secular works, whose stated aim was "to direct public opinion into agreeing with present political circumstances and the views of the government." Some 230 articles—in contrast to the forty-six of the 1804 statute—dictated procedures in detail and placed responsibility on the author, not the censor, should a duly censored text prove criminal once published. The new law also named a new cadre of censors: bureaucrats in the Education ministry rather than the university professors who had served Alexander I. When observers within and without the government ridiculed this "cast-iron" law as unworkable and counterproductive, Nicholas backed away from it, claiming he had signed it without reading it. The substantially more liberal April 22, 1828, statute ensued, governing all works of "literature, Science, and Art" that circulated within the Russian Empire, no matter what their language or place of publication. Issued the same day was a new ecclesiastical censorship statute. Besides requiring that censors be faculty members from ecclesiastical academies, this law gave the Holy Synod the right to ban any book, work of art, ceremony, musical composition, or theatrical performance detrimental to the Russian Orthodox Church.[2]

Under the companion statute for civil censorship, universities once again furnished censors, who resumed responsibility for the legality of whatever they approved. In a further concession to writers, no censor was to infer meanings from submitted texts nor change wording without the author's approval. With respect to foreign imprints, the 1828 law placed the Foreign Censorship Committee under the Main Administration of Censorship of the Ministry of Public Education in St. Petersburg (with subordinate committees in Riga and Odessa and individual censors elsewhere).[3] Each month this group issued a list of banned foreign works.

In keeping with his commitment to absolute paternalism, Nicholas secretly gave significant censorship power to the Third Section, his new political police, just three days after both censorship laws took effect. In what was clearly not an afterthought, he sent a confidential order on April 22, 1828, requiring officers of the Third Section to report any works "inclined to the spread of atheism or which reflect in the artist or writer violations of the obligations of loyal subjects." In 1829 official orders went out to all printers to provide the Third Section with copies of all the journals, newspapers, and anthologies produced in their shops. A year later, Nicholas added another layer of censors by requiring that his ministers approve in advance all published mention of their activities.[4]

Nicholas further tightened his grip when the French and Belgian Revolutions of 1830 confirmed for him that weak rulers invited mutiny. In 1831 he abruptly put down the Polish rebellion, crediting that show of strength with heightening Russian patriotism and loyalty to the throne. To consolidate that support, in 1832 Nicholas prescribed the system of ideas known as "Official Nationality" to guide his subjects and institutions (including censorship); its theme was that Russia would prosper if all loyally conformed to the dictates of the Imperial government, the Russian Orthodox Church, and a third, more intangible authority, Russian nationality.

Throughout the 1830s Nicholas deliberately limited private publishing. He personally approved or rejected applications for licenses for private periodicals, and the forty-two private periodicals of 1825 increased merely to sixty by 1845. (Small readerships also forced a number of licensed periodicals to close for lack of profits.) As for books, the few available statistics, dating only from 1837, indicate that the civil censorship in that year approved more titles (838) than in 1845 (804) and 1846 (810), although by 1847 the figures show a modest increase to 862.[5]

Threatening European-wide revolutions prompted Nicholas to inaugurate on April 2, 1848, a committee under D. P. Buturlin to further tighten censorship. That panel, infamously known as the Buturlin Committee, commenced the so-called censorship terror that lasted throughout its seven-year tenure to the close of the reign. In 1851 all previously uncensored wood blocks and plates used to produce popular prints known as *lubki* were ordered destroyed; censorship for them had begun in 1839. The outbreak of the Crimean War in 1853 was deemed to justify additional severe limits, with one typical order from P. A. Shirinsky-Shikmatov, minister of public education, requiring that all books for common readers be "penetrated with the living spirit of the Orthodox church and with loyalty to the throne, state and social order."[6] This order reflected rising official concern about increasing literacy, especially among the peasantry, as well as over the large number of cheap works that new Western printing technology fostered and that were feared could misdirect public opinion. In retrospect, censorship under Nicholas I ranks as the most invasive and dictatorial of any tsar after 1815. Even so, the university-based censors tended more to help than hinder writers of merit whom they respected, as will be shown in the sections on censors and writers.

Alexander II as Censorship Reformer, 1855–81

Coming to power at his father's death, Alexander II (1855–81) had first to deal with Russia's disastrous loss in the Crimean War, which he blamed on the country's social and economic backwardness, whose root cause he felt was the centuries-old system of serfdom that then held about forty million peasants in chattel bondage. An important sea-change in censorship consequently came from above, with no alteration of laws, once Alexander committed himself, in March 1856, to emancipation. Simply put, the tsar held that he must prod landowners into negotiating their own surrender of what were large and long-held assets; but, making little initial progress, he chose to apply outside pressure through a public airing of acceptable terms for freeing the serfs. Alexander therefore in December 1857 allowed private periodicals to print, without comment, two gentry proposals for liberation. A month later, his education minister ordered censors to allow "all purely scholarly books and articles which analyze and discuss economic questions about current and future arrangements for the landlords' peasants,"[7] thus lifting the de facto ban on printed comment about the peasant question, which no law specifically proscribed but censors had long forbidden.

As drafting of the Emancipation Act began in 1859, the emperor stopped all press comment on liberation but allowed a "correct" discussion of contingent reforms. Given that framework, some journalists urged an end to preliminary censorship, while others insinuated into print the need for representative institutions. With his enactment of emancipation in February 1861, Alexander II chose as overseer a new minister of the interior who distrusted journalists, P. A. Valuev. In an early report to the emperor, Valuev summed up the press as being "of one piece in its opposition to the government"; by November, he was attempting to wrest from the education minister control over censorship and rewriting its rules. While conceding the political need to shift from preliminary censorship to post-publication controls, Valuev held that judicial prosecutions could not alone stop uncensored publications from undermining the state.[8]

In March 1862 Alexander II pared down preliminary censorship by exempting Russian scientific, academic, and official publications and abolishing all screening offices outside the ministry of education. These reforms persuaded Valuev anew that firm controls would be needed to keep the press in check. In early 1863 he convinced the emperor that both censorship and the committee rewriting its rules should move to his interior ministry. Many of the changes favored by that committee required the Westernized court system that awaited the new judicial statute that took effect in December 1864; the long-awaited publishing statute followed on April 6, 1865.

In his implementing decree, Alexander II announced an "experiment" to give "relief and convenience to the national press" by lifting preliminary censorship for all periodicals in Moscow and St. Petersburg, all translations of 320 pages or more, and all original books of 160 pages or more.[9] Governmental and academic publications, whose screening had already ended two years before, were confirmed as freed. Should the content of any freed publication violate the criminal code, the emperor required judicial prosecution of those responsible. In addition, he prescribed administrative penalties for freed periodicals that broke no laws yet showed a "dangerous orientation." The implementing decree's guidelines warned that prosecutions would ensue against publications that printed, among other things, "insulting references to the laws operating in the Empire with the aim of undermining public confidence," works expounding "the harmful teachings of socialism and communism" or inciting "one class against another," and material that failed to "protect the inviolability of the Supreme Authority and its attributes," including "respect for members of the reigning house" or that "ridiculed entire classes or officials in the state or public service." Under the regulatory portion of the statute issued by the Council of State, the Chief Administration of Press Affairs (so named since the 1863 transfer of censorship to Interior) was to decide and impose administrative penalties—whether warnings, fines, suspensions, or closures. Subordinate Press Affairs staff were to screen works not freed and to read with equal care all freed works, once on the market, for content warranting an administrative penalty or referral to the judiciary for prosecution.

Prior censorship continued for shorter books, whose presumed wider audience made them potentially more harmful, as well as for all pictorial representations and for imported materials; during the next fifty years over 12,000 imported titles were banned and thousands of others were allowed only after censors had physically blacked out offending passages with ink, paste, and paper, or gutta-percha (popularly known as "applying caviar"). Reflecting the same particular concern with materials that might be relatively accessible to the poor, the 1865 censorship reform required peddlers to obtain licenses from local police. In 1869 the Ministry of Education decreed that only approved books could be read aloud to popular audiences (by 1901 the official catalog comprised 2,868 titles, although this constraint was lifted in 1906), and in 1872 the censors were told to be particularly vigilant when examining inexpensive publications.[10]

Of the eleven press-related trials that followed the 1865 press reform during the late sixties, judges upheld the charges of state prosecutors in only four, suggesting that the government and its judiciary significantly differed on defining illegal content. Made politically wary by rising terrorism in the seventies, the government avoided humiliating defeats in court by all but abandoning publishing-related trials. Instead high officials added and stiffened administrative controls for both freed and still-censored works. After April 19, 1874, for example, no book subject to pre-publication screening was accepted for review by a press affairs committee until all copies planned for the initial printing were ready for market. Behind that rule lay the assumption that the high cost of printing and binding so many vulnerable copies would force publishers to undertake no manuscript that a press committee might possibly ban.[11]

New financial penalties to counter freed but dangerously oriented newspapers included restrictions on their street sales and commercial advertisements. Temporary suspensions also cut profits; such were imposed ten times during 1865–69, on fourteen occasions between 1870 and 1874, and thirty times during 1875–79. In the second half of the 1870s, the minister of the interior began to single out censored papers and journals for additional administrative penalties, relying on authority granted his office before 1865 for warning and suspending censored but cumulatively dangerous periodicals since no such authority was granted in the 1865 reform.[12]

Alexander III and New Measures Against the Press, 1881–84

When the ultimate terrorist act—the assassination of Alexander II—stunned Russia on March 1, 1881, his son and successor Alexander III (1881–94) targeted the press as a plausible inciter of radicalism. Under measures of "intensified security" that August, the minister of the interior could unilaterally close any periodical that, in his judgment, threatened security. Similar authority was granted in August 1882, to the new Supreme Commission of Press Affairs, which could also punish responsible editors and publishers by temporarily banishing them from journalism. Commission-ordered newspaper closures amounted to seventeen between 1883 and 1904, and governmental officials temporarily suspended over thirty periodicals during 1881–89 and another fifty-five between 1890 and 1904. Partly due to such repression, between 1881 and 1889, the number of journals fell 22 percent and newspapers declined 11 percent.[13]

Using authority granted to him on June 16, 1873, to ban commentary on entire subjects in "unusual and rare circumstances," the minister of the interior forbade the press to discuss a growing list of topics, which reached 570 by 1904, including the "Jewish question," famine, and censorship. Between 1870 and 1904, twenty-three periodicals were temporarily suspended for violating such directives. During January 1883 the administrative arrest and exile of N. I. Mikhailovsky, then editor of the leading populist journal, *Notes of the Fatherland*, was ordered for criticizing the government in a speech to students at the St. Petersburg Technical Institute. Mikhailovsky continued to anonymously contribute, however, and by mid-1883 press affairs officials had "warned" the journal twice for its content. Early the next year came the arrest of three more staff members and then *Notes*' permanent closure for spreading "dangerous ideas." Charges against the editor then responsible, M. M. Saltykov, included allegedly authoring criminal articles for underground and foreign publications.[14]

By the 1880s, however, the relative public impact of the Russian-language journal—the enduring pulpit of the intelligentsia—had already fallen behind that of Russian-language newspapers. Although both stood equal in number (fifteen each) in 1860, by 1881 newspapers exceeded journals by more than two to one (eighty-three to thirty-five), and as both dipped in number during the crackdown following that year's assassination of Alexander II, papers increased their proportional edge, exceeding journals by a three-to-one ratio (seventy-nine to twenty-nine) by 1890. Newspapers also clearly reached far more Russians across more classes.

Circulation of the seven "serious" papers in St. Petersburg and Moscow during the seventies and eighties ranged from 20,000 to 30,000 copies. Daily and weekly papers throughout Russia in the late-1800s helped to quicken commercial life and their robust circulation reflected climbing literacy rates. Wide readership had become a reality in Russia, with all its positive and negative consequences for the autocracy.

Nicholas II and "Freedom of the Press," 1894–1914

At the accession of Nicholas II (1894–1917), journals and newspapers finally once more nearly matched the total operating when Alexander II was assassinated. Liberal journalists and lawyers, like those in 1881, urged a completion of the experiment launched by the 1865 statute: complete freedom for citizens to publish what they chose, subject only to the courts. Many high officials, however, held that pre-circulation screenings and administrative closures alone could prevent "criminal publications" from undermining the autocracy. Their view prevailed with Nicholas II during his first decade of rule, and the ratio of censored to uncensored periodicals remained fairly constant at about two to one.[15]

During the social and political turmoil of the Revolution of 1905, civil disobedience caught the government by surprise and nullified state controls over a wide range of activities, including publishing. When the government decreed in early October that no printing plant that bypassed press regulations could operate, St. Petersburg's printers simply paid no attention; the newly organized St. Petersburg Soviet of Workmen's Deputies even ordered printers not to work for bosses who obeyed the decree and achieved full compliance from the rank and file. Forced on all fronts to make concessions, Nicholas II issued his Manifesto of October 17, 1905, promising imminent freedom of expression and other reforms. What immediately followed was even greater anarchy during the so-called "days of freedom" through November, when printers imposed their own censorship by setting in type only those texts they approved—including polemics and manifestos from the Soviet's *News* (*Izvestiia*). In new rules issued to govern newspapers and journals on November 24, Nicholas claimed to be granting "one of the fundamental freedoms," the right to publish, subject only to the judiciary. "These regulations," he said, "remove all administrative rules in the area of the periodical press and restore decision-making to the courts in matters of criminal nature committed by the printed word."[16]

Yet shifting to judicial controls still gave the state sure means to suppress, at least temporarily, any work viewed as dangerous. The mere indictment of a publication alleged to be criminal mandated its confiscation pending a court's ruling, and the process that led to a decision could be protracted. Moreover, despite the emperor's avowed termination of all administrative measures, the government effectively continued some nonjudicial limits on publishing through supplemental regulations. One regulation, for example, which remained in place required that satirical journals submit their illustrations to one of the press affairs committees at least twenty-four hours before scheduled publication. Prosecutors would thus have sufficient time to issue indictments that enabled police to stage printshop confiscations to suppress all copies.

Court-ordered closures of periodicals figured prominently by late 1905. In December, eight St. Petersburg dailies that had published the local Soviet's "Financial Manifesto," a call for citizens to withhold tax payments to compel Nicholas to grant more concessions, were found guilty of inciting illegal behavior, despite their editors' defense that the document constituted "news." Penalties varied for those held criminally responsible: Publisher A. A. Suvorin of *Russia* (*Rus*) was sentenced to a year in prison, while L. V. Khodsky of *Our Life* (*Nasha Zhizn'*) was heavily fined. One source puts the number of periodical closures at sixty-three in the two months following the Financial Manifesto. Another indicates that altogether 1,270 newspapers suffered the same fate between 1905 and 1910 and that at least twenty-three editors were jailed after court convictions during this period.[17] However, owners commonly continued "closed" papers by registering them under revised names and new editors.

New rules on book publishing, effective April 26, 1906, also retained significant governmental power to limit expression. Because books of fewer than 160 pages still had to reach a press affairs committee several days before they were sent to bookstores, immediate indictments, as for satirical journals, enabled the pre-market seizure of all copies pending trial. Protests were raised that overuse of such indictments amounted to costly harassment; thus, in 1909 Russian publishers and booksellers complained that "the former [preliminary] censorship caused a mass of abuses for publishing, but it protected the editor and the bookseller from the annoyances of judicial prosecution."[18]

Marxist periodicals were especially plagued by prosecutions from 1905 to 1914. Indictments against the Bolsheviks' *Truth* (*Pravda*) and its various incarnations numbered 126 over 416 issues. Similarly treated was the Mensheviks' *Beam* (*Luch*) and its offshoots, which together received 130 indictments over 294 issues.[19] Underground works, and especially seditious papers like Lenin's *Spark* (*Iskra*) that were smuggled into Russia, were dealt with by the political police. As for ordinary foreign works, the Foreign Censorship Committee within the ministry of the interior worked continuously to 1917 to cite those with criminal content, with their seizure again being a matter for the police.

In sum, once private use and ownership of presses were finally legalized in Russia in 1783, imperial oversight of domestic publishing followed the pattern in Western Europe of initial preliminary censorship that eventually gave way to post-publication judicial and administrative controls. Russia experimented with the transition in 1865 and finally completed it in 1905. However, while in theory the Russian press was nearly as free as those in the West after 1905, in practice the degree of continuing judicial and administrative press harassment in Russia far exceeded that in other countries. Nonetheless, by World War I Russia press controls were losing effectiveness, at least partly because the immensity of Russian publishing made close monitoring increasingly difficult. Individual periodicals, which had passed the thousand mark in 1900, increased yearly; one book publisher alone, I. D. Sytin, produced nearly 5,000 different titles in 212 million copies between 1901 and 1910.[20]

CENSORS AND SETTING LIMITS ON EXPRESSION

Strictly speaking, regular censors were civil servants employed by the Imperial government or the Holy Synod in various censorship agencies to make certain that no inhabitant of the Russian Empire had access to dangerous information or ideas. These official full-time censors were not alone in fulfilling censorship responsibilities, however. What might be termed "irregular" censors also performed censorship functions, although their main professional responsibilities lay elsewhere. The "irregulars" ranged across Russian cultural establishments and could include editors of periodicals, directors of Imperial theaters and of art galleries, and the like. Also in the "irregular" category were officials of the political police and even the regular police whose duties extended into the censorship. Regular and irregular censors differed in that the former enforced specific rules and regulations while the latter operated more intuitively.

Regular Censors

Throughout the period under discussion, the censors were far from a disciplined thought police alert to the slightest deviation from political or religious orthodoxy. From the first statute on censorship in 1804 through much of the nineteenth century, many were academics or writers. Often they had two objectives: to nurture Russian culture and to protect their state and society from dangerous or deleterious words. As the lowest in the hierarchy of protectors, censors served local censorship committees under the empire-wide administrations already discussed. Belonging to the St. Petersburg committee carried the greatest weight, with membership on the committees of Moscow, Kiev, and Warsaw next in importance.[21] Favored with good pay and a place in the Table of Ranks, Russian censors were the initial screeners of books, journals, papers, pamphlets, calendars, and the like, as assigned by their chairman. They presented their recommendations in what were usually weekly meetings to enable the committee of the whole to vote a final decision.

On many occasions, censors advised writers how to improve both their writing and their prospects for publication. According to T. N. Granovsky, for example, the prolix writing of his friend V. G. Belinsky, Russia's leading literary critic of the nineteenth century, qualitatively benefited from cuts suggested by censors.[22] Censors also made possible the publication of works that fell outside established limits. One who stands out was the Moscow censor Prince V. V. Lvov, who, despite the de facto ban on discussing the peasant question in 1852, approved in that year *Sportman's Sketches* by Ivan Turgenev, which portrayed serfdom as an unjust institution and helped turn opinion in favor of liberation. Turgenev initiated publication by asking Lvov, a friend and fellow writer, whether the Moscow censorship committee might approve a book comprised of stories that had earlier appeared (except for one) with censorship approval in the weighty journal *Contemporary* (*Sovremennik*), as publishing them together would heighten their implicit criticism of serfdom and ensure them a wider audience. On Lvov's advice, Turgenev made minor changes and then sent his manuscript to the Moscow Censorship Committee, whose chairman assigned it to Lvov. Lvov recommended publication, and the committee agreed and informed Turgenev of its approval on February 28.

Coincidentally, Turgenev wrote a eulogy to the recently deceased writer, Nikolai Gogol, and submitted it to a St. Petersburg newspaper. The St. Petersburg censorship committee rejected the piece, which was approved in Moscow, however, and appeared in the March 13 *Moscow Bulletin*. When Nicholas I learned of this seeming maneuver around the St. Petersburg censorship, he was furious; he held Turgenev responsible, ordered him detained in a guardhouse in the capital for a month, and then ordered him exiled to his estate as an additional sign of imperial disfavor. (Turgenev used his time in the guardhouse to write one more story on serf mistreatment, "Mumu"; yet another Moscow censor, the humane and respected V. N. Beketov, approved it two years later for the March 1854 issue of *Contemporary*—and was reprimanded.) *Sketches* had meanwhile gone to the St. Petersburg censorship committee, as required for a new publication. Minister of Education Shirinsky-Shikhmatov condemned the book in mid-1852 and Nicholas dismissed Lvov from his censor's post (Lvov was reinstated early in the next reign). Officials now decided that Turgenev's book was a threat to social peace because of the sensitivity of the peasant question and banned a proposed new edition. Turgenev submitted the book again in March 1856 under the new tsar, Alexander II, but it was only reapproved in 1859, over a year after Alexander signaled his intention to end serfdom and only after another censor, the eminent novelist Ivan Goncharov, had championed a new edition.[23]

As liberal-minded authors and censors, Lvov and Goncharov exemplify the many with academic and literary credentials who stretched limits to approve controversial works with literary value. Inclined to do the same were some censors who might be termed professional bureaucrats. Typical of them was N. F. von Kruze, who joined the St. Petersburg censorship committee in 1855 and came into conflict with superiors by practicing what he called "cautious toleration" as censor of the *Russian Messenger*, founded in 1856 by the strikingly independent journalist Michael Katkov. One *Messenger* article in particular confirms Kruze's readiness to stretch limits: it recounted a banquet where writers repeatedly toasted the Emperor for his latest public step toward liberating the serfs before newspapers were permitted to discuss the terms of the liberation in early 1858. No punishment resulted then, but Kruze would be dismissed in December 1858 for overpermissiveness with the *Messenger*.[24]

Another censor who stands out for expanding limits on the printed word was A. V. Nikitenko. He become a censor during Nicholas's reign and eventually entered the Main Administration of Censorship. Within two months of Alexander II's accession, on April 3, 1855, Nikitenko successfully urged Minister of Public Education Norov to dismiss several "totally incompetent" censors, and he soon managed the replacement of one of them with Goncharov, whom, he noted "is intelligent, has great tact, and will be an honest and good censor." Of like mind was the new superintendent of the St. Petersburg educational district, Prince G. A. Shcherbatov, who succeeded in bringing about the dismissal of one of the old-line St. Petersburg censors, N. V. Elagin, because "for all his estimable qualities as man and citizen, [he] does not meet the stated requirements of the censorship" and whose decisions tended to provoke "the general displeasure of literary men."[25]

By the time the ministry of the interior assumed control over censorship in 1863, the government had replaced censors held over from the previous reign and turned more and more to employing as censors professional bureaucrats with a grasp of political, social, and economic issues appropriate to the changing character of the press. After the publishing statute of 1865 took effect, many new censors were chosen with at least some legal training at the university level. Because the new law made publishing-related violations of the criminal code subject to judicial prosecutions, censors needed to know when to recommend a prosecution and what evidence to provide to support it.

Writers could resort to a variety of methods to try to influence censors. As noted previously in discussing the censor Nikitenko, one technique was the blunt one of seeking his replacement. Thus, writer Nikolai Chernyshevsky managed to bring about the removal of the censor Rakhmaninov from responsibility for his journal *Contemporary*. Some censors were willing to cooperate with authors to increase their incomes. V. A. Posse, the editor of the legal-Marxist journal *Life* (*Zhizn'*) at the end of the century, wrote, "It is a good thing that the majority of censors took bribes, but to give bribes is repulsive." Posse complained to the head of the Main Administration of Press Affairs, Prince Shakhovskoi, that the notoriously unyielding censor Elagin had excised so many articles that he had material for only one monthly issue instead of three originally planned. Shakhovskoi removed Elagin and assigned to *Life* one Vorshev, who tried to be a most agreeable censor. Vorshev told Posse, "You know, Vladimir Aleksandrovich, I am an old man and I poorly understand the latest literary and political trends, and it is hard for me to decide under current conditions what to permit and what not to permit. I will sign everything that you put in front of me, but I ask you not to let me down and to exercise the greatest caution." For three or four months, says Posse, he avoided putting Vorshev in a corner; after that, Vorshev's superiors detected an absence of firm control over *Life* and reinstalled Elagin to monitor it.[26]

Another censor who was a notorious opponent of the printed word, M. P. Soloviev, typically denounced any publisher who issued works intended for a popular readership as a "hack." He was a favorite of the Procurator of the Holy Synod, K. P. Pobedonostsev, and headed the Main Administration of Press Affairs at the end of the nineteenth century. Soloviev was known in the publishing trade as the "Ignatius Loyola of the censorship" for his attempts to force conformity to officially approved ideas.[27]

Irregular Censors

Irregular censors dated at least from Nicholas I's use of Third Section secret political police to report any expressions in print, although already approved by censors, that endangered him or his rule. These officials qualify as censors because they looked for and reported illegal or dangerous expressions, although others decided whether to impose any penalties. Alexander II—like all nineteenth-century emperors—also doubted the regular censors' ability to cope with dissident publishing, and so he also turned to the Third Section to supervise the work of censors. By 1862, therefore, fourteen men in the Third Section's new "Fifth Bureau" read every issue of over 100 selected Russian publications and also surveyed major foreign papers and Russian theatricals. What they were looking for, the chief of the Third Section, Prince A. V. Dolgorukov, reminded them that year, ranged from antigovernment sentiment to useful ideas and commentary on social needs.[28] Censors of the Fifth Bureau sent reports on "unallowable words" to the executive director of the Third Section, who forwarded them, as a rebuke, to the head of the Chief Administration of the Censorship. By reintroducing the political police into censorship during the era of reform, Imperial officials showed their continuing concern about writers' threat to security.

Gendarmes—who were subordinate to the Third Section—had authority to investigate and approve editors for periodical publications. For instance, although publisher Vladimir Goldshtein had passed the necessary security clearance in 1861 to start his twice-weekly, tabloid-size *Voronezh Newssheet*, a local gendarme soon detected threats to state security in its contents, all of which a censor had approved. In a report to Dolgorukov, the head of the district gendarmes conveyed his subordinate's specific objection: that the newssheet editor was guilty of printing articles that denigrated "highly placed officials."[29] By 1864 repeated complaints from the gendarme district office about what was appearing in *Voronezh Newssheet* led to its eight-month suspension by the highest overseer of censorship, the minister of the interior, and the paper recommenced publishing only with a new editor. Gendarmes in this way exercised powerful authority over who edited provincial papers, what appeared in them, and even whether they published or not.

When censors found a writer or editor too hot to handle, they would send his material up the line, where it might even reach the tsar (who thus joined the ranks of the irregular censors). Ivan Aksakov, a Slavophil patriot and believer in a free press who edited the new Russian daily, *Day* (*Den'*), for this reason encountered repeated delays of his articles during the tenure of A. V. Golovnin, a leading government liberal and minister of public education (1862–66) who was attempting to reform the censorship. Censors in Moscow often sent Aksakov's articles to St. Petersburg for review. Some articles went only to the Main Administration, others to Minister Golovnin himself, who occasionally forwarded articles to Alexander II for his judgment. These delays were serious for the monthly thick journals, but they were disastrous for a newspaper working to meet daily deadlines.[30]

Aksakov found Golovnin even stricter as a censor than his predecessor, Admiral E. V. Putiatin, whom the tsar had appointed to impose discipline on universities. In 1862 Golovnin suspended *Day* for three months because Aksakov refused to reveal, even to the tsar, a source for a news report about public disturbances in the Baltic region, and he barred Aksakov from its editorship for the rest of 1862. Golovnin also fired a Moscow censor, A. P. Giliarov-Platonov, who had been unduly helpful to Aksakov and shared many of his views. Golovnin cracked down so harshly on Aksakov because he wished to placate conservatives in the government while he pushed forward a more liberal censorship statute.

Censors and the Challenges of New Ideas

Just as political journalism posed new problems for the censors during the 1860s, artists and scientists were also challenging traditional ideas. Summoning them to a crusade against established canons were two critics, well known because of their articles in *The Contemporary*, Nicholas Chernyshevsky and Nicholas Dobroliubov, who demanded that artists use science, not religion, to understand human beings, expose the world's flaws, and stimulate reform. So unyielding were Chernyshevsky and his fellow proponents of "social art" that they came to be known as "censors of the left." In promoting the study of biology, physiology, and psychology as the sole means to understand human beings, Chernyshevsky ran squarely into opposition from ecclesiastical censors who found these subjects threatening to religious explanations and wished to prohibit their discussion in the popular press. The civil censors and the courts understood, however, that Russian scientists and medical researchers had to maintain pace with European developments and so permitted the publication of even some of the most radical works on the new science that contained antireligious arguments. Wilhelm Wundt's *Lectures on the Soul of Men and Animals*, translated from German in 1866, drew the criticism of an ecclesiastical censor who found it demoted man "from his rightful place and included him in the common herd of animals, as they all, in the author's view, have the same soul as he, as the very title of the work demonstrates." The St. Petersburg Censorship Committee ordered the destruction of 3,000 volumes, but was overruled by a court acting under the reformed censorship law of 1865.[31]

Ivan Sechenov, a physiologist, attempted to publish an article in Chernyshevsky's *The Contemporary* in 1863 on the "Physiological Foundations of Psychic Processes," but the censorship rejected it in a journal so "widely read" (it had about 6,000 subscribers). The censor said that Sechenov was reducing the brain to nothing but a mechanism and was thereby subverting "all concepts of good and evil." Officials in the ministry of the interior, who recognized the scientific importance of Sechenov's work, directed the article to the *Medical Herald*, where they thought it would be seen only by specialists, but it was read widely and created a sensation.[32]

WRITERS AND THE CIRCUMVENTION OF CENSORSHIP

Because censors could strongly affect the fate of a periodical, a book, or a play, those who wrote, edited, and published in Russia cultivated censorship officials. An early publishers' target was Nikitenko, who, while a censor, accepted positions as editor of the journal *Son of the Fatherland* in the early 1840s and of *Contemporary* from 1846 to early 1848. After taking up the latter job, Nikitenko decided that the publishers were using him, hoping "to find in me a blind instrument" to allow them "to act independently under the cover of my name." He wrote later that he had intended to publish works "consistent with the existing order," but that he resigned quickly when the Menshikov Committee, assigned to check the work of the censors, detected "criminal" material in the journal.[33]

Writers had many techniques to circumvent the censorship. One was to wait for a censor to go on summer vacation and hope for favorable results from his replacement. The last years of the reign of Nicholas I appear to have been particularly onerous, and writers and playwrights waited for well beyond summer vacations for "better times." For example, the writer and playwright A. F. Pisemsky's novel *Boyarshchina*, a mordant picture of life in rural Russia, was turned down in 1847 but approved in 1858. Another technique was the artful scattering of controversial material in segments published in serial form, or, conversely, an author might choose to publish as an entirety a text he believed to be controversial because he feared the censor would be on his guard following the first installment. Turgenev proposed in 1876 to M. M. Stasiulevich, the editor of *Messenger of Europe*, that the latter print Turgenev's novel *Virgin Soil* in a single issue because the censor would see only at the conclusion that the book was not pro-populist. Stasiulevich decided instead to publish the novel in two parts in 1877; the censor had no trouble with the first part, and although he objected to the second he concluded that he could not ban the second part of a work by a well-known writer without creating an outcry. Turgenev discovered that the minister of the interior, A. E. Timashev, cast the deciding vote in favor of the second part while declaring "that, had he known the *whole* book beforehand, he would never have allowed its publication; but that it was now too late—and a kind of insult to the public—and a scandal—if the second part should be forbidden—or disfigured by omissions."[34]

Including a few innocuous pro-government statements might dispose the censor to approve a submission that contained controversial material. But sometimes the censor wanted even greater concessions. Thus, in 1855, when Leo Tolstoy submitted "Sevastopol in May," a powerful antiwar story from the Crimean front, he anticipated censorship objections by preparing for his editor optional wordings for some passages and mentioning others that might be deleted in order to satisfy the censor without destroying his work. When, without asking Tolstoy, the editor accepted other changes suggested by the censor, Tolstoy was furious: in print, his work had metamorphosed from an antiwar story to a patriotic one. Some writers left bait for their censors by including especially egregious material that the censor would have to cut in the hopes that the censor would then conclude that he had done enough and would permit other less controversial passages to appear. When a censor and a writer were not far apart in their assessment of a work, the writer frequently omitted language or changed a scene to appease the censor.[35]

Writers through experience well understood the work of censors and a number of writers became censors. The novelist Goncharov did so to increase his income. The lyric poet Fedor Tiutchev worked for the Foreign Censorship Committee for many years. Essentially, these writers as censors were sympathetic to literature and could be counted on to approve manuscripts if they possibly could. But the censorship was not ready to hire every writer who expressed an interest. Pisemsky was in perpetual conflict with the censorship. He conducted an extensive correspondence with censors, officials, writers, and even ministers over his entire literary career in attempts to persuade officials to approve his novels and plays. Pisemsky sought to be hired as a censor several times, arguing in a partly facetious manner that for the Ministry of Public Education "it would be very convenient to make censors from writers, leaving censorship judgments to the writers themselves."[36]

N. A. Nekrasov, the poet, editor, and publisher, regularly entertained censorship officials, especially those who sat on the directorate of the Main Administration of Press Affairs. One official, Lazarevsky, appeared at Nekrasov's dinners frequently and was said to have "won" goodly sums at convivial, postprandial card games. Even notoriously hostile censors were targets of publishers' blandishments. Censor M. P. Soloviev's eccentricities—his rages led to fainting spells—bore directly on his official acts; one observer declared, "This 'ill, hysterical, peevish man . . . completely discredited his department' by proving to be 'an exceptional despot.' "[37] Soloviev presented an especially difficult problem for the populist Moscow publisher I. D. Sytin, who required his permission to purchase a daily paper. To win over Soloviev, Sytin entered into an agreement with the censor to appoint one of Soloviev's friends and ideological allies, A. A. Alexandrov, editor of his paper. After gaining control of the paper, Sytin found a reason to remove Alexandrov, but gave him another job in his publishing company.

Sytin became the publisher of the largest Russian daily, *Russian Word* of Moscow, and found a job in his publishing company for the mistress of the new head of the Moscow Censorship Committee, Prince N. V. Shakovskoi. Sytin periodically admonished his journalists not to offend press officials, even when his paper was no longer subject to preliminary censorship, but he had trouble controlling one of his more outspoken writers, Grigory Petrov, so he paid Petrov's salary but hardly ever published his articles. When Petrov complained to Sytin, the latter advised an editor to make a gesture in Petrov's direction: "Petrov is terribly upset that nothing of his is printed [in *Russian Word*]. If possible, do me a favor and print something, but without violating conditions of censorship."[38]

By such deft maneuvering, Sytin was able to build a small reactionary paper into a "liberal" daily with a million readers by World War I, but he still had troubles with the regime. From 1906 onward, the Moscow censors sought to prosecute the editor of *Word* over thirty times for publishing allegedly criminal material, but never succeeded. Under special regulations to prevent disorders that followed the government's revision of the electoral law in 1907, Moscow press authorities fined *Russian Word* on forty occasions for a total of 22,700 rubles by 1915. Sytin's large newspaper and publishing company had became financially powerful and could survive harassment by press officials, however. Sytin recalled, "In the course of forty years of publishing, I experienced all the censorship penalties that there were."[39]

Candid discussions of sexual morality based on the new canons of realism posed special problems for Russian censors, and in one major instance Alexander III himself decided the question. Leo Tolstoy took up sexual passion in *The Kreutzer Sonata* in the second half of the 1880s, using explicit language to condemn marriage and depict sexuality as a wholly negative, uncontrollable force. Having learned of the story in advance but without having read it, E. M. Feoktistov, head of the censorship administration, in December 1889 told the publisher Haideburov, who had hoped to print the novel in his magazine *Week*, that he would prevent its publication, although *Week* was theoretically exempt from preliminary censorship.[40]

Undeterred, Sophia Andreevna, Tolstoy's wife, who wished to see the *Sonata* published as part of the thirteenth volume of Tolstoy's collected works, undertook to win support in high places. After the Foreign Censorship Committee banned a French edition published in Berlin in 1890, Sophia appealed without success to I. N. Durnovo, the minister of the interior. In the meantime, the story was becoming well known by means of private literary readings in the larger towns of Russia. Public interest grew, and the press began to publish articles about *Kreutzer Sonata*, although it had still not been published in Russia. The authorities then banned press commentary on what they declared was a topic of "state importance," but the ban was far from airtight. When Sophia proceeded to print volume thirteen in four separate editions, the smallest of which contained *The Kreutzer Sonata*, the Moscow Censorship Committee impounded the entire press run at the printing plant. She gained an audience with Emperor Alexander III, and he agreed to approve the release of volume thirteen on the understanding that it could be sold only as part of the collected works, declaring, according to Sophia, "Yes, as part of the collected works it can be permitted; not everyone can afford them; it won't be a matter of a large circulation."[41] Released from impoundment, volume thirteen sold so well that Sophia then reprinted it twice, as evidently did others in pirated editions, for very thin and inexpensive "volume thirteens" containing little more than *The Kreutzer Sonata* soon appeared in the bookstores. Only in early 1900—about a decade after the story was finished—did the Russian press affairs committee officially permit the separate publication of Tolstoy's *Sonata*.

By the early twentieth century, able journalists themselves expanded the bounds of press freedom as daily and weekly papers with growing subscription lists and street sales increasingly exercised an independent influence in Russian life, despite censorship restrictions. Journalists developed a style of "galloping" immediacy and wrote on subjects of interest to a broad audience, especially to urban readers in growing Russian cities. Vlas Doroshevich and A. V. Amfiteatrov, two of Russia's most popular journalists and drama critics, combined their talents to help create a St. Petersburg daily in 1901, *Rossia* (Russia), which quickly reached a circulation of 45,000 while specializing in indirect criticism of the government. Doroshevich later recalled this as a "happy time" when the "enemy was as obvious as serfdom [once had been]; now it was the bureaucracy."[42] When Doroshevich published his "Eastern Stories," about foolish Turkish viziers and Persian satraps, no one could miss that he was really ridiculing tsarist officials. Amfiteatrov wrote a biting satire on the Imperial family, published in 1902 as "The Obmanov [*obmanyi* = fraudulent] Gentlemen," which included homely details provided by an imperial household informant. Ridiculing the Romanov dynasty created a sensation; Nicholas II, without waiting for his censors and prosecutors, closed the paper and exiled Amfiteatrov to Siberia.

By 1905 journalists had lost all respect for the tsar and the imperial family. Several major disasters had devastated the public image of the Romanovs: the tragic trampling to death of almost 1,300 people during the tsar's 1896 coronation celebration; the "Bloody Sunday" massacre of hundreds of peaceful demonstrators in St. Petersburg on January 9, 1905; and the costly, humiliating, and losing Russo-Japanese War of 1904–5. Then, in response to a general strike in October 1905 amid the disorders of the 1905 Revolution, the tsar granted civil liberties, voting, and a legislative assembly, even as he continued to insist that he was Autocrat.

As censorship weakened under these revolutionary conditions, many satirical magazines appeared, especially in St. Petersburg and Moscow. The censors found them difficult to suppress, partly because of the press laws and the judicial system, and partly because of the persistence and inventiveness of writers and graphic artists. Between 1905 and 1908, at least 429 different satirical titles appeared in Russia (some of which were essentially the same journals publishing under different names).[43] Not until 1908 did the censors and courts suppress most of them.

Many of these publications were short-lived and of poor quality, but there were exceptions. *The Spectator* (*Zritel'*), which first appeared in June 1905 under preliminary censorship, was one of the best and boldest. Its targets were high Imperial officials, including Nicholas himself. Its methods relied on readers' detailed knowledge of the Russian political scene, since, as one journalist recalled, it specialized in "hints, not very subtle, but virtually harmless from a juridical point of view" that showed the monarch as a flawed and diminished figure and ridiculed his claims to majesty, authority, and leadership. In this vein, *Signal*, another satirical magazine, published the following "letter" to the editor: "Dear Editor: I very much want to subscribe to your journal, but Mama will not allow it. Kolya R." Every reader would know "Kolya" was the diminutive for Nicholas, "R" the initial for Romanov, and that "Mama" was Nicholas's wife, the Empress Alexandra Fedorovna. These few lines suggested to readers that Nicholas was childishly cowed by his wife, but they fell short of any clear-cut case for the censors or the courts.[44]

Censors carefully scrutinized political cartoons for hints of disrespect for the tsar, but found it no easier establish offenses, as references were satirical and only suggestive. For example, *The Spectator*'s cover in November 1905 showed a figure concealed behind a house of cards that he was constructing on a wobbly table. The title was "Our Constitution—Please Don't Blow." Only the high crinkled boots and tucked-in trousers, common to the tsar's attire, suggested that Nicholas himself was the personage depicted, but no Russian would have missed the reference to him. One especially biting cartoon led the government to act in late 1905, when *Machine Gun* (*Pulemet*) published the Tsar's October Manifesto covered with a bloody handprint in red ink entitled, "To this Manifesto General Trepov has added his hand." This unmistakable assertion that the St. Petersburg police chief was responsible for bloodily suppressing demonstrations that followed the publication of the Manifesto led Trepov to successfully sue *Machine Gun* for defamation; in addition, a court jailed the editor for a year. Writer Kornei Chukovsky was also successfully prosecuted and jailed at the end of 1905 for his satire in *Signal* and the government closed his magazine (but it soon reopened as *Signals* with a new editor).[45]

By the fourth issue of *The Spectator*, Trepov demanded that the assistant minister of the interior take steps to end the censors' laxness. Trepov insisted that the magazine "aimed to arouse passions and an oppositional spirit in the people," but the censors responded that they had rejected many stories and drawings submitted for *The Spectator*, but could expunge only legally prohibited material. In November, the government prosecuted the magazine's editor, Iu K. Artsybushev, but his lawyer successfully appealed to the Senate his original court-imposed sentence of two and a half years confinement, as the Senate found no direct evidence showing a connection between the satirical material and Nicholas. Although the government closed his journal in late 1905, Artsybushev was able to resume publication in 1908.[46]

CENSORING THE ARTS

Control of the Theater

Since the eighteenth century, the principal theaters and theatrical companies had been government institutions. Catherine II, herself a patron and writer of plays, set up the Imperial School of Theater in 1779 and the Academy of Theater in 1783. Only rural landlords wealthy enough to establish theaters on their estates staged theatricals outside of the official system, and major private companies appeared in cities only in the last quarter of the nineteenth century.[47]

Replacing past informal government control of theater, Nicholas I established a governmental agency for theater operating under strict rules. This first formal stage censorship, begun in 1828, was placed under the Main Administration of Censorship and approved all works intended for the stage, including plays and operas, first for publication and then for production. Censors also attended performances to ensure that the plays were produced as approved. The limits they set after 1865 came from the censorship statute of that year, but with greater strictures than the Press Affairs Committee applied to the written word. The cause was the perception that staged presentations had greater impact and were accessible to a broader spectrum of the population. The Imperial theaters inevitably reflected the tastes of the tsars about art. Alexander III favored foreign, especially Italian, opera and ballet, and these genres dominated the Marinsky theater in St. Petersburg and the Bolshoi in Moscow. When Russia signed a major treaty with France in 1891, French opera took precedence and the simultaneous rejection of the German alliance led to a dismissal of German works. The tsar himself was deciding what opera and ballet audiences could see on stage.[48]

Other members of the Imperial family freely intervened in the production of operatic performances, thereby layering censorship on top of censorship. Thus, when Grand Duke Vladimir Alexandrovich complained, after attending the rehearsal of Rimsky-Korsakov's opera *The Night Before Christmas*, that the composer "diminished my great-grandmother [Catherine II], as I see it," the opera was threatened with closure, although it was to be a benefit performance and all the tickets had been sold. Rimsky-Korsakov substituted another character for the Empress but stayed home in protest on opening night.[49]

This elaborate system of Imperial theaters under government administration provided a hurdle for playwrights and opera composers. Self-censorship and patronage flourished and resulted in a familiar repertoire of tested dramas, operas, and ballets. Playwrights who attempted to stretch the limits on theater would frequently wait years until the "time was right"—as it was said—to see a play published (it was Russian practice to publish the script of a play before it was staged), much less produced. Thus, during the tense year of 1848, censor Nikitenko wrote to the editor of the theatrical magazine *Pantheon* that he should not then attempt to publish P. G. Obodovsky's play, *Bogdan Khmelnitsky*, as he doubted that it would be approved: "It is about a rebellion of people, *although in favor of Russia*—but there are persons, scenes, that are very delicate for the present. You as an experienced editor understand all this without additional explanation."[50]

Plays completed late in Nicholas's reign often had to await the next reign. Although Turgenev completed *The Parasite* in 1847, the censors banned it and permitted its publication only in 1857 and its production in 1861. Turgenev's *A Month in the Country*, written in 1850, could be published only in 1869 and only staged in 1872. M. E. Saltykov-Shchedrin wrote *Death of Pazukhin* in 1859 and it was staged the same year, but then banned for thirty years and presented again only in 1893. Leo Tolstoy completed *The Power of Darkness* in 1886 and published it the next year, but it could be presented only after 1895 because Alexander III personally banned its production in response to a personal appeal from his advisor Pobedonostsev, the procurator of the Holy Synod. As late as 1903, more than 10 percent of the more than 2,300 plays submitted to the censors were forbidden.[51]

Playwrights themselves usually understood the prevailing limits quite well, but they lived with the knowledge that a censor might find unexpected objections. In presenting his play *Fanforon* to N. A. Nekrasov for publication in *The Contemporary*, Pisemsky sent a second, toned-down ending, advising Nekrasov that "if, unexpectedly, the censor creates difficulties, since [the play] touches on matters of state service," he should "pull out the other one (the one I most definitely would not like) as though it is all the same to me." After Pisemky's drama *Bitter Fate* was approved by a censor in 1859 despite the controversial theme of love between a landlord and a serf woman, he promptly published it in his journal *Library for Readers* (*Biblioteka dlia Chteniia*), but the censor Nikitenko warned Pisemky that the time was "unfavorable" to present it on stage as the peasant question was under intense scrutiny because of the impending emancipation of the serfs. In 1863, two years after the liberation of the privately owned serfs, *Bitter Fate* appeared on stage. Pisemsky's historical play *Lieutenant Gladkov* was never to appear on stage in his lifetime, although it was published in 1867. The play was about a tumultuous period in Russian history, 1740–41, during which court intrigues ultimately led to the unseating and jailing of Tsar Ivan VI and his family. High censorship officials upheld a ban on the play after one of the censors wrote that "one melancholy scene after another from our history" passed before one's eyes during it, including the display of the "universal confusion and debauchery of the power-loving officials and favorites" who jeopardized the throne of the Russian tsars, and that because of the "closeness of these events to our time," it was unfit for the stage. It was staged in Russia only after the 1905 Revolution.[52]

Beginning in 1888, the government issued special censorship restrictions on the so-called popular theaters (those with modest ticket prices), which opened in increasing numbers in the late nineteenth century; they numbered well over 350 and reached millions of Russians by 1905, when an official of the ministry of the interior warned in somber tones that theaters were "among the most powerful instruments of influence on the public" and were "penetrating the widest possible circles and becoming available at a cost everyone can afford." Censorship rules for the popular theaters demanded special alertness to issues of tsarist authority, peasant unrest, class conflicts, and morals, and hundreds of plays approved for the "educated" stage (more than 10 percent of the total in 1904) were banned from the popular theaters. For example, although Tolstoy's 1886 play *The Power of Darkness* was finally approved by the censors in 1895, it was restricted only to theaters catering to educated audiences until 1905. A 1905 vaudeville approved for regular theaters was banned from the popular stage because, the censor ruled, it "presents the Russian aristocracy in such a caricatured form that is undesirable for the people"; a 1908 educational drama about syphilis was treated in an identical manner by the censors because its upper-class setting might "give the people a false opinion of the privileged class as the spreaders of the disease." Such decisions apparently reflected fears like those expressed in 1868 by V. F. Adlerberg, the minister of the Imperial Court, who lamented that popular theaters "will be the most powerful and simplest means to cultivate in the people ideas hostile to the existing order," especially as the "press influences only the educated class, which is capable of discerning the truth and is not easily carried away," but "the theater can distort the comprehension of the simple folk and instill in them the germs of disorder." After 1905, the popular theater censorship eased somewhat and enforcement of censorship decisions seems to have gradually eroded: an investigation of one popular theater in Saratov province revealed that only 58 of the 245 plays performed there had been approved for such venues.[53]

Censorship and Painters

Among the imposers of cultural orthodoxy were the arts academies, although by the 1860s, the era of the great reforms, they began to lose their grip, and artists began to slip from the control of officially sanctioned organizations. Before then, Nicholas I totally subordinated to his personal will the Academy of Fine Arts, imposing his opinions on its artists, dismissing those out of favor, and passing judgment on works of art. Such attempts to control the fine arts long outlived Nicholas, but resistance developed by the 1860s. For example, in 1863, fourteen student painters at the Imperial Academy refused to compete for the gold medal and rejected the assigned theme, "The Festival of the Gods in Valhalla," with its required positioning of gods, moonlight, wolves, and ravens. Rather, they declared, they would paint what they chose.[54]

In 1870 a group of independent artists formed an association called the Wanderers to devote themselves to portraying the people, (i.e., the peasants), realistically. Denied access to exhibition halls controlled by officials, they took their paintings on the road, "to the people," as it was then said. Such dissent invariably aroused the authorities to action. Censors suppressed articles favoring this new school of art, and in the 1880s both the ecclesiastical and civil authorities began to subject art exhibitions to preliminary censorship. The censors, for instance, removed from a Wanderers' exhibit Ilia Repin's painting, *Ivan the Terrible* (completed in 1885), in which Tsar Ivan IV was shown holding his son, whom he had just mortally wounded in a fit of rage.[55]

Censorship and Music

Composers were beginning in the 1860s to write challenging librettos for musical compositions and the censors responded by scrutinizing them carefully. As a composer of high merit, Modest Musorgsky avoided the blatantly tendentious and propagandistic faults so evident in the works of minor artists bent on overthrowing established canons. But his works still fit well the critics' demand for popular and democratic themes and therefore the music and opera censors, as well as the ecclesiastical censorship, alert to possible antiautocratic and antireligious meaning in populist themes, subjected the works of composers like him to the same scrutiny that typified newspaper and book censorship. This was especially so as members of the Imperial family traditionally took a personal interest in opera and ballet.

Musorgsky first encountered the censors as soon as he completed both the music and the words for his romantic, comic song, "The Seminarist" in September 1866. The ecclesiastical censors would not approve the song because, they said, it profaned the clergy by depicting a theology student lusting after the daughter of a village priest. A version printed in Leipzig was forbidden in 1870 by the St. Petersburg Censorship, which announced that it "had the honor of announcing that this music cannot be authorized for public circulation."[56] Ultimately, on the advice of one of the censorship officials, Musorgsky won a small victory by petitioning for and receiving permission to distribute copies of "The Seminarist" to nine friends.

Musorgsky privately welcomed the combat with the authorities, writing, "Heretofore the censor let musicians be; the ban [of "The Seminarist"] shows that from dwelling on nightingales, leafy forests, lovers sighing in the moonlight, musicians have become members of human societies, and if they should ban *all my work*, I would not cease to peck at the stone, as long as I had strength; for 'brains cannot be tempted and prohibition creates in me a terrific eagerness.' "[57] At the same time he was encountering troubles over "The Seminarist," Musorgsky was negotiating to overcome a truly formidable problem of censorship: a tsarist prohibition affecting his opera *Boris Godunov*, which only a tsar could reverse. He began writing *Boris Godunov* in September 1866, based on the historical drama by poet

Alexander Pushkin that had been allowed in print but banned for the stage ever since 1826. Pushkin's supervising censor at the time he completed *Boris* was Nicholas I himself; after Pushkin told the tsar that he would have supported the suppressed democratically oriented 1825 Decembrist Rebellion, the tsar told Pushkin to continue writing, but that he would henceforth personally act as Pushkin's censor. The tsar assigned the actual assessment of the play to Pushkin's literary nemesis, Faddei Bulgarin. Bulgarin's complaint against *Boris* was based on precedent: "It goes without saying that it cannot and must not be performed, for we do not allow the Patriarch and monks to appear on stage."[58] The Empress Elizabeth had established this guiding principle of censorship in the middle of the eighteenth century.

In 1837 Nicholas imposed another prohibition that stood in the way of any opera based on Pushkin's play, declaring that he agreed to "the acceptance of dramas and tragedies but not operas, in which are represented on stage Russian tsars who ruled before the Romanovs, but excluding those who have been canonized, as for example, Alexander Nevsky." Thus, playwrights could portray some pre-Romanov tsars, but opera composers could depict no tsars at all. (Rimsky-Korsakov once asked the censor Fridberg about the prohibition on tsars, and was informed, "Suppose the tsar should suddenly sing a ditty? Well, it would be unseemly.")[59] Musorgsky therefore knew that to write an opera based on *Boris Godunov* was to confront head-on a well-entrenched prohibition of the censorship; moreover, his opera made its hero not Tsar Boris Godunov, but the peasantry, an approach certain to further antagonize the censors.

Repeated attempts to produce parts of *Boris* failed because of the subject-matter ban until a revised version of Musorgsky's original was permitted in September 1870. The censors still required that "the persons of the patriarch, of the abbot, and of monks in general, as well as monastery rites and all attributes of ecclesiastic and monastic rank, are to be excluded." However, concerning the tsar's depiction, Musorgsky finally triumphed due to the sheer drama and power of his work: Nicholas I's 1837 blanket prohibition gave way when the minister of the interior recommended and Alexander II personally approved the staging of the revised opera.[60]

Music written for the Russian Orthodox Church was another sensitive issue because of censoring powers of the Holy Synod and the Church itself. Stanislav Smolensky, writing in 1903 in the *Russian Musical Gazette*, recalled the effect of a Senate ruling on May 4, 1881, permitting the musical publisher P. Jurgenson to publish the score for Peter Chaikovsky's "Liturgy, opus 41": "I vividly remember the impression that this decision made on everyone who had felt the oppression of the musical censorship that existed up to that time."[61]

Chaikovsky first confronted a ban on his "Liturgy" in 1878, imposed by the choir director of the Imperial Court Chapel, Nicholas Bakmetev. The

Holy Synod had always exercised control over church music, and a special censorship had been introduced early in the nineteenth century as a means to limit Western influence on Russian church choral music. Reigning practice was that only works of composers who had a diploma from the Imperial Chapel were eligible for consideration, so although the original purpose of this stricture was to prevent the introduction of music seen as foreign to the liturgy of the Russian Orthodox Church, it also blocked out even the most talented composer who lacked the requisite diploma.[62]

Jurgenson, Russia's largest publisher of sheet music, decided to circumvent this monopoly on church music by printing the "Liturgy" abroad and then presenting it to the Moscow Ecclesiastical Censorship, an arm of the Holy Synod, for approval for sale in Russia. The Moscow committee approved the printed music, but Bakhmetev appealed to the Moscow Chief of Police, Kozlov, who seized whatever copies of the "Liturgy" that his constables could find on sale. Jurgenson promptly instituted a court case against both Bakhmetev and Kozlov and charged that they had exceeded their authority. The case reached the appeals section of the Senate two years later and resulted in an order to pay restitution to Jurgenson for the lost copies of the "Liturgy" and a ruling that neither the choirmaster nor the chief of police had any authority under law to proceed against Chaikovsky's composition. Bakhmetev had argued in the course of these proceedings that he had authority to act against music failing to meet ecclesiastical standards, but the Senate declared it could find no legal basis for this authority because only the ecclesiastical censorship committees of the Holy Synod could pass on religious music, and its Moscow branch had already ruled. Bakhmetev lost his claims to be censor of sacred music, claims that, however obscure their origin, the Imperial Court Chapel director had long exercised.

Censorship of Film

After the first two commercial movie theaters in Russia opened in Moscow in 1903, dire warnings appeared on every hand about the dangers of movie houses (where fires might break out and patrons lose their purses to thieves) and their corrupting influence. In particular, published criticism scored the new medium for its superficiality and foreignness and filmmakers for exploiting rather than educating their audiences. Government soon enlarged the role of the police as secular guardians of Russian morals by authorizing their selection, through censorship, of films shown commercially, based on moral, political, and legal standards. Late in 1908, the same year that the first film studio opened in Moscow, the Moscow police chief set up a censorship office in each district that housed one or more so-called electric theaters. According to his instructions, films were to be inspected weekly and each film, whether foreign or domestic, had to be numbered and entered in a record book along with a summary of its contents and the decision on its fate. Subject to ban was any footage that could "offend religious, patriotic, or moral feeling" or that contained "pictures of a tendentious and political character." He added, "It goes without saying that films are forbidden from showing criminal acts, either from the past or the present."[63]

Although at first local police made censorship decisions, leading to possible wide variances, even within each city, subsequently exhibitors obtained approved prints from special municipal executives in Moscow, St. Petersburg, and other major cities. Outright bans were imposed on all pictures of a religious or biblical nature (including any depiction of the bible, Orthodox priests, and Orthodox Church rites and sacraments) and (until 1910) on all films portraying members of the Imperial family; when this latter ban was relaxed special rules were imposed requiring that all films of the imperial family be shown without musical accompaniment and clearly separated from other films by a pause; moreover, apparently to avoid any improvised ridicule by proletarian projectionists or malfunctioning projectors, "the manager of the cinema must take particular care that the pictures be projected by hand, at a speed that ensures that the movements and gait of those represented on the screen do not give rise to any comments." Some of the other subjects that were forbidden included the French Revolution, all documentaries on the 1905 Russian Revolution, the execution of monarchs (even that of the sixteenth-century Scottish Queen Mary Stuart), or political upheavals of any sort. In 1913 tsarist officials demanded the "strictest attention" to films dealing with the "lives of workers" to ensure that "under no conditions whatever" might films depict "difficult forms of labor, agitational activity" or other scenes that "may arouse workers against their employers, films of strikes, of the life of indentured peasants, etc."[64]

But generally the Russian film industry, in emphasizing works of popular entertainment, avoided fundamental problems with the censorship. (Even the Holy Synod, after lengthy debate, voted 4–3 to allow priests to attend movies that had been approved by a church committee.) Movies not rejected were identified and forwarded to the appropriate theater with a police certificate of approval. It fell to local police constables to confirm that all films shown in their districts had the proper documentation, and, absent this, the police could close the offending theater. To prevent attempts to evade the censorship—in one case in 1913 an exhibitor in Riga re-edited a film back to its original form after the censors had done their work—banned material was publicized in an official municipal gazette for local police to check. But erring on the strong side of caution could carry a price: one zealous constable who independently closed a movie house for screening a farce spent seven days in the guardhouse when the owner proved he had censorship approval.

CONCLUSION

This summary of Imperial censorship from 1815 to 1914 concerns a period when accelerating literacy coincided with accelerating print technology and production. Nineteenth-century Russian officials consequently focused on publications as the medium of expression most requiring their control, especially given the capacity of printed works to publicize all other forums and outlets for ideas. During this same century—as private publishing modestly began and advanced to mass sales of multiple works from long-run presses—the absolutist Russian government remained essentially unchanged. By the late-1800s, nowhere more than in Russia did modern, popularly based journalism challenge the outmoded paternalism of autocracy.

Alert at mid-century to the need for reform, Alexander II in 1856 set about ending serfdom and, contingently, widened press freedom. His 1865 statute on publishing gave yet more leeway by replacing some preliminary censorship with judicial and administrative controls; with the latter came more openness about state actions to limit the press. Just as greater access to information raised expectations of freer expression, so did full disclosure of often vague and petty charges against the press cause the public to favor less state intervention. Press exposure of other repression by the state had the same effect, especially in light of more egalitarian rule in the West. With the abatement of the terrorism of the eighties came louder demands for liberal change. Although labor unrest ignited the Revolution of 1905, the issue of freer expression figured all through it. By early 1906 Nicholas II had ended preliminary censorship for printed works, which the state could henceforth challenge only in the courts. All told, in Russia between 1815 and 1914, individual writers, composers, and artists unquestionably suffered from censorship's shackles. But in this same period, even when state intervention was most severe, Russian literature, journalism, art, and music clearly flourished, proving that nineteenth-century Russian censorship was far from absolute—and absolutely failed to kill Russian creativity.

NOTES

1. K. Papmehl, *Freedom of Expression in Eighteenth-Century Russia* (The Hague, 1971), 54–56; Isabel de Madariaga, *Russia in the Age of Catherine the Great* (London, 1981), 291–94.

2. *Polnoe Sobranie Zakonov Rossiskoi Imperii*, ser. 2, 1, no. 403 (June 10, 1826), 571; ser. 2, 3, no. 1979 (April 22, 1828); *Polnoe Sobranie Zakonov*, ser. 2, 3, no. 1981 (April 22, 1828), 480–89. See A. Kotovich, *Dukhovnaia tsenzura v Rossii, 1799–1855* (St. Petersburg, 1909).

3. Marianna Tax Choldin, *A Fence Around the Empire: Russian Censorship of Western Ideas Under the Tsars* (Durham, N.C., 1985).

4. M. K. Lemke, *Nikolaevskie zhandarmy i literatura, 1826–1855* (hereafter Lemke, *Nikolaevksie*) (St. Petersburg, 1909), 39; *Polnoe Sobranie Zakanov*, ser. 2, 4, no. 3192 (September 25, 1829), 682; V. V. Stasov, comp., "Tsenzura v tsarstvovanie Imp. Nikolaia I," *Russkaia Starina*, 113 (1903), 306–7.

5. N. Lisovsky, "Periodicheskaia pechat v Rossii, 1703–1903 gg.," *Sbornik statei po istorii i statistike russkoi periodicheskoi pechati, 1703–1903* (St. Petersburg 1903), 15; *Zhurnal Ministerstva Narodnogo Prosveshcheniia*, 142, nos. 1–3 (1862), table following 47; N. Ablov, "K stoletiiu pervoi popytki 'ofitsialnoi' registratsii pechati v Rossi (1837–1855)," *Sovetskaia Bibliografia*, 1 (1937), 104.

6. "Tsenzura v tsarstvovanie," *Russkaia Starina*, 115 (1903), 425; 116 (1903), 173, 175.

7. *Prilozheniia k zapiske predsedatelia komiteta dlia peresmotra tsenzurnogo ustava, deistvitel'nogo statskogo sovetnika Berte, i chlena sego komiteta, statskogo sovetnika Iankevicha* (St. Petersburg, 1862).

8. See Daniel Balmuth, *Censorship in Russia, 1865–1905* (Washington, D.C., 1979).

9. *Sbomik postanovlenii i rasporiazhenii po tsenzure s 1720 po 1862 god* (St. Petersburg, 1862), 472–74; E. A. Swift, "Fighting the Germs of Disorder: The Censorship of Russian Popular Theater, 1888–1917," *Russian History*, 18 (1991), 7. For a complete English translation of the decrees, see Charles A. Ruud, *Fighting Words: Imperial Censorship and the Russian Press, 1804–1906* (Toronto, 1982), 237–52.

10. Swift, 10–11; Jeffrey Brooks, *When Russia Learned to Read: Literacy and Popular Literature, 1861–1917* (Princeton, N.J., 1985), 105, 304.

11. *Polnoe Sobranie Zakonov*, ser. 2, 49, sec. 1, no. 53398 (April 19, 1874), 667–68.

12. Ruud, 258; V. Rozenberg and V. Iakushkin, *Russkaia pechat i tzenzura o proshlom i nastoianshchem* (Moscow, 1905), 115–16, 140.

13. Ibid., 141–42; Ruud, 258; P. Zaionchkovsky, *Rossiskoe samoderzhavie v kontse XIX stoletiia* (Moscow, 1979), 281.

14. M. Lemke, "V mire usmotreniia st. 140 i 156 ustava o tsenzure i pechati," *Vestnik Prava* (July 1905), 97–106; "Zapiska o napravlenii periodicheskoi pressy v sviazi s obshchestvennym dvizheniem v Rossii," *Literaturnoe nasledstvo*, 87 (1977), 446–60.

15. A. Koni, "Vladimir Danilovich Spasovich (Rech v godovom sobranii S. Pet. Iuridicheskogo i obshchestva, 23 fev. 1903)," *Ocherki i vospominaniia (Publichnye chteniia. stati, i zametki)* (hereafter *Ocherki*) (St. Petersburg, 1906), 776; "Vypiska iz protokola . . . Imperatorskoi Akademii Nauk ot 24 fevralia 1903 goda," *Materialy . . . dlia sostavleniia novogo ustava o pechati* (St. Petersburg, 1907), 6; "K istorii russkoi tsenzury," *Moscow Bulletin*, 220 (1905), 4.

16. *Polnoe Sobranie Zakonov*, ser. 3, 25, sec. 1, no. 26962 (November. 24, 1905), 837.

17. E. Valle-de-Barr, *"Svoboda" russkoi pechati (posle 17-ogo oktiabria, 1905)* (Samara, 1906), 24; Louise McReynolds, *The News Under Russia's Old Regime: The Development of a Mass-Circulation Press* (Princeton, N.J., 1991), Table 14.

18. M. Lemke, ed., *Trudy pervogo vserossiskogo sezda izdatelei i knigoprodavtsev, 30 iiunia-5 iiulia 1909 goda v S. Petersburg* (St. Petersburg, 1901), 261.

19. Jacob Walkin, "Government Controls over the Press in Russia, 1905–1914," *Russian Review*, 13 (1954), 206–7.

20. C. A. Ruud, *Russian Entrepreneur: Publisher Ivan Sytin of Moscow, 1851–1934* (Montreal, 1990), 201.

21. I. P. Foote, "The St. Petersburg Censorship Committee," *Oxford Slavonic Papers*, n. s., 24 (1991), 60–120. For Moscow, see A. Sidorov, *Moskovskii komitet po delam pechati* (Moscow, 1912).

22. P. Annenkov, *The Extraordinary Decade: Literary Memoirs*, ed. Arthur Mendel (Ann Arbor, Mich., 1968), 133.

23. Lemke, *Nikolaevskie*, 204–13; Oksman, *Ot "Kapitanskoi dochki" k. "Zapiskam okhotnika"* (Saratov, 1959), 284.

24. N. Barsukov, *Zhizn'i trudy M. P. Pogodina* (St. Petersburg, 1888–1910), XVI, 405.

25. A. V. Nikitenko, *Dnevnik* (Moscow, 1955), I: 406–7, 415, 425; I. P. Foote, "Firing a Censor: The Case of N. V. Elagin, 1854," *Oxford Slavonic Papers*, n. s., 29 (1986), 124.

26. V. Posse, *Moi zhiznennyi put': dorevoliutsionnyi period* 1864–1917 (Moscow-Leningrad, 1929), 211.

27. S. Umanets, "lz proshlogo nashei tsenzury," *Nasha Starina*, 10 (1915), 956.

28. Instructions of February. 9, 1861, State Archive of the Russian Federation (hereafter GARF) (Moscow), 109/213/30, sheet 14.

29. "O gazete *Voronezhkii Listok*," GARF, 109/1292, 1861, 2, sheet 6.

30. I. Aksakov, *Ivan Sergeevich Aksakov i ego pismakh* (Moscow, 1896), 25.

31. Daniel Todes, "Biological Psychology and the Tsarist Censor: The Dilemma of Scientific Development," *The Bulletin of the History of Medicine*, 58 (1984), 533–35.

32. Ibid., 535–37.

33. Nikitenko, I: 301; V. Evgen'ev-Maksimov, *"Sovremennik" v 40–50 gg, ot Belinskogo do Chernyshevskogo* (Leningrad, 1934), 246.

34. I. P. Foote, "Counter-Censorship: Authors v. Censors in 19th-Century Russia," (hereafter Foote, "Counter-Censorship"), *Oxford Slavonic Papers*, n.s. 5, 27 (1994), 82.

35. Ernest Simmons, *Leo Tolstoy* (London, 1949), 139; Foote, "Counter-Censorship," 71, 91.

36. Pisemsky to Nikitenko, November 25, 1855, *Pisma*, 90.

37. Foote, "Counter-Censorship," 86; B. Glinsky, "M. P. Soloviev i S. I. Kossovich: Iz tsenzurnogo proshlogo," in Glinsky, *Svedi literaturov i uchenykh* (St. Petersburg, 1914), 443–44.

38. Sytin to Blagov, June 11, 1910, Russian State Archive for the Arts and Literature, 595–1-150, sheets 1–4.

39. Archive of the Main Administration of Press Affairs, Russian State Archive, St. Petersburg, fond 776, files 848, 853, and 854; Sytin, *Zhizn' dlia knigi* (Moscow, 1978), 153–54.

40. Peter Ulf Moeller, *Postlude to the Kreutzer Sonata: Tolstoy and the Debate on Sexual Morality in Russian Literature in the 1890s* (Leiden, 1988), 39–91.

41. Ibid, 75.

42. S. Bukchin, *Sud'ba fel'etonista: Zhizn' i tvorchestvo Vlasa Doroshevicha* (Minsk, 1975), 128.

43. V. Botsianovsky and E. Gollerbach, eds., *Russkaia satira pervoi revoliutsii, 1905–1906* (Leningrad, 1925), 210.

44. V. Botsianovsky, "Karikatura i tsenzura v nachale XX v. (Iz vospominanii redaktora satiricheskogo zhurnala)," *Byloe* (1924), 186; Botsianovsky, "Nikolai II v karikature," *Byloe* (1925), 231.

45. Margaret Betz, "Revolutionary Caricatures of Nicholas II: A Language of Hidden Symbols," in Hans-Jurgen Drengenberg, ed., *Bildende Kunst in Osteuropa im 20 Jahrhundert: Art in Eastern Europe in the 20th Century* (Berlin, 1991), 26–27; Botsianovsky, "Karikatura i tsenzura," 193. Sergei Isakov, *1905 i karikatura* (Leningrad, 1928) is largely devoted to political pictures from the era.

46. Botsianovsky and Gollerbach, *Russkaia satira*, 176–96, 201–2.

47. Marc Slonim expands on this subject in *Russian Theater: From the Empire to the Soviets* (New York, 1961), 17–37.

48. Abram Gozenpud, *Russkii opernyi teatr XIX veka* (Leningrad, 1973), 5.

49. N. Rimsky-Korsakov, *Letopis' moei muzykal'noi zhizni*, 8th ed. (Moscow, 1980), 262–63.

50. A. Koni, "M. N. Zagoskin i tsensura," *Ocherki*, 866.

51. *K. P. Pobedonostsev i ego korrespondenty* (Moscow, 1923), I: 648–51.

52. Pisemsky, *Pisma*, 66, 675.

53. Swift, 11, 35; Gary Thurston, *The Popular Theatre Movement in Russia, 1862–1919* (Evanston, Ill., 1998), 174, 177, 178; Thurston, "The Impact of the Russian Popular Theatre, 1886–1915," *Journal of Modern History*, 55 (1983), 262.

54. Elizabeth Valkernier describes the setting for this event in *Russian Realist Art: The State and Society: The Peredvizhniki and Their Tradition* (Ann Arbor, Mich., 1977), 20–22, 34.

55. Ibid., 35, 208.

56. Alexandra Orlov, *Musorgsky's Days and Works: A Biography in Documents* (Ann Arbor, Mich., 1983), 211–12.

57. *The Musorgsky Reader*, ed. Jay Leyda and Sergei Bertensson (New York, 1970), 152–53.

58. Caryl Emerson and Robert Oldani, *Modest Musorgsky and "Boris Godunov": Myths, Realities, Reconsiderations* (Cambridge, England, 1994), 92.

59. R. Taruskin, *Musorgsky: Eight Essays and an Epilogue* (Princeton, N.J., 1993), 150.

60. V. Iastrebtsev, *Rimsky-Korsakov: Vospominaniia* (Leningrad, 1959–60), I: 348.

61. St. Smolensky, "O 'Liturgii', op. 41, soch. Chaikovskago," *Russkaia muzykal'naia gazeta*, October 26, 1903, col. 1022.

62. *Musorgsky: In Memoriam, 1881–1981*, ed. Malcolm Brown (Ann Arbor, Mich., 1982), 96.

63. V. Dementiev, *Kinematograf kak pravitel'stevennaia regaliia* (Petrograd, 1915); N. Zorkaia, *Na rubezhe stoletii: U istokov massovogo iskusstva v Rossii 1900–1910 godov* (Moscow, 1976); B. Likachev, *Kino v Rossii, 1896–1926: Materaly k istorii* (Leningrad, 1927), I: 35–36.

64. Jay Leyda, *Kino: A History of the Russian and Soviet Film* (Princeton, N.J., 1983), 6; Yuri Tsivian, *Early Cinema in Russia and Its Cultural Reception* (London, 1994), 126–27; Tsivian, "Censure Bans on Religious Subjects in Russian Films,"

in Roland Cosandey et al. (eds.), *An Invention of the Devil? Religion and Early Cinema* (Lausanne, 1992), 71–80.

BIBLIOGRAPHICAL ESSAY

An early critic (1790) of the Russian censorship system under Catherine II, Alexander Radishchev, had a lot to say on the subject in his *Journey from St. Petersburg to Moscow* (Cambridge, Mass., 1958). Catherine II immediately prohibited the circulation of his argument that freedom of the press had "vast and boundless usefulness," and not until the preparation of the 1860s censorship reform was such direct criticism about censorship allowed. A summary of the ensuing press debate can be found in my history of the censorship: Charles A. Ruud, *Fighting Words: Imperial Censorship and the Russian Press, 1804–1906* (Toronto, 1982). Writer and attorney K. K. Arsenev collected a number of his commentaries on how tsarist legislation on the press departed from the reform in his 1903 book *Zakonodatel'stvo o pechati* (St. Petersburg). M. K. Lemke's detailed study of the era of mid-century censorship reform, including published legislation and supplementary regulations that were hitherto all but unknown to the public, followed the next year *(Epokha tsenzurnykh reform, 1859–1865*, St. Petersburg, 1904).

During the Soviet period, Russian historians wrote little about Imperial censorship because it inevitably raised the forbidden question of the pervasive Soviet censorship. However, during the 1960s Professor P. A. Zaionchkovsky of Moscow State University published two major works focusing on the defensive character of the tsarist regime as it sought to stifle threatening social change late in the nineteenth century: *Krizis samoderzhaviia na rubezhe 1870–1880 godov* (Moscow, 1964) and *Rossiiskoe samoderzhavie v kontse XIX stoletiia* (Moscow, 1970). The former appeared in English as *The Russian Autocracy in Crisis, 1878–1883* (Gulf Breeze, Fla., 1979). In a detailed study of the first ten years' operation of the post-1865 reformed censorship, I. V. Orzhekhovsky has argued that the new regulations in reality only masked new and ingenious ways to restrict the press: *Administratsiia i pechat' mezhdu dvumia revoliutsionnymi situatsiiami (1866–1878 gg.)* (Gor'ky, 1973).

Studies of the censorship appeared in the West also after 1960. For example, Benjamin Rigberg published three articles in *Jahrbücher für Geschichte Osteuropas* describing Nicholas II's censorship legislation as so loosely written that it enabled the press to flourish: "The Tsarist Press Law, 1894–1905," N.F. 13 (1965), 331–43; "The Efficacy of Tsarist Censorship Operations, 1894–1917," N.F. 14 (1966), 327–46; and "Tsarist Censorship Performance, 1894–1905," N.F. 17 (1969), 59–76. Professor. I. P. Foote has also published a series of articles focusing on nineteenth-century censorship: "Firing a Censor: The Case of N. V. Elagin, 1857," *Oxford Slavonic Papers*, n.s., 29 (1986), 116–31; "In the Belly of the Whale: Russian Writers and the Censorship in the Nineteenth Century," *Slavonic and East European Review*, 98 (1990), 294–98; "The St. Petersburg Censorship Committee," *Oxford Slavonic Papers*, n.s., 24 (1991), 60–120; and "Counter-Censorship: Authors v. Censors in 19th Century Russia," *Oxford Slavonic Papers*, n.s., 27 (1994), 62–105. Daniel Balmuth examined the period from 1865 to 1905, including extensive information from the central censorship archives now located in St. Petersburg:

Censorship in Russia, 1865–1905 (Washington, D.C., 1979). My own study *(Fighting Words*, cited above) gives an overview of the censorship against the history of the evolution of newspaper, journal, and book publishing in nineteenth- and early twentieth-century Russia. Marianna Tax Choldin's study of the Foreign Censorship Committee focuses on how the censors treated imported publications published in the west: *A Fence Around the Empire: Russian Censorship of Western Ideas Under the Tsars* (Durham, N.C., 1985).

Most studies and autobiographies of Russian writers include their censorship trials; many such stories are included in Ronald Hingley's lively *Russian Writers and Society, 1825–1904* (New York, 1967). Censor A. V. Nikitenko's published diary, with its rich commentary on press controls, appeared in Russian as *Dnevnik* (Moscow, 1955), and in an abridged English version as *The Diary of a Russian Censor* (Amherst, Mass., 1975). Other useful English-language books touching on nineteenth-century censorship include Jeffrey Brooks, *When Russia Learned to Read: Literacy and Popular Literature, 1861–1917* (Princeton, N.J., 1985); Effie Ambler, *Russian Journalism and Politics: The Career of Aleksei S. Suvorin, 1861 to 1881* (Detroit, 1972); Louise McReynolds, *The News Under Russia's Old Regime* (Princeton, N.J., 1991); and Charles A. Ruud, *Russian Entrepreneur: The Moscow Publisher Ivan Sytin, 1851–1934* (Montreal, 1990). George Kennan, *Siberia and the Exile System* (London, 1891) contains an appendix on tsarist censorship listing many penalties against the press.

On theater censorship, see E. A. Swift, "Fighting the Germs of Disorder: The Censorship of Russian Popular Theater, 1888–1917," *Russian History*, 18 (1991), 1–49; and Gary Thurston, *The Popular Theatre Movement in Russia, 1862–1919* (Evanston, Ill., 1998). Political cartoons and much information on caricature censorship and prosecutions from the Russian press of the early twentieth century can be examined in Cathy Porter and David King, *Blood and Laughter: Caricatures from the 1905 Revolution* (London, 1983). Censorship of films is discussed in Jay Leyda, *Kino: A History of the Russian and Soviet Film* (Princeton, N.J., 1983) and in Yuri Tsivian, "Censure Bans on Religious Subjects in Russian Films," in *An Invention of the Devil? Religion and Early Cinema*, Roland Cosandey et al., eds. (Lausanne, 1992), 71–80.

Index

Note: For additional information concerning index topics preceded by an asterisk (*), please also consult under the appropriate subentries under individual country listings (i.e., France, Spain).

About the Editor and Contributors

ROBERT JUSTIN GOLDSTEIN is professor of political science at Oakland University, Rochester, Michigan. He received his Ph.D. from the University of Chicago and previously taught at San Diego State University. Professor Goldstein is the author of numerous books and articles focusing on the history of civil liberties in Western democracies, including *Political Censorship of the Arts and the Press in Nineteenth-Century Europe* (London, 1989), *Political Repression in Nineteenth-Century Europe* (London, 1983), and *Political Repression in Modern America: From 1870 to the Present* (Boston, 1978).

JOHN A. DAVIS holds the Emiliana Pasca Noether Chair in Modern Italian History at the University of Connecticut. Professor Davis received his Ph.D. from Oxford University. He is the joint founding editor of the *Journal of Modern Italian Studies* and author of numerous studies on eighteenth- and nineteenth-century Italy, including *Conflict and Control: Law and Order in 19th-Century Italy* (London, 1988). He is currently editing the multivolume Oxford *Short Histories of Italy.*

LOTHAR HÖBELT teaches at the University of Vienna and received his doctorate there. He has published many books and articles on Austrian history, including *Parliamentary Politics in a Multinational Setting: Late Imperial Austria* (Minneapolis, 1992), *Österreich und die deutsche Revolution* (Austria and the German Revolution) (Vienna, 1998), and *Kornblume und Kaiserradler: Die Geschichte der deutsch-freiheitlichen Parteien*

Altösterreichs, 1882–1918 (A History of the Anticlerical Middle Class Parties in Austria, 1882–1918) (Vienna, 1993).

ROBIN LENMAN is senior lecturer at the University of Warwick, England. He was educated at Oxford University, where he received his Ph.D., and at the University of Marburg, Germany. His writings, which focus on the relationship between the state and the arts in imperial Germany and on aspects of modern German visual culture, include *Die Kunst, die Macht und das Geld: Zur Kulturgeschichte des kaiserlichen Deutschland, 1871–1918* (Art, Power and Money: Towards a Cultural History of Imperial Germany, 1871–1918) (Frankfurt-am-Main, 1994), and *Artists and Society in Germany, 1850–1914* (Manchester, 1997).

CHARLES A. RUUD teaches history at the University of Western Ontario in Canada. He received his Ph.D. from the University of California at Berkeley and also received degrees from Willamette University and Harvard University. His research has focused on journalism and civil liberties in nineteenth-century Russia. His publications include *Fighting Words: Imperial Censorship and the Russian Press, 1804–1906* (Toronto, 1982); *Russian Entrepreneur: Publisher Ivan Sytin of Moscow, 1851–1934* (Montreal, 1990); and (with Sergei Stepanov) *Fontanka 16: The Tsars' Secret Police* (Montreal, 1999).

ADRIAN SHUBERT studied at the Universities of Toronto, New Mexico, and Warwick before taking his Ph.D. at the University of London. He has taught at the University of Calgary and Stanford University and is currently Professor and Chair of History at York University in Toronto. He is the author of numerous books and articles on modern Spanish history, including *Death and Money in the Afternoon: A History of Spanish Bullfighting* (Oxford, 1999); (with George Eisenwein) *Spain at War: The Spanish Civil War in Historical Context* (London, 1995); and *A Social History of Modern Spain* (London, 1991).

HARDCOVER BAR CODE